D0071391

The Cambridge Companion to

James Joyce

This *Companion*, designed primarily for consultation on a range of topics (although it is organized so that it can also be read from cover to cover), will deepen and extend the enjoyment and understanding of James Joyce for the new reader.

The eleven essays, by an international team of leading Joyce scholars and teachers, explore the most important aspects of Joyce's life and art. The topics covered include his debt to Irish and European writers and traditions, his life in Paris, and the relation of his work to the 'modern' spirit of sceptical relativism. One essay describes Joyce's developing achievement in his earlier works (*Stephen Hero, Dubliners,* and *A Portrait of the Artist as a Young Man*), while another tackles his best-known text, asking the basic question 'What is *Ulysses* "about"', and how can it be read?' The issue of 'difficulty' raised by *Finnegans Wake* is addressed in an essay which takes the reader through questions of theme, language, structure, and meaning, as well as the book's composition and the history of *Wake* criticism. A leading Joyce editor discusses the production of the Joycean text; another contribution introduces the shorter writings (poems, epiphanies, *Giacomo Joyce,* and *Exiles*); and an essay on 'Joyce and feminism' considers the vexed question of the place of women in Joyce's work and creative life. There is also an extensive section on 'Further reading'. The whole volume is informed by current debates about literature and literary study, and it demonstrates the central place occupied by Joyce's revolutionary achievement in those debates.

This is the only convenient and affordable multi-author guide to Joyce for students and the general reader. One of its aims is to dispel the intimidation readers often feel when faced with Joyce's reputation as an arcane and difficult writer. It will enhance and enrich the reader's appreciation of Joyce's books without simplifying the multifaceted qualities of the writing. Advanced students and teachers will also find it a stimulating example of the usefulness of recent developments in Joyce criticism and scholarship.

The Cambridge Companion to
James Joyce

Edited by Derek Attridge

CAMBRIDGE
UNIVERSITY PRESS

Published by the Press Syndicate of the University of Cambridge
The Pitt Building, Trumpington Street, Cambridge CB2 IRP
40 West 20th Street, New York, NY 10011–4211, USA
10 Stamford Road, Oakleigh, Melbourne 3166, Australia

First published 1990
Reprinted 1993, 1996

Printed in Great Britain at the University Press, Cambridge

British Library cataloguing in publication data

The Cambridge Companion to James Joyce.
1. Fiction in English. Joyce, James, 1882–1941 –
Critical studies
I. Attridge, Derek
832'.912

Library of Congress cataloguing in publication data applied for

ISBN 0 521 33014 9 hardback
ISBN 0 521 37673 4 paperback

VN

Contents

vi   Contents

Contributors

DEREK ATTRIDGE is Professor of English at Rutgers University, New Brunswick. He co-edited *Post-structuralist Joyce: Essays from the French* (Cambridge University Press, 1984), and his most recent book is *Peculiar Language: Literature as Difference from the Renaissance to James Joyce* (Cornell University Press and Methuen, 1988).

CHRISTOPHER BUTLER is Tutor in English Literature and Student of Christ Church, Oxford. His books include *After the Wake: An Essay on the Contemporary Avant-Garde* (Oxford University Press, 1980) and *Interpretation, Deconstruction, and Ideology: An Introduction to Some Current Issues in Literary Theory* (Oxford University Press, 1984).

SEAMUS DEANE is Professor of Modern English and American Literature at University College, Dublin. His publications include *Celtic Revivals: Essays in Modern Irish Literature 1880–1980* (Faber, 1986), *A Short History of Irish Literature* (Hutchinson, 1987), *The French Enlightenment and Revolution in England, 1789–1832* (Harvard University Press, 1988), and a two-volume *Anthology of Irish Writing 550–1987* (Field Day and Faber, 1989).

HANS WALTER GABLER is Professor of English at the University of Munich. He is the editor of the 1984 Critical and Synoptic Edition of *Ulysses* (Garland) and of the 1986 Corrected Text (Bodley Head, Penguin, and Random House).

KAREN LAWRENCE is Professor of English at the University of Utah. She is the author of *The Odyssey of Style in 'Ulysses'* (Princeton University Press, 1981) and several articles on narrative and gender in Woolf, Charlotte Brontë, and Joyce. She is currently writing a book on British women travellers and travel writing.

JENNIFER LEVINE is Senior Tutor in the Literary Studies Programme at Victoria College, University of Toronto. She has published essays on the novel and on Joyce in *PMLA*, *UTQ*, and *JJQ*, and is presently at work on a study of *Ulysses* and reading.

VICKI MAHAFFEY is Associate Professor of English at the University of Pennsylvania. She has published a number of articles on Joyce, and her book, *Reauthorizing Joyce* (Cambridge University Press), appeared in 1988.

MARGOT NORRIS is Professor of English and Comparative Literature at the University of California, Irvine. She is the author of *The Decentered Universe of 'Finnegans Wake'* (Johns Hopkins University Press, 1976), and her forthcoming book *Joyce's Web: The Social Unraveling of Modernism* will be published by the University of Texas Press.

JEAN-MICHEL RABATÉ moved in 1992 from the University of Dijon to the University of Pennsylvania, where he is Professor of English. Among his books are *Language, Sexuality and Ideology in Ezra Pound's Cantos* (Macmillan, 1986), *James Joyce, Authorized Reader* (Johns Hopkins University Press, 1991), and *Joyce Upon the Void: The Genesis of Doubt* (Macmillan, 1991).

KLAUS REICHERT is Professor of English at the University of Frankfurt. He is the editor (with Fritz Senn) of the Frankfurt edition of Joyce's works in German (Suhrkamp, 1969–81) and of *Anna Livia Plurabelle* (Suhrkamp, 1970, 1982), and the translator of a number of Joyce's works. His collected essays on *Finnegans Wake*, *Vielfacher Schriftsinn*, were published by Suhrkamp in 1989.

JOHN PAUL RIQUELME is Professor of English at Boston University, and was an Alexander von Humboldt Research Fellow at the University of Constance in 1987–8. He is the author of *Teller and Tale in Joyce's Fiction: Oscillating perspectives* (Johns Hopkins University Press, 1983) and *Harmony of Dissonances: T. S. Eliot, Romanticism and Imagination* (Johns Hopkins University Press, 1991), and the editor of *Joyce's Dislocutions: Essays on Reading as Translation* by Fritz Senn (Johns Hopkins University Press, 1984).

Preface

One might think of *all* the numerous books and articles published about Joyce's work as companions, offering the reader a range of different services: accurate texts, possible interpretations, helpful information, interesting anecdotes about the artist and his models. But few readers have the time – or the desire – to sift through all this material in search of what they most need, and this volume is offered as a first resort for those who wish to deepen and extend their enjoyment and understanding of Joyce's writing. It does not attempt to make Joyce 'easy' (though one of its aims is to remove unnecessary apprehensions about Joyce's 'difficulty'); nor does it present a grand survey of the monuments of Joycean scholarship and criticism. It rests neither on the assumption that all you need in order to enhance your appreciation of a literary text is somebody else's close reading of it, nor on the assumption that the key to comprehension is a mass of inert biographical and historical facts. Joyce's works are approached as verbal artefacts that succeed in exploiting with an extraordinary fullness the potential for human insight and pleasure latent within the verbal and cultural fabric of the twentieth century (which includes its versions of previous centuries); equal attention is given, therefore, to the patterns and peculiarities of Joyce's language and to the threads that weave it into the world's history. Chapters deal with some of the most significant historical contexts within which Joyce's writing takes on its manifold meanings, with the problems and rewards of reading Joyce's texts, with the processes through which those texts came into existence, and with Joyce's place in the intellectual and political movements of the century. A guide to further reading points the way to more specialized companions.

Joyce is the most international of writers in English. He shares with

Shakespeare a global reputation, but, unlike Shakespeare, he crossed many national boundaries in his working career, in his outlook, and in his writing – extending his reach further and further until, in *Finnegans Wake*, he attempted to embrace the languages and cultures of the entire human community. Throughout his career, Dublin remained the other pole of his creative activity, but a Dublin constantly challenged and remade in the light of this internationalist distrust of patriotism and prejudice. A second feature of Joyce's work is the way it has intersected, and continues to intersect, with some of the most important transmutations of Western thought, both during his lifetime (one might include modernism, feminism, psychoanalysis, socialism, pacifism, secularism, and anti-colonialism) and after it (most notably in the movements known broadly as structuralism, post-structuralism, and post-modernism). The contributors to this volume reflect these two features of Joyce's writing: they are of many nationalities, and they all manifest in their different kinds of interest in Joyce an engagement with current intellectual and social changes. The volume as a whole also reflects the remarkable advances made in two areas of Joyce studies over the last decade: the excavations of scholars – textual, biographical, cultural, historical – and the explorations of literary theorists. I believe that the essays which follow demonstrate that the best writing on Joyce today takes advantage of both kinds of advance.

My task as editor has been made considerably lighter by the energy, commitment, and patience of my contributors. I would also like to thank Tom Furniss, Suzanne Hall, Jo Ramsey, and George Kearns for their help, and the students at Southampton, Strathclyde, and Rutgers Universities with whom I learned just how enjoyable reading Joyce can be. We are all, of course, indebted to scores of earlier readers and re-readers of Joyce, most notably James Joyce himself.

DEREK ATTRIDGE

Chronology of Joyce's life

1882   James Augustine Joyce, first child of John Stanislaus Joyce and Mary Jane ('May') Joyce, née Murray, born on 2 February in Rathgar, a suburb of Dublin.

1884   Birth of Stanislaus Joyce, who, of James's nine surviving siblings, was closest to him.

1888   Joyce family moves to Bray, a town south of Dublin. James enrolled in Clongowes Wood College, an élite Jesuit school. Downfall of Parnell (1890) makes a strong impression.

1891   Family financial difficulties cause the withdrawal of James from Clongowes, and a break in his schooling.

1892   Joyce family moves to Blackrock, in suburban Dublin.

1893   Further financial decline and move to the first of a series of more central Dublin addresses. James enrolled as a day student at Belvedere College, another Jesuit school.

1896   Becomes Prefect of the Sodality of the Blessed Virgin Mary.

1897   Wins academic prizes, including prize for best English composition in Ireland in his grade. Catholic faith dwindles.

1898   Enters University College, Dublin.

1899   Attends the riotous opening night of Yeats's *The Countess Cathleen*; supports Yeats.

1900   Publishes article on Ibsen in the *Fortnightly Review*; receives thanks from Ibsen. Reads paper on 'Drama and Life' to the Literary and Historical Society. Writes poems and plays, mostly destroyed.

1901   Writes 'The Day of the Rabblement', which is refused by a college magazine. Joyce publishes it privately.

1902   Graduates from University College; leaves Dublin for Paris, ostensibly to study medicine.

1903   Returns to Dublin in April on receiving news of his mother's illness. She dies on 13 August.

1904   Leaves the family home for a variety of residences, including the Martello Tower at Sandycove. Writes an essay entitled 'A Portrait of the Artist', and poems and stories for magazine publication (later to be included in *Chamber Music* and *Dubliners*). Starts work on *Stephen Hero*. Meets Nora Barnacle on 10 June, and leaves Dublin for the Continent with her on 8 October. Obtains job with Berlitz School in Pola, Yugoslavia, then under Austrian rule.

1905   Obtains job with Berlitz School in Trieste. Son Giorgio born on 27 July. Submits *Chamber Music* and *Dubliners* to London publishers Grant Richards. Stanislaus comes to Trieste to join the family.

1906   Moves to Rome to work as a bank clerk. Writes two more stories for *Dubliners*.

1907   Returns to Trieste. Daughter Lucia born on 26 July. *Chamber Music* published in London. Completes 'The Dead', the last story of *Dubliners*. Gives private English lessons and public lectures, and publishes newspaper articles. Starts rewriting *Stephen Hero* as *A Portrait of the Artist as a Young Man*, radically reducing its length.

1908   Finishes three chapters of *A Portrait*.

1909   Visits Dublin twice, to sign contract with Maunsel & Co. for *Dubliners*, and to set up a cinema. His sister Eva returns with Joyce to live with the family.

1912   Family trip to Galway and Dublin; this is Joyce's last visit to Ireland. Joyce battles with Maunsel editor George Roberts over censorship of *Dubliners*. Printed sheets of the book destroyed by the printer, fearing libel action.

1913   Ezra Pound makes contact with Joyce.

1914   *A Portrait* starts appearing in serial form in the *Egoist*. *Dubliners* published by Grant Richards. Joyce begins work on *Ulysses*. War breaks out, and Joyce faces internment in Trieste.

1915   *Exiles* completed. Joyce and family permitted to leave Trieste for Switzerland; they settle in Zurich.

1916   *A Portrait* published in New York.

1917   Completion of three chapters of *Ulysses*. First of many eye operations. Harriet Shaw Weaver starts supporting Joyce financially.

1918   *Exiles* published in London. *Ulysses* serialization begins in the *Little Review*.

1919   Return to Trieste made possible by ending of war.

1920   At Pound's suggestion, the family moves to Paris, where they will remain for twenty years at a number of addresses. Court case prevents *Little Review* from continuing to serialize *Ulysses*.

1922   *Ulysses* published in Paris by Sylvia Beach's bookshop, Shakespeare and Company.

1923   Begins 'Work in Progress', eventually published as *Finnegans Wake*.

1927   *Pomes Penyeach* published by Shakespeare and Company. 'Work in Progress' begins to appear in sections in *transition*.

1929   Publication of *Our Exagmination round His Factification for Incamination of Work in Progress*, by Samuel Beckett and eleven others.

1931   Marriage of James Joyce and Nora Barnacle in London. Joyce's father dies.

1932   First grandchild, Stephen James Joyce, born to Giorgio and Helen Joyce. Lucia has a mental breakdown.

1933   Court allows publication of *Ulysses* in USA. Lucia enters hospital in Switzerland.

1934   *Ulysses* published by Random House in New York.

1939   *Finnegans Wake* published by Faber & Faber in London and Viking in New York. On the outbreak of war, the Joyces move to southern France.

1940   Permission granted to leave France for Switzerland. Move to Zurich.

1941   Joyce suffers perforated ulcer; dies on 13 January, aged 58. Buried in Fluntern cemetery, Zurich.

1951   Death of Nora Barnacle Joyce in Zurich.

Abbreviations

Except in the case of the following abbreviations, full details of works referred to are given after each chapter, either in the notes or in a list of works cited.

Archive   *The James Joyce Archive*, ed. Michael Groden, Hans Walter Gabler, David Hayman, A. Walton Litz, and Danis Rose with John O'Hanlon, 63 vols. (New York: Garland, 1977–9)

CHI, II   *James Joyce: The Critical Heritage*, ed. Robert H. Deming, 2 vols. (London: Routledge, 1970)

CW   *The Critical Writings of James Joyce*, ed. Ellsworth Mason and Richard Ellmann (London: Faber; New York: Viking, 1959)

D   *Dubliners*, ed. Robert Scholes (New York: Viking, 1969)

E   *Exiles* (New York: Viking, 1951)

FW   *Finnegans Wake* (London: Faber; New York: Viking, 1939). References are to page and line numbers (these are the same in all editions), e.g. *FW* 213.28. Chapters are indicated by book and chapter numbers, e.g. II.3

GJ   *Giacomo Joyce*, ed. Richard Ellmann (London: Faber; New York: Viking, 1968)

JJ   *James Joyce*, by Richard Ellmann, revised edition (New York: Oxford University Press, 1982)

JJQ   *James Joyce Quarterly*

Letters I, II, III   *Letters of James Joyce*, vol. I, ed. Stuart Gilbert (London: Faber; New York: Viking, 1957; reissued with corrections, 1966); vols. II and III, ed. Richard

	Ellmann (London: Faber; New York: Viking, 1966)
P	*A Portrait of the Artist as a Young Man*, ed. Chester G. Anderson (New York: Viking, 1964)
SH	*Stephen Hero*, ed. Theodore Spencer, rev. John J. Slocum and Herbert Cahoon (Norfolk, CN: New Directions, 1963)
SL	*Selected Letters of James Joyce*, ed. Richard Ellmann (London: Faber; New York: Viking, 1975)
U	*Ulysses*, ed. Hans Walter Gabler with Wolfhard Steppe and Claus Melchior (New York and London: Garland, 1984; New York: Random House; London: Bodley Head; Harmondsworth: Penguin, 1986). References are to episode and line numbers, which are the same in all these editions, e.g. *U* 10.124.

In quotations, spaced points (. . .) indicate an omission, while unspaced points (...) occur in the original.

DEREK ATTRIDGE

1   Reading Joyce

Far more people read Joyce than are aware of it. Such was the impact of his literary revolution that few later novelists of importance in any of the world's languages have escaped its aftershock, even when they attempt to avoid Joycean paradigms and procedures. We are indirectly reading Joyce, therefore, in many of our engagements with the past half century's serious fiction – and the same is true of some not-so-serious fiction, too. Even those who read very few novels encounter the effects of Joyce's revolution every week, if not every day, in television and video, film, popular music, and advertising, all of which are marked as modern genres by the use of Joycean techniques of parody and pastiche, self-referentiality, fragmentation of word and image, open-ended narrative, and multiple point of view. And the unprecedented explicitness with which Joyce introduced the trivial details of ordinary life into the realm of art opened up a rich new territory for writers, painters, and film-makers, while at the same time it revealed the fruitful contradictions at the heart of the realist enterprise itself.

Of course, this momentous cultural shift, which can be said to have altered the way we understand and deploy systems of representation, was not achieved single-handedly and at a stroke by James Joyce. His changing understanding of the way language relates to the world, the work of art to its cultural situation, the commonplace and repetitive in life to the remarkable and the unique, was symptomatic of a wider mutation of thought which had begun before he started writing at the very end of the nineteenth century, and had its complicated roots in the social, economic, and political transformations that occurred before and during his lifetime.[1] But in the field of prose literature, this much broader set of movements found its most potent representative in

Joyce, and his own contribution helped to determine the particular form it took in this field.

There is a sense, therefore, in which we can *never* read Joyce 'for the first time'. Because of the ubiquity of his influence, anyone who now picks up a book of Joyce's already has at least some familiarity with the modes of his writing; and in addition the name 'Joyce' – and probably the name of the particular book – are likely to possess in advance a certain aura. This puts today's readers both at an advantage and at a disadvantage compared with Joyce's first readers. We are less likely to be baffled, dismayed, irritated, or intimidated by the strangeness of his writing (unless we have been led to expect something fearsomely difficult). On the other hand, we may miss some of its challenges to our own settled ways of thinking and making sense of the world because we muffle its unique voice: we can all too easily smother the text with our preconceptions about what it does and how it works, failing to perceive the things in it which are resistant to those preconceptions. If we do miss these challenges, we also miss some of the exhilaration, the humour, the pleasurable amazement that Joyce's work has to offer.[2]

I emphasize the pleasures of reading Joyce, because this is where any introduction to his work must begin; an account that loses sight of this fundamental point is in danger of forgetting why we read, or write about, Joyce at all. It is because his work has brought lasting enjoyment to so many people, even through translation into languages other than English or media other than print, that it has played such an important role in the world's cultural history. If we ever succeeded in fully explaining those pleasures, we would no doubt annul them, for they rely on qualities of inexplicability, unpredictability, inexhaustibility. But this is a danger we need not worry about: Joyce's texts are now so woven into the other texts of our culture that they constantly remake themselves as history moves inexorably on, and all our projects of explanation and interpretation get caught up in turn in this changing web, producing yet more transmutations in the very texts which they are trying to pin down.

If we can never read Joyce's works for the first time (though our pleasure may be enhanced if we always do our best to approach them with open minds), we can also never come to the end of our reading of them. We can never say, for example, 'A Portrait has yielded up all it has to offer me; I can put it down with a satisfying feeling of completion and finality'. As I have suggested, Joyce's texts change as our own

cultural surroundings change, which is one reason for their inexhaustibility; another (obviously related) reason is that they are unusually rich
texts – and that includes the apparently pared-to-the-bone stories of
Dubliners – which any single individual, even with the help of a whole
library of Joyce criticism, would be unlikely to squeeze dry. Doubtless
this inexhaustibility is to some degree characteristic of all the texts we
call 'literary', but Joyce's work in particular seems to have a built-in
principle of openness to further investigation, further interpretation,
further enjoyment. One aspect of this capacity for infinite self-
refashioning in Joyce's writing is the way it exposes and plays with the
very processes of sense-making that underlie all experiences of fiction,
so that the world in which we are invited to participate and find
pleasure when we read Joyce includes the world of our acts of reading
and comprehension. We cannot help making the attempt to come to the
end of a reading, to reach a stable point where it all makes coherent
sense, and we should never stop trying to achieve this moment; but it is
perfectly possible at the same time to enjoy the prospect of an endlessly
repeated failure to do so. Any critical text which claims to tell you (at
last) what a work of Joyce's is 'about', or what its structure, or its moral
position, or its symbolic force, 'is', has to be mistrusted, therefore; not
because it will not be useful to you in a reading of the work in question,
adding to your pleasure as you move toward that impossible goal of
total understanding, but because it is making a claim that, taken
literally, would exclude all other ways of reading the work, now and
in the unpredictable future.

II

Reading Joyce is an activity which extends from the small-scale
pleasures of appreciating the skilful organization and complex suggestiveness of a single sentence or phrase to the large-scale project of
constructing a model that will impart unity (provisionally, at least) to
an entire book or the entire *œuvre*, or even the entire *œuvre* together
with the history, personal and public, of which it is part. Reading a text
of Joyce's can be compared to playing a piece of music – it can be done
rapidly, skipping over opaque or repetitious passages to gain a sense of
the longer-range patterns and developments, or slowly, savouring the
words, puzzling over the conundrums, following up the cross-
references. (These two poles move further and further apart in Joyce's

work, until in *Finnegans Wake* the ability to jump over a page of apparent gibberish is as important as the ability to spend half-an-hour on a single word.) Other contributors to this book demonstrate ways of reading at many points on this continuum; here I want to exemplify some of the rewards of a reading that focuses on detail, and to touch on a few of the larger issues that arise from such a reading. In order to do this, I have chosen, more or less at random, two passages from the extremities of Joyce's writing career; there is not space to examine any examples in between, but much of the discussion holds good for the rest of Joyce's writing.

The first passage comes from one of Joyce's earliest stories, 'Eveline', written in 1904 for a Dublin magazine, the *Irish Homestead*, and published under the pseudonym 'Stephen Daedalus'. Joyce placed it, in a revised form, as the fourth story in *Dubliners*, and it is from this version that I am quoting. Most of the story is taken up with the twilight thoughts of a young woman who has consented to an elopement in order to escape her impoverished and stultifying life in Dublin. The following passage occurs at the story's halfway point:

She was about to explore another life with Frank. Frank was very kind, manly, open-hearted. She was to go away with him by the night-boat to be his wife and to live with him in Buenos Ayres where he had a home waiting for her. How well she remembered the first time she had seen him; he was lodging in a house on the main road where she used to visit. It seemed a few weeks ago. He was standing at the gate, his peaked cap pushed back on his head and his hair tumbled forward over a face of bronze. Then they had come to know each other. He used to meet her outside the Stores every evening and see her home. He took her to see *The Bohemian Girl* and she felt elated as she sat in an unaccustomed part of the theatre with him. He was awfully fond of music and sang a little. People knew that they were courting and, when he sang about the lass that loves a sailor, she always felt pleasantly confused.   (D 38–9)

At first sight, what is most remarkable about this writing is its unremarkableness; it hardly seems to be 'literary' language at all. But that does not mean that it is a mode of writing which is completely transparent, a truth-telling style whose sole aim is to convey as convincingly as possible the actuality of a specific, though presumably imagined, personal experience. There is no obvious reason why we should take pleasure in being exposed to the experience itself; it reveals no glories of the human spirit, and its view of the history and sociology of Dublin is fairly commonplace. Rather, the content (which we are accustomed to thinking of as the *raison d'être* of fiction) serves as a vehicle for the manner of the telling, the slow release of information, the hints and presuppositions that we are invited to elaborate on, the rhythm of mental deliberation that propels the narrative forward, and – our present concern – the controlled language that through its very spareness possesses a hair-trigger suggestiveness. This is not to say that Joyce has reversed the relationship between content and form as it exists in every other story, but rather that he has revealed, by going to an extreme, how unstable that relationship is; and if many readers remain convinced that their pleasure comes from being presented with the actual events of the story, for which the particular mode of writing is merely a skilfully contrived channel, this is probably because our activities as readers are usually more complex than the terms in which we represent those activities to ourselves. (We are less likely to misrepresent to ourselves the way we read, or attempt to read, *Finnegans Wake*, where, as we shall see, 'content' does not offer itself up for immediate apprehension.)

We have no difficulty as readers in identifying the close relationship between the sentences of this passage and the thoughts of the main character. The story's opening sentence has, in fact, introduced us to a narrator with an identifiable style: 'She sat at the window watching the evening invade the avenue'. The lack of any introductory story-teller's formula, the unspecific 'she', the simple past tense of 'sat', the use of a distinctive poetic register signalled by the metaphorical 'invade', the patterned sounds ('evening', 'invade', 'avenue') – all these announce the heightened realism of the dominant tradition of late nineteenth-century fiction, and the economical exposition of the conventional short story. But the style of the passage we are examining is markedly different, its rhythms graceless, its metaphors dead, its diction commonplace. We recognize a familiar novelistic device: the narrator's style has given way to one that mimics the speech and thought patterns of the character.[3] Much of the third-person past tense narrative can therefore be translated into first-person present tense with no difficulty. The third sentence, for instance, easily becomes: 'I am to go away with him by the night-boat to be his wife and to live with him in Buenos Ayres where he has a home waiting for me'. Eveline is rehearsing future events she can scarcely believe in – and the unreality of this future as she recounts it to herself, the strangeness of that name 'Buenos Ayres' surrounded by the ordinariness, to her, of Dublin names, is among the hints that she may find it a future that, when it comes to the moment of decision, is impossible to realize.

But this translation, like all translations, changes the text; to read the sentence as it actually occurs, in the third person and past tense, is to hover between hearing someone think aloud and hearing someone tell a story about a person's thoughts. If a clearly-identified narrator commenting on Frank were to state that Buenos Ayres is 'where he had a home waiting for her', and we had no reason to think of the narrator as a liar, we would take this as a fact, a given of the story; if a character *thinks* it, however, it has only as much validity as we feel we can ascribe to that thought. Has Eveline found a rescuer, or just another Dublin betrayer? How accurate is her assessment of him – for which the story gives no objective evidence – as 'kind, manly, open-hearted'? There is no way we can give final answers to these questions, and although part of the reading process is trying to reach some tentative conclusion by studying the evidence of the text, of Joyce's writing more widely, and perhaps of the social history of Ireland in this period, the inconclusiveness is something from which we can never escape, because it is built into the story. If a careful reading produces uncertainty, we cannot pluck certainty out of it; Joyce was not so hamfisted a writer as to be unable to make it clear, if he wanted to do so, that Eveline's hopes of a new life are either entirely valid or entirely baseless.[4]

Not all of this passage is equally amenable to translation into first-person thought, however, and we have to pick our way through continually shifting perspectives, relying as best we can on our sensitivity to individual words and turns of phrase. 'He was awfully fond of music': that 'awfully' could only be Eveline. The phrase '*see* her home' followed immediately by 'He took her to *see* . . .' would be clumsy writing in novelistic prose but a natural repetition in thought or speech. And an orthodox narrator would not write 'when he sang about the lass that loves a sailor' but 'when he sang "The Lass that Loves a Sailor"'; for Eveline, however, what is important is not whether this phrase is the title of the song, but what it states and signifies for her relationship with Frank. The reader's enjoyment lies in identifying this language as language normally excluded from literature, but functioning here just as efficiently as the most elaborate of styles to suggest with immense precision a mind, a social milieu, a series of emotions. The pleasure is in the precision, rather than what it is precise about.

There are even more subtle ways in which the illusion of intimacy with the character's own thoughts is created. Look at the repetition of 'Frank' at the beginning of the passage, for example. A narrator would be bound by the rules of English usage to substitute 'he' for the second 'Frank', but the dwelling on the name, the almost ritual quality of the mental statement 'Frank is very kind, manly, open-hearted', which is not a discovery but a moment of self-reassurance, belong to the blend of pride, excitement, and anxiety that comprises Eveline's complicated mental state. After that repeated proper name, notice the refrain of *she's* and *he's* as subjects of verbs: where a polished writer would introduce some variation, Joyce hovers just this side of a banality which would destroy the reader's pleasure altogether.

But reading this text is not entirely a matter of responding to immediately categorizable verbal details. What do we make of 'his hair tumbled forward over a face of bronze'? This is no longer the way Eveline might speak, though its clichés are not characteristic of the narrator either. Perhaps we can read it as the faint echo of a story Eveline has read, and this too might set alarm bells ringing – is she interpreting her experience according to the norms of romantic fiction? What about 'unaccustomed' in 'she felt elated as she sat in an unaccustomed part of the theatre with him'? A slightly posh word going through Eveline's mind to match the rather posh seat? Or a comment from the outside by the narrator, whose voice we might have detected already in the word 'elated'? Then there is 'pleasantly confused'. Our readerly enjoyment here includes some appreciation of the elegant and economical way in which the phrase sums up a complex and contradictory experience – not the kind of enjoyment that Eveline's own style usually offers us. Or is this interpretation just the kind of smug superiority which Eveline finds all too common in her Dublin environment? Joyce's writing – if we read it with sufficient alertness – here raises questions about our own processes of interpretation and judgement.

As readers, we are made hungry for information while traversing this sparse verbal terrain, and we seize on anything concrete, such as proper names – 'Buenos Ayres', *The Bohemian Girl*. We may not recognize the latter name, but its symbolic force is evident: a bohemian girl is exactly what Eveline is not, and the visit to the theatre with Frank obviously stands as a kind of rehearsal of the life she is imagining with him, at once a challenge to conventional mores and – if we take the force of the 'unaccustomed part of the theatre' – an introduction to a new position of affluence and respect. Of course the symbolism of the title may be entirely the author's: Eveline probably reminds herself of the exact name because of its fashionable resonance rather than because of its appropriateness to her situation. But there is nothing unusual, in a literary text, about language that emanates simultaneously from two sources, 'unrealistic' though this may be. Another example is the name 'Frank': within the fictional world and in Eveline's mind it is just a given, but as a word in a literary text it raises a question – is it an appropriate name (as it might have been in an older literary work), or is it ironically inappropriate?

Joyce is engaged in the double task which faces all realistic writers: on the one hand, he is working to produce the convincing effect of a certain kind of mind in a particular emotional state and, on the other, to contrive a narrative progression which gives the reader an active role in piecing together clues and wrestling with uncertainties and puzzles. The demands of naturalism are for a degree of incoherence, a completely nonliterary style, and a minimum of information (since the character has no need to verbalize to herself things she already knows); the demands of the narrative are for clarity, an original and forceful style, and the gradual provision of judiciously organized nuggets of information that will create an onward drive toward revelation and resolution. At a moment like this, Eveline would normally think 'he', not 'Frank'; so Joyce gives us the emphatically repeated 'Frank' both to suggest the character's conscious dwelling on the talismanic word and to furnish the readers with a necessary fact. Eveline has no need to go over the chain of events whereby she and Frank became acquainted, but we are prepared to accept her rehearsal of them as a deliberate basking in the memory of an experience she still cannot quite believe in, as well as part of the mental stock-taking appropriate for a critical moment such as this. At the same time, however, Joyce heightens our awareness of the techniques he so skilfully deploys by raising questions about our strategies of interpretation. And to be aware of how much is going on in this apparently simple style – this is part of Joyce's revolution – is not to puncture the illusion of reality but to enjoy the many-sidedness of language and story-telling, and to relish the readerly activity one is called upon to perform.

If we decide to pursue our craft as readers further than the text itself, we have many contexts to turn to, all of which have the capacity to enrich our experience. The story is part of a collection, and its setting in a specific time and place becomes more important when it is read in this context. Eveline's predicament is understood as a version of a more general problem afflicting Dubliners of a certain class, and this may reduce any tendency to pass judgement on her as an individual. Interconnections between this story and others become evident; for instance, the narrative technique of 'Clay' is a more complicated development of that used here, and Maria, the central figure of that story, might offer a glimpse of what awaits Eveline when she finds, at the end of the story, that she cannot leave Dublin. (Maria, as it happens, sings a song from *The Bohemian Girl*.) Read as part of Joyce's entire *œuvre*, 'Eveline' takes on further resonances. The 'Nausicaa' episode of *Ulysses* presents in Gerty MacDowell an elaboration of Eveline, building fantasies around a stranger whom she interprets in the terms of the romantic world she has read about, while the theme of the mariner whose words need to be treated with caution is comically expanded in the 'Eumaeus' episode. And in *Finnegans Wake* the visiting sailor who offers marriage becomes a Norwegian Captain paying court to a tailor's daughter in a hilariously elaborated anecdote (311.05–332.09).

Other contexts beyond Joyce's *œuvre* beckon as well. There is the social, political, and cultural history of Ireland; further information about *The Bohemian Girl*, for instance, reveals that it is highly relevant to Eveline's romantic hopes. Written by an Irishman, it nevertheless concerns Austrian gypsies, Polish nobility, and a family-romance plot of secret high birth and love triumphant over (apparent) social disadvantage – the very antithesis of what Joyce believed Irish art should be concerned with. And there is the close connection between 'Eveline' and important events and projects in Joyce's life: his intense courtship of a young working woman in Dublin, and his elopement with her to the Continent (less than a month after the publication of 'Eveline'); his fiercely-felt rejection of the narrowness and sterility of Ireland's political, religious, and cultural life; his struggle to forge a progressive European cultural outlook in opposition to the ideological fantasies and fabrications that were to contribute in his lifetime to two world wars. Admittedly, the blandishments of a wooing sailor with stories of a better life on the other side of the globe are a very long way from chauvinist and militarist propaganda, but what can be learned, so pleasurably, from Joyce's critical explorations of the potency of fiction and rhetoric within specific social and economic contexts may help to sharpen the linguistic and conceptual vigilance needed to combat the totalizing and totalitarian manipulations of language and thought still powerful today.

III

Unlike the language of *Dubliners*, that of *Finnegans Wake* casts no spell of realistic illusion. The following is part of a sentence that occurs in II.3:

> . . . our allies winged by duskfoil from Mooreparque, swift sanctuary seeking, after Sunsink gang (Oiboe! Hitherzither! Almost dotty! I must dash!) to pour their peace in partial (floflo floreflorence), sweetishsad lightandgayle, twittwin twosingwoolow. (359.35–360.03)

Here we are not inclined to ignore the medium whereby the content is transmitted; this is language at its least transparent – and this sentence is, for *Finnegans Wake*, relatively free from obscurity. Indeed, it is difficult to talk of a 'content' that is somehow behind these words, pre-existing and predetermining them, as Eveline's mental state might be thought to lie behind the words in the earlier passage: the meanings we discover in a passage like this are clearly the result of an interaction between the text and whatever expectations and knowledge the reader brings to them. This is what happens when we read *Dubliners* too, but there the process is masked by the discreetness and submissiveness of the style.

The newcomer to *Finnegans Wake* may not respond to this unashamed linguistic productivity with delight, however. And if he or she turns to a book about *Finnegans Wake* for help, the result is all too likely to be a sense of intimidation: to make any progress at all, the *Wake* reader, it might appear, needs to be at home in several languages and cultures, to have absorbed huge tracts of esoteric lore and historical fact, and to possess the verbal dexterity of a crossword-puzzle composer as well as the patience of a saint. But there is another way of looking at the *Wake*'s notorious complexity, density, and length: far from demanding exhaustive knowledge, it can be seen as offering every reader, from every background, *some* familiar ground to walk on, precisely because it incorporates so much of the world's linguistic, cultural, and historical knowledge. A wider range of expertise is something the reader can aspire to, if the initial encounter with the book is positive; and then the large number of secondary texts hold out the promise of further pleasures. But the richness of *Finnegans Wake* may be thought of as a comfort, not a threat, to the beginner, since Joyce's work is quite unlike those 'difficult' books which can be understood only if the reader is familiar with a particular body of knowledge. In order to appreciate the *Wake*'s reader-friendliness, however, one has to abandon two assumptions about the act of reading which frequently exist side-by-side (though they are, on the surface at least, contradictory). One is that reading is an act of mastery whereby the text is made to yield up all its secrets and allowed to hold nothing back; the other is that reading is a passive experience whereby the reader receives meanings unambiguously communicated by the text. The *Wake* will never be mastered, never dominated or exhausted by interpretation, nor will it ever offer itself up unproblematically as a single set of meanings; and if a sense of control and singleness of meaning is crucial to a reader's enjoyment, frustration will be the only result. More than this, however: the *Wake* teaches us, in a most delightful way, that *no* text can be mastered, that meaning is not something solid and unchanging beneath the words, attainable once and for all. All reading, the *Wake* insists, is an endless interchange: the reader is affected by the text at the same time as the text is affected by the reader, and neither retains a secure identity upon which the other can depend.

Another Wakean lesson is that different readers find different things in a text, making it impossible to hypothesize a 'typical' reader; and probably more than any other book in existence *Finnegans Wake* responds superbly to group readings. Each member of the group contributes his or her particular insights, which in turn trigger others, in a process which creates a growing network of meanings and patterns. Often a suggestion advanced tentatively by one member ('This seems ridiculous, but I can't help hearing ...') bears instant fruit as other members offer related perceptions of their own. What I wish to do is to imagine a group of new readers from different backgrounds tackling the book, armed with a minimum of prior knowledge but having available, for use as the discussion progresses, a good dictionary and a good encyclopedia.

There is no need to begin *Finnegans Wake* at the beginning; let us imagine that our group of readers decides to start with a passage which seems less crammed with multiple meanings than most (I have already quoted part of it), and that one member volunteers to read it aloud:

We are now diffusing among our lovers of this sequence (to you! to you!) the dewfolded song of the naughtingels (Alys! Alysaloe!) from their sheltered positions, in rosescenery haydyng, on the heather side of waldalure, Mount Saint John's, Jinnyland, whither our allies winged by duskfoil from Mooreparque, swift sanctuary seeking, after Sunsink gang (Oiboe! Hitherzither! Almost dotty! I must dash!) to pour their peace in partial (floflo floreflorence), sweetishsad lightandgayle, twittwin twosingwoolow. Let everie sound of a pitch keep still in resonance, jemcrow, jackdaw, prime and secund with their terce that whoe betwides them, now full theorbe, now dulcifair, and when we press of pedal (soft) pick out and vowelise your name.

(FW 359.31–360.06)

The response is a mixture of frowns at the stretches of apparent nonsense and chuckles as gleams of sense -- however absurd -- shine through. Some sort of purchase on the passage is obtained when the group quickly agrees that there is a syntactic scaffolding which, though interrupted by parentheses and elaborations, is quite firm, presenting a speaker who uses the first person plural to make a statement and to issue a command to a hearer or hearers addressed in the second person: 'We are now diffusing . . . the . . . song of the naughtingels . . . from their sheltered positions . . . whither our allies winged . . . to pour their peace . . . Let everie sound of a pitch keep still . . . and when we press of pedal pick out and vowelise your name.' Syntactic stability is characteristic of the *Wake*, and it often helps in the unpacking of a passage to trace the bare trellis on which the luxuriant verbiage is hung.

The second aspect of the passage on which members of the group quickly begin commenting is the clustering of related terms, some of which are half-concealed in puns and portmanteau words.[5] The most obvious of these clusters concerns birds: everybody hears 'naughtingels' as 'nightingales', and one person who has listened without looking at the text finds the same word in 'lightandgayle'. (When someone else is reading from the *Wake*, it is often helpful to put the book down, as the visual configurations can mask aural echoes.) With this lead to follow, one member of the group who speaks some Italian realizes that the strange word 'twosingwoolow' sounds rather like a badly-pronounced *'usignolo'*, which translates into yet another nightingale. No decoding is necessary to add to the cluster the terms 'winged', 'swift', 'sanctuary' (as in 'bird sanctuary'), 'crow', and 'jackdaw'; and someone suggests that 'Hitherzither' could be a description of the hither-and-thither movement of bird flight, perhaps that of the swift. But the group agrees that the main emphasis is on the sounds which birds make, and that a number of the repetitive phrases are reminiscent of conventional representations of birdcalls: 'to you! to you!' echoes 'to whit! to whoo!' (suggesting the additional presence of an owl, another nightbird to join the nightingales), and 'twittwin' suggests a twittering call. Other phrases seem built on similar models: 'Alys! Alysaloe!', 'floflo floreflorence'. Someone points out that the passage contains both 'song' and, buried in 'twosingwoolow', 'sing', while nightingales' song is often said to 'pour'. The syntactic framework is now taking on a body of sense, though that sense is beginning to overflow the rather limited possibilities provided by sequential English grammar. And each time a member of the group finds incomprehensibility suddenly yielding to meaning, or incongruity suddenly revealing a pattern, the discovery seems at once illuminating and ridiculous, satisfying and hilarious.

After a pause, someone notices that 'Florence' leads to another 'Nightingale', and this is picked up by someone else who spots a reference to the famous nineteenth-century soprano Jenny Lind (here apparently transformed into a place, 'Jinnyland'), known in Britain as 'the Swedish Nightingale' (which has become 'sweetishsad lightand-gayle'). The next suggestion, by a member with an interest in mythology, produces a discussion but no agreement: is 'terce' a reference to Tereus' rape of Philomela, who was subsequently metamorphosed into a nightingale? The cluster of birdsong references is rapidly expanding, it would seem: to human song, to women, perhaps to physical desire. Are the 'lovers' who are being addressed bird-lovers, lovers of opera and other human song, or lovers in the sexual sense? Again there is no consensus, since all these interpret-ations can be defended with reference to the passage – yet there is no way of holding the various possibilities together in an organic whole. No subtle tone of voice, no imagined human situation, could make all these meanings valid at the same time: *Finnegans Wake* explodes the belief that language, to be meaningful, must be subservient to a singleness of intention and subjectivity. (So too, we may remember, does 'Eveline'.)

Once the group is on the track of human song a new cluster of terms emerges. One member realizes that the initially puzzling 'rosescenery haydyng' introduces two of the most prolific of opera composers, Rossini and Haydn; another suggests that 'twosingwoolow' contains a version of 'sing willow', a refrain associated with songs of lover's grief (she cites Desdemona's 'Willow Song' in *Othello* and – reverting briefly to birds – Ko-Ko's song about a suicidal tom-tit in *The Mikado*); and a third, who is familiar with the traditions of the Western church, recognizes 'prime' and 'terce' as the names of the first two offices sung each day. He adds that 'vowelise' is close to 'vocalise', which as an English verb can mean to 'sing' and as a French noun is a singing exercise. As the discussion proceeds, human song broadens out to music and sound more generally: 'pitch' and 'resonance' obviously belong to this cluster, and someone who has picked up the dictionary informs the group that 'sequence' can mean 'a composition said or sung in the Western Church' as well as a melodic repetition, and that 'partials' are upper harmonics. Soon the group is picking out the instruments of a somewhat exotic orchestra in the passage too: a gong in 'gang', an oboe in 'Oiboe!', a zither in 'Hitherzither', a theorbo (a kind of lute) in 'theorbe', a dulcimer in 'dulcifair', and, by implication, a piano in 'pedal (sof!)'. And a different kind of organized sound produced by humans emerges from 'Almost dotty! I must dash!': Morse Code.

The proposal is made that the topic of sexuality should be followed up, to see if it also leads to a set of connected meanings. Several members comment together that 'naughtingels' contains not only 'nightingales' but also 'naughty girls' (or 'gels', if we imagine a certain kind of upper-class English accent), and soon other suggestions are forthcoming: 'waldalure' conceals 'allure' (and 'lure', perhaps, if sexual temptation is in the air) and 'twosingwoolow' contains 'woo'. Girls' names are a likely quarry for connotations of glamour and desirability, and the group may well pause on 'Alys! Alysaloe!,' which, backed up by 'allies', implies the presence of an Alice. Someone recalls that the author of 'Alice in Wonderland' (the originator of the term 'portmanteau word') liked to entertain and photograph little girls, and an enthusiast of the theatre tells the group about a 1930s stage beauty called Alice Delysio and a French revue artiste named Gaby Delys. At this point, a sceptical participant objects that Joyce could not possibly have put all these meanings into the text, and two answers are forthcoming: one is that we cannot know for certain in any specific case that he did not, and the other is that even if we could, it need not make any difference, since Joyce has deliberately created a text with the power to generate more meanings than he had in mind.

While this discussion has been going on, one member of the group has been noting suggestions of seclusion (especially in natural surroundings) and darkness, which relate both to the nightingale cluster and to the hints of sexual impropriety. 'Dewfolded' implies both night and enclosure; 'sheltered positions' needs no deciphering; 'rosescenery hayding' gives us concealment in a rose-garden in addition to the composers already discovered there; and 'other' is appropriately transformed into 'heather'. A German speaker adds to the list the German word for 'forest' – 'Wald' – in 'waldalure'; and a French speaker notices that 'duskfoil' combines the fall of darkness with leaves ('feuilles'). There is obviously a park in 'Mooreparque', and this is followed by the 'sanctuary' that has already been mentioned; then there is a sunset, or 'Sunsink', with perhaps an echo of the German word for the same phenomenon, 'Sonnenuntergang', in 'Sunsink gang'. The suggestions of darkness draw the group's attention to words indicative of blackness – 'Moor' (triggering another association with Othello), 'pitch', 'crow', 'jackdaw' – as well as an allusion to 'Jim Crow'. The dictionary reveals that this last phrase, although it became associated with racism in this century, was originally the name of a Negro plantation song of the early nineteenth century; and the group considers whether this fact can be related to the presence of the words 'gang', 'pick' and 'hoe' (in 'whoe'). Of course it can be related, once the connection has been noted; whether it is a little entertaining dead-end or leads into a new exfoliation of meaning can only be determined by further reading – sometimes a tiny cluster like this can remain dormant for years until one suddenly finds that it is part of a pattern of linked terms running through the chapter or the entire book.

Someone now comments, 'I can't help feeling that the passage is also about battles, though the only example I can point to is the reference to Florence Nightingale, who became famous in the Crimean War.' Others chip in: 'The word "peace" is there'; 'And "allies" suggests a military force'; 'What about the Morse Code we mentioned earlier? – that could go with army signalling.' The group studies the passage for a few minutes, sensitized to this new potential sequence of terms, until light suddenly dawns: 'Of course ... "waldalure" must be Waterloo!' And a member with some knowledge of that battle picks up the idea: 'Yes, it must be, because "Mount Saint John's" is Mont St Jean, a village near the battlefield whose name the English army used – it's where they built the Waterloo museum. And now I can see an extra reason for the word "allies": on the Continent the battle was often named after another village on the site, La Belle Alliance.' Someone else adds, 'When the passage was read aloud, "sound of a pitch" came over to me as "son of a bitch", but I didn't think it could be relevant – but it *is* the sort of thing you'd be called on an army parade ground. And maybe "pick out and vowelise your name" is an order to speak out and identify yourself.'

A question is now posed by one of the group: 'Is there a specific place where we can situate all this activity?' The answer, the group agrees, must be no, in that the passage traverses a wide range of countries; at the same time, those who have read Joyce's work insist that Ireland, and Dublin in particular, always have a special place in Joyce's writing. Someone who has read *Ulysses* remembers Leopold Bloom's meditations on 'Dunsink Time' – the local Dublin time determined at the Dunsink Observatory – and notices its form adumbrated in 'Sunsink gang'. ('Time', someone notes paranthetically, 'is also there in "secund" and the canonical hours, "prime" and "terce"'.) Another Irish connection is pointed out in 'swift', now not a bird or an adjective of speed, but the Irish writer Jonathan Swift; and the encyclopedia provides the information that the estate in England where Swift was employed for a time was called 'Moor Park'. Swift, the group also recalls, went 'almost dotty'.

The word 'dewfolded' also arouses comment: although the group has noted the appropriateness of both 'dew' and 'folded' to the thematic concerns of the passage, the portmanteau word they make in combination still has to be explained. It sounds as if 'dew-folded' has been combined with 'twofold', and this provides yet another thread for the group to follow. The exclamations (evocations of birdsong?) always come in pairs: 'to you! to you!'; 'Alys! Alysaloe!'; 'Oiboe! Hitherzither!' 'Almost dotty! I must dash!'; and there is doubling in 'floflo' and 'floreflorence'. 'Twittwin' not only involves doubling, but the word 'twin', and it is immediately followed by 'two'. Two famous women figure in the passage, both Nightingales. However, there is clearly a triple principle at work in 'prime and secund with their terce that whoe betwides them', even if 'betwides' still contains a hint of doubleness in '-twi-' (a prefix we are particularly familiar with in 'twilight') as well as an oscillation between 'between' and 'beside'. This pattern of twos and a three seems to be important, but the group is unable to take it further – until it turns to other passages in the book.

The passage is now glowing with interconnected meanings, but a number of portmanteau words remain unexplained. As long as there is an element in a word unaccounted for there is something more to think about (not that the process would stop if all the deformations could be explained). It is all too easy, having unearthed one or more familiar expressions from a baffling portmanteau, to forget that the distortion itself needs explanation. Having identified 'Moor Park' in 'Mooreparque', for instance, the group still has to ask why it has undergone this transformation. The spelling 'parque' suggests Frenchness to everybody, with an obvious appropriateness to a passage dealing with Waterloo, but the French speaker also proposes that its meaning, 'fate', is connected with the warning 'woe betide them' in 'whoe betwides them'. And the spelling of 'Moore' with an 'e', someone observes, may be a reference to the Irish poet Thomas Moore – a suggestion that is clinched when someone else detects, in 'full theorbe, now dulcifair', the title of one of Moore's songs, 'Fill the Bumper Fair'. (We now have two Irish poets to go with the two Nightingales.) The group still has not come up with an explanation of the spelling of 'Oiboe!' (though the Italian speaker might have a suggestion), 'everie', or 'sof!'; it has not established whether 'in partial' echoes 'impartial' or 'in resonance' 'in residence'; and it remains undecided as to a possible cluster of tools that would include the jemmy and the crowbar of 'jemcrow' and the 'pick' near the end of the passage.

But it is time to pause and recapitulate. The passage presents a voice which describes the song of nightingales from their hiding places in dark vegetation; we, the readers (or listeners) are asked to keep quiet, and then to join in a singing exercise. Clearly this 'content' is of very little interest in itself, like so much of *Dubliners*. But other implications crowd in upon that voice, which we have to treat as only one element in a text that is speaking to us in ways that ordinary speech, with its linear simplicity, cannot achieve. The nightingales (perhaps two of them) are related to other birds associated with dusk, night, or blackness – owls, swifts, crows, jackdaws – and beyond that to women, especially women who sing and women who conventionally represent sexual temptation (though they may, like Desdemona, be innocent). All this takes place within an international context: languages and geographical references take us to Sweden, Germany, Italy, France, Belgium (for Waterloo), England, the American South, the Crimea; and although international co-operation is implied by this free market and by the evocations of many kinds of music, we also detect sounds of battle, hints of slavery, warnings of doom. Sexual difference, it seems, is mapped onto national difference, and sexual encounters onto military ones. (Or vice-versa: there is no certainty about what is literal and what figurative in the *Wake*.)

To have got this far is to have transformed an opaque block of language into an almost-too-meaningful complex of ideas and associations; this in itself is a pleasing achievement, and the experience of finding more and more of the obscurity clearing is a fascinating and fulfilling one. In moving through the passage several times, with different thematic clusters in mind, our group has found many of the words and phrases accumulating a number of meanings, like pictures that look different from different perspectives – and this happens not just with portmanteau words and obvious puns, for the *Wake* encourages the reader to scrutinize *every* word for possible openings onto new meanings. From here the group might move to other passages, which would be illuminated by the discoveries made in this one, and on returning to this passage would find yet more in it. Members might also consult some of the secondary material on *Finnegans Wake*, such as the books mentioned in the section in this volume on 'Further Reading', or examine transcriptions and facsimiles of earlier drafts (not that these will furnish 'solutions' to problems of interpretation, but they can suggest fresh pathways to follow), or talk to someone who has spent longer on the *Wake* and has a sense of its recurrent patterns and concerns.

One context that can hardly be ignored is the chapter in which the passage occurs (II.3); like all the *Wake*'s chapters (and like those of *Ulysses*), this has its own distinctive character. It was one of the last major works Joyce completed before his death in 1941: seventy-four pages of Wakean language at its most multidimensional and its most comic, bombarding the reader with a constantly proliferating evocation of sounds and sights somewhat uncertainly localized in a Dublin bar-room and featuring both rowdy conversation and broadcasts from a television set and a radio. Armed with this knowledge, the reader will immediately recognize that the passage is based on a radio transmission. The presence of Morse Code hints at this, as does the inclusion of the French term for 'broadcast' – '*diffusion*'. A specific historical framework emerges once we learn that among the BBC's most popular programmes in the 1930s were live transmissions of nightingale songs. (The superior English accent we detected earlier could be that of the early BBC.) Indeed, if our group had started with the secondary material on the *Wake*, it might well have read the passage with the BBC broadcasts dominating its interpretation – a preconception which might have obscured some of the other leads that were followed up. The immediate context of the passage also makes possible a tentative psychological interpretation, since it concerns accusations of a sexual nature levelled against a male figure (usually referred to by the initials HCE): it may be that even the radio broadcast, to HCE's ears, becomes a further accusatory voice.

Ranging more widely, other passages in the book provide a number of constantly repeated motifs, scenarios, and anecdotes which enrich and clarify our reading of this passage. HCE's crime, never given a definitive form but recurring in a multitude of versions, seems to involve two young women committing an indiscretion – perhaps just peeing, perhaps more – in a park, usually Dublin's Phoenix Park (notice its ornithological name), and the whole incident's being observed by three soldiers. The park incident and its ramifications have been developing since the beginning of the book – should we choose to start there. We hear on the first page of 'sesthers wroth with twone nathandjoe' (3.12): these sisters are also Esthers, and Swift had two woman-friends who both bore this name. (Unscramble 'nathandjoe' to find 'Jonathan'.) So in our passage Swift and the two girls in the park are not as unconnected as we might have thought, especially if we know that it was at Moor Park that he met one of the Esthers.

Read in this context, our passage seems more obviously concerned with sexual indiscretions than it did on its own; the 'naughtingels', the reiteration of 'two' and the presence of 'three', the emphasis on the bosky seclusion and dewy darkness of the scene, the coexistence of military and sexual imagery, and the fact that the sounds emanating from this hidden place are being publicly broadcast, all resonate with the book's many other versions of a sexual misdemeanour made public, and from there to considerations of transgression, guilt, accusation, and defence. (Other important versions of the incident in the park include the anti-British Phoenix Park murders of 1882, Eve's temptation of Adam in the Garden of Eden, and, as our passage suggests, the Battle of Waterloo – that word functioning as both a proper and a common noun, just as 'Frank' in 'Eveline' is both a name and an adjective.) Knowledge of the indiscreetly urinating girls also enables us to add a further meaning to the phrase 'pour their peace'. And very little that we have found in the passage is not repeated many times, in altered forms, elsewhere in *Finnegans Wake*.

The main point of the communal reading process I have imagined is not, it must be stressed, to demonstrate the complexity of a passage of the *Wake*; it is to show how that complexity holds open numerous entrances to the text, each of which will provide a thread of meaning, together with satisfaction and amusement, and each of which can be traced beyond the passage without the necessity of waiting until every word has been explained. The group I have imagined is obviously a rather exceptional one (though many of the leads I have indicated could have been provided by judicious use of secondary material); but what is important to realize is that it is not essential to an enjoyment of the *Wake* that all these meanings emerge. Since reading the *Wake* is a never-ending activity, it would be quite enough for the time being to register this passage as a radio interlude of birdsong, or as a tranquil evocation of nature, or as a version of the girls' misdemeanour in the park, or as an allusion to the Battle of Waterloo – and it would do no harm to skip it altogether.

If we do choose to linger on the passage, to draw out as many of the threads as we can, we may spend a considerable time, in a group or as individuals, saying the words over and over, listening to their sounds, studying their letters, allowing them to resonate to the furthest reaches of our memory; probably no literary text encourages as full an engagement with all the features of language and all the processes of reading as *Finnegans Wake*. New readers seldom appreciate just how much of the *Wake* remains unaccounted for in spite of the abundance of books and articles that it has generated, and feel that they are stumbling behind what other people have done when they may in fact be breaking completely new ground. One of the pleasures of reading the *Wake* is that it is impossible to predict when an item of apparently useless knowledge will suddenly illuminate a shadowy corner, since each of us is in possession of a somewhat different segment of the cultural treasure-house (or midden-heap, to use one of the *Wake*'s own images) which the text endlessly turns over. We may also want to spend time in the library with guides and reference books, in order to build on the work of others; this is how the individual reader can become the member of a group with a range of specialized knowledges. Some potential readers may question this expenditure of time, so far beyond that demanded by other works. But is not time spent per line of print a crude, because purely quantitative, measure? If we are going to think quantitatively, it might be more appropriate to consider the time Joyce spent in writing the *Wake*: a rough calculation would give us an average of nine days' creative labour per page; or three days for our passage. An hour or two seems rather little to devote to its interpretation and enjoyment.

Our exercise of reading has also revealed how many of our usual novelistic expectations we have to suspend in reading the *Wake*: expectations that we will find a 'narrative voice', some 'characters', a 'plot', some kind of 'truth'. But it is not that these are absent; rather, they are present in *Finnegans Wake* in much greater abundance than we are used to. Several voices can be heard in this passage; there are a number of 'characters' (including birds, armies, singers, and lovers); plots are thick on the ground (stories of warfare, seduction, exhibitionism); and if there is no truth to be had, there are constant insights into the way language relates to meaning and to itself, the way cultures interconnect, the way history throws up coincidences and repetitions, the way guilt and temptation influence language and thought (and vice versa), the way stories, gossip, reportage, and a hundred other uses of words construct the world in which we live, love, fight, and dream.

All this does not make *Finnegans Wake* utterly unlike any other literary work, however. The kinds of reading to which it responds are only an extreme version of what we do with all literary texts. We have already seen that in 'Eveline', as plain a piece of writing as one could wish for, there are conflicting points of view between which we have to – yet cannot – decide; there is more than one implicit story being played out (the romance with the happy ending, the betrayal of the innocent victim, the escape route blocked by obligations to others); there are words and phrases that resonate in several directions ('face of bronze', '*The Bohemian Girl*', 'pleasantly confused'). Reading *Finnegans Wake* may seem a far cry from reading *Dubliners*, but the same attention to every aspect of every word, the same open-mindedness about possibilities of interpretation, the same curiosity and persistence can produce similar rewards.[6]

By beginning with a short passage in this way, we have avoided what is perhaps the more usual approach to the *Wake*: the application of a simple framework derived from an external source, used as a key to reading. Many readers pick up the book with the expectation that they will be reading about a dream, or about a family called Porter who live above a pub in Dublin, or about a night to complement the day of *Ulysses*; and they are inevitably disappointed when they find that pages go by without any apparent reference to their framework, which was supposed to unlock for them the mysteries of the text. Much more helpful, and derivable from a careful reading of passages rather than from Joyce's remarks to friends or the guesses of early commentators, is an awareness of the interconnected series of patterns, structures, relationships, anecdotes, and myths such as those we discovered at work in our passage. The publican's family is one such structure, but it does not hold the entire book together; the notion that the whole thing is a dream may provide a sense of reassurance when all seems obscure but does not give much assistance when a particular passage has to be elucidated. That Freud's *Interpretation of Dreams* is relevant and illuminating is unquestionable; but it functions like so many other books in the *Wake* – the Egyptian *Book of the Dead*, for instance, or Vico's *New Science* (or Freud's books on jokes and slips of the tongue, for that matter) – as a quarry for ideas, structures, phrases, formulae. Only the reader who spends enough time with the book to grow familiar with all its chapters needs to begin asking questions about total structure; how the coming of darkness depicted at the end of I.8 relates to the sporadic references to evening in Book II (including those in our passage), night in Book III, and dawn in Book IV; why the seventeen chapters are divided into eight, four, four, and one; whether the 'concluding' monologue offers any kind of vantage point from which to survey the whole text.[7] Here again the *Wake* demands that we suspend our usual practice in reading a literary work. Normally we start constructing a hypothesis about the possible organization and meaning of the whole (whether in terms of plot, symbolic structure, moral lesson, or a combination of these) as we start reading, and as we go on we continuously revise this hypothesis, interpreting each detail in terms of it; the end of the book then comes as the revelation of its true form and thereby of the true meaning of all the details we encountered along the way. The *Wake* helps us to see that this is not the only way to read a novel; that the details may undermine or be in excess of any overall structuring principle, and that the structure may be something we create out of rather than derive from the elements offered by the text.

At the same time, the *Wake* makes it evident that we cannot read *without* creating structures, sequences, and relationships; that is what interpretation is. One reader will trace through the book all the references to night and the sleeping body, another will become hyper-alert to family and gender roles, a third will mine the text for impulses of desire and guilt on the model of psychoanalysis. All will produce valid and valuable readings, capable of enhancing the text for other readers; all will leave most of the *Wake's* resources untapped. No single mind could give all the possible meanings of the *Wake* equal and simultaneous weight, and there is no need to assume that Joyce, brilliant verbal artist though he was, ever did. To create a text as full of interconnections as *Finnegans Wake* is, connections within itself and with the weave of human culture of which it is both simulacrum and constituent part, is willingly to lay aside the reins of intentionality and let the text's meanings work in the world to which it belongs.[8] The willingness to relinquish authorial control is an evident property of *Ulysses* as well; and is it not also true, to some degree at least, of 'Eveline', and, for that matter, of any literary work that engages with the texts, cultural, historical, political, commercial, psychological, or technical, of its time and ours? Reading Joyce is only one of many ways to pursue an interest in the unceasing traffic – in both directions – between words and the world, but it is one that can throw light on all the others, and offer as it does so the pleasures of an undogmatic and regenerative comic awareness.

IV

Reading Joyce's *œuvre* is, as an ever-renewed activity, more than a lifetime's work (or play); and when we take into account the massive heap of books written about that *œuvre* towering around it – and growing larger at an ever-increasing rate – the task of even beginning to feel at home with Joyce may make the newcomer quail. But there is no need for alarm: none of those books is essential to the reader of Joyce in search of pleasure and understanding, and at the same time all of them are potential allies. Although complaints about the overproduction of secondary commentary on Joyce (as with Shakespeare) will always be heard, it is a real problem only for the diligent librarian or the obsessive scholar. It is possible to think of the growing pile of books 'on Joyce' as neither a threatening rampart casting deeper and deeper shadows over the original brightness of Joyce's genius nor a heroic monument to the task of total elucidation whose final moment draws nearer and nearer. This metatextual mountain is not in any simple way *outside* Joyce's own writing at all: it could be seen as continuous with the text it surrounds, extending that text to something much larger and richer than it was when Joyce first wrote it; and there is also a sense in which it is *inside* Joyce's original text, interleaving and interlineating it, dilating it to many times its original size. Take the library shelves which hold a hundred books containing interpretations of Joyce: they also hold, inside those same books, much of Joyce's text itself, quoted, paraphrased, fragmented, dispersed, rearranged, expanded. In reading through those books you are reading, and rereading, the Joycean text itself, seen from constantly-changing viewpoints and enhanced by ever new juxtapositions.

However, there is no need to move beyond the original work at all to experience its special rewards. Help in reading Joyce is not confined to the books that surround his own; his texts themselves teach us how to read them, provoking laughter at our *naïveté* when we fall into the trap of thinking of the world they create as a world that existed before they brought it into being, encouraging us to do without our need for singleness of meaning or certainty of position, showing us how our language is a powerful, and powerfully funny, determiner – but also underminer – of our thoughts and acts. Many of the most influential literary theorists of the past twenty years, whose views have percolated into thousands of classrooms, have testified to the importance of reading Joyce in the development of their ideas.[9]

So Joyce's work has actually been growing over the years, and the number of ways of reading it has also been growing, all of them of some value, none of them final or definitive. There could not possibly be a 'correct' way of reading, or even starting to read, the textual mass that consists of Joyce's texts themselves, all the texts of which *they* are readings (and we are only just beginning to appreciate how many of Joyce's words come not freshly-minted from his brain but copied out from other books[10]), all the works of Joycean criticism and biography which read *them*, all the transcripts and facsimiles of manuscript material, and all the other texts which have a potential bearing on Joyce. At one extreme are the readers who will read one or two of Joyce's books, relying entirely on the general familiarity I have already mentioned to help them find enjoyment and stimulation; at the other extreme are the professionals and the monomaniacs, who may attempt to read not only the Joycean texts themselves several times but, impossibly, all the other works with which they interrelate. In between are a multitude of options, all of them valid and valuable; there is no justification for saying that a reading of *Ulysses* by a Dubliner born towards the end of the nineteenth century is 'better' or 'truer' than one by a reader born in 1970 who has never set foot in Ireland, and the same applies to readers who have and who have not read the rest of Joyce's work, or biographies of Joyce, or the available manuscripts, or a pile of critical books, or a cross-section of early twentieth-century fiction, or the history of Europe. But what is undoubtedly the case is that all these encounters with Joyce are different, and to keep coming back to Joyce after detours through these and other readings (whether readings of books or of the world outside books) is to keep on engaging with recreated texts and thereby discovering new pleasures. If there *is* a way of reading Joyce that could be thought of as less than fully worthwhile, as something of a waste of human energy, it would be one that fails to bring together an active and curious attention to the words on the page with whatever store of knowledge and experience the individual reader has accumulated.

What I have been saying about the relation between Joyce's texts and the texts that surround them holds true for the different parts of Joyce's *œuvre* as well. The reader returning to a work of Joyce's after having read, or reread, another one finds it a different work (or, to put it another way, finds that he or she has become a different reader). Several of the essays in this volume discuss the interconnectedness of all Joyce's productions: not just the way the early texts prefigure the later texts, but the way the later texts rewrite the early texts, and in so doing proffer readings of those texts that would not otherwise emerge – and that Joyce himself, when he wrote those early texts, may not have been in a position to appreciate. To take one example: the beginning of *Ulysses* both continues and retroactively transforms the ending of *A Portrait*, exposing Stephen Dedalus's heroic ambitions as an artist at the close of the earlier text to the possible accusation of self-deceived posturing when we learn in the later text of their unimpressive outcome.

Something similar happens *within* the covers of Joyce's books, too: 'The Dead' can be regarded as a reading of all the stories of *Dubliners* that come before it, and thus offers the reader a fresh perspective on them; the later chapters of *Ulysses* reread and thereby remake the earlier chapters. And even the boundaries between works become porous; in some ways the first three chapters of *Ulysses* belong more with *A Portrait* than they do with the last three chapters of *Ulysses* – which in turn might be said to be a prelude to *Finnegans Wake*. To begin a work of Joyce's at the beginning and to read to the end is therefore to exercise only one of many options. New readers of *Ulysses* may find their first reading less arduous if they begin at chapter four (the opening of the second part of the book), then move from the end of chapter six to chapters one to three before proceeding to chapter seven. There will be some losses in doing this, but some gains as well; and we need not fear that the irate ghost of Joyce will come to haunt us with an insistence on linear integrity, since his texts themselves undo such a notion. One of the great pleasures of being a lifetime reader of *Ulysses* or *Finnegans Wake* is singling out one episode and treating it as a relatively independent work; many of these chapters are, after all, as long as a medium-sized novel. As a way of freeing oneself from too rigid a notion of the organic and self-sufficient work of art (a notion that Joyce expounds but also ironically exposes in *A Portrait*), it is sometimes worth trying to think of Joyce as the author of around sixty distinct works – with interesting interconnections – that happen to have been bound together as the chapters of a number of differently-titled volumes.

Equally, the unpublished and the published texts of Joyce interlock in ways which make the separation between these categories somewhat artificial (and render the notion of a 'definitive' edition an impossible one). Thus, for example, a kind of 'Greater *Finnegans Wake*' is emerging, consisting of the final text and the mass of notebooks from which it was drawn, carefully preserved by Joyce so that they could be read by posterity and now widely available in the facsimile edition of the *James Joyce Archive*. To give another example, the reader who reads *A Portrait* together with *Stephen Hero*, the surviving fragment of its predecessor which Joyce abandoned, has a complex experience that cannot simply be described in terms of 'preliminary' and 'final' versions of the same text. One way of approaching *Stephen Hero*, in fact, is as an addendum to *A Portrait* exemplifying the type of novel that the Stephen of the end of *A Portrait* would have written – and then, by the time of *Ulysses*, abandoned.

As this example might suggest, there is a similar fluidity at the borderline between fiction and biography; the various Stephens of *Stephen Hero*, *A Portrait*, and *Ulysses*, together with the Shem of

Finnegans Wake, are related in interesting (and ultimately unspecifiable) ways not only to one another, but also to the consciousness we perceive – with increasing difficulty – as the 'author' in each of these books, as well as to the individual named 'James Joyce' whom we meet in the biographical accounts by, say, Stanislaus Joyce or Richard Ellmann. (We might recall that Joyce's early pen-name was Stephen Daedalus.) And the Dublin in which most of Joyce's fictions are set is neither wholly identifiable with nor wholly distinguishable from the real city, just as the 16 June 1904 we encounter in *Ulysses* is and is not a day in history of which the newspapers bearing that date provide some record.

Yet another permeable boundary is that between the works as published and the commentary which Joyce deliberately circulated to guide early interpreters. For instance, *Ulysses* carries no chapter-titles, but the reader who is aware of the titles which Joyce gave to friends, knowing they would be made public, and which have become standard in commentaries on Joyce, will have a different experience from the reader who has not come across them. We cannot say whether or not these 'are' the titles of the episodes, however; all they offer us is a possible way of reading the book, one which is based on a decision to ignore the striking blankness at the top of the initial page of each chapter. (Accepting the titles does not lead automatically to a single interpretation of the chapters that follow, however.)

As readers, then, we cannot divide up the Joycean text into absolutely leakproof boxes: original/quotation, *Dubliners/A Portrait/ Ulysses/Finnegans Wake*, published/unpublished, fictional/historical, internal/external, and so on. Part of Joyce's revolutionary achievement in literature, and in the understanding of literature and other cultural forms, was his demonstration of the interrelations and interpenetrations of such categories. And we cannot come to the end of making sense of the Joycean text, finding patterns and structures in it, following tracks through it, and – by the same token – deriving pleasures from it. It entices us into repeated acts of interpretation by proffering us keys and promising us conclusions, but it proffers and promises with such teeming generosity that no single key or conclusion can stand for very long. In one sense, this makes it an extraordinary *œuvre*, pushing to the limits all the traditional features of the novel as a genre such as characterization, narrative voice, plot, symbolization, and ethical or political significance; but at the same time this is what makes it such a *typical* literary *œuvre*, revealing just what a self-contradictory institution literature is, and just how much pleasure is generated by those contradictions in the ordinary act of reading. One result is that reading Joyce can make a difference to all one's reading, enriching, complicating, and perhaps even undermining it (at least until it becomes possible to substitute a fuller sense of what reading is for the narrow one that often prevails in educational establishments).

The number of entrances to the Joycean mansion, therefore, is potentially infinite; the main requisites for a visit are a sharp eye and ear, a willingness to be surprised, and of course a sense of humour. The chapters of this book provide introductions to some of these ways in, and will suggest many more in passing. Different readers will, of course, find some approaches more congenial than others: if you like crossword puzzles you may enjoy piecing together the scraps of information about the characters' lives scattered through *Ulysses* or constructing a plausible plot that might undergird the linguistic extravagances of *Finnegans Wake*; if you value the textures of language that poets have traditionally exploited you can relish the carefully modulated patterns of Joyce's sounds and syntax; if you find coincidences, human oddities, and unexpected incongruities funny, Joyce will provide endless amusement; if you enjoy the novelist's capacity to convey the motions of thought and feeling or the sensory experiences of the body, there will be mimetic pleasures in abundance for you; if you have an interest in history, in culture, in politics, in the problems of the artist, in literary theory, you will find that any of these will open doors in Joyce's works. But these are only ways in: Joyce's writing can reveal sources of fascination and exhilaration which you were not expecting to find, and if you feel at times that Joyce is laughing at you just as much as you are laughing at him, you have begun to appreciate the delightfully unsettling energies of his art.

NOTES

1 Other chapters of this book trace some of the ways in which Joyce's achievement was both shaped by and helped to shape a wider complex of cultural movements: see especially chs. 2, 3, 4, and 11.

2 Joyce's shorter published works – his collections of poetry and the play *Exiles* – are, at least on the surface, more obviously conventional than his four major works, *Dubliners*, *A Portrait of the Artist as a Young Man*, *Ulysses*, and *Finnegans Wake*; but some of the texts which remained

unpublished during his lifetime, notably *Giacomo Joyce*, also demand unusual strategies of reading (see Vicki Mahaffey's contribution to this volume).

3 This device goes by many names – free indirect discourse, narrated monologue, empathetic narrative, *style indirect libre, erlebte Rede* – and is perhaps best regarded as a cluster of techniques ranging from precisely recoverable thoughts to a slight colouring of the narrator's style by that of the character. (A related device, in which specific thoughts are not implied, goes by the name of 'The Uncle Charles Principle': see Hugh Kenner, *Joyce's Voices* (Berkeley: University of California Press, 1978), ch. 2.) Earlier examples, such as those in Jane Austen's fiction, usually involve the thoughts of more highly educated and sophisticated characters than Joyce chooses. Joyce's revisions of 'Eveline' for *Dubliners* involved many substitutions of words and phrases more appropriate to Eveline's limited mental world than the ones he first used (see *Dubliners*, Viking Critical Library edition, ed. Robert Scholes and A. Walton Litz (New York: Viking, 1969), pp. 238–40).

4 The most vigorous proponent of the view that Frank is a liar has been Hugh Kenner; for a discussion of Kenner's various accounts of the story, and a counter-argument, see Sidney Feschbach, '"Fallen on His Feet in Buenos Ayres": Frank in "Eveline"', *JJQ* 20 (1983), 223–7. In a traditional narrative, of course, the truth would be revealed in the denouement.

5 The portmanteau words of *Finnegans Wake* – Joycean inventions which fuse two or more words, sometimes in different languages – probably constitute the most alarming feature of the book for new readers; they are also central to its operation and the pleasures to be had from it. For further discussion, see Derek Attridge, *Peculiar Language: Literature as Difference from the Renaissance to James Joyce* (Ithaca: Cornell University Press, 1988), ch. 7.

6 There are, of course, many passages in *Dubliners* with more elaborately contrived subtleties than the relatively simple example we have examined. See also John Paul Riquelme's discussion of the language of *Dubliners* in ch. 5, pp. 123–8 below.

7 For an interpretation of the *Wake*'s structure which discusses these matters, as well as making valuable use of Freudian dream theory, see Margot Norris's contribution to this volume.

8 It is worth pondering why *Finnegans Wake* is as long as it is – could not Joyce have achieved the same results in a much shorter work? One answer would be that only a work of massive proportions could produce such rich and overdetermined interconnections that it escapes any possibility of interpretative mastery, and achieves an openness to all possible futures akin to that of the human brain itself.

9 Jacques Derrida discusses his indebtedness to Joyce in 'Two words for Joyce', in Derek Attridge and Daniel Ferrer, eds., *Post-structuralist Joyce: Essays from the French* (Cambridge: Cambridge University Press, 1984), 145–59; Hélène Cixous wrote her doctoral dissertation – and many later essays – on Joyce; Julia Kristeva has paid special attention to Joyce in her theoretical writings on literature; Jacques Lacan devoted one of his famous seminars to Joyce; Northrop Frye, Wolfgang Iser, Umberto Eco, Fredric Jameson, Stephen Heath, Raymond Williams, and Colin MacCabe have all written important texts on Joyce. Even those who have reacted vigorously against Joyce – like Georg Lukács and Carl Gustav Jung – have recognized his importance.

10 The study of manuscript materials is currently revealing how much of Joyce's writing is built up from jottings made in notebooks while he went through other books; see Hans Walter Gabler's contribution to this volume, and Margot Norris's discussion of the genesis of *Finnegans Wake* (pp. 170–2 below).

2 Joyce the Irishman

In *Stephen Hero*, the abandoned forerunner to *A Portrait of the Artist as a Young Man*, the undergraduate artist-hero attacks the Irish educational system and gives promise of his rebellion against it and the culture it represents:

> The deadly chill of the atmosphere of the college paralysed Stephen's heart. In a stupor of powerlessness he reviewed the plague of Catholicism . . . The spectacle of the world in thrall filled him with the fire of courage. He, at least, though living at the farthest remove from the centre of European culture, marooned on an island in the ocean, though inheriting a will broken by doubt and a soul the steadfastness of whose hate became as weak as water in siren arms, would lead his own life according to what he recognised as the voice of a new humanity, active, unafraid and unashamed. (*SH* 194)

Joyce's repudiation of Catholic Ireland and his countering declaration of artistic independence are well-known and integral features of his life-long dedication to writing. Yet he was formed by the Ireland he repudiated and his quest for artistic freedom was itself shaped by the exemplary instances of earlier Irish writers who had, in his view, failed to achieve that independence which he sought for himself, an independence which was at once the precondition and the goal of writing.

When we survey his achievement in retrospect, it seems surprising that the uncertain and fragmented accomplishment of nineteenth-century Irish literature should have reached a culmination in his fiction and in the poetry of Yeats. It seems quite inexplicable that an oppressed and turbulent country, which had lost half its population and its native language only forty-five years before Joyce was born, could have begun to produce literature of world importance as he reached his early teens. But some explanations are forthcoming when we look more closely at Irish literary culture in the nineteenth century. Most importantly, an understanding of some of the stresses and strains of that literature help us to understand why Joyce produced works like *Ulysses* and *Finnegans Wake* in his maturity. The deformations of the English language and of the traditional form of the novel which we encounter in these are anticipated in the conflict between Irish, Hiberno-English and standard English which is a feature of the Irish writing Joyce knew.

The most important of Joyce's Irish predecessors was the poet James Clarence Mangan (1803–49), whose tragic and miserable life was represented by Joyce as an emblem of the characteristic alienation of the true artist. More significantly, Joyce exaggerated the extent to which Mangan had been ignored by his countrymen after his death. For, as Joyce saw it, Mangan also represented the artist who was spurned by his countrymen in a typically treacherous fashion, largely because he had identified his own multifarious woes with those of his suffering country. Joyce's obsession with betrayal manifests itself in unmistakable fashion in the lectures he delivered on Mangan, in Dublin in 1902 and in Trieste in 1907. Wherever he looked, in Irish political or literary history, he found that the master-theme was betrayal. The great political crisis which dominated his early life – the fall of Parnell – probably governed this reading of his country's past and helped to define for him the nature of the embattled future relationship between him and his Irish audience. Parnell was, in Joyce's view, a heroic spirit brought low by his own people, who sold him 'to the pharisaical conscience of the English Dissenters' (*CW* 196) or, in a more famous formulation, listened to Parnell's plea that they should not throw him to the English wolves. 'They did not throw him to the English wolves; they tore him to pieces themselves' (*CW* 228).

It may be that betrayal was a Joycean obsession; certainly it provided him with a way of reading the Irish past as a series of narratives which led to the same, monotonous denouement. But betrayal implies a preceding solidarity, a communion between the victim and his treacherous countrymen. The most appealing and dangerously seductive form of solidarity in Irish conditions was that offered by Irish nationalism, in all its variant forms, from the United Irishmen of 1798 to the Young Ireland movement of the 1840s and the more recent Fenian and Home Rule movements. It was Mangan's downfall as an artist that he could not free himself from the tragic history of his nation. 'The history of his country encloses him so straitly that even in his hours of extreme individual passion he can barely reduce its walls to ruins' (CW 185). Mangan's art is, therefore, caught in the toils of a political crisis from which it can never be freed until that crisis has been resolved. So 'the most significant poet of the modern Celtic world' (CW 179) has suffered oblivion in his own land because he is, on the one hand, not national enough, and, on the other hand, too national ever to be appreciated for his own individual and remarkable qualities as a poet. This paradox leads to Joyce's declaration that if Mangan is to achieve the posthumous recognition he deserves, it will be without the help of his countrymen; and if he is ever accepted by the Irish as their national poet it will only be when the conflicts between Ireland and the foreign powers ('Anglo-Saxon and Roman Catholic') are settled. On that day 'a new civilization will arise, either indigenous or completely foreign. Until that time, he will be forgotten' (CW 179). The history of Mangan, his miserable life and the oblivion Joyce claimed had descended upon him after his death, was a carefully construed cautionary tale for the Irish artist who wished to elude the fickle acclaim of his treacherous countrymen. The portrait of Mangan is one of Joyce's early fictions. It is his portrait of the artist as a Young Ireland man.

But the portrait reduces the importance of other aspects of Mangan's career which have a direct bearing on Joyce. We are told how competent a linguist Mangan was, how he knew the languages and literatures of Italy, Spain, France, Germany, England and, of course, Ireland. In addition, he had some Sanskrit and Arabic. In a passage which could be a description of Joyce himself, we are told:

The learning of many lands goes with him always, eastern tales and the remembrance of curiously printed medieval books which have rapt him out of his time, gathered day by day and woven into a fabric. He knows twenty languages, more or less, and sometimes makes a liberal show of them, and has read in many literatures, crossing how many seas, even penetrating into the land of Peristan, which is found in no atlas.   (CW 181–2)

This is Mangan disguised as Joyce. Mangan's linguistic competence was not of this order at all. But the central fact about Mangan's poetry is that so much of it is offered to us as translation, often from exotic sources, Turkish, Coptic, Arabic, which were beyond his reach. Mangan is a characteristic nineteenth-century Irish author in his fascination with translation as an act of repossession. He betrays other languages into English, the better to possess both them and the English in which he writes; but his ultimate 'betrayal' is that of his own authorship. He is not the original author, merely a secondary, intermediate author. He is an artist whose relationship to his material is oblique, regarding it as something rare and strange which passes over into language that cannot but be secondary, insufficient. In this respect, he is indeed a central figure in the literature of the period in Ireland. For the role of translation in Irish letters had, at least from the beginning of the nineteenth century, become crucial in a country in which the riches of the native literature were being made accessible in the English language as part of the effort of the new cultural nationalism which had emerged after the Act of Union in 1800. This movement was led by Sir Samuel Ferguson (1810–86) and others in the pages of the *Dublin University Magazine*, founded in 1833, and then by Thomas Davis and his allies in the pages of the *Nation*, the newspaper which spoke for the nationalist Young Ireland movement. Mangan's poems appeared in both these publications. Moreover, he was for a time employed in the Ordnance Survey Office in Dublin, from which the 're-mapping' of Ireland was being carried out. In this remapping, Irish place-names, of every description, were to be re-rendered in English equivalents.[1] Mangan was, in other words, centrally involved in a series of movements in which translation played an important part, the translation of ancient literature and names into an English which would be, simultaneously, an estrangement from the original and also a means of repossessing that which had been lost.

Joyce's own career as a writer is dominated by the same linguistic anxieties. He could write the spiritual history of his own country, but only when he found that mode of English appropriate to Irish experience, through which the Irish could repossess their experience in an English which was unmistakably an Irish English. In that light, Mangan was bound to be as important to him as was William Carleton to Yeats.[2] Yet Mangan's essential alienation from the nationalist cause, to which he had been recruited by the Fenian rebel John Mitchel (see the latter's introduction to the *Poems of James Clarence Mangan* (1859), reprinted with the centenary edition of the *Poems* in 1903), had great appeal for Joyce. Although he shared the general view that Mangan was a nationalist poet, he also recognized that the poetry would not be seen for what it truly was as long as the two imperialisms,

British and Roman Catholic, prevailed. Nor did he believe that nationalism was anything other than an extension of those imperialisms, despite its apparent antagonism to them. Like Mangan, he could find no alternative to imperialisms and nationalism other than an attitude of fierce repudiation.[3] In his disaffection, he sought to show that the theme of betrayal, which dominated the political narrative of nationalism, also characterized translation, its preferred method of cultural repossession.

Thus, in Ireland, the problem of being a writer was in a very specific sense a linguistic problem. But it was also a political problem. The possibility of maintaining one's integrity as an artist while being involved with a community's enterprise was, initially at least, looked upon with scepticism by Joyce. Yet the achievement of that integrity could only be complete when it was expressed as an indication of communal and not merely personal possibility. In that respect, Joyce's project went beyond what Mangan represented.

The essential loneliness and apartness of the artist was tragically epitomized by other writers, and in other conditions. If Mangan served as the primary Irish example in Irish conditions, Oscar Wilde was the most notorious Irish example in English conditions. Joyce does not give particular stress to Wilde's Irishness, although it is an element in his interpretation of Wilde's fate. Instead, he chooses to read the life and work of Wilde in a religious, specifically Catholic, light. Wilde died a Roman Catholic – he 'closed the book of his spirit's rebellion with an act of spiritual dedication' (CW 203). For Joyce, there is a peculiar fitness in this last act of the life. For it was in accord with

. . . the pulse of Wilde's art – sin. He deceived himself into believing that he was the bearer of good news of neo-paganism to an enslaved people. His own distinctive qualities, the qualities, perhaps of his race – keenness, generosity, and a sexless intellect – he placed at the service of a theory of beauty which, according to him, was to bring back the Golden Age and the joy of the world's youth. But if some truth adheres to his subjective interpretations of Aristotle, to his restless thought that proceeds by sophisms rather than syllogisms, to his assimilations of natures as foreign to his as the delinquent is to the humble, at its very base is the truth inherent in the soul of Catholicism: that man cannot reach the divine heart except through that sense of separation and loss called sin.   (CW 204–5)

Once more, we see Joyce translating an author into his own image, or, at least, into the image of his own protagonist, Stephen Dedalus. Wilde is a type of the heroic artist brought down, like Parnell, by the mob. But his life, like Mangan's, contains within itself a spiritual truth which has been obscured by the public version of his career. In Wilde's case, the secret of that truth was best represented in his novel *Dorian Gray*. Wilde is, as an artist, no more the preacher of the new paganism to an enslaved people than was Mangan the preacher of freedom to an oppressed community. In each case, the truth is more fundamental than that. In each case, the truth is to be found in the apartness, the separateness of the artist, a separateness which is experienced only because it was preceded by a repudiation of fake solidarity. Wilde's mother, Lady Wilde, was a fierce Irish nationalist who wrote for the *Nation* newspaper under the pen-name 'Speranza'. Little trace of that nationalism remains in Wilde's writings. His rejection of middle-class culture is even more complete. His peculiar blend of socialism and dandyism and his assiduous attempts to create a myth of himself have their affinities with Mangan's careful creation of an adversarial and tragic version of his own life. Mangan's 'translations' from the Arabic, indeed his re-siting of his poetry within the frame of the Orient, are analogous to Wilde's revision of the bourgeois society in terms of classical Greece and the 'new paganism' which he derived from it. Like Mangan, Wilde assimilates natures foreign to his own, producing the fiction of a new and revolutionary community both as an alternative to existing social and political forms and as an antidote to and an assertion of separateness. Once more, we are involved in an act of translation. An original state of belonging is exchanged for a secondary state of separateness which then, by assimilation and translation of 'foreign' materials, tries to reconstitute a more genuine communality.

For Joyce too, this is a central problem. He returns to it in the opening chapter of *Ulysses*, in which Buck Mulligan, the poor man's Wilde, mouths the doctrine of Wilde's 'new paganism' (*U* 1.176). Mulligan, Wilde's 'Irish imitator' (*Letters II* 150) is, of course, a betrayer, the 'Usurper' (*U* 1.744), the quoter of Wilde's prefatory aphorism to *Dorian Gray*, translated into the new emblem of Irish art. He refers to Caliban's rage at not seeing his face in a mirror and exclaims to Stephen, 'If only Wilde were alive to see you', which evokes Stephen's bitter retort that the mirror is a symbol of Irish art, 'The cracked lookingglass of a servant' (*U* 1.143–7). In Irish conditions, mimesis is a double problem. The mirror that is held up to nature is cracked and it belongs to a servile race, a race of imitators, a people that cannot bear to see its own sorry reflection in the glass, nor bear to see that its authentic nature is not reflected in the glass. It is either a distorted image or it is no image. Joyce, therefore, gives an extra twist to Wilde's dicta in the Preface to *Dorian Gray*:

The nineteenth century dislike of Realism is the rage of Caliban seeing his own face in a glass.
   The nineteenth century dislike of Romanticism is the rage of Caliban not seeing his own face in a glass.

Joyce, in his reading of Wilde, recognizes that the issue of representation is critical for the Irish artist. Mangan's art was recognizable to the extent that it seemed to represent nationalism in art; Wilde's to the extent that it represented the 'new paganism'. But these representations are merely analogues for what each was trying to represent. Someone like Buck Mulligan intensifies the problem by being himself a false representation, an imitator, of Wilde. He embodies the servility of the Irish imagination. Joyce himself, on the other hand, sees his role as that of the artist who will not, like Mangan, be distorted in the glass of communal desire. He will be the true artist. He will escape false representation and, in doing so, come to terms with the medium in which this representation has been made – the vexed medium of a language which carries within itself the idea of the re-presentation in one form of a culture which initially existed in another, earlier form. In a newspaper article of 1907, 'Ireland at the Bar', Joyce protested at the misrepresentation of Ireland to the world and chose, as an illustration of his theme, the story of a namesake, Myles Joyce, who was executed for a murder he did not commit. Myles Joyce was tried in an English-speaking court, but knew no English. His language was Irish. For James Joyce, he is a symbol, one he will revert to again in *Finnegans Wake*. 'The figure of this dumbfounded old man, a remnant of a civilization not ours, deaf and dumb before his judge, is a symbol of the Irish nation at the bar of public opinion' (*CW* 198). Representation is a language problem; but it is also a problem to decide what is to be represented. The civilization of Myles Joyce is not that of James Joyce. What civilization, then, does James Joyce possess?

   In *The Decay of Lying* (1891), one of Wilde's personae had confronted the inversion of the belief that Art imitates Life.

I can quite understand your objection to art being treated as a mirror. You think it would reduce genius to the position of a cracked looking-glass. But

you don't mean to say that you seriously believe that Life imitates Art, that
Life in fact is the mirror, and Art the reality?

In bending forward to see himself in the cracked mirror which
Mulligan has taken from the maid's room at his aunt's house, Stephen
sees himself as others see him. Genius is thus reduced. What looks at
him from the servant's mirror is 'Life'; the consciousness that surveys
this reflection is 'Art'. The mirror is offered by the mock-Wildean, the
fake artist who steals from the servile the emblem of reality. This, of
course, is part of Joyce's objection to the Irish Literary Revival,
expounded with considerable force and bitterness in his pamphlet of
1901, 'The Day of the Rabblement'.

The artist who 'courts the favour of the multitude' (CW 71) becomes
a slave to it. In words similar to those he used in the passage from
Stephen Hero (quoted above), Joyce goes on to say that such an artist's
'true servitude is that he inherits a will broken by doubt and a soul that
yields up all its hate to a caress; and the most seeming-independent are
those who are the first to reassume their bonds' (CW 72). Enslavement
to the 'rabblement' is the governing condition of representation. This
truth had made itself evident in Mangan and had been seen by Wilde;
both had been cruelly victimized by it. Now, in 1901, it was
manifesting itself again in the work of the Irish National Theatre and its
concession to folk-art, a sorry collapse after a promising beginning.
Once more, truth was betrayed.

Although Joyce was opposed to the folkish, even folksy, elements of
the Irish Revival, he is himself a dominant figure in that movement.
Officially, he stands apart, as ever. Yeats, George Moore, Edward
Martyn, Lady Gregory, Synge, Padraic Colum and their supporters
seemed to him to be dangerously close to committing themselves to a
version of the pseudo-Irishness which had once been the preserve of
the stage-Irishman of nineteenth-century England and was, by the last
decade of the century, becoming the property of the Celtic Irishman of
the day. Yet, despite his difference, Joyce had much in common with
these writers. In the work of all of them, Ireland, or an idea of Ireland,
played a special role. For the revivalists, who were intent on turning
nationalist political energies into cultural channels, the idea of Ireland
was an invigorating and positive force. It embodied vitality and the
possibility of a new kind of community, radically different from the
aggregate crowds of the industrialized democracies. The distinction

was enhanced by the predominantly rural character of Irish society, transformed by the writers into something very different from its harsh reality. For instance, Synge, in *The Playboy of the Western World*, could make Mayo, the home of the Land League and the Agrarian War of the 1880s, into the site of the self-realization through language of the 'stuttering lout', Christy Mahon. However, Joyce, like Wilde and Shaw, was a Dublin writer. For him, as for them, Ireland was a negative idea, a place which threatened the artist's freedom and integrity, in which gifts were wasted and language was used as a deadly weapon. All three of them came from families that had been broken by various forms of fecklessness, alcoholism and squalor. They too transformed that bitter reality. Wilde became a dandy, Shaw became GBS, and Joyce became the professional exile from a home he never, imaginatively speaking, left. Yet these three cosmopolitan writers, like the cultural nationalists of the Revival, produced work of a self-conscious linguistic virtuosity in which English was manipulated to the point at which mastery over it began to sound like the mastery that can be achieved over a foreign language. Like Mangan, Joyce and his contemporaries wore their linguistic rue with a difference. Their language did not represent an identifiable world beyond itself. It represented the ways in which the idea of Ireland represented the reality of Ireland. It was, in effect, an exercise in translation.

Joyce made it clear that, in his opinion, the Revival was conceding to public pressure by allowing the caricatured, but popular, version of Ireland to become the abiding image of the Abbey Theatre. This was wrong on a number of grounds. It deprived the artist of his independence; it nurtured provincialism; and it did this in the guise of a return to the 'natural'. Exile safeguarded independence; cosmopolitanism helped to avoid provincialism; and the return to the natural was to be achieved, not by a romanticizing of rural and peasant life, or of the idea of the Celt and his lost language, but by an unflinching realism which, like that of Ibsen, stripped the mask from the pharisaic middle-class society of urban Europe and exposed its spiritual hypocrisy and impoverishment. In that respect, Ireland was indeed a special country. It lived under the political domination of England and the religious domination of Rome while it espoused a rhetoric of freedom, uniqueness, especial privilege. Ireland was, in fact, especially underprivileged and was, on that account, more susceptible to and more in need of an exemplary art than any other European country. It was in Joyce's art that the interior history of his country could be, for the first time, written. Joyce set himself up as the anatomist of Irish illusions, but this did not in any sense inhibit him from believing that, under the 'lancet of my art', 'the cold steel pen' (*U* 1.152–3), the soul of the country would be revealed. He medicalized the condition of his culture and subjected it to a surgical analysis. But the surgeon in Joyce attended upon the corpse of a dead or moribund country; the priest in Joyce attended upon the soul that was released from its terminal condition.

Ancient Ireland is dead just as ancient Egypt is dead. Its death chant has been sung, and on its gravestone has been placed the seal. The old national soul that spoke during the centuries through the mouths of fabulous seers, wandering minstrels, and Jacobite poets disappeared from the world with the death of James Clarence Mangan. With him, the long tradition of the triple order of the old Celtic bards ended; and today other bards, animated by other ideals, have the cry.   (*CW* 173–4)

If Ireland was to be seen, it would be in the full light of an Ibsenite dawn, not in the glimmer of a Celtic twilight. The Revival was, from its inception, an anachronism. It was a bogus attempt to revive the old Gaelic culture which lay beyond the pale of the modern consciousness.

Joyce's civilization was not, therefore, that of Myles Joyce, of Yeats and Lady Gregory and the Abbey Theatre, or of Mangan. Equally, it was not that of the comic dramatists, Sheridan, Goldsmith, Wilde, and Shaw, all of whom performed the role of 'court jester to the English' (*CW* 202). It was the civilization of Catholic Dublin, related to but distinct from that of Catholic Ireland. Joyce tried to persuade the publisher, Grant Richards, that his collection of stories, *Dubliners*, was about a city that still had not been presented, or represented, to the world. He insists, on many occasions, on the emptiness that preceded his own writings about that city. It is an historical but not yet an imaginative reality. Although Dublin has been a capital for thousands of years and is said to be the second city of the British Empire, Joyce claims that no writer has yet 'presented Dublin to the world'. Furthermore, 'the expression "Dubliner" seems to me to have some meaning and I doubt that the same can be said for such words as "Londoner" and "Parisian"' (*Letters II* 122). In the following year, 1906, the same publisher received from Joyce a sequence of famous letters, defending his text from charges of indecency and suggestions for changes, and declaring the importance of this 'chapter of moral history' as 'the first step towards the spiritual liberation of my country'. Richards is asked to 'Reflect for a moment on the history of the literature of Ireland as it stands at present written in the English language before you condemn this genial illusion of mine . . .' (*Letters I* 63). 'It is not my fault', he writes a month later, 'that the odour of ashpits and old weeds and offal hangs round my stories. I seriously believe that you will retard the course of civilization in Ireland by preventing the Irish people from having one good look at themselves in my nicely polished looking-glass' (*Letters I* 63-4). The mirror held up to Culture was going to reflect a reality no-one had presented before. Dublin would find it an unwelcome sight, but Dublin and Ireland would be liberated by it. Joyce is an author without native predecessors; he is an artist who intends to have the effect of a missionary.

By insisting that Dublin had not been represented before in literature, Joyce was intensifying the problem of representation for himself. He abjured the possibility of being influenced by any other Irish writer, because there was, in effect, none who belonged to his specific and peculiar version of his civilization. He was bound, therefore, to find a mode of representation that was, as far as Irish literature was concerned, unique. But the literature of Europe did offer possible models, and Joyce repeatedly spoke of Dublin – as in the letter to Grant Richards – as a European city. Indeed, he saw it as a city that inhabited three spheres of civilization. The first was that of the British Empire; the second that of Roman Catholicism; the third that of the ancient Europe to which Ireland had made such an important contribution. All three of these co-existed in Dublin, the only major European city which had not yet been commemorated in art.

So Dublin was the second city of the Empire, the seventh city of Christendom, the first city of Ireland; rich in history, it was now to become famous in art. The art would have to be similarly hospitable in its range; it could not be provincial, but it could have provincialism as one of its themes. To be truly European, the art would have to represent the city as an inheritor of the Judaeo-Greek civilization, in a language which would be as diversified and varied as the city's dense and intricate past.

First, provincialism had to be exposed and explained as a disease, a paralysis of the will. In one sense, the clinical and 'scrupulous meanness' (*Letters II* 134) of the style of *Dubliners* is perfectly competent 'to betray the soul of that hemiplegia or paralysis which many consider a city' (*Letters I* 55). But Joyce's enterprise was founded on a paradox. Dublin was an absence, a nowhere, a place that was not really a city or a civilization at all. It was a Cave of the Winds, like the 'Aeolus' chapter in *Ulysses*, the home of the cosmetic phrase, the Dublin rouge on the faded cheek of the English language. Joyce wanted to dismantle its provincialism and its pretensions; yet he also sought to envision it as the archetypal modern city, as the single place in which all human history was rehearsed. It had to be both nowhere and everywhere, absence and presence. Somehow, he had to find the language which would register both aspects of the city. He had to scorn it for its peripherality and praise it for its centrality. Between these two possibilities, his strange language vacillates and develops.

Like the other Irish writers of the turn of the century, Joyce learned the advantages of incorporating into his writing the various dialects or versions of English spoken in Ireland. This was not simply a matter of enlivening a pallid literary language with colloquialisms. He went much further than that. He incorporated into his writing several modes of language and, in doing so, exploited the complex linguistic situation in Ireland to serve his goal. The chief features of that situation included a still-living oral tradition which had begun to influence the writing of fiction in Ireland more than sixty years before Joyce was born, in the work of novelists like Gerald Griffin, the Banim brothers and, above all, William Carleton. The English spoken by the mass of the Irish people and partly recorded in the works of these writers, was oral-formulaic in its compositional principle and closely related to Irish. Much misunderstanding of this language and its supposed misconstructions was created by the application to it of the conventions of a literate print-culture. Certainly, the English language, as spoken in nineteenth- and early twentieth-century Ireland, was profoundly altered in its syntax, grammar and vocabulary by the migration of Irish speakers from a predominantly oral culture. The linguistic collisions and confusions which were an inevitable consequence were often taken to be characteristic of a particularly 'Irish' cast of mind. This could lead, especially in times of political crisis, to a malign stereotyping of the Irish; equally, it often led to a benign view of Irish 'eloquence', quick-wittedness and linguistic self-consciousness.[4] Joyce would have felt the impact of this linguistic interchange in the standard clichés of the stage Irishman, but he would also have known its more sophisticated variations, in the work of Wilde and Shaw and in the Revival's declared objective of reinvigorating the English language with the energetic speech of the Irish peasantry. His own work is itself part of the history of Ireland's complicated linguistic condition.

Dublin was a strange mix of the oral and the literate cultures. It prided itself on its reputation for wit, good conversation, malicious gossip, oratory, drama, and journalism. Joyce's work reflects this aspect of the city's culture. It is a mosaic of set pieces – sermons, speeches, stories, witticisms, rhetorical extravaganzas, and mimicries. The culture of print is also reproduced and parodied. The 'Nausicaa' and 'Oxen of the Sun' episodes in *Ulysses* are among the best-known examples. Pulp-literature and 'high' literature are equally subject to this form of mimicry; language is always being proffered as a species of performance. In fact, the histrionic nature of Joyce's achievement aids and abets his peculiar combination of pedantry and humour. The weighty and arcane learning of a Stephen Dedalus has to be worn lightly if he is to keep his local reputation on the Dublin stage as 'the loveliest mummer of them all' (*U* 1.97–8). Moreover, it is one of the most important of all the Joycean performances that a character should take possession of the language of others, the public language, and render it as his inimitable own. This is one of the several functions of quotation in Joyce's work. The ability to incorporate the words of others into one's own particular language-system is a sign of a 'character', a presence on the Dublin scene. In the first few pages of *Ulysses*, Buck Mulligan quotes Latin, Greek, Wilde, Swinburne, and Yeats, besides singing a song and blending all of this into his 'hyperborean' (*U* 1.92) conversational assault on Stephen. Quotation is one of the structural principles of *A Portrait of the Artist as a Young Man*. Stephen collects words and quotations with increasing eagerness until the novel finally becomes a quotation from Stephen's own writings. We are to presume that the world which gave itself to him in words has now become junior to his own word-world. To make the world conform to words is a characteristic aspiration of a culture which has found it for so long impossible to make its words conform to the world. The speaker of Irish-English in the world of increasingly Standard English finds it too difficult to conform to the imperial way. He takes as his script the advice: 'When in Rome, do as the Greeks do.' There is a certain scandal in such behaviour. It is a linguistic way of subverting a political conquest.

Subversion is part of the Joycean enterprise. However, the bitterness attendant upon it is accompanied by the joy of renovation. There is nothing of political or social significance which Joyce does not undermine and restructure. Dublin and Ireland are dissected and yet both are revitalized; the English language is dismembered and yet reinvigorated; Catholic hegemony is both destroyed and reinstated; the narrowness of Irish nationalism is satirized and yet its basic impulse is ratified. Even the most deadening features of his culture yield priority to its enlivening, creative aspects. He is one of the few authors who legitimizes the modern world, seeing its apparent randomness and alienation as instances of an underlying diversity and communion. If Dublin offered him nothing else, it at least provided him with the experience of a modern city which was also a knowable community. That sense of community, city-wide and country-wide, was possibly more alive and more widespread in his generation than in any since. His interest in Irish politics confirmed his sense that the Irish community was susceptible to a reformulation of the idea of its essential and enduring coherence.

One of Joyce's undergraduate friends, Constantine Curran, has described how effectively Joyce suppressed in his fiction the intellectually vital aspects of life at University College, Dublin, and how carefully nurtured was the fable of his refusal to sign the student protest against Yeats's play The Countess Cathleen in 1899.[5] Similarly, it has been demonstrated how Joyce concentrated on the more derelict areas of Dublin in his effort to portray the city as the centre of paralysis and squalor.[6] In fact, despite the impression given by Joyce's early fiction, Dublin was experiencing a revival of energies which outmatched anything known since the Act of Union in 1800. He was not, of course, unaware of this. When he spoke or wrote of it, he tended to concentrate on its political manifestations. In various articles he wrote on Irish political matters, Joyce shows himself to be a supporter of the Sinn Fein movement, which had been founded by Arthur Griffith, and a rather uncritical admirer of Fenianism and its formidable influence. The most notable of these are the 1907 essays, 'Fenianism', 'Home Rule Comes of Age' and 'Ireland at the Bar', the 1910 article, 'The Home Rule Comet' and the 1912 piece, 'The Shade of Parnell'. The collaboration between old Fenianism and the new Sinn Fein had, he believed, 'once more remodelled the character of the Irish people' (CW 191). But the Irish parliamentary party which sat at Westminster and which had overthrown its great leader Parnell in 1890 seemed incapable of recognizing that this remodelling had happened at home; instead they naively believed that the transformation of Ireland's fortunes would come from legislative changes in the English system – like the breaking of the veto of the House of Lords. The Irish national character had indeed altered; but the English were their old, unreconstructed selves and would never willingly yield to any separatist doctrine preached in Ireland. Yet the Irish themselves had their own, irredeemably fatal flaw. They could not be faithful to anything. Ireland's willingness to make common cause with British democracy, Joyce claims, should neither surprise nor persuade anyone: 'For seven centuries she has never been a faithful subject of England. Neither, on the other hand, has she been faithful to herself' (CW 212–13). Ireland has entered into the British domain but has never really been part of it; the conqueror's language has been adopted but his culture never assimilated; the Irish 'spiritual creators' have been exiled, only then to be boasted about back home. The governing motif of betrayal and the association between Ireland's treatment of its political and artistic heroes, although significant, is perhaps less important than the implied reason for Ireland's traditional unfaithfulness. Having exiled her spiritual creators, she has no 'soul', no mode of existence in which faithfulness is a meaningful category. Instead of her true soul, she has surrendered all to the authority of the Church, a foreign institution which operates as a political system, disguised as a spiritual one. Ireland has remained faithful to that faithless master only because she has been incapable of remaining faithful to her true self. That self, created by the artist, has no existence. Now it must be invented. Its invention demands that a certain view of Dublin, of University College, of Joyce's parents, of Mangan, Wilde, Yeats and all the others must be accepted as an authentic version of the inner spiritual void in which the Irish artist – James Joyce – must function, creating out of nothing, fascinated by stories which recount the intricacies of betrayal, of the self and of others, as well as opposing stories of fidelity and solidarity. Treachery and fidelity are the terms which determine the development of Joyce's fiction, as they determine his reading of Ireland's past and present. The remodelling of the national character, undertaken by groups like Sinn Fein and the Irish Revival, is indeed a heroic enterprise, but it is a futile one unless it accepts that the remodelling has to begin with the problem of fidelity to Rome rather than with the problem of fidelity or infidelity towards the British system. It is Rome, not London, which rules the Irish mind. London will readily use Rome for its purposes. But the Roman imperium is the more subtle and pervasive because it encroaches on the territory which should be ruled by the artist.

If proof were needed, the developments in Irish political history seemed to provide it. Once Ireland had shaken off the shackles of British rule, Church rule became ever more dominant. 'The Church has made inroads everywhere, so that we are in fact becoming a bourgeois nation, with the Church supplying our aristocracy . . . and I do not see much hope for us intellectually.'[7] Yet Joyce's views on the spiritual thraldom of Catholicism are a good deal less interesting than the methods he employed in his fiction to dramatize the profound conflicts which the pressure of Catholicism could generate in those brought up in its all-encompassing ambience. The hostility of the Church towards almost all movements for Irish liberation, from the United Irishmen to the Fenians, Parnell and beyond, is only the most superficial manifestation of these conflicts. At a deeper level, the challenge of Catholicism is to individual liberation, and Joyce, well-trained by the Jesuits and compelled by an attraction for the faith he wished to repudiate, envisaged that particular struggle in terms of the revolt of the artist heretic against official doctrine. Sometimes he modified this into a struggle between an aesthete-heretic against a provincial and philistine church which had taken possession of the mob mind. But, at root, the conflict was even more painful. It was a conflict between a son and his parents – cultural, religious, biological – and a desperate attempt to go beyond the terms set by such a conflict by producing a theory of the self as its own parent, or, less desperately, a desire of the self for alternative, surrogate parents who would permit the imagination to live its necessarily vicarious existence. This is the plight of Stephen Dedalus in *Ulysses*.

There are two forms of Catholicism in Joyce's work. One is European, the other Irish. European Catholicism, as he has Stephen speak of it in *Ulysses*, is based on the doctrine of the Trinity; Irish Catholicism, influenced in this respect by the Italians, is a more sentimental faith, based on the idea of the Holy Family, the vulgar version of the Trinity. For all his undergraduate extravagance, Stephen is enacting a central Joycean dilemma. Catholicism provides him with two versions of parenthood and of community, Trinity and Holy Family. Literature provides, in the life of Shakespeare, matching versions. The Trinitarian version is that whereby Shakespeare is the author of the play *Hamlet* which contains Hamlet the Father and Hamlet the Son; but it also contains Gertrude who is the mark in the play of Ann Hathaway's infidelity to Shakespeare. With Claudius and young Hamlet, she helps to create a grotesque version of the Holy Family. Equally, Trinity and Family can be replaced by Greek and Jew, and the relation between these can veer from much nodding in the direction of the Wildean attempt to preach a new Hellenistic paganism to Judaic-Biblical England, to the prurience of Bloom, staring at a Greek statue in the National Museum, observed and described by the pseudo-Greek, fake Wildean, Buck Mulligan, who turns to Stephen and says, 'He knows you . . . O, I fear me, he is Greeker than the Greeks' (*U* 9.613–15). In this ninth episode, the obsession with betrayal merges with the anxiety to find a basis within oneself for origin. The association between homosexuality and cuckoldry, clearly indicated in this and subsequent passages, includes the association between Greeks and Jews (via Wilde and Swinburne as modern Greeks, and Bloom as modern St Joseph). Further, the 'Greek' homosexuality is the 'Love that dare not speak its name' (*U* 9.659), while the 'Jewish' love is linked to the Holy Family, itself a betrayal of the doctrine of the Trinity and carrying within it the inevitable heterosexual betrayal which leaves Joseph a cuckold. In the true beginning, of which Christ's birth is the duplication, was 'the Word'. All through the 'Scylla and Charybdis' episode, the motif of naming, of losing or hiding the name of the father or of the origin, recurs as Stephen weaves his extraordinary theories. Yet for all the Greek and Jewish references, the ultimate reference is to Stephen himself and to Ireland, to Wilde and to Mangan (one of whose best-known poems is 'The Nameless One'), and even, by insinuation (in *U* 9.660–1), to Thomas Moore, who notoriously 'loved a lord' in the sense that he loved English society, and wrote a song, 'O Breathe Not His Name', about Robert Emmet, the rebel, who pleaded that his epitaph not be written until his country took her place among the nations of the earth (see *U* 11.1274–94). All these sexual references finally achieve their full political dimension as Bloom enters Barney Kiernan's pub to confront the Citizen in episode 12, 'Cyclops'.

The notion of self-authorship, creation of the self by becoming one's own father, is entertained by Stephen in a series of reflections which begin with the invocation of a parent – God the Father, Shakespeare – and move to the notion of the father betrayed – King Hamlet, Saint

Joseph – to the repudiation of the betraying woman, thence to the idea of homosexual, all-male love, and finally to the 'economy of heaven' where, as Stephen says, with a flourish, 'there are no more marriages, glorified man, an androgynous angel, being a wife unto himself' (*U* 9.1051–2). The four participants in this conversation, Mulligan, Best, Eglinton and Stephen, are all bachelors. When Bloom leaves, passing between Mulligan and Stephen, Mulligan whispers: 'Did you see his eye? He looked upon you to lust after you' (*U* 9.1209–10). The role of Wilde (and Swinburne) has a clear function in the series of homosexual and literary allusions which punctuate the discussion. Homosexual love, of which he and Swinburne and the Shakespeare of the sonnets are representatives, is here presented as the Greek alternative to the heterosexual love, celebrated in marriage, to which the Jews are more given than any others. 'Jews . . . are of all races the most given to intermarriage' (*U* 9.783–4). As the conversation breaks up, it is the shadow of the cuckold, Bloom, which passes between the two young bachelors. If betrayal is to be avoided, parenthood, origin, must be removed from others to oneself. It is an impossible position, but then Stephen is, as Mulligan says, 'an impossible person' (*U* 1.223).

Every heretic mentioned in the text (Sabellius, Photius, Arius, Valentine), every author, every contrasting opposition, signals parenthood, priority, origin. The point is that Stephen is caught in a dream of origin which can never be realized. There is no ultimate beginning, there is only the desire for it, for a total independence from all and everyone else. This desire is itself generated by fear of betrayal which, in turn, is associated with sexual infidelity. Ireland has betrayed itself over and over again, most recently and memorably in the sexual scandal of the Parnell affair; the Catholic Church betrayed its founding mystery, the Trinity, by substituting for it the story of the Holy Family, in which Joseph is betrayed into the position of the merely nominal father of God. Stephen and Bloom are both involved in parental and marital betrayals which are, in their turn, closely associated with religious affiliation, Christian and Jewish, while the 'Greek' Mulligan is the ultimate betrayer who cannot even recognize his own treachery towards Stephen. Just as he reads the Irish political tradition in the light of this theme, Joyce, through Stephen, reads Shakespeare and the English literary tradition in the same way. Church, State and Culture are the betrayed remnants of an originary purity towards which Stephen, as artist, dedicates himself. In such a situation, only art is beyond betrayal. It is the only activity to which Stephen can give his fidelity because it is a form of production in which his own authorship is secure. The problem is, of course, that Stephen is always about to be an artist. He has his theory complete, but it does not fit with the circumstances of flawed paternity which surround Bloom.

Ulysses is as concerned as is *Dubliners* with failure. The form of the failure is more brilliant, because it is the result of sophisticated, exotic, ingenious readings of the past and of the present which are finally disabling for the readers – Stephen and Bloom in particular. The semiotic systems of Dublin, Irish history, literature, are all read under the sign of a betrayal which, while it exposes, does not reveal. That is to say, failure is exposed but the way to success is not revealed. Stephen, remembering his meeting in Paris with the exiled Fenian, Kevin Egan, and the stories of the Fenian escapades and associated Irish political enterprises, thinks of them all as phantasmal, failed and fading attempts. 'Of lost leaders, the betrayed, wild escapes. Disguises, clutched at, gone, not here' (*U* 3.243–4). In his 1907 lecture, 'Ireland, Island of Saints and Sages', Joyce declared, 'It is well past time for Ireland to have done once and for all with failure' (*CW* 174). Yet much of his own work is precisely on this theme. He analyzes the psychology of subjection in his people by showing the paralysis which has overtaken them in their endless, futile quest for an origin which will provide them with an identity securely their own. Such an origin is always beyond history, since history, as we have seen, is for him a sequence of betrayals, the effect of which is to leave the Irish people leaderless, subjected to an authoritarian Church, bereft of that spiritual life which only the artist, in his quest for origin, can provide.

Characteristically, when Joyce does find the originary story, it involves a betrayal. The legend of the Fall of Man is an extra-historical narrative, a kind of metacommentary, which is repeated in endlessly diverse forms throughout human history, which both derives from and returns to it. At the centre of this mass of historical material is Irish historical experience. It has the fall of man deeply inscribed upon it, from the story of the fall of the High King Rory O'Connor, to the execution of the radical Republican Rory O'Connor in 1923. It moves from the era of Saints and Scholars to the Devil Era of the great modern leader, De Valera. Repetition is the law of this universe; in every event, the originary event reappears. Origin is always with us. Yet the origin is visible only when the story is told in the language which contains all languages, in the Ur-speech which is the language of the dreaming or subconscious mind of HCE, Everyman, who Haveth Childers Everywhere. *Finnegans Wake* is Joyce's Irish answer to an Irish problem. It is written in a ghost language about phantasmal figures; history is haunted by them and embodies them over and over again in specific people, places and tongues. If Ireland could not be herself, then, by way of compensation, the world would become Ireland. Thus is the problem of identity solved. Irish history is world history *in parvo*. The mutilated sequences of war, failure, disaster, lost language, broken culture, are brought under the governance of a single, mastering story which renders everything thought to be unique as typical.

Yet just as *Ulysses* had made real order out of apparent chaos, *Finnegans Wake* sustains individuality within the frame of the archetypal. The Earwicker family, for instance, is a version of Joyce's family; yet the figures within it are always coalescing 'through the labyrinth of their samilikes and the alteregoases of their pseudoselves' (*FW* 576.32–3). The events of the Irish War of Independence against the British, the signing of the Treaty, the civil war which followed, and the subsequent entry of De Valera into parliamentary politics are all presented in fractured form as specific happenings in themselves and also as representative events. We can see here, a little more clearly, how Joyce grappled with the problem of representation. Individual items, which by themselves might be meaningless, gain significance when seen as part of an overall pattern. Therefore, if the pattern is sufficiently hospitable, everything can be represented within a system and everything therefore has whatever meanings the system is able to produce. Nevertheless, the governing pattern has, in itself, an originary meaning which is replicated throughout all subsequent variations. We have seen that, for Joyce, in his readings of Mangan, Wilde, Irish politics, and so forth, the theme of betrayal was the repeated meaning which linked all the aspects of Irish experience together. His task was, in part, to demonstrate that this was indeed a given, originary pattern rather than a retrospective, enforced one. In *Finnegans Wake*, the linking theme of transgression and betrayal is legitimized by the nature of language itself. Repetition, puns, homonyms, resemblances, echoes, carefully arranged, reveal or are proposed as revealing, a cousinship between the events which these sounds describe. Alliance between word-sounds reveals an alliance between those things which the word-sounds represent. Joyce is involving himself and us in a stupendous act of retrospective translation, whereby the distinctions and differences between words and languages are collapsed into a basic, originary speech native to the subconscious, not the conscious, mind. This is his version of the lost language of Ireland; it is also the lost language of the Irish soul, that entity which had not been articulated into existence before Joyce. In effect, what this lost language tells is the story of the transgression which led to its loss, the story of the life of the soul lost to the life of the conscious mind, the narrative of an Edenic Ireland which, through sin, became postlapsarian and British.

Here we have the Mangan position transfigured. Where he made all his texts 'secondary' by positing a real or imaginary 'original' from which they derived, Joyce makes all other texts secondary by actually producing the original language of which they are the later derivations. Thus the divine thunder which inaugurates civilization, according to the theory of Vico, who plays a role in *Finnegans Wake* similar to that of Homer in *Ulysses*, can be translated, so to say, into the gunfire of an ambush in the Irish War of Independence or the boom of the guns at the Battle of Waterloo. The reader must go forward to the individual instance and back to the originating example. This is, after all, a dream which we are interpreting, and the language of dreams must, as Freud had shown, go through a series of readings before they can yield a meaning we can recognize, even though the meaning was already there in the original 'language'. This is what Joyce himself had done in reading the careers of Mangan, Parnell, Wilde, the Fenians. The Irish had dreamt in their own language and then betrayed the dream into the English language in such a manner that the original meaning had been lost, misread; as a consequence, for this transgression, they had been punished. English did not translate the dream because the Irish did not possess, had, indeed, refused to accept, the culture which English represented. So Joyce, following in the steps of all of those who had been busily translating Irish material – especially legendary material – into English, went very much further than the second-hand Carlylese of Standish O'Grady, or the Kiltartan dialect of Lady Gregory, or the peasant speech of Synge, who takes a drubbing, chiefly from Mulligan, in the 'Scylla and Charybdis' episode.

Joyce translated in the other direction. He brought English and as many other languages as he could manage – including Irish – back to the literary equivalent of the Indo-European from which they had all sprung. In doing this, he confronts the problem of parenthood, as well as the problem of translation and betrayal, on the level of language itself, not merely on the level of language-as-narrative.

Given this, Joyce can indulge as freely as he likes in detail. The minutiae of Dublin life, ever-present throughout *Ulysses*, now undergo a second transformation. The geography of the city and the history of the country were readable there in specific, if generous, contexts. Dublin could be the Mediterranean, Irish history could be a version of episodes from the Greek legends or from Biblical history. But in *Finnegans Wake*, Dublin's Phoenix Park can be anything from the Garden of Eden to the field of Waterloo, including the site of a phallic rebirth represented by the Wellington monument, the '*duc de Fer's* overgrown milestone' (*FW* 36.18). In the hands of 'Maistre Sheames de la Plume' (*FW* 177.30), the poor old Iron Duke and his obelisk can take on almost any meaning. The strangest effect of this titanic effort of translation is that the text is never revealed; rather, it is produced by the reader. There is no question any longer of a skeleton key which will turn in all the locks. This translation does not translate. The thousands of proper names in the text are so interwoven that even the minutest knowledge of Irish affairs (and the more minute the better, given that so many of the names are of Irish provenance) does not legitimize, say, a reading of the text as a version of Irish history in a Babylonian dialect. Names specify, but these are names that also typify. Even in *Dubliners*, the anorexic opposite to this Rabelaisian carnival, Joyce kept offering specifications that seemed treacherous. Is there any significance in the fact that the miching episode in the story 'An Encounter' culminates at three o'clock on a Friday afternoon? Perhaps there is a reference to the Crucifixion, perhaps not. Support can be gathered from all sorts of details. But is that a possible reading, or a deliberately implanted possible misreading? The bareness of the short stories is a challenge to elaborate interpretation; the richness of *Finnegans Wake* is a challenge to a reading that might be too basic, a reading that says everything here is the same but different, that all we see are multiple, fused versions of the Fall of Man. The treachery which obsessed Joyce is fundamental to his practice of writing. For he leaves us to wonder if the text that he offers is one which has been so fully articulated that it can go no further; or if it is a text which is so blurred that it awaits and invites full articulation. This was not only a problem for him. He saw it as the problem of his culture. Dublin had never been represented in literature before. Perhaps he was the first to represent it; or perhaps he was the first to show that it was not representable.

For all that, Joyce was, and knew himself to be, part of the Irish Revival. A remodelling of the idea of Ireland was under way and, although his sense of the problem of finding a new representation for what had not yet come into existence was more acute than that of his contemporaries, he could see that people as diverse as Yeats, Pearse, De Valera, and Synge were extending the process which had been made most manifest in the earlier generations by writers like Mangan and Wilde, and by political figures like Thomas Davis and John O'Leary. That sense of renewal is clear throughout *Finnegans Wake*. The country and culture he repudiated was also the country and culture he re-imagined. The absence could become a presence. Time and again in his writing Joyce characteristically salutes and bids farewell to the Ireland he had left and to the Ireland he created in his absence from it and its absence from him.

NOTES

1 See Frank O'Connor, *The Backward Look: A Survey of Irish Literature* (London: Macmillan, 1967), pp. 150ff.; Seamus Deane, *A Short History of Irish Literature* (London: Hutchinson, 1986); J. H. Andrews, *A Paper Landscape: The Ordnance Survey in Nineteenth Century Ireland* (London: Oxford University Press, 1975). See also Brian Friel's play *Translations* (London: Faber, 1982), for a contemporary treatment of this theme.

2 William Carleton (1794–1869) published his *Traits and Stories of the Irish Peasantry* between 1830 and 1833. He is renowned as the first writer in English to provide an authentic account of the life and speech of the Irish peasantry. Yeats wrote an introduction to his own selection, *Stories from Carleton* (London: W. Scott, 1889).

3 See David Lloyd, *Nationalism and Minor Literature: James Clarence Mangan and the Emergence of Irish Cultural Nationalism* (Berkeley, Los Angeles, London: University of California Press, 1987), p. 209.

4 See Alan Bliss, *Spoken English in Ireland, 1600–1740* (Dublin: Dolmen Press, 1979).

5 C. P. Curran, *Under the Receding Wave* (Dublin and London: Gill and Macmillan, 1970), pp. 96–110. See also his *James Joyce Remembered* (London: Oxford University Press, 1968).

6 J. C. C. Mays, 'Some comments on the Dublin of *Ulysses*' in Louis Bonnerot, ed., *Ulysses: Cinquante ans après* (Paris: Didier, 1974), pp. 83–98.

7 Arthur Power, *Conversations with James Joyce* (London: Millington, 1974), p. 65.

3   The European background of Joyce's writing

In 1904, Joyce left Ireland for a life of permanent exile in continental Europe; but by that date he had already responded fully and vigorously to the major intellectual developments of the wider cultural environment into which he was transplanting himself. He had become thoroughly dissatisfied with Ireland, whose atmosphere of nationalist parochialism had become distasteful to him. As Gabriel Conroy in 'The Dead' would burst out some ten years later: 'I'm sick of my own country, sick of it!' (*D* 189). It was a comparatively large number of intellectual figures and movements he had absorbed – 'modern' thinkers as well as historical figures reinterpreted by the nineteenth century – only some of which can be dealt with in this survey. I have concentrated on those influences that were to remain important throughout his writing career. Even though the later Joyce frequently adopted an ironic attitude to many of the ideas and heroes of his early years, they were never dismissed.

Young James Joyce grew up, as every child does, in an ambience of commonly shared values. In his case these were the values associated with Catholicism, nationalism, and bourgeois morality, reinforced by an appropriate canon of works of art and literature. Reading Joyce's early writings – notably his essays and *Stephen Hero* – one becomes aware of the scathing and uncompromising reaction against the totality of these values that marked his late teens and early twenties. What was the use of a church that did nothing to alleviate the spiritual or physical needs of her sheep, but encouraged an attitude of awe and obsequiousness? What was the good of the rising nationalism that turned out to be as authoritarian and intolerant as the oppressors from which it had set out to liberate its people? As for middle-class values such as respectability, decency, and strict sexual morality – how was one to

55

account for the very opposite qualities that one could see if one looked just a little bit under the surface? Was not *hypocrisy* the common denominator to all these values?

This spirit of unrest and revolt, of insubordination and a 'revaluation of values', pertinent to the spirit of adolescence as it is, was at the same time in accordance with certain 'counter-cultural' movements that had emerged 'out in Europe' (*SH* 35) throughout the nineteenth century, and that had come fully to the fore towards its end. To someone brought up, like Joyce, by Jesuits who watched his every step lest he deviate from the right path of belief, the new science of historical biblical criticism must have come as a revelation. Young Joyce read the scandalizing *Vie de Jésus* (1863) by Ernest Renan (1823–92), and the equally notorious *Leben Jesu* (1836) by David Friedrich Strauss (1808–74) that had prepared its way, books that had dealt a deathblow to some of the most fundamental assumptions and traditions of the Church – in the name of science, based on facts and documents, things that could be proved. The insistence on 'facts' – things 'as they are' and not what they are supposed to be – became an obsession with Joyce, from his iconoclastic shattering of idealizations and 'systems' (after all, as he was fond of saying, the Catholic Church was built on nothing but a pun (*JJ* 546)) to his insistence on the accuracy of fictional details.[1] Stanislaus Joyce noted in his *Dublin Diary* (18 July 1904): 'The Jesuit influence, not their system, is educational, because it trains those under it to educate themselves.'[2] Once alerted to the fact that there were two sides to the coin, Joyce did not simply turn his back on the Church: he set out for himself to discover that other side, the things covered up, distorted or silenced by the official traditions of the Church. He turned to the reformist Franciscan writers of the Trecento, to Joachim, abbot of Fiore, to the Spanish mystics of the sixteenth century such as St Teresa and St John of the Cross, all of whom had in their own time been thought of as heterodox or had even been condemned as heretics, yet had become, each in his or her own way, rejuvenators of an ossified system of thought. But their challenging ideas had gradually been smoothed over and neutralized. Was it possible to rekindle some of that extinguished fire?

A special case in point is that of Dante (1265–1321), whose influence pervades all Joyce's writing.[3] Dante is the greatest of Catholic poets, the verbal architect of the hierarchical edifice of the church. But are we justified in 'reducing' him to that revered status? Hardly, if we are prepared to look at the 'facts'. Dante was to Joyce what may now be termed a 'committed' writer, a political poet, who is never cowed by authority, whose Hell teems with popes and cardinals and bishops displaying every kind of mental aberration. There is nothing saintly or benign about Dante that could make him a useful member of 'the Church': he is partisan and belligerent, full of the ire that comes from a lacerated heart, one who detects fraudulence, treason, meanness everywhere and castigates it severely. Dante is not a moralist in any vague sense of the term. Whatever he sees, he describes and judges in its uniqueness, and only then does he place it within the framework of his premeditated system. Concrete instance and general plan seem to be in balance. This could *technically* be learned from Dante by any writer willing to look for himself rather than relying on the guidance offered by the schoolmen. Thus, far from discarding tradition but equally far from adhering to it in the spirit that was expected of him, Joyce 'rescued' from Dante those things that could make him usable for a modern writer. (In *SH* he was to say provokingly: 'No esthetic theory . . . is of any value which investigates with the aid of the lantern of tradition' (212).) Moreover, it may not have been unimportant for the shaping of Joyce's mind that Dante was an *exile*, expelled from his home town for political reasons, but that his whole thinking kept focusing on this very city, the moral corruption of which he set out to expose – as Joyce was to do in *Dubliners*. This anti-Catholic view of Dante, incidentally, need not have originated with Joyce. It was in keeping with the rediscovery of Dante by such Romantic poets as Byron and Shelley, and with the re-assessment of the poet by the highly influential Victorian critic Thomas Carlyle (1795–1881) in his lecture series on *Heroes, Hero-Worship and the Heroic in History* (1841). As the century drew on, Dante became one of the great challenges to orthodox Catholic tradition even for the larger reading public.

Perhaps even more important than Dante as an example for Joyce among early Italian writers, and certainly the most conspicuous example of Catholic counter-tradition, was Giordano Bruno (1548–1600). Born in Nola, he had entered the Dominican Order in Naples but had soon come into conflict with the Inquisition. Fleeing Italy after being charged with heresy, he gained favour with King Henri III in Paris. He then accompanied the French ambassador to England where he wrote and published the six Italian dialogues upon which his fame rests, among them the *Spaccio della Bestia Trionphante* which

Stephen alludes to in a discussion with his Italian teacher Father Artifoni (*SH* 170). Bruno taught for some time at Oxford, the stronghold of Aristotelianism, the premises of which he dared to question; as a result, after some fiery disputes, he was compelled to leave. He then had a spell in Germany, but was forced to leave again – this time by Calvinists – and was eventually lured back to Italy, where he fell into the hands of the Inquisition, was brought to Rome, tried for eight years, and finally burned at the stake on 16 February 1600. ' – You know, he [Father Artifoni] said, the writer, Bruno, was a terrible heretic. – Yes, said Stephen, and he was terribly burned' (*SH* 170).

Father Artifoni's view was, however, no longer the generally accepted one. It was the nineteenth century that had rediscovered Bruno as a victim of the Church, not so much as a dissenting Catholic but, along with Copernicus and Galileo, as a hero of modern science, for which he alone had been made a martyr. On 16 February 1889 a monument was erected to Bruno on Campo dei Fiori, the very same place where he had been burned, at one and the same time a symbol of the liberation from the Church State and of the triumph of science. Joyce felt drawn to Bruno because of his uncompromising spirit, his constant questioning of authority (religious, philosophical, and scientific), his rebelliousness, his adherence to what he held to be the truth, even at the peril of his life. Yet it was also the *writer* Bruno that appealed to Joyce, the irascible and witty satirist, as sarcastic as Swift, who poured his scathing remarks on anything pedantic or seemingly acceptable that, out of the sheer sluggishness of thought, had simply not been doubted. And it was equally the elegant stylist, erudite poet, and careful builder of structures,[4] who demonstrated to Joyce that complicated philosophical thoughts could be expressed in a language 'full of invention', that is a joy to read. It may not be unimportant to note that the only Bruno text young Joyce mentions is the *Triumphant Beast*, the one dialogue that is not concerned with cosmological or neoplatonic speculations but with concrete moral reform – which Bruno set forth by means of a total revaluation of those values that were held dear by Christian tradition. The dialogue is iconoclastic – not out of moral fervour only, but also out of encyclopedic erudition – yet at the same time it constructs an ethically renewed universe that leaves behind the petty controversies of Western religions, in the name of 'scientific' truth. This truth, howsoever enigmatically formulated, could be expressed only from the newly postulated spaces of the multitude of worlds, in isolation and solitude. This is what Joyce sensed when he began his essay 'The Day of the Rabblement' (1901) with the words: 'No man, said the Nolan, can be a lover of the true or the good unless he abhors the multitude; and the artist, though he may employ the crowd, is very careful to isolate himself' (CW 69). At this point Joyce was not aware of the fact that Bruno would be more than a spiritual example for him: one of the connections between the two men would also be a physical one – the condition of exile.

As for the typical middle-class values against which Joyce rebelled – sexual repression and taboos, the ideal of monogamous marriage, male dominance, and so on – again, 'out in Europe' there had been authors who had seriously questioned them and analysed their devastating effects upon the human psyche.

The first name that comes to mind is that of Sigmund Freud (1856–1939),[5] who, at the turn of the century, was beginning to show in Vienna that it is precisely the things repressed which structure our thinking and behaviour and are at the root of many of our mental illnesses. More specifically, it is the things that we desire and the things we fear, both sexual in origin, that are relegated to the unconscious, from where they may re-emerge in 'normal' behaviour in various distorted forms such as dreams, slips of the tongue, jokes, or false memories, or as physical or psychic 'symptoms' that indicate an illness. Freud showed that it is impossible to draw a strict line between normal and abnormal behaviour, because everybody participates in both inasmuch as we are conditioned by forces beyond our control that are nonetheless formative parts of our psychic structure. What happens on the surface, what finds its expression in actions, can usually be attributed to the machinations of the sexual drives. In short, Freud dealt a death-blow to bourgeois morality, which he analyzed as a thinly disguised cover-up of the things society wants to ignore and negate because it feels them to be threatening to its structures of power and control. And at the same time it is this very morality that drives people into illness to the point of insanity.

True, Freud had no influence on young Joyce, though he was very important later in Joyce's life.[6] Joyce probably first heard of him when he arrived in Austrian Trieste in the autumn of 1904. Yet there are so many striking resemblances between the two that we may be allowed to refer to some 'spirit of the age': Joyce *sensed* the things that were

happening 'out in Europe' and worked on them in his own way. In his
early concept of 'epiphany' he looked for something hidden, something
underneath the glossy surface of the most commonplace things,
something latent that might suddenly cut through to reveal an
underside that had been kept 'repressed', but that alone could give an
intimation of the truth of the phenomenon observed.[7] To be sure, Joyce
expounded his theory of epiphanies by referring to what he called the
'Esthetic' of 'applied Aquinas' (*SH* 77),[8] using such quaint terms as
'quidditas', the 'whatness' of a thing (*SH* 213), to define what became
suddenly manifest when the proper analysis (the word is both Joyce's
and Freud's) had been made: the true identity of something. But his
insistence on analysis, that is, on the cognitive procedures rather than
on mystical empathy (even though this latter is not absent), his belief
that latent entities can explain the specific appearance of manifest ones,
or, more generally speaking, his search for hidden motivations of
actions and expressions – all of this shows Joyce to be on the same
'track' as Freud, in spite of the lack of direct influence during Joyce's
formative years. And there is another striking parallel worth mention-
ing: both Freud and Joyce discovered the significance of the apparently
insignificant. It is minute gestures or facial expressions, sudden turns of
phrase, unintentional actions, in short, things that usually go unnoticed or that are discarded as irrelevant, that have a revelatory quality
precisely because they are not governed by intentions or the censorship of consciousness, and it is these that allow glimpses of the true
nature of a person, of his or her repressed 'real' self, to the observer.
Joyce's preoccupation with the small, the marginal, the insignificant
details of everyday life, in order to build his characters upon them, may
be seen throughout his work, from his early epiphanies – experimental
sketches of trivial situations – through *Dubliners* to *Ulysses*. (Why does
Maria, in the story 'Clay', sing the same stanza twice? Why does Bloom
forget where he left his hat in the 'Calypso' episode of *Ulysses*?)

How is it that Joyce could develop something analogous to Freud's
discoveries within a totally different frame of reference? Part of the
answer certainly is that an approach valorizing a focus on the minutest
details was 'in the air' in various fields at the turn of the century. There
was, for instance, the fashionable science of archaeology[9] (of the utmost
importance to Freud) that had underlined the significance of the
smallest potsherd, and had shown that it was possible to reconstruct a
totality out of seemingly random fragments, even though 'essential'
parts might still be missing (parts which could mentally – or

'analytically' – be supplied by the ingenuity of the assembler). Then there was the German art critic Morelli (also quoted by Freud) who had concentrated on the execution in paintings of such details as fingernails, earlobes, and nostrils in order to identify the artist without having to take into consideration such broad – and therefore misleading, possibly 'borrowed' – features as design, colour, subject-matter, 'style'. Both examples serve to show that there were precursors of the *method* of Joyce as well as of Freud.

There are also abundant examples in literature – precursors or parallels – of the concerns of Joyce and of Freud: the questioning of bourgeois morality, the discovery of the force of sexuality, of hidden motivations, of the functioning of the unconscious.

There had been Gustave Flaubert (1821–80) and Leo Tolstoy (1828–1910). Flaubert, in *Madame Bovary* (1857), and Tolstoy, in *Anna Karenina* (1877), had both shown that there is a causal nexus between sexual negation, under cover of marital obligations, and adultery. In both cases there is a close relationship between the power of repression and the force with which the things that have been repressed eventually erupt, sweeping everything into the resulting maelstrom. Both women end in destruction and catastrophe: there is no place in society for this kind of deviant behaviour. In France, Emile Zola (1840–1902) had adhered to the new scientific spirit of positivism and attempted to show in his numerous novels that human beings are entirely determined by the social conditions, the 'milieu', in which they had grown up: all the so-called higher ideas – religion, national-ism, love – were just fictions and disguises to cheat the mind and make it accessible to all kinds of fraud. In Italy, the novelist, poet and dramatist, Gabriele D'Annunzio (1863–1938) had stressed, from a different angle, the importance of sense data, the givens of 'sensuous-ness', for the shaping of concepts. The dramatist and prose writer Arthur Schnitzler (1862–1931), like Freud a medical doctor working in Vienna, had discovered, independently of Freud and to the latter's surprise, the importance of the sexual drives, and had exposed the hypocrisy of upper-class morality, especially in matters of marriage and the sexual abuse of people from lower classes. (It was Schnitzler, incidentally, who wrote the first full-length interior monologue in his novella *Leutnant Gustl* (1901), a text Joyce knew, although we do not know when he read it or heard about it.)

Most important of all upon the shaping of Joyce's mind was the work of the Norwegian dramatist Henrik Ibsen (1828–1906).[10] Nobody ever held greater sway over Joyce than Ibsen. His brother records: 'The other influences he had felt, though he had accepted them, had been imposed; this [Ibsen's] arose within him, keen and exultant, as if in answer to a call.'[11] His influence can be found throughout Joyce's work, most markedly in its early stages, and at one point in his early career he even styled himself Ibsen's successor.[12] In *Stephen Hero* Joyce describes the indebtedness of his autobiographical hero at some length (the time referred to is equivalent in Joyce's career to the years 1898–9):

It must be said simply and at once that at this time Stephen suffered the most enduring influence of his life . . . [H]e encountered through the medium of hardly procured translations the spirit of Henrik Ibsen. He understood that spirit instantaneously . . . [T]he minds of the old Norse poet and of the perturbed young Celt met in a moment of radiant simultaneity. Stephen was captivated first by the evident excellence of the art: he was not long before he began to affirm, out of a sufficiently scanty knowledge of the tract, of course, that Ibsen was the first among the dramatists of the world.   (40)

What it was that drew Joyce to Ibsen may be seen in the characterization of the dramatist that follows:

But it was not only this excellence which captivated him: it was not that which he greeted gladly with an entire joyful spiritual salutation. It was the very spirit of Ibsen himself that was discerned moving behind the impersonal manner of the artist: a mind of sincere and boylike bravery, of disillusioned pride, of minute and wilful energy.[13] Here and not in Shakespeare or Goethe was the successor to the first poet of the Europeans, here, as only to such purpose in Dante, a human personality had been found united with an artistic manner which was itself almost a natural phenomenon: and the spirit of the time united one more readily with the Norwegian than with the Florentine.
                (41)

These characterizations, in particular their insistence on an 'artistic manner' and an 'impersonal manner', are a most peculiar way of representing Ibsen, and they have probably more to do with the growing self-stylization of the artist Joyce than with the Norwegian. Ibsen's scandalizing provocation of middle-class values in the latter part of the nineteenth century was certainly not due to the cultivation of the 'impersonal manner of the artist', a fact which did not escape Joyce at all, as he testifies elsewhere. It was perhaps Ibsen's uncompromising attack upon everything sanctioned by, and dear to, Western civilization that attracted Joyce to him in the first place.

In many ways Ibsen's life shows parallels to that of Joyce. He grew up in Christiania, a pre-modern provincial capital similar to Dublin. His youth was poverty-stricken. He had a biting, satirical, and defiant temperament, full of disdain for the hypocrisy that surrounded him. His early publications were condemned for their lack of 'higher ideals', their bitter attack on commonly shared values. He felt sure that as a writer he could never survive in his home country, and he therefore chose to go into exile, living for the greater part of his later career mainly in Germany (in Berlin, Dresden, and Munich). As Georg Brandes wrote: 'He left his people; his home country became the sum total of insignificance, inertia and dispiritedness. He grew used to feeling at home in homelessness.'[14] And Brandes goes on: '. . . moral *distrust* became his muse. It inspired him to ever more daring inquiries.'[15] His probing eye was that of a scientist. Although he has been called an iconoclast, which he certainly was, this is only one part of the picture. It is true that he denounces the fraudulent eroticism of the philistine, exposes the so-called idylls of marriage – the holiest cow of nineteenth-century Europe – as repressive, is the first to point to the abominable status of women in society, attacks the hypocrisy of religion and the egotistic dogmatism of political parties of all colours. In the high-strung words of youthful Joyce, reviewing the French translation of Ibsen's earliest play, *Catilina*, his 'breaking-up of tradition, which is the work of the modern era, discountenances the absolute' (*CW* 100). It was, of course, this questioning of commonly approved values that led in turn to a condemnation of Ibsen by those who felt that they were in charge of these very values. Thus, when Joyce had finished his student paper on 'Drama and Life', the hero of which is Ibsen, he had to submit it to the President of University College; the President promptly turned it down and would not allow him to read it before the Literary and Historical Society of the College. Joyce went to see him, and gives an ironic account of the meeting in *Stephen Hero* (90–8). The arguments the President puts forth are, indeed, hardly more than the clichés of general disapproval launched against Ibsen throughout his career: 'free thinking . . . atheistic . . . garbage of modern society . . . free living . . . unbridled licence . . . Ibsen and Zola who seek to degrade their art, who pander to a corrupt taste . . . That is not art.' (Arguments, to be sure, that would later be launched against Joyce's own writings.) But Stephen can show that the arguments are quite irrelevant. Ibsen, he contends, is an objectivist writer; he works without any preconceived 'specific code of moral conventions'. He sees things as they are, not as they are thought to be or ought to be. If society is corrupt, he feels it his task to examine the corruption, as a scientist does. It is this that Stephen will later call – and claim as his own method of procedure – 'vivisective': 'The modern spirit is vivisective. Vivisection itself is the most modern process one can conceive' (*SH* 186). It implies that there is nothing which is beneath the dignity of the writer to observe and examine: filth and dirt, bodily functions and animal drives, are just as much part of life as are emotions and thoughts, and there may even be close connections between the two – indeed, the one may be the foundation of the other. The spirit of vivisection demanded of the author that nothing which life presented should be shunned, but rather that it should be rendered in the most objective, most disinterested terms possible.

Here we may come back to Stephen's initial characterization of Ibsen: 'the impersonal manner of the artist'. Ibsen presents things as he sees them, without commenting on them, leaving their evaluation to the reader or the audience. Since he lets his characters speak for themselves he is never in danger of denouncing them, of painting them in black or white. His handling of relationships between characters has been called 'dialectical'. For example, in *A Doll's House*, the tragedy of married life, Helmer, the husband, is a 'positive' character: he is good, amiable, loving, caring, well-educated, sensitive. And yet Nora, his wife, is his victim in an increasingly intolerable situation. The reverse dialectic is at work in *Ghosts*: there is a debauched, morally irresponsible husband, and yet the morality of society and religion obliges his wife to give herself to him.[16] Thus Ibsen does not so much blame the individual characters: we are rather made to feel compassion for each one in turn, we can 'understand' them; what he blames, rather, are the conventions, the commonly shared values of society and religion *behind* them that compel them to act as they do. At the same time Ibsen is most specific in letting his characters express themselves; he evokes an authentic picture of Norwegian society in the latter half of the nineteenth century, down to the minutest details of domestic duties, everyday routine, insignificant actions, presented in an unpretentious colloquial language and precisely described settings. This close attention to the minute details of speech and of everyday things – most often apparently trivial, commonplace or marginal – is something Joyce would take over and carry to extremes in his own art. From the point of view of the writer's craft there was another thing Joyce learned from Ibsen: his economy. Ibsen manages to compress into the space of a few hours or one or two days the whole lifespan of his characters[17] – as Joyce would do in 'The Dead', in *Exiles*, in *Ulysses*, and perhaps in *Finnegans Wake*. This connects him with the technique of Greek tragedy and the so-called Aristotelian unities derived from it, as Brandes had seen.[18] In 'Drama and Life' Joyce, to the great dismay of his hearers, places the two side by side.

Yet, as Joyce states in his review of *When We Dead Awaken* (1900):

Ibsen's plays do not depend for their interest on the action, or on the incidents. Even the characters, faultlessly drawn though they be, are not the first thing in his plays. But the naked drama – either the perception of a great truth, or the opening up of a great question, or a great conflict which is almost independent of the conflicting actors, and has been and is of far-reaching importance – this is what primarily rivets our attention. Ibsen has chosen the average lives in their uncompromising truth for the groundwork of all his later plays.

(*CW* 63)

Again, this reads like an anticipation of what he was to do himself. It has been said that there is no character in literature we know more about than we do about Leopold Bloom; he may be a bore as Joyce contends Ibsen's characters may be (*CW* 65), yet at the same time he is Everyman, in his different roles as husband, father and son, cuckold and seducer, and Nobody (as Odysseus, whose wanderings Bloom unknowingly re-enacts, chose to call himself): petty domestic drama and grand mythic design at one and the same time.

The double function of local specificity and 'universal import' (*CW* 45) only works if a third party is taken into account: this is where the role of the artist – the artificer who joins things together and has them reciprocally point to each other – becomes of prime interest. Joyce raises the 'impersonal manner of the artist' he has discerned in Ibsen to the height of religious vision. In his review of Ibsen's last play he states that the author sees the theme of his play 'steadily and whole, as from a great height, with perfect vision and an angelic dispassionateness, with the sight of one who may look on the sun with open eyes' (*CW* 65). This elevation of the artist to an angelic rank is driven even further by Joyce when he has Stephen give his famous definition in *A Portrait*: 'The artist, like the God of the creation, remains within or behind or beyond or above his handiwork, invisible, refined out of existence, indifferent, paring his fingernails' (P 215). Thus Joyce probably saw Ibsen as the precursor, like John the Baptist, of a greater one who was to come. The high rank of the artist had of course its consequences in the petty world of society: his uniqueness singled him out and set him apart from the multitude or what Joyce was to call 'the rabblement'. What he had attributed to Ibsen – 'his profound self-approval . . . his haughty, disillusioned courage' (SH 41) – he was to assume for himself: 'Stephen had begun to regard himself seriously as a literary artist: he professed scorn for the rabblement and contempt for authority' (SH 122–3). He cultivated this attitude, derived not only from Ibsen but also, as we have seen, from Bruno, and carried it to extremes, as his early writings all the way through to A Portrait (where the manner is ironically exposed) bear ample testimony. In the words of his brother Stanislaus, Joyce had the feeling 'that he belonged to the elect company of those who mould the conscience of their race'.[19] Or again, in reaction to some incident Stanislaus recounts, 'My brother was beginning to experience in his own person the truth that the hearty Dr Stockmann had blurted out in An Enemy of the People: that the strongest man is he who stands most alone.'[20] The most haughty formulation of this attitude occurs in a passage in the essay 'A Portrait of the Artist' (1904) which he clearly liked (he alludes to it in 'The Holy Office' (1904) and he took it over in full when he rewrote the essay as Stephen Hero): 'Let the pack of enmities come tumbling and sniffing to my highlands after their game. There was his ground and he flung them disdain from flashing antlers' (SH 34–5). The logical consequence of this attitude was to go into exile, as his master had done before him, and become, as he was to call Ibsen later, an 'egoarch' himself.[21]

Ibsen was never as provokingly arrogant about the status of the artist as Joyce interpreted him to be, and it is highly probable that his interpretation blends in ideas he had picked up from Nietzsche's concept of the Superman and D'Annunzio's cult of art as religion. But for a more specific model, we may turn to Gerhart Hauptmann (1862–1946), who was a more literal successor of Ibsen than Joyce was to become, and who had offered his own full-scale version of the portrait of an artist. This portrait had a great influence on Joyce, even to the point of identification.

As Joyce had learned Danish in order to read Ibsen in the original, although his work was available in the translation of William Archer (with whom Joyce corresponded and who became a valuable advisor in his early career[22]), so he learned German apparently for the sole reason of reading Hauptmann, who was not available in translation. Hauptmann was, together with Hermann Sudermann, the German representative of the so-called naturalist movement initiated by Ibsen. But where Ibsen had presented middle- or upper-class characters – characters who belonged to the same class of society as Freud's patients did – Hauptmann had turned to the lower class, had peopled his stage with labourers, servants, petty craftsmen, peasants, outcasts of society, and had painted the reverse side of the prosperous German 'Gründerjahre' after the foundation of the 'Reich': its sordidness, misery and despair, and the poverty and ugliness of a segment of society that had never before been deemed worthy to serve as the subject of literature. Where Ibsen had employed the everyday language of educated people who could express themselves in complete sentences, Hauptmann had used the speech of common people who could express themselves only 'by fits and starts', in broken phrases and exclamations. Hauptmann was careful to have his characters reveal themselves by the language they used, usually by resorting to his native Silesian dialect, or, if that seemed inexpedient, by inventing special kinds of colloquialism; each had his or her own 'speech mask' as a mark of identity ('We recognize that it is *that* thing which it is', as Stephen's definition of the epiphany runs (*SH* 213)). From there it is not difficult to understand how Joyce could see Hauptmann as a successor of Ibsen, and where he would find the potential to go even further. That he clearly placed himself in this line of descent can be seen from the concluding statement of his essay 'The Day of the Rabblement' (1901): 'Elsewhere there are men who are worthy to carry on the tradition of the old master who is dying in Christiania. He has already found his successor in the writer of *Michael Kramer*, and the third minister will not be wanting when his hour comes. Even now that hour may be standing by the door' (*CW* 72).

In the summer of 1901 Joyce translated two of Hauptmann's plays – *Vor Sonnenaufgang* (*Before Sunrise*; 1889) and *Michael Kramer* (1900) – hoping that the Abbey Theatre would perform them. (It did not.) Whereas the first of these is a pure naturalistic drama in the strict sense of the term – it presents the moral corruption in a village community suddenly grown rich after the discovery of a coal mine – the other play, *Michael Kramer*, is multilayered and full of symbolic overtones. It is the tragedy of a father and a son who are both artists. The father, Michael

Kramer, lives in the frigid sphere of solitude and absolute devotion to his art. He may be seen as the fully-developed artist of the type postulated by young Joyce. Although the play is, again, naturalistic in that the everyday life of the painter is depicted with great care, it is to be read at the same time on the plane of religious symbolism. Kramer's studio is likened to a church, but instead of a crucifix there is the death-mask of the one artist who was worshipped like a god in nineteenth-century Germany, Beethoven. Kramer struggles with his art as Jacob did with the angel. For seven years he has been trying to paint a picture of Christ which nobody is allowed to see. The happiness of his wife and daughter has been offered upon the altar of his art; they lead no lives of their own. Yet this unique, though ultimately sterile, devotion is countered and challenged by the painter's son, Arnold. In his sullen and morose passiveness he rebels against his family and the bourgeois values of respectability that even his father's art has been made part of (Michael Kramer is a professor), but he is too weak to rebel openly. He is physically repulsive, grimaces at himself and at others, neglects himself, ridicules other people and is in turn ridiculed by them, keeps late nights, drinking and becoming attached to a girl 'beneath' him who shuns his advances. In short, he is the counter-type of his father in everything; and yet he is the greater artist. Behind his ridiculous outer appearance he hides a sensitive soul that is permanently hurt – by the strictures and demands of his father who does not understand him, and by the pompousness of the pillars of society in the pub, who physically hunt him to death, 'slay him like a dog', as his father says. The despised and expelled Arnold bears a resemblance to Christ, and his end is the end of a martyr. What Michael Kramer fails to see is that the likeness of Christ he is striving for and never achieves lives in his midst and cries out to him for recognition. During the course of his play Hauptmann unfolds a whole panorama of thwarted artistic ambitions, of futility and sterility, and of the mean, vulgar, and brutal superiority of those who are respected members of society. They are shown to be the living dead. But the one character who has been expelled because he does not fit in anywhere and because he terrifies all the others by dint of his very otherness, his strangeness, the deeply felt uncanniness of his genius, is he who by his very death stays alive in the end. His living spirit hovers over everything and lets the aspirations of his father appear as what they really are: ambitious and sterile.

It is obvious what interested Joyce in this drama. There is, first of all, a simultaneity of minute naturalistic detail and spiritual or symbolic meaning, which he could not have seen handled with such consequence in any play of Ibsen's. There is, as in Ibsen, the terrifying role of convention, of self-righteousness, of the pressure of family expectations. There is the new theme of the living dead or, as its reverse, of the superiority of the dead over the living, a theme Joyce would make use of in his story 'The Dead'.[23] And finally, there is the theme of the artist. It must have been illuminating for Joyce to find Hauptmann dividing the role in two: that of the strong, spotless, uncompromising, absolutely devoted father, a true 'egoarch', who nevertheless has lost contact with 'the sluggish matter of the earth' out of which alone he would be able to forge 'a new soaring impalpable imperishable being' (P 169), and that of the weak son, even more talented than his father, yet dubious, reckless, inconsiderate, unable to discipline himself. Hauptmann seems to imply that a reconciliation between the two artist types is inconceivable: that one will fail for lack of sincerity, the other perish because society will not let him exist. For Joyce this may have acted as an antidote to his high exaltation of the artist figure. In any case the eccentric type represented by Arnold became more congenial to him. In Stephen Hero, in the fifth chapter of A Portrait, and perhaps again in the figure of Shem in Finnegans Wake he pictured the Arnold type – reckless, disdainful, sarcastic – and he even cultivated it himself, at least in his outward appearance.[24] When the artist reappears in the first chapters of Ulysses his attitude is the same but the tone is different and he is ironically distanced. The artistic problems with which the book is concerned are not any longer those of Stephen, and Joyce deals with them on other levels: the artist has become 'invisible, refined out of existence' (P 215).

As I have mentioned already, Joyce's concept of the artist may also be indebted to Nietzschean ideas. This is difficult to prove because nowhere in his early writings does he actually quote or refer to Nietzsche (1844–1900). In his story 'A Painful Case', finished in August 1905, he makes Mr Duffy a reader of Nietzsche (an affinity which also shows in this gentleman's character), and Joyce's Triestine library lists three of Nietzsche's books,[25] but it may safely be assumed that he read the German philosopher at a much earlier date, possibly along with Ibsen and Hauptmann before the turn of the century, and that it was to Nietzsche that he owed the radicalness, the fierce impetuosity and the acid irony of his early essays. It would have been highly inopportune, however, for Joyce to allude to Nietzsche in the climate of University College, because, if Renan and D. F. Strauss criticized Christianity on historic principles, it was Nietzsche who actually tried to destroy it by pouring his caustic scorn on what he regarded as a religion invented to breed slaves and not human beings worthy of life.

In any case, Nietzsche was the most notorious intellectual in late nineteenth-century Europe – incomparably more scandalizing than Ibsen or, say, Wagner – and his influence, whether acknowledged or not, could be felt everywhere, in philosophy and science (in Freud, for example), in philology and historiography, in the arts, in criticism and literature. Nietzsche was the titanic iconoclast who, with his sledge-hammer ('How to philosophize with the hammer' is the title of one of his tracts), destroyed what came to be called (by Wagner's son-in-law Houston Stuart Chamberlain) 'The Foundations of the Nineteenth Century': the god of the Christians, the radiant image of the Greeks established by Winckelmann and the German classical writers, the traditional concepts of morality, the equalizing spirit of democracy, and, perhaps most importantly, at least in the context of his own time, the peculiar German ideal of education (*Bildungsideal*). This ideal was an abstraction created by philistine schoolmen and professors which culminated in the reduction of history to a heap of archival facts and thus was utterly useless and without life. Instead, Nietzsche advocated atheism and nihilism as proper expressions of the dignity of a free human being, showed the dark underside of the supposedly serene Greeks (regarding their mad ecstasies and exuberant irrationalities as a precondition of their culture), proposed an amorality 'beyond good and evil', suggested a counter-education beyond schools and universities that would take into account the givens of life in its complexity, and, most notoriously of all, expounded the theory of the Superman, that supreme being living in the icy sphere of absolute seclusion, disdaining the rabblement, 'Unfellowed, friendless and alone . . . Firm as the mountain-ridges . . .',[26] a law only unto himself: in sum, a total revaluation of all values – the phrase is Nietzsche's – in comparison with which every artistic revolt of his time shrinks to a special case within his grand design.

With *The Birth of Tragedy* Nietzsche blasted his way onto the European stage. Written in a dithyrambic prose never heard before in Germany, least of all in a book by a scholar, Nietzsche brushed away

Winckelmann's and Goethe's 'noble simplicity, calm grandeur' of the Greeks and argued 'that the achievements of the Greeks generally, and their tragedies in particular, cannot be understood adequately so long as we do not realize what potentially destructive forces had to be harnessed to make them possible'.[27] It is this for which Nietzsche uses the term 'Dionysian', the terrifying, boundless, and yet pleasurable life-force which is held in check by the measure and harmony of the 'Apollonian' form of tragedy, but of which we are constantly kept conscious by the chorus out of which tragedy grew. As Nietzsche says in section seven: ·

The metaphysical comfort – with which, I am suggesting even now, every true tragedy leaves us – that life is at the bottom of things, despite all the changes of appearances, indestructibly powerful and pleasurable – this comfort appears in incarnate clarity in the chorus of satyrs, a chorus of natural beings who live ineradicably, as it were, behind all civilization and remain eternally the same, despite the changes of generations and of the history of nations.   (p. 59)

I have given this quotation at length for two reasons: it contains Nietzsche's philosophy of history in a nutshell – the eternal return of the same under the disguise of different shapes and appearances – which may have been an initial spark for the emergence of Joyce's own concept of history, formulated later with the help of Vico's theory of historic cycles[28] and Edgar Quinet's dictum about the everlasting presence of a life-force in contrast to the eternal flux of man-made things.[29] The second point is that by way of the chorus Nietzsche connects tragedy with the fullness of life, in all its aspects of frenzy and insanity, exuberance and joy, irrationality and sensuous drives, thus pointing to those layers of life that had been covered up, or 'rationalized away', by civilization, and that would be drawn to the light some thirty years later, in a calmer mood, by Freud. This *affirmation* of life in its totality – an 'everlasting Yea' – would become the final note of *Ulysses*. But as early as his paper on 'Drama and Life' Joyce had differentiated between 'literature' and 'drama' – the former being concerned with 'accidental manners and humours', whereas drama, the 'real' art, has to do with that which is changeless: 'Drama has to do with the underlying laws first, in all their nakedness and divine severity' (*CW* 40). That these Nietzschean-sounding changeless laws are perhaps synonymous with his own concept of life may be implied in the very title of Joyce's paper, or when he says, further on: 'I believe . . . that drama arises spontaneously out of life and is coeval with it' (*CW* 43).[30] In the 'Attempt at a Self-Criticism' which Nietzsche added to the 1886 edition of his early book, he distanced himself from many things he had said or conclusions he had drawn, and in particular he criticized the heavily overwritten, rhapsodic or 'romantic' manner of its style. But he held firmly to the connection he had established between art and life, art *in* life. What he had done in the book was – and he had this printed in italics – '*to look at science in the perspective of the artist, but at art in that of life*' (p. 19).

Another point Nietzsche stresses and reformulates dogmatically in his 'Self-Criticism' is his concept of the artist. In the early book he had spoken about the abdication of the subjectivity of the artist: the artist gave voice to a reality within or behind or beyond or above him. 'The artist has already surrendered his subjectivity in the Dionysian process . . . The "I" of the lyrist . . . sounds from the depth of his being: its "subjectivity" in the sense of modern aestheticians is a fiction.' When the poet says 'I', 'this self is not the same as that of the waking, empirically real man, but the only truly existent and eternal self resting at the basis of things, through whose images the lyric genius sees this very basis' (pp. 49–50). Only by surrendering his Ego the artist may come in touch with the eternal laws that allow him to create. This implies, in Freudian terms, a recognition of the unconscious aspects of creativity, but it is not yet quite the 'impersonal manner of the artist' that Joyce saw in Ibsen. For this we must turn to the 'Self-Criticism'. Here Nietzsche points somewhat apologetically – and this is not altogether dissimilar from the way Joyce would expose his earlier self in the representation of Stephen in *A Portrait* – to 'the moodiness of youth, independent, defiantly self-reliant even where it seems to bow before an authority and personal reverence . . .', and speaks of the arrogance of his book 'that sought to exclude right from the beginning the *profanum vulgus* of "the educated" even more than "the mass" or "folk"' (pp. 18–19). But what he never takes back or ironizes, what turns out to be the central idea of the book, is that 'art, and *not* morality, is presented as the truly *metaphysical* activity of men'. He continues with a summary of his argument:

In the book itself the suggestive sentence is repeated several times, that the existence of the world is *justified* only as an aesthetic phenomenon. Indeed, the whole book knows only an artistic meaning and crypto-meaning behind all events – a 'god', if you please, but certainly only an entirely reckless and amoral artist-god who wants to experience, whether he is building or destroying, in the good and in the bad, his own joy and glory.　　(p. 22)

And he goes on to rail against the Christian hostility to life which he sees as bound up with its exclusively moral interpretation of the world, measured against which 'life *must* continually and inevitably be in the wrong, because life *is* something essentially amoral . . .' (p. 23). The principal themes of Joyce's concept of the artist are here: his amoral disposition perhaps first of all (we should remember Stephen's dispute with the President), which allows him to see life in the totality of its forms, and consequently his detachment, the 'impersonal manner' which allows life 'to come through', beyond his subjectivity or objectivity, from the sources of his unconscious. Then there is the defiance, the self-reliance, the abhorrence of the multitude. And finally there is the equation of god and artist who first replaces the forbidding god of Christianity as a figure of veneration but who gradually becomes – in Nietzsche's Superman, in Joyce's triumphant definition of the artist in *A Portrait* – a figure of identification.

Nietzsche dedicated his book to Richard Wagner (1813–83), whom he regarded as his 'sublime predecessor on this path', that is, in the idea 'that art represents the highest task and the truly metaphysical activity of this life' (pp. 31–2). In his essay Nietzsche first analyzes the birth of tragedy 'out of the spirit of music', as the subtitle to the first edition ran, then its decline under the impact of the rise of Socratic philosophy.[31] But then he goes on (for ten more sections; the whole book has only twenty-five) to describe the rebirth of tragedy which had become manifest to him in the music drama of Wagner. He was later to regret bitterly his high praise of Wagner, but our concern is not with this changing relationship. We turn our attention to Wagner because he too was important for the shaping of Joyce's mind. In contrast to the silence as far as Nietzsche is concerned, there are abundant references to Wagner's operas in Joyce's writing, and the Triestine library not only contains some scores and libretti, but also editions of letters, pamphlets, and an English edition of the Prose Works of 1892 that included Wagner's famous essay on 'Art and Revolution' (1849).

As a young man Wagner had been a political agitator, had taken an active part in the German revolution of 1848, had built barricades, and as a consequence had to go into exile after the revolution had failed. But he carried the spirit of revolution over into art, postulating that it had to be revolutionary in order to bring about a change of consciousness and through that a change of society. In his 'Art and Revolution' he started, as Nietzsche would after him, with the Greeks, praising their efforts 'to bring about the highest possible work of art, drama'. 'Such a day of tragedy was a feast of the god . . . The poet was his high priest who really, even physically, was part of his own creation.'[32] But Greek art could be '*conservative* because it was a valid and adequate expression of the public conscience; with us true Art is *revolutionary* because its very existence is opposed to the ruling spirit of public opinion' (p. 295). Yet the perfect work of art, i.e. the Drama, had not yet been 'reborn', and it is this that Wagner set out to achieve in his 'music dramas' (as he preferred to call his operas). The artist, however, at least as Wagner conceived him in his early tracts (notably in 'The Artwork of the Future' (1849)), was nothing but a mediator: the real, the only artist was 'the Folk'. Such a contention was opposed to Ibsen's view of the artist as an aristocrat and isolationist. In 'The Day of the Rabblement' Joyce seemed to have sided with Ibsen. Yet in his essay on 'Drama and Life' he recognized that drama fulfils this communal role and urged his countrymen to 'criticize in the manner of free people, as a free race, recking little of ferula and formula. The Folk is, I believe, able to do so much' (*CW* 42). The artist as mediator: he was to reach through to the uncreated conscience of his race, liberate the dormant forces and raise them to the light in his creations. Joyce said in 'Drama and Life': 'Every race has made its own myths and it is in these that early drama often finds an outlet. The author of Parsifal has recognized this and hence his work is solid as a rock' (*CW* 43). The observation is not quite correct. Wagner certainly drew on myths, usually Germanic ones, or what he held to be Germanic ones, but the interesting thing is what he did with them. Existing myths he only used as his raw material, as a quarry out of which he *created* myths that were entirely of his own making. (Nobody would mistake his Siegfried, for instance, for the Siegfried of the Middle High German epic poem.) His reasons for doing so are rather complicated. He believed that the myths that had been given literary form in the Middle Ages were still part, however shapelessly and unknowingly, of some kind of collective unconscious of his people, and that they thus structured and conditioned their behaviour. Or vice versa: under the various shapes of outer appearance (of 'characters' as well as of institutions) could still be seen the old forms and motivations at work. It is easy to see what use Joyce would make of an approach to myth of this sort. He clearly sensed what he called 'universal import' when he said, again in 'Drama and Life', that the drama of Lohengrin which 'unfolds itself in a scene of seclusion, amid halflights, is not an Antwerp legend but a world drama' (CW 45). But Wagner never intended such general applicability of the myths. His intention was to a large extent political: he wanted to confront *his* people with their *own* myth, with clear indications of how it could be put to use. His Siegfried is a pretty obvious exemplification of the new type of hero – a dreamer, a bit of a fool, living more in the amorphous realm of his unconscious than in the light of reason, in sum, a German prototype who would spurn the lure of Jewish intellectualism (Mime) or of bourgeois capitalism (the hoard of the Nibelung) and fight his way through, even if it were to lead him to his own destruction and to the destruction of the world.

Joyce certainly did not see the full implications of the Siegfried figure when he had Stephen partially identify with him. Stephen, too, brushes aside the claims of his home, his country and his church. Before he does so, in his conversation with Cranly, he hears the bird call from *Siegfried* as a kind of an incentive which causes him to muse: 'How could he hit their [i.e. the Irish patricians'] conscience or how cast his shadow over the imaginations of their daughters, before their squires begat upon them, that they might breed a race less ignoble than their own?' (P 238). Although he does not forge the new sword, Nothung, as Siegfried does in the smithy of Mime, he sets out 'to forge in the smithy of his soul the uncreated conscience of his race' (P 253), thus, in a way, reinterpreting what Siegfried hoped to achieve with his sword. Yet in the 'Circe' chapter of *Ulysses* Stephen brandishes his ashplant and, with the cry 'Nothung', smashes the chandelier of the brothel in an act that signifies the 'ruin of all space' (U 15.4241–5). The glaring design of Wagner is now exposed in its ridiculousness.

It is, however, the *technique* of Wagner from which Joyce seems to have profited most. Wagner worked from relatively small musical units – of melody, of chords, of rhythm, of instruments – which he assigned to the different themes and characters (or groups of characters) of his operas. They are introduced in such a way that from them the listener can immediately recognize the themes or characters; thus the listener knows that when a certain horn signal sounds a certain character is about to enter the stage. This is the technique that Wagner called the 'leit-motif'. This relatively simple device of musical givens of course allows for an infinite variety of highly intricate combinations that can express the complex stages in the unfolding of characters and themes. Thus, when a character sings one thing, a chord, a melody, a rhythm in the orchestra can make the listener aware that, for instance, the character has something else in mind or something is taking shape in his unconscious that he does not yet know about or something or somebody is present in some layer of his self which he has tried to repress. In this way Wagner is able to evoke simultaneously the multilayered totality of his characters (in Freudian terms: their unconscious, conscious, and super-ego) at any given moment, recording at the same time the quick or gradual changes in what is becoming dominant or latent in the psyche by the minutest alterations in orchestration, tone-colour, dynamic, or pitch. Never before had opera achieved such comprehensive and differentiated presentation of character which at the same time reaches through to the deeper layers of the 'uncreated conscience', or the myth, of the people out of which this character has emerged: at once ontogenesis and phylogenesis. This would never have been possible if Wagner had only been a composer. He was, and felt himself to be, also a poet, and what he intended was what he called a *Gesamtkunstwerk*, a total artwork. That is, without language, without the cognitive faculty, there would not have been any understanding of his characters in the abstract medium of music. And in addition to this he used the overall effects of the staging, the setting, the lights – written down with meticulous care to preclude any arbitrariness on the point of future directors – in order to approach the totality of theatre as it had been realized by the Greeks and was to be reinstituted by himself.

When Joyce composed *Ulysses* he certainly had some kind of *Gesamtkunstwerk* in mind. He did not only make use of all literary genres – poetry and drama, satire and parody, different styles of narration – but also made language audible by using its 'material' parts, sounds and rhythms, and 'composed' them according to musical rules (as in the 'Sirens' chapter). He further wanted to embrace the totality of sensory impressions, and this is why he included smells and tastes, the lower bodily functions, and the physiological effects of inebriation ('Eumaeus'), not in simple descriptive terms but transposed completely into features of language, such as syntactic procedures. And like Wagner he wanted to reach through to the collective unconscious of his characters: Bloom was to be Everyman, Molly all women, without – or perhaps deliberately set against – the nationalistic confinements of Wagner. Most important however was what he could technically learn from Wagner: the technique of the leit-motif which allowed him to introduce comparatively small units of language into the text, to work from and to expand, in order to establish an evergrowing system of references and cross-references. This is quite obvious from the moment Joyce was in full possession of his artistic powers, from the first pages of *Dubliners* and *A Portrait* (notice, for instance, the adjective 'nice' that structures the first chapter of *A Portrait*). As he went on to *Ulysses* the Wagnerian technique taught him how to present the multi-layered facets of his characters. He learned from Wagner how a simultaneous presentation of character – at once focusing on both conscious and preconscious or unconscious layers – was to be achieved on the various planes of language. Seen from the point of view of technique or, equally, the point of view of the unheard-of possibilities that extended the boundaries of the arts so immeasurably, it was, I believe, Wagner who had the most fundamental and the most lasting influence on the writing of Joyce.[33]

Missing from this survey, of course, are a great number of authors who also figured in Joyce's development. From Ibsen we could have moved to Björnsterne Björnsen or Jens Peter Jacobsen, two other Scandinavian writers read by Joyce and very much *en vogue*, like everything Scandinavian, at the turn of the century. When speaking about the high exaltation of the artist, his status of highpriest or god, we might have discussed the aestheticism of Gabriele D'Annunzio and his cult of beauty. Joyce read most of his many novels, plays and poems,[34] and took some with him to Trieste, notably the English edition of *The Child of Pleasure* (1898), which had an interesting 'modernist' preface by Arthur Symons. Symons had been important for Joyce in other respects, as the mediator of the French Symbolist movement, and, personally, through his assistance to Joyce in getting his first book of poems, *Chamber Music*, published.[35] Also of immense importance were the great Russians Leo Tolstoy (whom we have considered briefly), Ivan Turgenev (1818–83), and Mikhail Lermontov (1814–41). For Tolstoy he always had the highest praise, and it is possible that he got some initial ideas about the technique of the 'interior monologue' from such stories as 'Sebastopol' or 'Master and Servant'.[36] He compared

Lermontov's *Hero of Our Time* to his own efforts in writing a novel about himself, that is, the early draft of *A Portrait*.[37] About Turgenev he had reservations and found him only 'useful technically',[38] which seems strange because there are interesting parallels between their lives and writings: Turgenev, too, was an exile, and made Russian nationalism, the Slavophile movement that wanted to cut off the ties to Western European thought, the target of his criticism. In his stories he concentrated upon ordinary people, the weak, the insignificant, the superfluous; nothing unusual ever happens, and his manner of narration is detached, letting the things described speak for themselves without comments or judgements. Perhaps Joyce's cautious reaction was because there were too many points of contact. After all, he kept Turgenev's Complete Works in eleven volumes in his Triestine library, in addition to many single editions.

A full description of the intellectual development of the young Joyce would have to treat of the authors just mentioned, and some others besides. The importance of the Russians, in particular, has never been fully studied. But this selective survey has singled out those figures whose influence on Joyce became manifest at an early age and who exerted an influence traceable throughout his work, all the way down – or up – to *Finnegans Wake*. There is, moreover, a common denominator that unites these, widely differing, figures with Joyce. With the exception of Hauptmann all of them were exiles – they had either chosen exile because of the hostility of their countries to their work (Ibsen, Nietzsche) or they had been expelled by their countries (Dante, Bruno, Wagner). At the same time they remained absolutely fixated upon their countries, pouring hate or scorn upon them, exposing their vices and rottenness, but at the same time indicating possibilities of renewal. All of them were revolutionaries who at no point in their lives succumbed to the spirit of compromise. Each broke with tradition in such a way that the future could not ignore or reverse their achievements, since they had changed the course of history in their respective fields: Dante created 'Italian' as literary language; Bruno envisioned an infinity of worlds anticipating modern physics, and formulated as a universal law the coincidence of opposites, anticipating Hegelian dialectics; Ibsen proposed the 'objectivity' of drama, its 'scientific' disengagement, precluding the artistic self-expression of its maker and paving the way for a concept of art that centres on its textuality; Nietzsche offered an antisystematic alternative to school philosophy which is still influential in contemporary philosophical movements, and anticipated much of what psychoanalysis, comparative mythology, and anthropology were to bring to light; and Wagner revolutionized compositional procedures by introducing leit-motifs and by presenting the complexities of his operatic characters in the totality of their psychic layers. All these different strands and movements converged in the mind of Joyce – philosophy and history, myth and music, physics and psychology, art and various literary forms – and made possible the uniqueness of his own art.

NOTES

1 For instance, he criticized George Moore's *Untilled Field* as follows: 'A lady who has been living for three years on the line between Bray and Dublin is told by her husband that there is a meeting in Dublin at which he must be present. She looks up the table to see the hours of the trains. This on DW and WR where the trains go regularly: this after three years. Isn't it rather stupid of Moore' (*Letters II* 71).

2 *The Dublin Diary of Stanislaus Joyce*, ed. G. H. Healey (Ithaca: Cornell University Press, 1962), p. 112.

3 See Mary T. Reynolds, *Joyce and Dante: The Shaping Imagination* (Princeton: Princeton University Press, 1981). Vicki Mahaffey discusses the importance for Joyce of Dante's *Vita Nuova* and *Inferno* in ch. 8 of this volume (see pp. 204–5).

4 The *Spaccio* is composed of ten parts: an 'Epistola esplicatoria' and three dialogues, each subdivided into three parts, each corresponding to its equivalent part in the other two sections. Here, as in Dante, Joyce met with writing as composition: each part was interrelated with the others in the totality of the construction. Dante's *Commedia* and Bruno's *Spaccio* may have provided the germ of Joyce's constructive principle.

5 For further discussion of Freud's importance for Joyce see Christopher Butler's chapter in this volume (ch. 11, pp. 271–3).

6 In his Triestine Library we find Freud's *Psychopathology of Everyday Life* and his essay on Leonardo. But he certainly knew other works by Freud, including *The Interpretation of Dreams*, *Jokes and Their Relation to the Unconscious*, and the 'Wolf-Man' case history (see Daniel Ferrer, 'The Freudful couchmare of Λd', *JJQ* 22 (1985), 367–82).

7 His famous definition runs: 'By an epiphany he meant a sudden spiritual manifestation, whether in the vulgarity of speech or of gesture or in a memorable phase of the mind itself. He believed that it was for the man of letters to record these epiphanies with extreme care, seeing that they themselves are the most delicate and evanescent of moments' (*SH* 211).

8 For the importance of Thomas Aquinas in Joyce's writing see Father T. Noon, S.J., *Joyce and Aquinas* (New Haven: Yale University Press, 1957) and Jacques Aubert, *L'Esthétique de Joyce* (Paris: Didier, 1973).

9 The most conspicuous name that comes to mind is that of Heinrich Schliemann (1822–90) who had dug up, in 1870–82, what he held to be the Troy of Homer, proving that 'fiction', down to the minutest detail, was based on 'facts', an idea that appealed to Joyce strongly. Joyce was also interested in Samuel Butler's theory about *The Authoress of the 'Odyssey'* (1897), with its pinning down of Homeric localities; and in Victor Bérard's discovery of actual trade routes at the back of the Odyssean wanderings. For Bérard and Butler see Michael Seidel, *Epic Geography: James Joyce's Ulysses* (Princeton: Princeton University Press, 1976).

10 For a full study see B. J. Tysdahl, *Joyce and Ibsen* (Oslo: Norwegian University Press, 1968).

11 Stanislaus Joyce, *My Brother's Keeper*, ed. Richard Ellmann (London: Faber, 1958), p. 102.

12 He states in his letter to Ibsen of March 1901: 'Your work on earth draws to a close and you are near the silence. It is growing dark for you . . . You have only opened the way – . . . But I am sure that higher and holier enlightenment lies – onward' (*Letters I* 52).

13 The original wording after the colon had been: 'Ibsen with his profound self-approval, Ibsen with his haughty, disillusioned courage, Ibsen with his minute and wilful energy' (*SH* 41).

14 The Danish critic Georg Brandes, well known to Joyce, also lived in Germany; he chose to write in German. I have paraphrased those sentences from his Ibsen essay (1883) that bear some resemblance to Joyce's attitude towards his own country. In the original they read: 'Er ist ausgeschieden aus seinem Volk; . . . Heimath als Inbegriff der Unbedeutendheit, Schlaffheit und Muthlosigkeit . . .' ('Schlaffheit', which I have rendered as 'inertia', may also connote 'paralysis'). '. . . er hat sich daran gewöhnt, sich in der Heimathlosigkeit heimisch zu fühlen' (*Moderne Geister. Literarische Bildnisse aus dem XIX. Jahrhundert* (Frankfurt: Rütten und Loening, 2nd ed., 1887), pp. 416–17). Joyce may have known the English publication of Georg Brandes, *Henrik Ibsen and Björnstjerne Björnson* (London, 1879).

15 '. . . moralisches Misstrauen [ward] seine Muse. Es inspirierte ihm immer kühnere Untersuchungen' (*Moderne Geister*, p. 420).

16 Both plays were interpreted in this way by Brandes (*Moderne Geister*, pp. 459–60).

17 Joyce actually noted this in his review of 'Ibsen's New Drama', published in the *Fortnightly Review*, 1 April 1900. 'His analytic method is thus made use of to the fullest extent, and into the comparatively short space of two

days the life in life of all his characters is compressed. For instance, though we only see Solness during one night and up to the following evening, we have in reality watched with bated breath the whole course of his life up to the moment when Hilda Wangel enters his house' (*CW* 50).

18 *Moderne Geister*, p. 463.
19 *My Brother's Keeper*, p. 102.
20 *My Brother's Keeper*, p. 108.
21 Letter to Stanislaus, 4 April 1905, *Letters II* 205.
22 See Archer's letter to Joyce, especially his criticism of Joyce's (lost) play, *A Brilliant Career*, in a letter of 15 September 1900 (*Letters II* 8–11).
23 See Hugo Schmidt, 'Hauptmann's *Michael Kramer* and Joyce's "The Dead"', *PMLA* 80 (1965), 142.
24 Stanislaus Joyce noted in his diary on 14 September 1904: 'I hate to see Jim limp and pale, with shadows under his watery eyes, loose wet lips, and dank hair. I hate to see him sitting on the edge of a table grinning at his own state.' And again: 'He likes the novelty of his rôle of dissipated genius' (*Dublin Diary*, p. 76).
25 *The Birth of Tragedy* (edition of 1909), *Joyful Wisdom* (1910) and *Wagner, Nietzsche contra Wagner* (1911).
26 From Joyce's early poem 'The Holy Office' (*CW* 152).
27 Walter Kaufmann in the introduction to his translation of Nietzsche's *The Birth of Tragedy and the Case of Wagner* (New York: Vintage Books, 1967), p. 10. Quotations are from this edition.
28 On Vico – who had been discovered for Germany by Herder and for France by Michelet and thus may have been known to Nietzsche – see Donald Phillip Verene, ed., *Vico and Joyce* (Ithaca: Cornell University Press, 1987). See also John Bishop, *Joyce's Book of the Dark* (Madison: University of Wisconsin Press, 1986), ch. 7, 'Vico's "Night of Darkness"': *The New Science* and *Finnegans Wake*'.
29 For a brief summary of the difference between the theories of Vico and Quinet see the introduction of Giorgio Melchiori to the Italian translation of *Finnegans Wake* (Milan: Mondadori, 1982), pp. xxi–xxiv.
30 Joyce goes on: 'Every race has made its own myths and it is in these that early drama often finds an outlet. The author of Parsifal has recognized this and hence his work is solid as a rock.' The fact that he points to Wagner in this connection seems to be a clear indication that he had Nietzsche in mind for his concept of 'Drama and Life', since it is Wagner whom Nietzsche sees as the renovator of Greek tragedy.
31 When tragedy died, the so-called New Attic Comedy emerged. In this connection Nietzsche gives an extremely illuminating hint about the change and deterioration of one character, Odysseus, that may have been taken up by Joyce and may have helped to shape the figure of Bloom:

'Odysseus, the typical Hellene of the older art, now sank, in the hands of the new poets, to the figure of the Graeculus, who, as the good-naturedly cunning house-slave, henceforth occupies the center of dramatic interest' (p. 77).

32 'Die Kunst und die Revolution', in Richard Wagner, *Dichtungen und Schriften*, Jubiläumsausgabe in 10 Bänden, hg. von Dieter Borchmeyer, v (Frankfurt: Insel, 1983), 275–6. References are to this edition. The translation is my own.

33 See also Mahaffey's discussion of the indebtedness of Joyce's *Exiles* to Wagner's *Tristan and Isolde* in this volume (pp. 202–7).

34 Stanislaus Joyce lets us feel what his brother thought of D'Annunzio around the turn of the century: '*Il Fuoco*, which my brother considered the highest achievement of the novel to date' (*My Brother's Keeper*, p. 154). And apropos *Le Vergini delle rocce* Stanislaus writes: 'The exaltation of an ardour of life, manifested in a diversity of forms by the development of each one's native energies, appealed strongly to him at this early stage of his development. The thought expounded in those pages is that the elect are those few spirits who, conscious of their gifts, endeavour by a self-imposed discipline to become the deliberate artificers of their own style of life; and that they owe obedience only to the laws of that style, to which they have willingly bent their free natures in pursuit of a personal ideal of order and beauty' (pp. 171–2). Mahaffey discusses the importance of D'Annunzio for *Exiles* (pp. 206–7 below).

35 Arthur Symons's *The Symbolist Movement in Literature* was first published in 1899 and many times re-issued. There is a reprint with an introduction by Richard Ellmann (New York: Dutton, 1958).

36 Stanislaus saw a link between the *Sebastopol Sketches* and the interior monologue (*Letters III* 106). Tolstoy may also have alerted Joyce to the importance of minute physiological changes in the formation of cognitive decisions. In an essay on the effects of tobacco and alcohol, 'Why do men stupefy themselves' (in his *Essays and Letters* (London: Grant Richards, 2nd impression, 1904), and found in Joyce's Triestine library), Tolstoy contends that it is by the most tiny movements and steps that the mind works. 'Tiny, tiny alterations – but on them depend the most immense, the most terrible consequences' (p. 29).

37 'The only book I know like it [*Stephen Hero*] is Lermontoff's *Hero of our Days* . . . There is a likeness in the aim and title and at times in the acid treatment', Letter to Stanislaus, about 24 September 1905 (*Letters II* 111).

38 Letter to Stanislaus (*Letters II* 90).

4 Joyce the Parisian

'*Trieste – Zurich – Paris*, 1914–1921'; 'PARIS, 1922–1939'. Anyone who has read Joyce will recognize the famous dates and place names which link the writing of *Ulysses* and *Finnegans Wake* to a particular context, to circumstances whose importance is not merely anecdotal but, if only to judge from the recurrence of these very names in Joyce's last book, structural. Joyce's exile, recaptured by the three cities which, each in its turn, saw the inception of new developments in the writing of *Ulysses*, was to end in Paris. Does this make him a 'Parisian'? If we speak of Joyce as a 'Parisian', two images, two contrasting clichés, immediately come to mind: Joyce as part of the Bohemian crowd of the 'Expatriates', the Irish genius adding his own tenor voice to the hoarse chorus of drunken American 'Pilgrims' wandering between Odeonia and the cafés of Montparnasse; or the secretive writer, living only with his family and a small group of devotees, pent up in an ivory tower, completely indifferent to his surroundings, absorbed by the drawn out *tour de force* of having to finish his universal history before the real apocalypse of the century comes... If both clichés indeed contain an element of truth, I shall try to show first that they correspond to different phases of Joyce's Parisian life, and then, that they misconstrue the very organic relationship he had established with his elected Ithaca. Neither, say, Hemingway's version, nor Arthur Power's,[1] can manage to convey the specific role of Paris for Joyce, who may well be called, as *Finnegans Wake* coins it, a 'paleoparisien' (*FW* 151.09) – that is, first of all, an 'arch-parisian'.

'Arch-parisian' Joyce was bound to be, and in two senses; in the historical sense of his feeling very early an attraction to Paris – called by Paris, almost a 'calling', which receives momentous mythological overtones in *Ulysses*; and in the transcendental sense of a 'principle' underlying the anarchic tendencies implied by the nomadism of perpetual exile. It is true that Joyce's early and brief stay in Paris was not to prove entirely satisfactory. His surprising decision to register there as a medical student for the academic year 1902–3 was soon turning all his energies to the practical strategies of survival; he experienced hunger and solitude much more than the lively atmosphere of the *carabins* of the Latin Quarter. The Bibliothèque Sainte Geneviève saw him poring over the dusty pages of Aristotle's works more than on the newest publications of the post-Symbolist avant-garde. And when he discovered *Les Lauriers sont coupés* by Dujardin in a station kiosk, it was because he remembered that George Moore had mentioned him, not because of any awareness of the literary trends in Paris.[2] Yet, when the moment came for a second departure which he knew would be a final exile from Dublin, his mind was still fixed on Paris. When planning the great 'adventure' of eloping with Nora Barnacle, he writes to her on Michaelmas Day 1904: 'I do not like the notion of London and I am sure you won't like it either but at the same time it is on the road to Paris and it is perhaps better than Amsterdam . . . It amuses me to think of the effect the news of it [our adventure] will cause in my circle. However, when we are once safely settled in the Latin quarter they can talk as much as they like' (*Letters II* 57). As it turned out, the Berlitz school had only a position in Italy to offer, which Joyce accepted; but his adolescent dream – to be able to live with Nora as a 'man' – was realized sixteen years later when Pound suggested that he should come to Paris in order to finish writing *Ulysses*. Although his acceptance of Pound's suggestion seemed reluctant, he was in fact making good what he had failed to experience when a poor Irish student in Paris, soon called back by the news of his mother's fatal illness.

Paris therefore immediately provides a myth, aptly evoked by the phrase 'the Latin Quarter'; however, this does not imply that it is the artistic or intellectual glamour of Paris that attracts the young Joyce. From the very start, Paris has been identified with 'life', a mystical force which ought to be perceived in Dublin but remains thwarted by the general air of Irish corruption or paralysis. In another letter of the same crucial period preceding his departure with Nora in 1904, and following shortly after the day later to be commemorated as 'Blooms-day', Joyce writes about Paris. He starts with a meditation on Grafton Street by night:

The street was full of a life which I have poured a stream of my youth upon. While I stood there I thought of a few sentences I wrote some years ago when I lived in Paris – these sentences which follow – 'They pass in twos and threes amid the life of the boulevard, walking like people who have leisure in a place lit up for them. They are in the pastry cook's chattering, crushing little fabrics of pastry, or seated silently at tables by the café door, or descending from carriages with a busy stir of garments soft as the voice of the adulterer. They pass in an air of perfumes. Under the perfumes their bodies have a warm humid smell' –

While I was repeating this to myself I knew that life was still waiting for me if I chose to enter it.   (*Letters II* 49)

The sensuous pleasure taken in a contemplation of the night crowds on Grafton Street has to be relayed by an even more sensual awareness of these Parisian prostitutes, in what was first written as a Paris epiphany, later included in *Giacomo Joyce*, finally to be reworked as part of Stephen's memories of his student days and of his strolls on the Boulevard Saint Michel in *Ulysses*. The sexual 'entering' this letter calls up is a first step away from Dublin, a preparation for the proud flight away from the Irish nets, and it also provides a new superimposition of several cities: the glitter of Dublin's most fashionable area is transformed into a more salacious Parisian evocation, which later encompasses Trieste. The following vignette occurs in *Giacomo Joyce*: 'Trieste is waking rawly: raw sunlight over its huddled browntiled roofs, testudoform; a multitude of prostrate bugs await a national deliverance. Belluomo rises from the bed of his wife's lover's wife: the busy housewife is astir, sloe-eyed, a saucer of acetic acid in her hand...' (*GJ* 8). It is followed two pages later by another Parisian motif: 'In the raw veiled spring morning faint odours float of morning Paris: aniseed, damp sawdust, hot dough of bread: and as I cross the Pont Saint Michel the steelblue waking waters chill my heart. They creep and lap about the island whereon men have lived since the stone age...' No wonder all these carefully remembered scenes contain hints of a mystical 'stream of life' and even adumbrations of a 'wake' – especially as the second vignette alludes to a service in Notre-Dame, the gothic cathedral to which Joyce at a later stage compares his writings.

When the same motifs reappear in *Ulysses* ('Paris rawly waking, crude sunlight on her lemon streets . . . Belluomo rises from the bed of his wife's lover's wife . . . Faces of Paris men go by, their wellpleased pleasers, curled *conquistadores*' (*U* 3.209–15)), the connection between the clichés of 'raw' naturalism and subtle mythical overlayering is clinched in an apotropaic image evoking at the same time the judgement of Paris – his choice of Aphrodite leading to the rape of Helen and the Trojan war – and the fall of Icarus: 'Seadeath, mildest of all deaths known to man. Old Father Ocean. *Prix de Paris*: beware of imitations. Just you give it a fair trial. We enjoyed ourselves immensely' (*U* 3.482–4). (The 'Prix de Paris' is a horserace still famous today.) But, even if there was some enjoyment in the Paris Joyce knew, the 'Prix de Paris' turned out to be a certain price he had to pay for – precisely – staying in Paris: the price of fame, of pure innovation and radical experimentation, may indeed have been high, and Joyce could wonder whether, in a derisive echo of Henri IV's boast that Paris was worth his conversion to Catholicism, 'was Parish worth thette mess' (*FW* 199.08–09).

Of course, when Joyce arrived in Paris in 1920 for what was to be a stay of two decades, it was a far different place from the Latin Quarter he had glimpsed as a student in 1902–3. It was a city which had taken the lead in artistic experimentation in an unprecedented fashion, and as a number of young Americans had stayed on after the war, attracted as much by the rate of exchange which enabled them to live very cheaply as by the more exciting night life it provided (by contrast with a Puritan America carried away by Prohibition), it had also become the capital of the English-speaking community abroad. The names of Hemingway, Stein, Scott Fitzgerald, McAlmon, Antheil, Pound, to name but a few celebrities, are among those who made Paris into a paradise for all expatriates. Joyce, who had known, if only tangentially, the artistic avant-garde in Zurich during the war, whilst refusing to be included in any group, probably missed the intellectual stimulation this had provided when he returned to Trieste in 1919. Besides, Joyce would not have come to Paris without Ezra Pound's insistence. Much more than Joyce, Pound was in search of a 'capital' from which he could launch new schools and movements and create the new 'Renaissance' he attempted to bring about almost single-handedly. Just as Joyce was increasingly dissatisfied with a post-war Trieste in which a nationalist crisis was brewing, Pound had only felt growing rancour and anger against the still Victorian London he had inhabited since 1908. Pound signalled his break with London in two poems, *Homage to Sextus Propertius*, in which he used the mask of the Latin poet to rail at British Imperialism, and, more decisively, *Hugh Selwyn*

Mauberley, which marks his abandonment of the aesthetic pose he had
kept for a few years among the Georgian poets. Pound was a foreign
correspondent of *The Dial*, and his visit to Paris in June 1920 was to
provide the material for his 'Island of Paris' reports, in which he argued
that the only place that was intellectually and artistically alive in
Europe was Paris.

It was also in the same month of June 1920 that Pound and Joyce
finally met in Italy. Joyce, disgusted with Trieste, even thought of
leaving for Ireland (as he writes, in order to buy cheaper clothes!);
Pound was unsure of where he would go next, even contemplating a
return to the United States. Thus Pound could suggest that Joyce
should stop in Paris on his way to London, promising to pave the way
for him, inculcating all his acquaintances with the idea that they would
soon have to do everything to help a very needy family of Irish people,
a family which also contained his latest discovery. For a long time,
Joyce thought his stay in Paris would be temporary, hesitating between
London and Rome as his next destination. A letter Valery Larbaud sent
to a friend in May 1921 (that is about eight months after Joyce had come
to Paris) still stresses the provisional nature of his Paris settlement:
'*Ulysses* is not finished yet. Joyce is working on the last two episodes,
Eumaeus (sic) and Penelope. He thinks he will be through in May and
will then leave for Rome with his family.'[3] It is interesting to see Rome
vying with Paris for pre-eminence in Joyce's mind, since the common
point of the two capitals, besides being important ideological centres, is
that they had been the places of unpleasant short stays (1902–3 being in
many ways parallel to 1906–7, when Joyce worked as a bank clerk in
Rome). Perhaps he hoped to redeem these unrewarding experiences.
Paris, at any rate, was more central than Rome, since Joyce could see
himself roughly situated mid-way between Trieste and Dublin, Zurich
and London, which were the main cities where his European
correspondents lived.

Another irony of these crossed exiles is that Pound duplicated with
Joyce what he had done with Eliot, who was to reap the benefits of the
literary revolution they had brought about in London by just
remaining there: having installed Joyce in Paris and introduced him to
all his friends, Pound soon grew as dissatisfied with Paris as with
London, and then decided to settle in Rapallo in order to be a closer
witness to what he took for a Fascist Renaissance in Italy. On the other
hand, during the twenty years or so of their French stay, the Joyces

remained faithful to the deep imprint of their Trieste sojourn by speaking only the Triestine dialect of Italian in the family, a fact which astounded new Italian friends living in Paris, like Nino Frank.

However, although they lived in one city, a list of the Paris addresses of the Joyces will give a sense of their deliberately perpetuated exile. This has been described by friends such as Louis Gillet, who explains that one cannot say that Joyce 'settled' in Paris 'for he continued wandering between Passy and the Gros-Caillou, Montparnasse and Grenelle, not counting the escapades, the eclipses, the letters which without warning showed him to be in London, Folkestone, Basel, Copenhagen. His page in my address-book is filled with numerous erasures. I never saw him in the same lodgings for more than six months.'[4] Louis Gillet exaggerates slightly there, for Joyce did stay more than six months in a few places, as the following list of moves to new addresses shows:

1920	July	9, rue de l'Université (VIIe)
	July	5, rue de l'Assomption (XVIe)
	November	9, rue de l'Université (VIIe)
	December	5, Boulevard Raspail (VIe)
1921	June	71, rue du Cardinal Lemoine (Ve)
	October	9, rue de l'Université (VIIe)
1922	November	26, Avenue Charles Floquet (VIIe)
1923	August	Victoria Palace Hotel, 6 rue Blaise Desgoffe (VIIe)
1924	October	8, Avenue Charles Floquet (VIIe)
1925	June	2, Square Robiac (192, rue de Grenelle) (VIIe)
1931	April	Hotel Powers, 62 rue François Ier (VIIIe)
	September	'La Résidence', 41 Avenue Pierre Ier de Serbie (VIIIe)
	October	2, Avenue Saint Philibert (XVIe)
1932	April	Hotel Belmont et de Bassano, 28–30 rue de Bassano (VIIIe)
	October	Hotel Lord Byron, Champs Elysées (VIIIe)
	November	42, rue Galilée (VIIIe)
1934	September	7, rue Edmond Valentin (VIIe)
1939	April	34, rue des Vignes (XVIe)
	October	Hotel Lutetia, Boulevard Raspail (VIe)[5]

The second address (rue de l'Assomption) and the fifth (rue du Cardinal Lemoine) are the two flats which were offered rent-free, for a short period, to Joyce, the first by Madame Bloch-Savistsky, a friend of

Pound's who was to translate *A Portrait*, the second by Larbaud, on whose friendship I shall comment later. All these addresses indicate a preference for the left bank, but always in its most fashionable areas, plus a few incursions into Passy and the sixteenth arrondissement. 'Reeve Gootch was right and Reeve Drughad was sinistrous!', as *Finnegans Wake* confirms (*FW* 197.01). Yet, even if they are mostly located around the 'lootin quarter' (*FW* 205.27), these were not the kind of addresses one would associate with a writer 'down and up in Bohemian Paris'. Two addresses stand out as having been kept much longer than the others, the one in Square Robiac used from 1925 to 1931, and the rue Edmond Valentin one (almost five years). Although Nora was prone to abuse her husband and reproach him for his heavy tipping and drinking at night, the general lack of stability became a fact of their lives and she learnt to put up with it. But the decisions to leave these two addresses, in 1931 and in 1939, determine specific periods marked by their own crises.

Joyce had come to Paris with one main wish: to be able to complete *Ulysses* in a relative quiet which he could not find in Trieste. Thanks to the almost unlimited generosity of Harriet Weaver, he had no further money problems and could spend all his time writing. While finishing *Ulysses* (which took him longer than he had expected), he had to arrange for its publication and see to the French translations of *Exiles* and *A Portrait*; and then he had to deal with the translation of *Ulysses*. This corresponds to a relatively frantic period in Paris which lasted until the late twenties, the moment when Joyce really enjoyed his '*vie parisienne*'... Meanwhile he had to concentrate again on the writing of 'Work in Progress', which was initially published in instalments, first in the *transatlantic review* in 1924, then in various places (*Contact Collection of Contemporary Writers, Criterion, Navire d'Argent, This Quarter*) in 1925, until the appearance of *transition* provided a steady outlet for the serial publication (thirteen instalments from April 1927 to the end of 1929) of a work which baffled the editors of other, less experimental magazines. The publication of *Anna Livia Plurabelle* by Faber and Faber in 1930 signals the end of this first period; Joyce had produced a text which could justify the claims of his new work, stand on its own and be appreciated as a new type of prose-poetry. Furthermore, doubts over his writing, renewed eye troubles, the increasing strangeness of Lucia, capped by the death of his father (29 December 1931), led to a crisis in 1931–2 during which Joyce wrote very little or with great difficulty.

Such a crisis found direct expression in a desire to leave Paris. In a very dejected mood, Joyce wrote to Harriet Weaver in March 1931:

I understand that both Miss Monnier and Miss Beach have written to you to come over for the séance on the twenty-sixth which for all I know may celebrate the close of my Paris career, just as that of the 7th of December, 1921, opened it . . . So to conclude I shall probably go into a small furnished flat in London and then perhaps go to Zurich and then perhaps go back to London and then perhaps go somewhere else and then perhaps come back to Paris.

(*Letters I* 302–3)

But along with the despair and the incertitude, there appeared a few encouraging elements; Joyce adds this revealing remark: 'The second good point is that I think if the séance of the twentysixth is successful it will probably break the back of the english resistance to Work in Progress as they usually follow a Paris lead over there' (303). The séance alluded to was a reading of *Anna Livia* on 26 March 1931, in French by Adrienne Monnier and in English by Joyce. In his typically superstitious way, Joyce was once more attempting to give a definitive pattern to his life by splitting it into decades, and he had decided that his Parisian decade had come to an end.

Joyce rightly surmised that this decade of almost steady successes leading to worldwide recognition had to be linked for himself and for posterity with the efforts of Sylvia Beach and Adrienne Monnier on his behalf. Adrienne Monnier had started her own lending library and bookshop in 1915, during the war, and her American friend Sylvia Beach had in 1919 opened a bookshop which was primarily an English-speaking lending library close by. Beach's need to sacrifice herself for a good cause and her devotional approach to her job were to find in Joyce an idol whom she 'worshipped' (as she admitted herself), and to whom she was to devote more and more of her time, until Joyce's callousness provoked Adrienne's resentment. At one point, Sylvia Beach jokingly referred to Shakespeare and Co. as the 'Left Bank', implying that she had become Joyce's (and other artists') personal banker...[6]

One of the high moments in the crusade led by these two sincere and enthusiastic women in favour of *Ulysses* was the lecture referred to in Joyce's letter; given to more than two hundred people by Larbaud in Adrienne Monnier's bookshop on 7 December 1921, this event launched the reputation of the book in France. Joyce had responded to the pressure put on him by the lecture and the accompanying translations by hurrying to finish the novel, so that he and his friends were also able to celebrate the forthcoming publication undertaken by Sylvia Beach,[7] with the help of Maurice Darantiere, the Dijon printer. Subscriptions began to pour in, and when the book was published in 1922, it was almost immediately a best-seller in Sylvia Beach's bookshop. 'Bloomsday' very soon became the pretext for festivities and commemorations among the little group of friends of both bookshops.

Thus Joyce was right to recollect the date of 1921 as a turning-point in his life. But during the crisis of 1931, what was really at stake was his wish to inscribe himself in a symbolic legitimacy at last, by renouncing the still Luciferian stance that had been his until then. This he hoped to achieve through a departure from Paris and a step by step return to Dublin. The first step was the embarrassingly belated marriage with Nora, which took place in London in July 1931. Along with the planned marriage went the concept of a 'fifth hegira' (*Letters III* 217) to London – an idea which Beach, for instance, did not approve of: 'It is useless to discuss my present condition with Miss Beach. As she does not know what my motive is . . . she naturally regards my acts in a wrong light' (*Letters III* 215). It is therefore time to consider more carefully the 'fourth hegira', the move to Paris in 1920, in order to understand the milieu Joyce found when he arrived there and the way in which it sustained his work for nineteen years.

The first happy coincidence noticed by Joyce after his arrival in Paris was the fact that everyone seemed interested in Homeric parallels: 'Odyssey very much in the air here. Anatole France is writing *Le Cyclope*, G. Fauré the musician an opera *Penelope*. Giraudoux has written Elpenor (Paddy Dignam). Guillaume Apollinaire *Les Mammelles de Tirésias*' (*Letters III* 10). He himself felt enthralled by 'Circe', an episode which he insisted he had to write in Paris. After he had rewritten 'Circe' for the sixth or seventh time (Larbaud told him that this episode alone would suffice to establish the reputation of a French writer), he stayed on until the book was finished. However, my main contention is that Joyce was not so deeply absorbed in his own Odyssey that he could not perceive the main literary trends in Paris. And if he did finally stay in Paris till the last moment, until, that is, the German threat in 1940 forced him to leave, it was because he felt in Paris a unique blend of respect for tradition and playful love of experimentation. Moreover, he kept a very keen eye on what was written around him; once he had been made aware of Giraudoux's parallel Homeric attempts, he had to know more about him, and in this particular case his verdict was extremely negative. 'Giraudoux belongs to the school of poets whose day has passed, the so-called rhetoricians, and waits in vain for his Du Bellay and his Ronsard to come to life again. Never have I come upon a writer who was such a brilliant bore', he told Jan Parandowski in 1937.[8]

However, it seems indubitable that Joyce had first access to the French literary circles thanks to the network of friends gathered by Adrienne Monnier, and that he eventually shared her tastes: she had an instinctive dislike of surrealism, more precisely of André Breton whom she immediately rejected, while she and Sylvia Beach remained on good terms with Aragon, whose excellent command of English enabled him to be a staunch customer of Beach's bookshop. Beach herself stresses the fact that her French friends were the first and the last supporters of her venture. The main enthusiasm of Monnier and Beach (for they made a point of selling only books which they liked, often becoming personally acquainted with their authors) were Valery Larbaud, who called himself the bookshop's godfather, Léon-Paul Fargue, whose obscene wit was peerless, and the more established Valéry, Gide, and Claudel.

Joyce's relationship with Larbaud unhappily remained somewhat instrumental; as with Pound, Joyce seemed to have little interest in his writings, and to consider Larbaud primarily as an excellent translator. Larbaud is now thought of as a good modernist poet, but at the time he was above all interested in translation (an art on which he has written some of the most intelligent statements to date). Joyce did not have to court Larbaud as he later did Gillet; Larbaud came to him of his own will, and was immediately 'raving' about *Ulysses*. Larbaud's support opened the door of the *Nouvelle Revue Française* to Joyce, in spite of the reservations of the editor, Jacques Rivière (who would be similarly hostile to a publication of Artaud's poems in 1923). Thus, Larbaud's lecture was published in 1922 in what was the best literary magazine in France, and was soon translated into English in Eliot's *Criterion*. This triggered a series of translations and articles, so that the year 1922 can be called a 'Joyce year' in Paris: the *Ecrits Nouveaux* published 'Arabie' a few days after the publication of *Ulysses*, while the March issue of *La Revue de Genève* contained 'Un incident regrettable' ('A Painful Case'). The critical acclaim of Joyce, largely due to the atmosphere of scandal surrounding his recent book, was kept up by the translation of *A Portrait of the Artist as a Young Man* as *Dedalus* in March 1924, followed by the first issue of the new magazine *Commerce* (with Valéry, Larbaud, and Fargue as the editors), which in the summer of 1924 offered the initial publication of passages from *Ulysses* in translation. And to crown it all, the university was made aware of the Joyce phenomenon by a bilingual essay written by one of the leading professors of the period, Louis Cazamian, who wrote *L'Oeuvre de James Joyce* in 1924.[9] This extremely rapid recognition contrasted strongly with the reluctance of the literary milieux in England and Ireland.

Besides, help was to come from an unexpected quarter: the staunchly conservative *Revue des Deux Mondes*. The first article on Joyce to be published there, dated 1 August 1925, was 'Du côté de Joyce', stressing the link between Proust and Joyce, a point later reiterated to satiety. The article was rather hostile, but nevertheless showed an understanding of Joyce's techniques which was then quite remarkable. Joyce on the whole was happy with the article, knowing that such hostile criticism brought excellent publicity. What he could not imagine was that the author, Louis Gillet, subtly coached by Sylvia Beach, was slowly to change his mind, becoming within five years one of Joyce's most ardent advocates, and a very close personal friend. The total surrender of 'our review of the two mounds' (*FW* 12.19–20) indicated a major recognition, and it is necessary to read the whole of Gillet's *Stèle pour James Joyce* in order to appreciate the depth of such a critical reversal.[10] This occurred precisely at the time of Larbaud's disaffection with Joyce's 'Work in Progress', which he called a 'divertissement philologique'.[11]

It is clear that in the strategy employed by Joyce to convert Gillet to his side he attempted to become more French than the French, declaring for instance about *Ulysses*: 'In the wooden horse borrowed from Dujardin I put the warriors I stole from Victor Bérard'.[12] Joyce has been accused by his brother Stanislaus and by Mary Colum of using Dujardin as a decoy to hide more relevant borrowings from Freud or Dostoevsky; but if he systematically publicized his debt to *Les Lauriers sont coupés* (an undistinguished piece of prose revery, even if it indeed 'invents' a continuous stream-of-consciousness technique), to the point of sparking off a revival for an older and forgotten writer whom everyone associated with fin-de-siècle symbolism, it was his way of inscribing his cultural roots in France. No doubt Joyce could have acknowledged an 'Ich stamm aus Flaubert', as Pound would have it; he even saw in Larbaud another heir to Flaubert and to his own novels: 'Larbaud result of JJ. & GF.' (Notebook VI.B.8–88). But the French heritage he modestly claimed for himself had also to be proudly invented; this went as far as his name: he confided to Gillet that 'the name of Joyce is an old French word, in which one finds the name of M. de Joyeuse'.[13] Joyce could also have commented on the way French people called him 'Monsieur Joasse' (a pronunciation of his name not too far from that of 'Jolas', and one which would make him synonymous with 'very happy' (*'joice'* or *'jouasse'* or *'joasse'*) in French slang). Joyce was not only trying to look as French as possible in order to win over a conservative French critic, by a trick exposed in *Finnegans Wake* ('Parysis, *tu sais*, crucycrooks, belongs to him who parises himself' (*FW* 155.16–17)), he was busy finding confirmations of his decision to become a Parisian by organizing a system of felicitous coincidences and mystical prophecies. This implied that his new identity should be more than a mask, since it entailed an awareness of a rich and ancient tradition. It is the image of this culture which should occupy us.

Joyce may have surprised Parandowski when referring to Giraudoux as a 'poet', but this was consistent with his view of French culture as a whole. Louis Gillet was no less surprised when he heard Joyce explain that the French language was not, as English-speaking people are prone to say, primarily the language of analytic prose, but the language of poetry: 'Contrary to all expectations, the musical language *par excellence* for him was French, because of the softness of intervals and the quantity of silent syllables that gave to it something airy and diaphanous, which Claude Debussy felt so well, something *soluble dans l'air* as the delightful Lelian says.'[14] This is a far cry from what the young Joyce had had to say about French poetry during his first stay in Paris: 'Paris amuses me very much but I quite understand why there is no poetry in French literature' (*Letters II* 24). It is not that French poetry was something Joyce discovered when he came to Paris for the second time; his encounter with Valéry, whom he admired, probably had little to do with his preference for a purely French musicality. It seems that he had studied French poets systematically when still in Trieste: a large notebook with his Trieste address contains poems in French by Samain and Rimbaud, and prose excerpts of Mallarmé's 'Divagations'.[15] Joyce professed an unbounded admiration for the softest and most musical French poet, Verlaine, and knew many of his texts by heart. Wyndham Lewis told Richard Ellmann how they had drinks with prostitutes in local Paris cafés, and how Joyce was called 'le poète' because he would quote Dante and Verlaine to their astounded ears. One night, Joyce had only had to quote Verlaine in French to the bartender to be recognized and allowed in after closing time (JJ 515–16).

Among the contemporaries, Joyce enjoyed the poems of Valéry, Fargue and Soupault, and he could recite the famous opening of 'Ebauche d'un serpent'[16] (with its characteristic mute 'e's) although he deplored Valéry's inability to read his own verse musically. Only an Irish tenor could do justice to the music of French poetry! One of the earliest Finnegans Wake notebooks (VI.B.5, composed in 1924) bears the traces of this fascination for the 'Serpent', thirty-four lines of which are copied in a neat handwriting. Valéry represented for Joyce the Mallarmean line of descent, a heritage that had been intellectualized in an effort to bridge the gap between poetry and science. But his poetics did not preclude rich clusters of images close to the unconscious. The neo-Platonic meditation of Valéry's 'Ebauche d'un serpent' on the 'error' or 'sin' (faute) of a creation which masks the sun of absolute truth has lent a few overtones to the cosmogony of the Fall in the Wake, and precipitated the association of S (the Serpent as devilish tempter) and Sistersen among the Wake sigla.

Joyce's knowledge of French poetry was not limited to the writers he usually met in the rue de l'Odéon; he was able to comment on the mistake of omitting Maurice Scève's 'Poèmes à Délie' from a Danish translation of French love poems before 1800. This evinces not only excellent taste, but also a familiarity with the French hermetic tradition which culminates with Mallarmé (JJ 693). Joyce's relation to the French language as a whole is surprisingly similar to his relation to music: in both cases he shows relatively classical tastes and a love of the spoken voice which are nevertheless buttressed by an understanding of a tradition which reaches back to the Renaissance and the mediaeval period. This mixture of sophisticated historical knowledge and lack of sophistication in the direct enjoyment of the medium's materiality is typical of the effect Finnegans Wake was meant to achieve. And it is not a coincidence if the musicality of the last pages of the Wake is meant to climax on an almost silently whispered 'the'...

Thus it is no surprise to see that Joyce was generally impatient with the surrealists, who, unlike Valéry, could not intellectually justify every word, every letter in their collages packed with wild images. He was much more indulgent towards contemporary French novelists, especially Gide and Proust. He told Power and other friends that he admired Gide, not for the experimental novelistic technique of *mise en abyme* with which he is generally associated, but for the purity of his style. (Joyce always had a priggish grammarian's awareness of stylistic correction in French, as his slightly sophomoric comments on Flaubert reveal (*JJ* 492).) He offered *La Symphonie pastorale* to Power, with the words 'Let it be your model'; he praised *La Porte étroite* for being 'a little masterpiece', 'as fine as a spire on Notre Dame' (*CJJ* 76–7). The one book he could not abide was *Corydon*, a kind of Platonic dialogue in which Gide attempted to give biological grounds for pederasty.[17] Hence, Gide appears as 'Gidding up' (*FW* 347.27) in the Butt and Taff episode of the *Wake*, in which he is turned into a French counterpart of Oscar Wilde.

Joyce's reverence for Proust (whose funeral he attended in 1922 after a missed opportunity for a direct conversation (*JJ* 508–9)) could be hedged by reservations, but at times could find a less guarded expression, as with Power, precisely because the latter did not like *La Recherche*: 'He is the best of the modern French writers, and certainly no one has taken modern psychology so far, or to such a fine point' (*CJJ* 78). And he refused to acknowledge that Proust had indulged in mere 'experimentation', explaining that his stylistic 'innovations were necessary to express modern life as he saw it . . . Proust's style conveys that almost imperceptible but relentless erosion of time which . . . is the motive of his work' (*CJJ* 79). Unoriginal as these remarks are, they testify to the sympathy Joyce felt for the French writer, since the terms he uses for him are taken up almost verbatim in a defence of his own artistic ambitions (*CJJ* 95).

Joyce could have found an echo or some support among the French writers who were promoting a revival of Catholic literature in the late twenties, as suggested by François Mauriac's fervid reaction to the reading of the translation of *A Portrait of the Artist*. Mauriac writes to the translator in May 1924: 'With what emotion have I finished *Dedalus*! Madame, perhaps you have read some of my pages, and thus were able to guess that this frightening book [*ce livre terrible*] was meant for me . . .'[18] But support was unavailable from this side, essentially because of Claudel's fierce opposition. Though he remained a friend of

Gide (in the steady hope of converting him!) and of Adrienne Monnier, Claudel always expressed the most vehement rejection of Joyce, and when Monnier sent him a copy of the French translation of *Ulysses* while he was in the diplomatic service in Washington, he sent it back. It was a book which to him did not 'offer the least interest', but smacked of heresy. In his diary and letters Claudel gives a harsh description of Joyce, who, he says, 'inspired a true revulsion' in him: '*Joyce was a man eaten up by insects* ['*un homme en proie à l'insecte*', an astonishing phrase with hints of 'incest']. He made me think of arboraceous plants devoured from the inside by bostrychidae . . . A man who separates himself from the source of life and who only lives on himself, as they say, is *autophagous*! The last phase was this second book in which I read a few passages, the verb turned back upon itself, feeding and burning itself.'[19] No-one else was as violent, but a few testimonies left by other Parisian literary figures such as André Suarès, who took Joyce to task for his uneducated arrogance and his middle-class mind,[20] show that negative impressions were not peculiar to English people like Wyndham Lewis. It is important to remember this fact, which justifies Joyce's exaggerated politeness and painful silences: such strategies were not only symptomatic of a withdrawal from life, but defence tactics in the mandarin world of French letters.

On the other hand, one needs only to read Adrienne Monnier's essay on Joyce's *Ulysses* to realize that the French intellectual circles also had first-hand introductions to Joyce's works, and intelligent, informed, and sympathetic accounts of Joyce's major novel. As if to answer Claudel's accusations of 'blasphemies' uttered by a 'renegade',[21] she stresses Joyce's 'charity', his mysticism of the human, and his fundamental humility: 'The overwhelming task that [Joyce] imposed upon himself, that invention of the sensible world – an inventory that supposes, that calls for a classification – no doubt has nothing to do with traditional saintliness, but it nevertheless has something saintly about it, even in the Christian sense, which distinguishes it from the ordinary enterprises of philosophy or literature.'[22] One of the young intellectuals who used to frequent her bookshop no doubt followed the hint: Jacques Lacan, when barely seventeen, met Joyce in Adrienne Monnier's bookshop, and when just twenty, heard Larbaud's 1921 lecture on *Ulysses*. Lacan's title for the long seminar he devoted to Joyce in 1975–6 memorializes him as 'Joyce the Symptom' ('Joyce le Sinthome'), which, along with a pun on Aquinas ('saint Thomas'), also means 'Joyce the Saintly Man' of literature.[23] But if Lacan was able to pay off an old debt by such a masterly reading, the debt perhaps derives from the fact that, from very early on, the founder of the Paris Freudian School may have owed to Joyce a central concept, that of the capitalized Other – just as he found it nicely formulated in Louis Gillet's commentary on the Shakespeare theories developed by Stephen Dedalus: 'In *Hamlet*, Joyce would argue that the main character, the character who dominates everything, who is the real hero, is not Hamlet but the Ghost; it is not the living one, it is the Other [*c'est l'Autre*]; not the mortal but the immortal presence.'[24]

At any rate, even if Joyce is not the father's ghost looming large behind Lacan's Paris School, he himself took some pains to prove the 'Catholic' nature of his works, commissioning McGreevy to write an essay on the theme for the collection on *Finnegans Wake* published in 1929.[25] Some of his efforts must have seemed amply rewarded when, in 1940, he discovered a favourable review of the *Wake* in the *Osservatore Romano* (*JJ* 739). By this time he had found a *cénacle*, a set of apostles, and two authorized commentators: Eugène Jolas and Jacques Mercanton. Jolas had an intense, mystical relationship to literature; he was basically a Romantic and a Jungian, all of which may have been foreign to Joyce's linguistic and historic preoccupations. But Jolas had a keen eye for any kind of verbal experimentation, he had no political bias, and he was ready to open his magazine not only to sections from 'Work in Progress' (they were published in almost every issue of *transition* for ten years, from the first number in 1927), but also to commentaries, discussions, and tireless defences and illustrations of the new synthetic polyglossary invented by Joyce. Jolas soon became a kind of prophet, heralding the death of the King's English, thus showing himself to be the first critic to act out the implications of the parodic Bible contained in *Finnegans Wake*. Even if Joyce did not endorse the most extreme statements or the manifestoes announcing the 'Revolution of the Word' in *transition*, there were enough points of contact to let the main contributors to the magazine stand as the official interpreters of the *Wake*, and to give Joyce a renewed sense of rootedness in Paris. But if Jolas was very quickly entrusted with a general plan of the work, it was Mercanton, the Swiss writer, who was deemed the appropriate successor to Stuart Gilbert as the authorized commentator on *Finnegans Wake*. However, this last development belongs to Joyce's sixth hegira in 1939, to a final exile which took him back to Switzerland, but alas, did not last very long...

Even before these last troubled years, in which all his energies were devoted to the completion of the *Wake*, Joyce could note the bleak changes affecting Paris: 'Paris is frightfully dear and has become, they say, the ugly duckling of the great capitals. Most of the foreign colony has fled', he wrote in 1935 (*Letters I* 362). In spite of what has been said about Joyce's lack of political commitment (belied by the active help tendered to Jewish friends), his political sense was extremely acute, as witnessed by the remark he made to Mercanton in 1938: 'In a year France will be Fascist. But there is reason to believe that she will not have to call in fascism from the outside; it will come to her from within.'[26] It is perhaps as well that Joyce did not live long enough to see his prediction come true.

With a sad blindness as to the real cause of her husband's organic disease, Nora complained during one of the last summers which they spent in Paris that her husband had 'fits' and nervous 'pains' in his belly whenever she managed to drag him away from Paris (*JJ* 710); it was clearly an undiagnosed stomach ulcer which killed Joyce, and not his being taken from Paris for too long – but being away from Paris meant above all not being able to write his final testamentary opus, *Finnegans Wake*, which had become Joyce's sole obsession. By the same token, when the book was finished, Joyce did not show the same desperate wish to survive which had borne him through terrible personal tragedies. Besides, thirteen years earlier, in a letter to his father written in 1923, Joyce blames on Nora the fact that they cannot leave Paris and go to a sunnier and cheaper city: 'If I had my way I should live in a quiet place near Nice on the Mediterranean Sea but Nora dislikes it and she has some friends here and so has Giorgio and so has Lucia.' But then he immediately connects their immobility to the positive influence of Parisian intellectual circles: 'Moreover it cannot be denied that the greater part of my reputation is due to the generous admiration of French writers here' (*JJ* 541).

The question that now remains unavoidable is whether the admiration that was lavished on Joyce in Paris – which at times seemed singularly unfounded when it came from people who could not understand his aesthetics or even his language – spoilt him. Stanislaus Joyce seemed to believe that the pernicious influence of Parisian coteries had prompted his brother to emulate Gertrude Stein in obscurity and daring. The answer to such a question depends on how far one is willing to follow Joyce to the end, to accept that the *Wake* is the logical development of *Ulysses*. I do not mean, of course, that one should re-open the old debate concerning Joyce's opacity or hermeticism. Even if he is shown by certain Parisian accounts as awkward or scheming, regally isolated in a close circle of prejudiced friends, taking shelter in silence and exaggerated politeness – in certain cases to the point of prudishness – it must be said that his monstrous work could not have been produced in any other milieu; the word 'milieu' does not simply refer to exceptional private circumstances, but also maps out a whole intellectual history which Joyce traversed with an extremely far-seeing gaze.

Joyce told Arthur Power, in a meaningful understatement on which he refused to comment further, that Paris was 'a very convenient city' (CJJ 50). Power was wrong to conclude that 'the surrounding French life with all its brilliance and attraction seemed to pass over him': if it is true that Joyce was not interested in the erotic glamour of la vie parisienne which so mystified his Irish friend, he had had more than his share of vital nourishment among the Parisians. He declared to George Moore: 'Paris has played an equal part in our lives' (JJ 617), but was still more to the point when he said: 'In my heart Paris is the second city after Dublin.'[27] If he had written Ulysses while still a Dubliner at heart, describing Dublin so accurately, as he claimed, that one could reconstruct it a thousand years after some all too imaginable catastrophe, who else but the last Irish Parisian of l'entre-deux-guerres might have had the courage and the dedication to reconstruct universal history for all the generations to come? Paris may well have been 'the last of the human cities' (JJ 508) for him, the last conch in which one could hear the murmur and prattle of all the languages of man.

NOTES

1   For a popular account of the life of American 'Pilgrims' in Paris during the twenties, see Ernest Hemingway, A Moveable Feast (London: Jonathan Cape, 1964). Arthur Power's recollections of James Joyce in the twenties make it plain that Joyce did not want to have anything to do with the crowd of hard-drinking aesthetes, to the point of determinedly avoiding their favourite cafés and of sticking to his own three restaurants, Les Trianons, Fouquet's and Chez Francis. See Arthur Power, Conversations with James Joyce, ed. Clive Hart (London: Millington, 1974); hereafter referred to as CJJ.

2   See Richard Ellmann's invaluable biography in its revised edition, JJ 126.

3 Valery Larbaud – Marcel Ray, *Correspondance 1899–1937*, III (1921–37), ed. Françoise Lioure (Paris: Gallimard, 1980), p. 15.

4 Louis Gillet, 'Farewell to Joyce', trans. G. Markow-Totevy, in Willard Potts, ed., *Portraits of the Artist in Exile: Recollections of James Joyce by Europeans* (Portmarnock: Wolfhound Press, 1979), p. 167.

5 I have slightly modified the list established by Bernard Gheerbrant in the exhibition shown during the 5th Symposium Joyce in Paris, in Jacques Aubert and Maria Jolas, eds., *Joyce & Paris 1902...1920–1940...1975*, I (Lille: CNRS and Université de Lille III, 1979), p. 135.

6 Noel Riley Fitch, *Sylvia Beach and the Lost Generation: A History of Literary Paris in the Twenties and Thirties* (London: Souvenir Press, 1984), p. 88. See also Shari Benstock, *Women of the Left Bank: Paris 1900–1940* (Austin: University of Texas Press, 1986), pp. 194–229.

7 As Noel Fitch has proved it had been at Joyce's instigation, not at Beach's. See *Sylvia Beach and the Lost Generation*, p. 78.

8 Jan Parandowski, 'Meeting with Joyce', in Potts, *Portraits of the Artist*, p. 156.

9 See the whole recapitulation given by Francine Lenne in 'James Joyce et Louis Gillet', Jacques Aubert and Fritz Senn, eds., *Cahier de l'Herne James Joyce* (Paris: L'Herne, 1986), pp. 151–75.

10 Louis Gillet, *Stèle pour James Joyce* (Marseille: Editions du Sagittaire, 1941).

11 Quoted by Dougald McMillan in *Transition 1927–38: The History of a Literary Era* (New York: George Braziller, 1976), p. 180.

12 Joyce's Letter to Louis Gillet, 20 November 1931, quoted in *Cahier de l'Herne James Joyce*, p. 161.

13 *Stèle pour James Joyce*, p. 101.

14 Louis Gillet, 'The Living Joyce', in Potts, *Portraits of the Artist in Exile*, pp. 196–7.

15 *Archive 2, Notes, Criticism, Translations, & Miscellanous Writings*, prefaced and arranged by Hans Walter Gabler, pp. 375–83.

16 Paul Valéry, *Oeuvres* I, Pléiade edn. (Paris: Gallimard, 1957), p. 138.

17 Jacques Mercanton, 'The hours of James Joyce', in Potts, *Portraits of the Artist in Exile*, p. 223.

18 Letter to Ludmila Savitzky shown in Gheerbrant's 1975 exhibition 'James Joyce et Paris'. See Aubert and Jolas, *Joyce and Paris* I, p. 121.

19 *Cahier de l'Herne James Joyce*, p. 91. This comes from a letter written to Louis Gillet and never sent by Claudel. See the complete text in Paul Claudel, *Oeuvres en prose*, Pléiade edn. (Paris: Gallimard, 1965), pp. 1485–6. Claudel, by an ironic twist of fate, was to take Louis Gillet's seat at the Académie Française (see *Oeuvres en prose*, pp. 634–58).

20 See the introduction by Jacques Aubert and the unpublished diary by André Suarès in *Cahier de l'Herne James Joyce*, pp. 139–50.

21 *Cahier de l'Herne James Joyce*, p. 129.

22 Adrienne Monnier, 'Joyce's *Ulysses* and the French public', in Richard McDougall, *The Very Rich Hours of Adrienne Monnier: Translations and Commentaries* (New York: Charles Scribner's Sons, 1976), p. 124.

23 Jacques Lacan's original opening lecture for the Paris James Joyce Symposium, in which he gives these biographical indications, has been published in *L'Ane* 6 (Fall, 1982), 3–5. See *Joyce avec Lacan*, ed. Jacques Aubert (Paris: Navarin, 1987). For an account of Lacan's literary interests, see Elisabeth Roudinesco, *La Bataille de cent ans, Histoire de la psychanalyse en France* II, 1925–85 (Paris: Seuil), 1986.

24 *Stèle pour James Joyce*, p. 151.

25 Thomas McGreevy, 'The Catholic element in *Work in Progress*', in Samuel Beckett *et al.*, *Our Exagmination Round his Factification for Incamination of Work in Progress* (1929) (London: Faber, 1972), pp. 119–27. See also Beryl Schlossman's excellent book, *Joyce's Catholic Comedy of Language* (Madison: University of Wisconsin Press, 1985).

26 Jacques Mercanton, 'The hours of James Joyce', Potts, *Portraits of the Artist in Exile*, p. 241.

27 Jan Parandowski, 'A meeting with James Joyce', Potts, *Portraits of the Artist in Exile*, p. 159.

5   *Stephen Hero, Dubliners,* and *A Portrait of the Artist as a Young Man*: styles of realism and fantasy

TOWARDS A STYLISTIC HISTORY: FROM *STEPHEN HERO* TO *ULYSSES*

Near the end of what has survived of Joyce's unfinished draft of an autobiographical novel, *Stephen Hero* (written in 1904–5), the central character, Stephen Daedalus, claims that one function of writing is 'to record . . . epiphanies with extreme care', since 'they . . . are the most delicate and evanescent of moments' (*SH* 211). In the same passage he defines an epiphany as 'a sudden spiritual manifestation, whether in the vulgarity of speech or of gesture or in a memorable phase of the mind itself'. Stephen's statement makes clear that his interest in writing evocative prose vignettes, the sort Joyce himself wrote, is wholly aesthetic.[1] Like the real author, the artist character in *Stephen Hero* and in *A Portrait* (written 1907–14) has been strongly influenced by the writings of older contemporaries, especially Walter Pater, whose famous 'Conclusion' to *The Renaissance* (1873) emphasizes the special status of art as providing the most direct access to experiences of the highest intensity.[2]

The Paterian influence is one that Joyce clearly moved beyond, in part by producing in the realistic style of *Dubliners* (written 1904–7) an antithesis to Pater's lush, late-Romantic writing. But it is less clear exactly how far beyond Pater's influence Stephen moves in either *Stephen Hero* or *A Portrait*. Toward the end of part IV of *A Portrait*, for instance, he thinks admiringly of 'a lucid supple periodic prose' (*P* 167) of the sort Pater wrote, and in the climactic scene on the beach that follows, the narrator renders Stephen's thinking in a vividly Paterian style full of 'ecstasy' and 'trembling' (*P* 172). Based on some of their experiences, thoughts, and actions, it is possible, despite the Paterian allegiance, to see Stephen Daedalus and, especially, his counterpart in *A Portrait* and *Ulysses*, whose last name is spelled Dedalus, moving tentatively toward the production of original writing comparable in quality to Joyce's and different in kind from Pater's. But numerous readers have come away from their encounter with Stephen with quite a different impression.[3]

The evidence concerning Stephen's potential as an artist is mixed, and the problem of judging him is a difficult one for several reasons. We may, in fact, be dealing with two distinct characters about whom different judgements can be made, since the narrative of *Stephen Hero* differs in important ways from the narrative of *A Portrait*. The difference goes deeper than the spelling of the character's surname. And yet, these characters have a great deal in common. A further complication arises in *Ulysses*, for Stephen's experiences and views from *A Portrait* do not carry over with any great force, though they are sometimes in evidence. Given these factors but also the common first name among the three characters, it seems reasonable to identify them only provisionally, as I do in the discussion to follow, and to keep in mind that some sharp distinctions need at times to be made. Another difficulty arises because Joyce assigned so many details from his own life to Stephen. In addition, there is the odd fact from the early publishing history of the *Dubliners* stories that Joyce sometimes used the pseudonym 'Stephen Daedalus' (*JJ* 164). Joyce's frequent intimate renderings of his characters' thinking, as in the Paterian passages of *A Portrait*, also make it hard to distinguish the narrator's perspective from the character's thoughts even though the narration occurs in the third person. Since Joyce is writing fiction and not pure auto-biography, it is important not to identify the real author in any absolute way with the young artist character; nevertheless, the texts frequently encourage us to consider the alignment.

In presenting Stephen's development prior to *Ulysses*, Joyce employs the two epiphanic modes of stark realism – 'the vulgarity of speech or of gesture' – and visionary fantasy – 'a memorable phase of the mind itself' – as delimiting extremes in his character. In both *Stephen Hero* and *A Portrait*, Stephen alternates between allegiances to the visionary and to the material, between internal fantasy and external reality. In *Dubliners*, by contrast, the visionary has been largely displaced by the grim limitations of living and dying. Stephen, however, continues to be attracted by visionary possibilities until very nearly the end of *A*

Portrait, and is clearly influenced by them when he writes both his villanelle and his journal.

The evocations of Stephen's alternative allegiances differ substantially in the two narratives that focus primarily on him. In *Stephen Hero* Joyce portrays Stephen as both ruthlessly analytical and visionary. At a crucial moment in his development, his encounter with the disturbing reality of death intensifies both his critical bent and his visionary yearnings. In *A Portrait,* by contrast, Joyce presents the two perspectives of realism and fantasy not primarily as aspects of character but fundamentally as aspects of style. Having now emerged as mutually modifying and mutually challenging attitudes, these styles of Stephen's thinking and of Joyce's writing vie with one another for predominance as they merge and diverge. The realistic and the visionary components become much more complexly intertwined than in *Stephen Hero,* for they begin to become elements in a style that emphasizes memory. The double temporal orientation of this later style indicates the direction Joyce will take after *A Portrait* in the more allusive initial style of *Ulysses.*

We can begin sketching Joyce's stylistic progress, and some of the changes his artist character experiences, by considering Stephen's remembrance in *Ulysses* of his former commitment to an art that captures spiritual manifestations. Since the recollection concerns Paterian attitudes, it bears on Stephen's potential for becoming an artist and on his possible similarity to Joyce. During the recollection, which occurs in the third episode of *Ulysses,* Stephen is again on the beach and may be remembering his former allegiance to a spiritual, Paterian notion of art because the surroundings remind him of the earlier beach scene in *A Portrait.* An important event has occurred, however, between these two scenes, since Stephen's mother has died during the unnarrated period following the end of the journal in *A Portrait* and preceding the beginning of *Ulysses.* During the day of *Ulysses,* the fact of her death almost exactly one year earlier is the often unstated background for all Stephen's thinking, including this memory. In the presentation of Stephen at the beginning of *Ulysses,* Joyce returns to an encounter with death, like the one involving Stephen's sister in *Stephen Hero,* as he composes an alternative for both realism and fantasy. Those earlier styles evoked in *Stephen Hero* in relation to the epiphanies are being complicated and displaced by a style of play that involves a recognition of death. The alternative to those styles emerges as Stephen engages in a kind of mental play that eventually affects his more public performances as well as his thoughts. The newly developed playfulness involves an altered attitude toward audience.

Stephen's remembrance focuses on his epiphanies:

Reading two pages apiece of seven books every night, eh? I was young. You bowed to yourself in the mirror, stepping forward to applause earnestly, striking face. Hurray for the Goddamned idiot! Hray! No-one saw: tell no-one. Books you were going to write with letters for titles. Have you read his F? O yes, but I prefer Q. Yes, but W is wonderful. O yes, W. Remember your epiphanies written on green oval leaves, deeply deep, copies to be sent if you died to all the great libraries of the world, including Alexandria? Someone was to read them there after a few thousand years, a mahamanvantara. Pico della Mirandola like. Ay, very like a whale. When one reads these strange pages of one long gone one feels that one is at one with one who once......

(U 3.136–46)

This brief, mocking remembrance indicates that as an aspiring artist Stephen has taken his epiphanies wholly seriously, as Joyce likely did himself at one time. But the importance he attached to these snatches of sometimes lyrical prose is clearly in the past. The passage gives us part of the context for Stephen's production of epiphanies, and it mixes in new ways elements from earlier presentations of him. It also provides stylistically one of the positions Joyce reaches soon after A Portrait, a position markedly different from his preceding styles. There is nothing quite like this allusive, parodic, internal dialogue in either Stephen Hero or Dubliners. The style of A Portrait comes much closer to it, prepares the way for it, but does not fully reach it.

In this extended moment of self-mockery, Stephen retrospectively places the writing of epiphanies among his grandiose, youthful literary projects, projects he now sees as no more than adolescent fantasies. In all Stephen's references to the mystical traditions, he turns them to ironic purposes. The famous library at Alexandria exists, for instance, only in imagination, since it was destroyed in the first century BC, but it once apparently formed part of Stephen's imagined audience for his writings. Because of its permanent place in a timeless, visionary realm, that audience ostensibly solves the problem of mortality for the immature artist by providing an eternal repository for his writings at his death. As the memory makes clear, the only real audience for Stephen's narcissistic performances was himself. The implied isolation is also evident in both Stephen Hero and A Portrait when Stephen searches, largely unsuccessfully, for a responsive audience for his activities.

Stephen is passing a negative judgement on himself, especially with the reference to Hamlet's whale-like cloud. The final sentence of the passage, however, evokes *stylistically* another kind of negative judgement, one that shows the double effect the aesthetic tradition of the 1890s has had on Stephen. The sentence parodies quite openly Pater's use of the impersonal pronoun 'one' in his essays, as for instance in this sentence from 'Pico della Mirandola': 'He will not let one go; he wins one on, in spite of one's self, to turn again to the pages of his forgotten books . . .' (Pater, 67). And it mocks Pater's notion that the writing and reading of texts provides a virtually unmediated access to the past. Pater claims in his essay on Pico, for example, that 'to read a page of one of Pico's forgotten books is like a glance into one of those ancient sepulchres . . . with the old disused ornaments and furniture of a world wholly unlike ours still fresh in them' (Pater, 62). Stephen has clearly read this essay and others in *The Renaissance*, a collection that had an immense influence on his older contemporaries in Dublin, especially W. B. Yeats and his circle. He has sufficiently mastered Pater's style through careful, and presumably enthusiastic, study to be able now to transform it into an expression of his distance from it. The earlier styles of *Stephen Hero* and *A Portrait*, on the contrary, present Stephen's enthusiasm for Pater and for aesthetic, mystical writings and experience with much less (if any) irony. In *Stephen Hero*, Yeats's prose of the 1890s has a powerful effect on Stephen, as Pater's presumably has in *A Portrait*, and he shows no self-irony or restraint about the enthusiasms. The difference is reflected in the way Stephen thinks and what he thinks about in each text.

The passage from *Ulysses* concerning the epiphanies exemplifies a pattern evident in the earlier texts. This is not the first time Stephen has given himself to an enthusiasm and to impulses, only to turn away from them. The turning away is always only partial because the effect of the influence, which was powerful, remains. The most obvious example of the pattern is Stephen's commitment to the Catholic Church. As many critics have pointed out, his childhood and early adolescent religious experiences, including especially his education by the Jesuits, continue to inform the way he thinks, including the way he tries to reject the object of his former commitment. The traces of that commitment linger.

The mixture of intimate knowledge and scepticism in the Ulyssean

Stephen's thoughts, his former attraction but present aversion to the intensely serious, even mystical, aesthetic reverence that was the impetus for the epiphanies, points to one of Joyce's major stylistic achievements. We find Joyce developing this double temporal perspective, the perspective of memory, in the works written before *Ulysses*, especially in *A Portrait* but to some extent in *Dubliners* as well, particularly in 'The Dead'. By means of this double perspective we can experience simultaneously both scepticism and the deeply-felt impact of thoughts and events in the central character's changing sensibility. The inherently double, or multiple, interiorized style is the vehicle Joyce invents to render the deep ambivalence and dissonance of Stephen's mental life, especially in the interplay of critical self-scrutiny and vivid recollection. As Joyce complexly presents them, ambivalence, dissonance, and interplay inform the mental process of creativity.

We can see some of Joyce's strategies and perspectives emerging in the early fiction by noting differences between the episodic fragments of *Stephen Hero*, the starkly realistic stories of *Dubliners*, and the discontinuous narrative and flamboyant narration of *A Portrait*. The new style that Joyce produces in *Ulysses* as one outcome of his earlier endeavours requires new strategies for reading, which we acquire as we encounter the stylistic changes from book to book and even within each book. The shift is from either fantasies or seemingly objective, realistic presentations to recollections or other moments of mental activity, structured like memories, that are neither fantastic nor objective. Stephen's memory of his epiphanies, for instance, is not itself a fantasy; and rather than being neutral, through its tone it expresses a judgement about the earlier activities. The mediation announces itself stylistically, often through obscure allusions and personal references that hinder as well as enhance our understanding; this style is opaque rather than transparent.

By contrast, both fantasy and objective description present themselves as transparent language that carries its own interpretation with it.[4] The heightened language of fantasy announces its immediate access to an extraordinary spiritual realm whose status we perceive because of its difference from the limitations of ordinary reality. Its meaning is the denial of conventional meaning, and once we recognize that ordinary experience is being transcended, no further questions are necessary or perhaps even possible. The quite different, referential language of objective realism promises apparently direct, uncomplicated access to that limited, ordinary reality. The mediated, allusive style of the passage from *Ulysses*, on the other hand, invites and enables readers to respond to its complications by doing more, often playfully, than they are encouraged to do by a comparatively transparent style. We are asked to clamber over, under, around, and through the obstructions to understanding that it places in our path and to enjoy our energetic motions. Because of the differences from the earlier narratives, including stylistic ones, the passage from *Ulysses* gives us a version of Stephen's development through and away from mystical aestheticism against which we can gauge the other versions. The trajectory for that development is toward allusive mental play and self-mockery.

The fragments of *Stephen Hero*, for instance, present Stephen's interest in the occult quite differently and indirectly, through his reverence for some of Yeats's mystical short stories.[5] In chapter XXII, during Stephen's second year at the university, he studies even less than before and spends more time on his literary enthusiasms, which include Yeats's stories, especially 'The Tables of the Law', concerning Owen Ahern, Michael Robartes, and mystical excess. Stephen's reading of these stories, with their emphasis on a mode of life wildly at variance with societal conventions, dovetails with his whimsical research into Renaissance Italian writings at a little-used Dublin library. His recollection in *Ulysses* of reading 'the fading prophecies of Joachim Abbas' 'in the stagnant bay of Marsh's library' (*U* 3.107–8), which occurs just before the memory of the epiphanies, refers explicitly to this period in his life. Stephen's attraction to Ahern and Robartes is made clear in *Stephen Hero* in ways that it is not in the later works. In *A Portrait* they are barely mentioned, and in *Ulysses* Stephen openly distances himself from other artists who show interest in them. In *Stephen Hero*, however, he is easily able 'to believe in the reality of their existence' since he found himself 'in such a season of damp and unrest' (*SH* 178). Because they are 'outlaws' (*SH* 178) who possess secret wisdom, Stephen can take a stand against the restrictive conventions of Irish culture by identifying with them. He takes the same stand when he begins writing epiphanies.

STEPHEN HERO: FROM RESTRAINT TO EXTRAVAGANT DEFIANCE

In the narrative of *Stephen Hero*, the encounter with Yeats's writing signals an important turning point for Stephen that is rendered almost entirely in terms of his character rather than being evoked primarily through style. The difference in emphasis in the rendering marks a major contrast between *Stephen Hero* and *A Portrait* and between our impressions of their central characters. With the reading of Yeats's stories, Stephen becomes more extravagant in his determined protest against the restricting conventions of Irish culture. He is learning here to follow a Blakean revolutionary precept, that 'the road of excess leads to the palace of wisdom', or, in Oscar Wilde's irreverent version, that 'nothing succeeds like excess'. As had many English and Irish artists of the 1890s, Stephen chooses the road of excess to protest middle-class conventions. We see that excess as extravagance in various scenes in *Stephen Hero*, but first in Stephen's desire to recite publicly from memory Yeats's story, 'The Tables of the Law'. Even though he feels 'acutely the insidious dangers' in his behaviour, presumably the dangers of losing control and becoming insane, 'a dull discharge of duties' would be even more dangerous and frustrating (*SH* 179). Stephen chooses fantasy and the impulsive behaviour that accompanies it over the dull grind of conventional reality. From this point onward in the narrative, 'A certain extravagance began to tinge his life' (*SH* 179).

Starting in this chapter, not only does Stephen's extravagance become more frequent, it begins to take exaggerated forms. His uninhibited behaviour reaches a memorable climax at the end of the next chapter when he interrupts his Italian tutorial and runs after Emma Clery to propose a night of lovemaking. In his discussion of the incident with his friend Lynch (*SH* 200), Stephen's evident lack of humour or self-irony about it seems typical. Even though the narrator does not provide an explicit judgement, Stephen's self-serious attitude can be seen as a fault. In both *Stephen Hero* and *A Portrait*, Stephen's regular tendencies to think abstractly and with concentration, to practise discipline (though at times selectively), and to turn a serious face to the world do often seem unattractive. But the implications and results of his behaviour are mixed in both narratives. His reasons for responding with dead seriousness are not limited to emotional frigidity, and he responds at times in a different way.

'The Tables of the Law' and the spiritual aestheticism it represents are not the cause for Stephen's change in behaviour but rather the first artistic focus he finds for his intense anger toward Irish culture. That anger emerges in the aftermath of his sister's illness and death, for which there are no equivalents in *A Portrait*. Despite his unconventional views, his eccentricities, his frustration, his isolation, and his arrogance, Stephen's public conduct before her death remains largely within the bounds of convention, and he behaves neither erratically nor with absolute seriousness. In the half dozen chapters leading up to Isabel's death, there are many examples of Stephen's independence in thought and action but also of his sensible, circumspect conduct. Even though he baits Father Butt with a question about unseemly passages in *Twelfth Night* (*SH* 28), Stephen's tolerance for the contradictions he experiences in his culture remains for a time fairly high. He can react to them with amusement (*SH* 29). Later, when the paper he delivers at the Debating Society is attacked, he can still respond in a restrained way, then decide gradually to withdraw without clamour from the groups and activities he earlier frequented. A mixture of prudence and tolerance serves Stephen well until he realizes that the issues are too important for him to continue restraining his responses.

Stephen comes to this realization through the experiences in and around chapter XXII. Immediately after Stephen's presentation to the Debating Society, his younger sister, Isabel, returns home due to a serious illness. The situation with Isabel is mentioned for several chapters until she dies in Stephen's presence at the beginning of chapter XXII. Though the references to her illness are brief, the descriptions suggest unambiguously the deep effect on the entire family, but on Stephen in particular: 'The lingering nature of her illness had spread a hopeless apathy about the household and, though she herself was little more than a child, she must have been aware of this' (*SH* 161). Her condition is so severe that she whimpers when left alone or when she has to eat. Her few moments of animation come in response to the playing of the piano downstairs. We hear only of Stephen playing that piano. She has become his audience, albeit temporarily. It is important that she has, since Stephen has had difficulty finding appropriate audiences. Except for his brother, Maurice, Isabel is the only auditor with whom Stephen is able to establish good communication. By this point in the narrative, he has largely given up not only on the Debating Society but on the group of young people who gather regularly at the Daniels' household, a group for whom he would sometimes sing and play. The moribund Isabel provides a particularly striking contrast to the robust Emma, to whom Stephen's singing at those gatherings had been largely directed. During Stephen's final visit to the Daniels' house shortly before Isabel's death, in an unambiguous, though still mild, gesture of protest, he refuses to perform when asked (*SH* 158).

Stephen's playing for Isabel is obviously motivated by neither desire, which he feels for Emma, nor rebellious, intellectual comradeship, which he shares with Maurice. There is desperation and determination, as well as pathos, in Stephen's pretence that Isabel is not near death. As part of that pretence he 'preserved his usual manner of selfish cheerfulness and strove to stir a fire out of her embers of life': 'He even exaggerated and his mother reproved him for being so noisy. He could not go to his sister and say to her "Live! live!" but he tried to touch her soul in the shrillness of a whistle or the vibration of a note' (*SH* 161). Stephen cannot save her, but they achieve a special kind of understanding when 'once or twice he could have assured himself that the eyes that looked at him from the bed had guessed his meaning' (*SH* 161). In these scenes we witness Stephen putting on his mask of seriousness for a more humane purpose than self-protection. It enables him to undertake a work of kindness and establish communication with an audience that matters to him. Like Isabel, the success is short-lived, and Stephen's moods of selfish indulgence keep recurring, at times in a style that is the precursor for the Paterian ending of part IV of *A Portrait*: '. . . in his soul the one bright insistent star of joy trembling at her wane' (*SH* 162).

The breaking point for Stephen occurs with Isabel's death. At the end of chapter XXI, in a passage that draws on one of Joyce's realistic epiphanies, Stephen's mother interrupts his self-communion at the piano with the disturbing news that 'There's some matter coming away from the hole in Isabel's ... stomach' (*SH* 163). Not only do Stephen's reveries not disappear after her death, his commitment to the kind of spiritualized art he finds in Yeats emerges in part because of it. But the situation has changed. In a way that is exceptional in *Stephen Hero*, Joyce renders the change briefly through style by describing the funeral in chapter XXII realistically: 'Standing beside the closed piano on the morning of the funeral Stephen heard the coffin bumping down the crooked staircase' (*SH* 166–7). Given the piano's regular appearance and its importance in the previous chapter, the closed instrument reiterates the shift indicated stylistically by the grim details. After the funeral, Stephen finally breaks significantly with decorum by choosing to drink a pint with the carriage drivers rather than having a more genteel drink with the middle-class mourners. The gesture does not go unnoticed by Stephen's father, who gives him a hard look at the time (*SH* 168) and upbraids him much later for his conduct (*SH* 228). This is a new kind of public performance for Stephen, marking an irrevocable shift in his conduct, his relationships within the family, and his attitude toward the family's Irish social context.

By means of brief uses in *Stephen Hero* of a Paterian style and, in tandem with it, a realistic style, Joyce is able to suggest Stephen's difficult, contradictory situation and the opposing extremes of his attitudes in a way that is the forerunner for his extended use of those styles for similar purposes in *A Portrait*. But neither style is suitable for capturing the energy with which Stephen sometimes thinks and reacts in *Stephen Hero* and in the later books. That energy emerges as clowning and laughter in numerous scenes both preceding and following Isabel's death. In response to a self-deprecating story Maurice tells him, for example, he 'exploded in laughter' (*SH* 59). He has to resist the impulse to express his antic disposition to the President when they discuss the censoring of his paper (*SH* 94–7). During a Good Friday sermon, he indulges 'his gambling instinct' by trying to outpace the priest's various translations of *Consummatum est,* running quickly through a list of possibilities, wagering 'with himself as to what word the preacher would select' (*SH* 120). Much later, well after Isabel's death, Stephen and Lynch have a funny conversation about love and sex (*SH* 191–2), and he parodies the mechanical catechism of his Italian lessons by composing his own humorous alternative (*SH* 192–3).

Joyce moves in such passages toward presenting Stephen not only as serious but as energetically engaged in the way he sometimes is in parts IV and V of *A Portrait* and in *Ulysses*. When Stephen deceptively wears a mask of seriousness to cover a mocking interior response, he has already begun pursuing his scheme of surviving by 'silence, exile, and cunning' announced in *A Portrait* (*P* 247). But Joyce has yet to find an adequate style for presenting at length Stephen's 'scornful mind scampering' (*SH* 97) in active dialogue with itself and its surroundings. By contrast with the condensed, allusive internal dialogue we have already seen in the early part of *Ulysses*, Stephen's thoughts in *Stephen Hero* have a ponderous, awkward quality that does not capture the energy he sometimes humorously expresses.

His self-reflections regularly take the form of self-doubts in which Stephen recognizes that he, like his culture, is full of inconsistencies. He thinks about or experiences vacillations at various times, including a moment near the end of chapter XXI, just before the scene in which his mother informs him of the disturbing new development in Isabel's degeneration. There, as elsewhere, the contradictions emerge in Stephen's doubts about himself: 'Even the value of his own life came into doubt with him. He laid a finger upon every falsehood it contained' (*SH* 162). Such misgivings are presented more extensively shortly after the culminating episode with Emma in a segment (*SH* 204–6) that is stylistically unusual in *Stephen Hero* because it seems to present at length, though awkwardly, an internal colloquy. 'An embassy of nimble pleaders' from the Church state their positions (*SH* 204), but these 'ambassadors' must be internal ones, since Stephen is involved in 'reflections'. The implications of the passage for Stephen's character are clear. He is engaged in self-criticism and self-testing, motivated by residual fear and insecurity in the face of continuing temptations to conform and succeed. In short, he has yet to move entirely beyond the crisis of his break with the Church.

Joyce attempts in this passage to capture Stephen's predicament, but he lacks the stylistic techniques for presenting it vividly and directly as the shifting to-and-fro of thinking. The report of Stephen's thoughts mixes third and second person, but not first person, in a logical discourse composed of propositions, questions, and direct address. Many of the sentences would not be out of place in an actual dialogue: 'However sure you may be now of the reasonableness of your convictions you cannot be sure that you will always think them reasonable'. By contrast with Stephen's thinking in *Ulysses*, the passage lacks the signals Joyce developed later to indicate interior language: frequent colons, exclamation marks, multiple allusions, and condensed or grammatically fragmented statements.

Stephen's tendency toward self-doubt points to ambivalences that are different in kind from those he perceives and despises in his culture, in part because he is willing to consider that he himself may be self-deceived. By recognizing the self-deception around him, he has become sensitive to the potential for it within himself. After Isabel's death, Stephen's encounters with the cultural contradictions elicit some new responses. He recognizes, for instance, that the members of the Debating Society 'revered' the 'memory of Terence MacManus', a revolutionary patriot, 'not less . . . than the memory of Cardinal Cullen', an ultra-conservative clergyman who spoke out against the nationalists (*SH* 173). Earlier Stephen might have responded with restrained amusement, but his response takes considerably stronger forms instead: total withdrawal and sarcasm.

Stephen's sensitivity to contradictions leads him to undertake literary projects, including his love verses and his epiphanies, that allow him to position himself against his society by admitting and working with opposing elements set in combination. We first hear about Stephen's love poetry, on which he labours instead of pursuing his academic studies, between the death of Isabel and his infatuation with Yeats's stories. Inspired by Dante's *Vita nuova,* 'in his expressions of love he found himself compelled to use what he called the feudal terminology', but also 'to express his love a little ironically': 'This suggestion of relativity, he said, mingling itself with so immune a passion is a modern note: we cannot swear or expect eternal fealty because we recognise too accurately the limits of every human energy' (*SH* 174). In his typically ambivalent fashion, Stephen sees both loss and gain in transforming the idealizing literary language of love. What it loses in 'fierceness' it gains in 'amiableness'. Stephen strives to humanize his love poetry by tempering overstatement with a sense of human limitations.

It is important that Stephen articulates such a goal for his poetry at this point in the narrative, just before he discovers Yeats's mystical stories about mystical temptations. His doing so indicates in advance an attitude that should protect him from following the path of eternal, visionary fantasies for too long. The later history of Stephen's verses suggests that he has developed a sufficent sensitivity to his own excesses and the alternatives not to rest permanently content with the attitudes he strikes. In chapter xxiv he continues 'making his book of verses in spite of' distractions (*SH* 208) at a time when his differences with his friend Cranly and his parents appear no longer to be reconcilable. but in the next chapter, he tells Maurice he has 'burned them' because 'they were romantic' (*SH* 226). Though the tone and style of the statement are different, this is the kind of judgement about his earlier efforts we see Stephen making about his epiphanies in *Ulysses.*

The concept of the epiphanies, introduced late in *Stephen Hero,* provides another way for Stephen to proceed by means of contradiction in his literary work. In writing them, he can employ both stark realism and visionary experience in a mode that, like his love poetry, has the potential for being internally differential. In the representing of a vacuous reality, the artist recognizes and rejects its superficialities; in the evocation of visionary realities, the artist displaces debased, ordinary reality with a spiritual alternative. There is no evidence in *Stephen Hero*, however, that Stephen can transform his dual epiphanic procedure into something more than a double gesture of defiance. An exaggerated swerving between extremes could even become the vertiginous hyperbole of madness, about which Stephen himself expresses concern. The passage from *Ulysses* ridiculing the epiphanies suggests that they were indeed excessive and narcissistic, a form of writing to be left behind. But the epiphanies hold out distantly the possibility for juxtaposing and perhaps even merging opposites stylistically in a mutually modifying way that might serve to present the to-and-fro of the mind in process. That possibility is one that Joyce is able to actualize only after abandoning *Stephen Hero*.

A PORTRAIT OF THE ARTIST AS A YOUNG MAN: OSCILLATIONS IN STYLE AND NARRATIVE

Despite the self-indulgent and potentially self-destructive qualities of the epiphanies, Stephen's working by contraries is a step toward achieving the interplay, or oscillation, of perspectives that we encounter in aspects of his thinking and his life in later works. His putting into practice of Blake's precept that 'Without Contraries is no progression' has only just begun in *Stephen Hero*. The results of that practice emerge much later, when the alternation tending toward a process of extremes merging and mutually modifying one another becomes an important structural principle in Joyce's subsequent writing. By using styles that often work by means of oppositions in order to present a character whose thoughts and experiences regularly involve opposing forces, Joyce enables readers to recognize a variety of possible resemblances and differences between the writer and the character. The same language pertains simultaneously, though in different ways, to the writer who has learned to work successfully with contrasts and to the character whose life is filled with them. Various judgements about Stephen become possible. The reader attempting to make them based on *A Portrait* and *Ulysses* encounters a much richer, more complex stylistic and structural texture than is the case with *Stephen Hero*. Part of the new complexity arises from Joyce's developing a differential style for capturing the shifting quality of memory; part of it arises from a narrative structure that emphasizes repetition rather than continuous, chronological development.

In *A Portrait* we see the swerving in Stephen's life more clearly and more regularly than in *Stephen Hero*.[6] That swerving resembles the abrupt shift in *Stephen Hero* at the end of chapter XXI and the start of chapter XXII from Stephen's high-flown meditations and self-doubts to the material details of Isabel's death and funeral. In *A Portrait* Joyce takes maximum advantage of the strong contrast such a shift can evoke when he uses it not just once, as in *Stephen Hero*, but repeatedly at the narrative's major junctures. At the end of each of *A Portrait*'s five parts, Joyce uses elevated language to suggest that Stephen achieves a momentary insight and intensity through a transforming experience: his communion with nature and his fellow students after complaining to the Rector at the end of part I; his sexual initiation in the encounter with a prostitute at the end of part II; his post-confession, pre-communion peace at the end of part III; his commitment to art climactically presented as an encounter with an idealized woman at the end of part IV; and the exclamations about hopes for the future in the book's final sentences at the end of Stephen's journal. At the start of each succeeding part, Joyce counters and ironizes the intensity of the preceding conclusion by switching immediately and unexpectedly to a realistic style and realistic details: the bad smell of Uncle Charles's tobacco in part II; the craving of Stephen's belly for food in part III; the mechanical, dehumanized character of Stephen's religious discipline in part IV; and in part V the dreary homelife that is the daily context and one frame of reference for Stephen's aesthetic ambitions. The pattern of contrasts is also repeated at various minor junctures in the narrative, for instance, at the end of the first section and the beginning of the second section of part II, when Stephen's revery about Mercedes is followed by the 'great yellow caravans' (*P* 65) arriving to remove the family's belongings. By alternating and starkly juxtaposing extremes, Joyce arranges the events of Stephen's life without relying primarily on continuity of action. Like *Stephen Hero*, *A Portrait* is episodic, and often there is little or no transition from one situation to another, but the later work provides an orienting pattern for Stephen's development. Emphatic presentation of that pattern actually depends on abandoning narrative continuity in order to make moments that are separated in time contiguous in the narration.

Even within the individual, juxtaposed moments of elevated, climactic insight and countering, realistic perception, a pattern of contrast and possible merger sometimes appears. When this happens, a highly complex process of reading can ensue that may be understood to mimic Stephen's process of recollection. The possibilities for this kind of reading emerge most emphatically late in the narrative, once the reader has come to know Stephen's thinking, especially the language of his thinking, well. It would seem that Stephen remembers at some level his earlier experiences, which have become connected with one another and tend at times to merge. The situation is complicated because he apparently remembers and connects elevated moments of insight not just as a group but in some relation to the moments of realistic perception that always follow them. And he remembers and combines other experiences as well. Joyce does not present Stephen explicitly remembering and linking the opposing moments. He depends instead on the reader's remembering, connecting, and anticipating. And he presents Stephen's thoughts in language that, by repeating aspects of earlier scenes, suggests that a remembering and crossing-over may be taking place.

A kind of feedback is created whereby Stephen's later experiences, which are in some ways repetitions of earlier ones, are not in fact exact repetitions, in part because they occur against the background of what has gone before. The reader has access to this feedback through the increasingly mixed language that leads back to earlier scenes of different kinds. Because the language is complexly layered, the reader comes to every scene with frames of reference derived from earlier elements of the narrative, but each scene in turn results in new retrospective framings of what has gone before and new prospective framings of what is to come, and so on until the various frames overlap or nest within one another. The highly unusual effect, which is difficult to describe in an expository way, mimics the process of Stephen's remembering his complicated, differential past as he encounters each new experience, but it depends on the reader's active recollection of earlier passages.

An example may help clarify the complex possibilities the style offers. In the closing pages of part IV, Stephen has an intense experience on the beach, reported in vivid Paterian language, after which he naps in a nest-like, sandy nook. Having decided to lie down, he feels the heavens above him 'and the earth beneath him' (P 172). When he wakes, 'recalling the rapture of his sleep' (P 173), Stephen holds these oppositions together briefly. He imagines a merging of two realms in his image of the moon embedded in the earth: 'He climbed to the crest of the sandhill and gazed about him. Evening had fallen. A rim of the young moon cleft the pale waste of the sky like the rim of a silver hoop embedded in grey sand; and the tide was flowing in fast to the land with a low whisper of her waves, islanding a few last figures in distant pools' (*P* 173). Visionary and material, heaven and earth, sea and land, process and stasis merge and interact in a promise of harmonious union not nearly so evident in Joyce's earlier narratives. Not only do heaven and earth merge as silver blends with gray, but the tide, though flowing fast, has been humanized: her waves whisper.

The conjunction of opposites extends and fulfils the intense experience Stephen has had on the beach. As with the earlier moments of intensity, this one is quickly followed by its stylistic and experiential opposite at the beginning of part v. There Stephen drinks 'watery tea', chews 'the crusts of fried bread that were scattered near him', stares 'into the dark pool of the jar' of tea, remembers 'the dark turfcoloured water of the bath in Clongowes', and rifles idly with 'greasy fingers' through a box of pawntickets, whose lid is 'speckled with lousemarks' (*P* 174). As at the beginning of the three preceding parts, a debunking takes place through style. But the situation is more complicated now, because the language at the end of part IV already anticipates some details from the realistic passage that follows it. There are pools of liquid in that earlier passage as well, but also some past participles ('fallen', 'embedded') that anticipate the numerous past participles in the first paragraph of part v ('fried', 'scattered', 'scooped', 'rifled', 'scrawled and sanded and creased'). The pool of tea is in part an ironic recollection of the pools of water on the beach, but the additional recollection of Clongowes makes clear that these later pools are all embedded in a past and in memories that make any simple contrast of two isolated moments impossible.

The overlap between the two scenes creates a stylistic double helix, in which the experience of visionary intensity with its elevated language and the experience of a grimy reality with its material details mutually frame one another. They have become styles of memory, and part of what they recollect, or help us recollect, is one another. We begin to see each through the lens of the other, and that is an important development because it suggests that Stephen may have begun seeing them in that odd fashion as well.

Joyce provides abundant material for the reader to recognize and work with the complexities by including a kitchen scene (*P* 163), shortly before the scene on the beach, that contains elements common to both the Paterian and the realistic scenes that follow. The description of the light and the singing there anticipates the light and Stephen's singing on the beach (P 172). But this earlier scene in a littered kitchen that involves Stephen's family, specifically his siblings, is obviously echoed in the later kitchen scene. The 'knife with a broken ivory handle . . . stuck through the pith of a ravaged turnover' (P 163) that Stephen sees there anticipates the later scattered breadcrusts, but it also anticipates the moon embedded in the sand. And that latter anticipation does not necessarily have an ironic implication. Stephen on the beach may himself be recalling the earlier image as he half-perceives and half-creates the later one. In so doing, he can be understood to reaffirm what has taken place in the kitchen on his return home after having decided not to become a priest, when, perhaps to his own surprise, he joined his ragamuffin brothers and sisters in their singing. It seems, oddly, that at the time he rejects a religious vocation and chooses art, Stephen is aligning himself, if not exactly committing himself, to the grim realities represented by the family situation and not just to visionary experience.

To the extent that Stephen's perception of the moon carries a memory of the broken knife and the family along with it, the family situation nests within and contributes to the visionary scene rather than simply debunking it. The two kitchen scenes frame and implicitly comment on the beach scene that comes between them, but since the framed and framing scenes overlap, the implications are multiple and not altogether determinate. Joyce's language invites the reader to pursue those implications.

The thorough imbricating of these various passages gives us access to the complicated network of intertwined elements making up Stephen's life. It does so in a way that enables us to recognize and explore multiple, simultaneous perspectives for understanding and combining those elements as we respond to the narration's twists and turns. If we have recognized some of the repetitions connecting these passages, when we encounter a scene later in which Stephen awakens in ecstasy after a dream and composes a villanelle (P 217–24), the resemblances to the beach scene create a further framing, in this case for the second kitchen scene, which falls between them. A soup-plate from the previous night's supper remains on the table as a link to the description of the kitchen (P 218). Stephen, however, intends his writing to involve 'transmuting the daily bread of experience' (P 221). He is intent on 'shrinking from' the ordinary world of 'common noises, hoarse voices, sleepy prayers' (*P* 221), though his memories during the writing of the poem keep thrusting that world into his thoughts.[7]

In this section, even more fully than earlier, the two apparently antagonistic styles of visionary intensity and grim realism merge, though they continue to alternate as well. Both have become characteristic of Stephen's consciousness in Joyce's unusual attempt to represent the mental act of aesthetic creation. In creativity, as Joyce here presents it, fantasy, perception, and memory all mingle and merge as imaginative production. Rather than serving a common purpose of protesting convention, as in the epiphanies, or of mutually debunking one another, fantasy and realism converge in a form of play that is the attempt to produce something new. The convergence occurs in part under the auspices of memory, whose work is presented throughout the section either explicitly or inscribed in the repetition of phrases from earlier sections. With this convergence, the style of Stephen's thinking not only in *A Portrait* but also in *Ulysses* becomes possible. The style of visionary intensity has its antecedents in Yeats's 'The Tables of the Law' and in the writings of Walter Pater, whose style Stephen's thoughts mimic at the end of part IV and parody in *Ulysses*. In the 'Conclusion' of *The Renaissance*, Pater characterizes art as the most important of experiences and defines 'success in life' as maintaining ecstasy and burning 'always with this hard, gemlike flame' (Pater, 222). The flame Stephen attempts to keep burning as he writes his poem is at once the visionary intensity of his dream and the emotion he feels for a real woman. His flame-tending proceeds next to a table on which, in the midst of composing, he notices a real, burnt-out candle, 'its tendrils of tallow and its paper socket, singed by the last flame'; he must write out his poem as best he can on the back of a torn cigarette packet (*P* 218). The two styles have been conjoined.

As those styles interact in *A Portrait,* they carry forward from *Stephen Hero* and begin actualizing the suggestion of a potential in Stephen for self-recognition and self-correction that may enable him eventually to break successfully from the conventions he inherits and the enthusiasms that for a time occupy him. We see such a break starting to occur at the end of *A Portrait* when Stephen's oscillations and reversals culminate in self-criticism, as well as intense commitment, in his journal. He explicitly distances himself there, for instance, from his earlier enthusiasm for Yeats's visionary heroes: 'Michael

Robartes remembers forgotten beauty and, when his arms wrap her round, he presses in his arms the loveliness which has long faded from the world. Not this. Not at all. I desire to press in my arms the loveliness which has not yet come into the world' (*P* 251). It is not at all clear, however, how exactly that loveliness differs from Michael Robartes's 'forgotten beauty'.

The criticism in the journal is at times not only self-directed but also humorous. Although we encounter regularly in *A Portrait* the energy of Stephen's thinking, we do not see his humour as often as in *Stephen Hero*. Its emergence at the end of the later work is something of a relief, perhaps for Stephen as well as the reader. He even makes fun of his own ambivalent tendency to re-evaluate his experiences when he writes: 'Then, in that case, all the rest, all that I thought I thought and all that I felt I felt, all the rest before now, in fact… O, give it up, old chap! Sleep it off!' (*P* 252). This kind of comment comes as a relief because of Stephen's evident tendency toward emotional frigidity. We see this tendency more clearly in *A Portrait* than in *Stephen Hero*, though Stephen's serious demeanour and disciplined responses in both texts create the impression of coldness. In part IV of *A Portrait*, at the end of Stephen's period of religious fervor, the emotional absence is evident even to him: 'He had heard the names of the passions of love and hate pronounced solemnly on the stage and in the pulpit, had found them set forth solemnly in books, and had wondered why his soul was unable to harbour them for any time or to force his lips to utter their names with conviction' (*P* 149). It is, in fact, a positive sign that he recognizes the problem, for that recognition influences his decision not to follow a religious vocation that would likely reinforce his emotional deadness. Although Stephen's coldness diminishes in the remainder of the book, especially in the journal, even there, the penultimate entry emphasizes what he has yet to learn, at least according to his mother: 'She prays now, she says, that I may learn in my own life and away from home and friends what the heart is and what it feels. Amen. So be it' (*P* 252). Stephen's emotional potential, like his artistic talent, remains to be actualized when he writes the last, hopeful entries in his journal.

DUBLINERS AND BEYOND: FROM REALISM TO MEMORY AND PLAY

In creating the impression of Stephen's coldness in *A Portrait*, Joyce excised material that holds an important place in *Stephen Hero*, especially the intimacy between Stephen and his siblings, Maurice and Isabel, who do not appear in the later work. The absence of Isabel's death, with its strong impact on Stephen, is arguably the most significant of many alterations Joyce made. He also chose not to include the death of Stephen's mother, which occurs after the writing of the journal. Even in *Ulysses* that death, like Molly Bloom's adultery, is not directly presented as part of the realistic narrative. Only in the fantastic scenes of the episode in Nighttown are we given the act of adulterous copulation and the body of May Dedalus, ravaged by cancer. Such moments of death, ecstasy, and betrayal are so powerful in themselves and in their effects that they defy adequate representation in language. They signal certain limits that even Joyce, with his great skills as a stylist, did not attempt to cross in a realistic style.

In Joyce's hands, however, the limits of realistic writing are very wide indeed, so wide that the realistic style becomes a complex means for presenting memory that leads eventually to the allusive style of *Ulysses*. There is no trace in *Dubliners* of the Paterian style that Joyce later uses in *A Portrait* to suggest Stephen's values and attitudes. By avoiding that style entirely and focusing on the limitations of life in Dublin, Joyce responds critically to the mystical writing, such as Yeats's stories, that Stephen fervently admires. With his remark concerning Michael Robartes in his journal, Stephen begins to shift away from an art emphasizing vision and fantasy, as he continues to do in *Ulysses*. In the seventh episode of *Ulysses*, centred on the newspaper office, he even narrates a realistic vignette that counters stylistically the highly rhetorical, elevated styles that some of the other characters have used. Joyce went much further in this critical direction even before the writing of *A Portrait* by focusing resolutely in *Dubliners* on the grimy surface of ordinary life. He includes, as well, however, some indications of a potentially richer interior life.

Of the two epiphanic modes, the fantastic and the realistic, it is the latter with its 'vulgarity of speech or of gesture' that leads to *Dubliners*, whose stories are all narrated in a realistic manner. The stories and their style share with the epiphanies the goal of criticizing and unmasking a culture that Joyce despised because he considered it paralytic (*Letters I* 55). The opening story, 'The Sisters', involves paralysis literally, and some of the later stories include it at significant moments as a mental condition. At the end of 'Eveline', for instance, the central character is so torn between her desire to escape her dreary life in Dublin and her fear of doing so that she cannot move. And at the end of 'A Painful

Case', James Duffy's mental life reaches a moment of emptiness and stasis, the paralyzing result of his earlier behaviour. Despite the absence of overt commentary by the narrator, an absence that is characteristic of Joyce's fiction, the characters and their culture are generally presented in a harsh light. Many details of the eleven stories from 'Eveline' through 'Grace' provide material for a severely negative judgement of the events, characters, and society presented in them.

The same is not entirely true of the opening and closing stories of the volume, though they project no strong optimism about Irish culture. The first three stories, 'The Sisters', 'An Encounter', and 'Araby', and the concluding story, 'The Dead', differ in some important respects from the stories they frame. Because of the difference, which is in part stylistic, the collection as a whole creates effects that no one of the stories can when read separately. The central figures in the beginning and ending stories differ from most of the other central characters because they are more aware, at least in retrospect, of their situations and possible alternatives. It is the retrospective orientation in these stories that sets them largely apart from the others and that makes them early precursors for Joyce's later, more elaborate style of memory.

Among the other stories, only 'A Painful Case' also presents a central figure who clearly develops a retrospective self-understanding, but for James Duffy the time has passed for self-knowledge to result in a beneficial change in his life. Like Stephen Dedalus and like Gabriel Conroy in 'The Dead', Duffy affects a mask of seriousness and has difficulty feeling, recognizing, and expressing emotion. He comes to recognize his own limitations, as does Conroy, through an experience that brings him into contact with death. But by the end of his story, Duffy's case is closed, whereas the outcome for Conroy and the young boy of the first stories is still unclear when their narratives end. As in many of the other stories, the implicit irony of the perspective offered to the reader in 'A Painful Case' carries a finality that precludes hope for something better in the future.

By contrast with all the stories that follow them in *Dubliners*, the first three are narrated in the first person and may all concern the same young boy. As with Stephen in the three narratives in which he appears, the continuity of the central figure in the separate narratives can only be tentatively maintained, especially since he is never named in any of them. But there are also no details indicating unambiguously that the boy is different in any of the stories. The question of continuity aside, all three stories are retrospective narrations, told by an 'I' who provides little in the way of overt commentary and explicit judgement but whose narrating skills and vocabulary clearly set him apart from the young boy who is his earlier self. The fact that the boy is much younger than any of the later protagonists contributes to the comparatively more hopeful implications of these first stories. The retrospective form of the narration indicates at the least that he has a future that may consist of more than continuing paralysis, though we do not know what exactly that future will be.

While there is irony in the retrospective narration, particularly in the presentation of the boy's 'foolish' (*D* 30) adolescent romantic desires in 'Araby', the distance between narrator and character is never as great as in the stories told in the third person prior to 'The Dead'. The combination of first-person narration, a relatively innocent, young central character, and an intimate style for rendering his thinking creates a potential for sympathy that is largely lacking in the stories that follow. The intimacy of the narration is evident in all three stories, since the narrator regularly presents the character's thoughts seemingly directly without summarizing or explaining them in language that seems inappropriate for the character. The adjectives in 'Araby', for instance, are sometimes descriptive in a psychological rather than an objective way; they originate in the child's thinking rather than in the narrator's. Near the story's ending, when the boy sees 'the magical name' (*D* 34) on the building, it is 'magical' only from his adolescent perspective. Having by this point in *Dubliners* already encountered many similar indications of thinking, the reader will likely realize, even though there is no comment from the narrator, that the word emanates from the child's mind.

The opening sentence of 'The Sisters', with its references to a person and a situation about which the reader as yet knows nothing, presents the character's thinking in a less understated way: 'There was no hope for him this time: it was the third stroke' (*D* 9). It is only after we become acquainted with some details of the boy's life that we understand that 'him' refers to an old priest who has befriended the boy and 'stroke' refers to the priest's illness, not to a clock. Whereas a realistic style can often seem transparent, apparently giving us direct access to the details of a world that is independent of the style's language and fully intelligible, Joyce here produces a relatively opaque realistic style. It draws attention to its own language because the illusion of transparency is not maintained. In this particular instance, even once we understand the references, there remains the question of the specific circumstances in which the statements are made. These are never clarified. In producing a style that presents memory at work and raises more questions than it answers, Joyce has turned his realistic writing into an allusive style of memory.[8]

In 'The Dead' Joyce brings his early realistic style equally close to his later style when he employs a wide range of strategies for presenting thought in the third rather than the first person. Although Joyce uses many of these strategies in the other stories told in the third person, especially the more complicated ones, such as 'A Painful Case', in this one the effect of the narration resembles the intimate effects of the stories narrated in the first person. The kinds of techniques used and the specific ways they are used affect the reader's sense of distance or irony with regard to the characters. In first-person narration a sympathetic response is almost automatically created, unless of course what the character thinks and feels is obviously unpleasant and unattractive. One of Joyce's great achievements as a stylist is his development of third-person narrating strategies that create an effect of intimacy essentially similar to the effect of first-person techniques. By the end of 'The Dead', his mastery of these strategies is evident.

In part because the story is longer than the others, in 'The Dead' the narrator can rely on the reader's having become sufficiently acquainted with Gabriel Conroy's life and his thinking for an intimate, allusive presentation of his thoughts to be possible. By the time Gabriel and his wife, Gretta, have reached their hotel room after his aunts' party, we have already learned a great deal about his values and the circumstances of his life. Much of the information suggests his limitations, particularly in dealings of an emotional sort. He has failed in his attempt to be friendly with Lily, the caretaker's daughter who is acting as maid at the party, and he has botched his encounter with his colleague, Miss Ivors, who has criticized his anti-nationalist attitudes. It is no surprise that Conroy's attempt to evoke an affectionate response from Gretta is also a failure. It is surprising, however, that he seems to learn something about his own deficiencies from the final encounter. He admits, for instance, that 'He had never felt like that himself towards any woman but he knew that such a feeling must be love' (D 223). Conroy's realization about this lack and his decision to help Gretta tell her story are bound up with his new sense of communal relations.

Those relations are based on a common mortality he has, until now successfully, tried to forget.

Equally surprising is the lengthy passage rendering Gabriel's thoughts, which begins 'She was fast asleep', and with which the story closes; this passage brings the reader in a sustained way into the sometimes ambiguous texture of Gabriel's thinking. Unlike the opening sentence of 'The Sisters', the one about Gretta's sleeping has an immediate, though subtle, effect even though the person referred to is not named. There is no need for a name; we know the character's thinking well enough that a pronoun will do. As in 'Araby', we understand some of the adjectives as Gabriel's interior language. When we read that the tears filling his eyes are 'Generous' (*D* 223), however, the word can elicit a more complicated response than the adjective 'magical' in 'Araby'. There the discrepancy between the narrator's view and the character's created some sense of distance and irony. Here the word, with its combined psychological and physical meanings, which the reader is invited to recognize as ambiguously conjoined, cannot so easily be assigned to the character's view only. There may not be any irony, since the word can be the narrator's description, too, rather than evoking the character's perspective only, or both character's and narrator's perspectives as somehow separable. The kind of intense activity that such a style encourages from the reader as it captures the multiple, shifting perspectives of the character's thinking in its relations to the narrator's language is typical of Joyce's later writing as well.

That activity is a kind of play, a transformational process that takes many elements and perspectives and combines them variously, at times in a fashion that is nearly aleatory. It is surely no coincidence that the complexities of style that give rise to this activity in *Dubliners* occur most insistently in such stories as 'The Sisters', 'A Painful Case', and 'The Dead', all of which involve encounters with death and retrospective views. In *Stephen Hero*, Stephen responds to his sister's death by turning toward realism and fantasy as modes of protest; realism that depicts coldly and without illusion the apparent limits of ordinary experience and fantasy that claims to exceed and escape those limits. The Ulyssean Stephen, who is older but perhaps no better able to respond to death, realizes that fantasy, too, has its limits. He may be on the way to learning that there are alternatives to defensive, self-enclosed, and self-protective styles of writing and thinking. Joyce gives us one form those alternatives can take when he produces a style of recollection, one that recovers and revivifies as it invites engaged responses. By writing stories in a style that evokes memory, Joyce can focus on mortality and yet ask for and enable an active redefining of the apparently unalterable limits all of us face.

NOTES

1 Vicki Mahaffey discusses the epiphanies in ch. 8 of this volume.
2 Walter Pater, *The Renaissance* (Cleveland and New York: The World Publishing Company, 1961). Hereafter referred to as 'Pater'.
3 Wayne Booth discusses the difficulty the reader faces in judging Stephen without explicit guidance from the narrator in a widely reprinted essay, 'The problem of distance in *A Portrait of the Artist as a Young Man*', in *The Rhetoric of Fiction* (Chicago: University of Chicago Press, 1961), pp. 323–36. Robert Scholes also discusses the difficulty in 'Stephen Dedalus, poet or esthete?', *PMLA* 89 (1964), 484–9. Hugh Kenner, whose negative judgement of Stephen has been influential, discusses Stephen in 'The *Portrait* in perspective', in *Dublin's Joyce* (London: Chatto and Windus, 1955), pp. 109–33, which has also been widely reprinted. He extends his argument in a more convincing later essay, 'The Cubist portrait' in Thomas F. Staley and Bernard Benstock, eds., *Approaches to Joyce's 'Portrait': Ten Essays* (Pittsburgh: University of Pittsburgh Press, 1976), pp. 171–84. S. L. Goldberg provides a more sympathetic judgement of Stephen in his *James Joyce* (Edinburgh and London: Oliver and Boyd, 1962). I argue for a positive judgement of Stephen in *Teller and Tale in Joyce's Fiction: Oscillating Perspectives* (Baltimore and London: Johns Hopkins University Press, 1983).
4 Many critics have emphasized one aspect of Joyce's language over another by arguing that his writings are essentially naturalistic, that is, filled with straightforward, external detail, or essentially symbolic, that is, filled with seemingly straightforward details that actually involve spiritual revelations. The terms were set long ago by Edmund Wilson in his seminal book, *Axel's Castle: A Study in the Imaginative Literature of 1870–1930* (New York: Charles Scribner's Sons, 1931). William York Tindall's interpretations in *James Joyce: His Way of Interpreting the Modern World* (New York: Charles Scribner's Sons, 1950) and in *A Reader's Guide to James Joyce* (New York: Farrar, Straus & Giroux, 1959), for example, assume that Joyce's narratives are to be read symbolically. Kenneth Burke convincingly challenges the critical tendency toward symbolic readings in his essay on *A Portrait*, 'Fact, inference, and proof in the analysis of literary symbolism' (*Terms for Order*, ed. Stanley E. Hyman (Bloomington: Indiana University Press, 1964),

pp. 145–72), in which he outlines a critical procedure that pays careful attention to the shifting meanings of words. More recent critics have also frequently challenged the emphasis on symbols. In *James Joyce: The Citizen and the Artist* (London: Edward Arnold, 1977; Stanford: Stanford University Press, 1977), for instance, Charles K. Peake takes exception to symbolic interpretations and provides well-reasoned, detailed commentaries on all Joyce's early fiction. In the present essay I argue that we witness in the early fiction a shift in Stephen's allegiances away from a symbolic art toward an art that grapples more directly with the sufferings and uncertainties of mortality.

5 Readers need to be aware of an error in the chapter numbering in all editions of *Stephen Hero* to date (edited by Theodore Spencer in 1944, revised by John J. Slocum and Herbert Cahoon in 1955 and 1963). Hans Walter Gabler explains the error in his 'Preface' to *Archive 8, 'A Portrait of the Artist as a Young Man' – A Facsimile of the Manuscript Fragments of 'Stephen Hero'*:

> The eleven chapters of the University College episode in the manuscripts are numbered [xv] to xxv. Theodore Spencer's edition mistakenly numbers twelve chapters as xv to xxvi. The editorial error arises in chapter xviii. Halfway through the manuscript chapter xviii, at the bottom of page 610, appears the note 'End of Second Episode of v' in a large scrawl of red crayon. The text it obliterates is repeated in the margin of the subsequent leaf. This leaf is again headed 'Chapter xviii' in blue crayon. These as we now know, are markings related to the composition of *Portrait* and do not constitute a revision of *Stephen Hero*. Yet, unfortunately, Theodore Spencer assumed a revisional new chapter division and, introducing 'xix', renumbered all subsequent chapters. Users of the *Stephen Hero* editions must be warned that chapters 'xviii' and 'xix' consecutively are one chapter, chapter xviii, and the chapters 'xx' to 'xxvi' should be correctly numbered xix to xxv. Only with this correction can the editions be matched with the manuscript and Joyce's comments on the novel in his letters. (p. xi)

I refer to the corrected chapter numbers throughout my discussion. The order in which the surviving fragments of *Stephen Hero* are printed in the revised edition can also cause confusion. The fragments published at the end of the volume, which are from the middle of the original manuscript, should precede the much longer segment that comes before them in this edition. A freshly edited critical edition of *Stephen Hero* is in preparation.

6 Hugh Kenner was probably the first critic to discuss the pattern of triumph and undermining in the five parts of *A Portrait* in 'The *Portrait* in perspective', cited above.

7 The best-known critical discussion of Stephen's villanelle is Robert Scholes's essay, 'Stephen Dedalus, poet or esthete?', cited above. Dorrit

Cohn provides an alternative perspective in her brief discussion of narration in *A Portrait* (in her book *Transparent Minds: Narrative Modes for Presenting Consciousness in Fiction* (Princeton: Princeton University Press, 1978), pp. 30–3). Although her book is not primarily about Joyce's fiction, it provides some useful strategies for describing Joyce's varied attempts to present thinking as a process in his writing.

8 Fritz Senn was the first critic to argue for a close relationship between Joyce's later style and the apparently simpler style of *Dubliners*. He makes that argument briefly in '"He was too scrupulous always": Joyce's "The Sisters"', *JJQ* 2 (1965), 66–72.

6   *Ulysses*

What do we need to know in order to read *Ulysses* properly? An intimidating question, perhaps, by which to introduce a notoriously intimidating book. But reading of any kind, whether of *Ulysses* or of *Goldilocks and the Three Bears*, never takes place in an entirely blank or virgin mind. Other discourses are always implicated. Unlike *Goldilocks*, however, *Ulysses* poses the question of prior knowledge with some urgency because it can make us feel so unknowing, and with such devastating speed, and because sometimes a small bit of information available outside the novel, or inside it but hundreds of pages further on, can just as quickly unravel pages of confusion. One of the questions raised by such difficulties is central to literary studies in general: what is inside the literary object? What lies outside it? Can the border lines be drawn with any certainty? My intention is not to proclaim boundaries, nor to choose between right or proper readings, and wrong ones, but only to indicate the kinds of knowledge that *Ulysses* seems to require. My survey is brief, and hardly exhaustive. It is a preface to the major focus of this essay: what is *Ulysses* 'about', and how can it be read?

When T. S. Eliot wrote about Joyce's work soon after its publication in 1922 he argued that its use of *The Odyssey* as both subtext and pre-text 'made the modern world possible for art'.[1] He might also have said that *The Odyssey* has a similarly enabling function for Joyce's readers: that it makes *Ulysses* possible for a modern audience. For us, now, familiarity has naturalized the title. Wrenched out of its original Homeric context (it is the Roman version of 'Odysseus'), the name 'Ulysses' seems entirely Joycean. But that title is a provocation. Imagine for a moment that this seven hundred page novel is called *Hamlet* and you will regain a sense of it as a text brought into deliberate collision with a powerful predecessor. Leaving aside the question of whether that meeting is heroic or satirical it is obvious that even the initial decision to give each episode a name sets a whole interpretive machinery into play. Readers of *Ulysses* – however much they might disagree about what it means or what it is worth – have agreed to refer to each episode by a Homeric title (as Joyce did in correspondence, yet which he chose not to use when *Ulysses* appeared in print, first in *The Little Review* between 1918 and 1920 and then as a book in 1922). Thus the fist episode is known as 'Telemachus', the second is 'Nestor', the third 'Proteus', the fourth 'Calypso', and so on: 'Lotus Eaters', 'Hades', 'Aeolus', 'Lestrygonians', 'Scylla and Charybdis', 'Wandering Rocks', 'Sirens', 'Cyclops', 'Nausicaa', 'Oxen of the Sun', 'Circe', 'Eumaeus', 'Ithaca', and 'Penelope'. Further, again by common consent, section I (the first three episodes, focusing on Stephen Dedalus) is known as the Telemachiad, section III (the last three), as the Nostos, or return. Section II (the twelve middle episodes) is the Odyssey proper, displaced in time and space to the streets of Dublin at the beginning of our century: 16 June 1904, to be precise.

The Homeric parallels are irresistible. Granted, we do not need the *Odyssey* to tell us that Stephen is a young man troubled by the fact that he is a son, and has a father, nor that Bloom is haunted by memories of the son who never really was – his second child, Rudy, having died only days after his birth. But it sharpens our sense of the potentially filial relationship between them to see them also as Telemachus and Odysseus. (They are not simply that, of course. Stephen may be cast as Telemachus, but he thinks he is playing Hamlet.[2] One might argue that he never does find out he is emoting on the wrong stage.) Similarly, it is obvious enough that Bloom is odd man out in Dublin: he does not drink; he does not buy drinks for others; he does not bet (though he is suspected of doing so); he is a Jew (and doubly alien from his Jewishness, for he has chosen to become both Catholic and Protestant). In the effusive round of greetings that punctuate the Dublin day, Bloom is pointedly unacknowledged. Yet when we recall that Odysseus proclaims his name as *outis*, nobody, and that he draws on that facelessness for his own tactical advantage, we recast Bloom's uncomfortable place in society and invest him with a certain power – the power, for example, to escape the blinkered and bullish nationalist in the 'Cyclops' episode, just as Odysseus outwitted the bloodthirsty Cyclops. Like Odysseus, Bloom seeks after knowledge, though the scale of his curiosity is endearingly domestic. 'Wonder what I look like to her', he thinks as he feeds the cat. 'Height of a tower? No, she can jump me' (4.28–9). If we know even the bare bones of the Odyssean plot, the texture of *Ulysses* thickens. Certainly Molly Bloom's assignation with Blazes Boylan resonates against Penelope's legendary faithfulness. The more detailed our knowledge of Homer's epic, the stronger the echoes with *Ulysses*. The more precise, too, our sense of difference.

Caveat lector, therefore. In resorting to Homer, even by calling a chapter 'Penelope' or 'Nestor', we are insisting on something that Joyce himself took care to tone down by deleting chapter headings – though certainly, allusions to the *Odyssey* remain scattered throughout the work. The reader of *Ulysses* should not insist on parallels – Homeric or other – with too much vehemence. Bloom, after all, does not kill his wife's suitor(s). In fact he is careful to stay away during the hour of adultery. The nearest thing to a confrontation between him and Boylan is the one dramatized in 'Circe' where Bloom, as flunky and voyeur, is instructed to apply his eye to the keyhole and play with himself while his rival offhandedly announces his intention to 'just go through her a few times' (15.3789). Abjectly, Bloom offers 'Vaseline, sir? Orangeflower...? Lukewarm water...?' (15.3792–3) and asks 'May I bring two men chums to witness the deed and take a snapshot?' (15.3791–2). For 'Circe's' Bloom, there is intense erotic pleasure in betrayal: '(*his eyes wildly dilated, clasps himself*) Show! Hide! Show! Plough her! More! Shoot!' (15.3815–16). The passion here is very different from the avenging fury of Homer's text, and defines the role of the patriarch/husband in ways for which the epic writer would probably feel contempt. It might even be argued that the task of killing off the suitors is not so much neglected as given over to Molly, who picks them off one by one with dismissive wit in the closing episode.

The first generation of Joyce's readers affirmed his standing as an artist by insisting on the heroic premeditation of the Homeric allusions (a scenario by which Joyce becomes the epic hero of his own literary Odyssey). Stuart Gilbert's pathbreaking study, for instance, is based on a set of correspondences which Joyce himself had provided.[3] Each episode is assigned its own precise time, place, symbol, colour, body part, literary technique, and Odyssean subtext. But readers tempted by symmetries like these should know that Joyce gave another commentator/friend, Carlo Linati, a rather different outline, and with a similar authorial 'guarantee'.[4] More recently, with Joyce's legitimacy no longer in question, critics have been less anxious to reveal hidden correspondences, and more interested in the way *Ulysses* flirts with disconnection. There is a certain point at which the tactful reader holds back, wary of saying that this or that will unlock *Ulysses*'s secrets.

Homer offers the most obvious 'key' to *Ulysses*, but Shakespeare and Dante are similarly between the lines.[5] Although it does so with some irony (particularly in 'Oxen of the Sun'), *Ulysses* makes it clear that it places itself within – perhaps at the end of – a long line of literary history, and that this is one of the contexts in which it is to be read. It follows that the ideal reader would be extraordinarily well versed in the Western literary tradition. But few of us can claim that kind of knowledge: education demands both more and less at the end of the century than at the beginning. Happily for us now, a number of specialized guides to *Ulysses* have been produced in the interim. Still, each reader has to decide how often, and when, to consult such materials. This is a strategic choice, for the knowledge gained by stopping to find a reference or establish an allusion must be balanced against the urge to read on. The narrative impetus also offers solutions, though of a different kind. One of the interesting things about *Ulysses* is that it can be read at two speeds, fast or slow, and at every possible combination of the two. The institutionalization of Joyce's work, the fact that *Ulysses* has become a 'great book', more often than not encountered as a set text at the university level, means that there is considerable pressure to opt for the fixed (and often delayed) moment of knowledge. The danger is that *Ulysses* begins to be read as an elaborate conundrum, a literary jigsaw puzzle that can only be addressed if every piece is put in place in consecutive order, left to right, top to bottom. Sometimes the need to know what everything 'means' in *Ulysses* should be resisted.

Joyce's own earlier writing is very much a part of the intertextual network that *Ulysses* draws on. Readers coming to *Ulysses* with a knowledge of *A Portrait of the Artist as a Young Man* and *Dubliners* are at a considerable advantage. When Bloom steps into the carriage at the very beginning of 'Hades' they too will recognize and acknowledge his fellow-mourners: Martin Cunningham and Jack Power from the short story 'Grace' and Simon Dedalus, still on the long slide down begun in *A Portrait*. In 'Cyclops' there will be another recognition. On its own, the episode hardly draws attention to the drunk blubbering in the corner and trying to ingratiate himself with the Citizen's dog

(12.486–97). But this drunk has a name – Bob Doran – and readers of 'The Boarding House' will recognize in him the grey little man set up by his formidable landlady and her daughter Polly (who might, or might not, also be a victim). That story of entrapment, now given a new, more bitter closure, foregrounds Doran's brief appearance. He is totally befuddled by both drink and marriage. And yet, though the judgements in this episode are not to be taken at face value, there is also the intriguing possibility that mild Mr Doran was always potentially as low as the Mooneys: 'lowest blackguard in Dublin when he's under the influence' (12.384–5) – and that *Ulysses* rewrites *Dubliners*.

The earlier texts are most significant in the case of Stephen Dedalus for they project a history onto a character who is now back in Dublin, utterly penniless, recalled by his father's telegram to a dying mother. He was last seen (at the end of *A Portrait*) in rather different circumstances: setting out on his heroic journey to forge the uncreated conscience of his race. (Clearly, *Ulysses* picks up on the less savoury implications of 'forging': the artist's making is inherently a kind of deceiving, an idea that *Finnegans Wake* will develop extensively.) Readers familiar with *A Portrait* will also know, in spite of the opening pages' attention to Mulligan, that the one to watch is Dedalus: quite flat and undramatic in comparison, but potentially explosive. It is worth considering here the dramatic parallel with *Hamlet*. In the court scene that introduces both Hamlet and Claudius, it is Claudius who hogs the show. He wears brilliant royal robes, stands centre stage, and holds the full attention of his court while he speaks, and speaks, and speaks. Hamlet meanwhile, dressed all in black, stands to the side, and says very little that is not private and for his own ears only. In the first pages of *Ulysses* every gesture and utterance of Mulligan's is emphasized with an adjective, an adverb, or a richly descriptive verb. Stephen, in contrast, 'displeased and sleepy', looks 'coldly' at him, merely steps up, follows him 'wearily', and asks 'quietly'. Mulligan, in the first two pages, 'intones', calls out 'coarsely', gurgles 'in his throat', adds 'in a preacher's tone', gives 'a long slow whistle', and laughs 'with delight'. He says a great number of things, by turn 'sternly', 'briskly', 'gaily', 'frankly', 'thickly', and, at last, 'quietly'. Stephen is silent for almost fifty lines until he finally 'says': first 'quietly', then 'with energy and growing fear'. In between, he merely 'says'. Like Hamlet, however, he will soon gather all eyes and ears to himself. At least till Bloom's entry in 'Calypso'.

The kinds of knowledge I have discussed so far are essentially literary. But there are other worlds, beyond the literary, by which readers have set their course through *Ulysses*. The range of languages and codes within which *Ulysses* is inscribed has a great deal to do with Joyce's sense of himself as a citizen. Irish history, Catholicism, the Celtic Revival, popular culture, Dublin geography, and a certain slice of middle-class Dublin life in the years before and after the turn of the century all play their part.[6] Real Dubliners are written into *Ulysses*, not always with the benefit of a new name. Nor does Joyce spare himself: details of his own life (many of them less than flattering) are drawn into the portrait of Stephen Dedalus. A great deal of what we consider to be safely inside the fictional frame only makes sense if you can go outside it. For instance, if you know that the ancestor whose parliamentary record Mr Deasy quotes in 'Nestor' to prop up his claim to being a 'true' Irishman and a patriot actually voted in precisely the opposite way, you realize that Deasy is convicting himself out of his own mouth (2.278–80). In 'Sirens', where only fragments from 'The Croppy Boy' (sung by Ben Dollard (11.991–1141)) are given in the narrative, you need to be able to hear the whole song in your head, and to understand the historical context out of which it comes, in order to catch the subtle ironies by which national and marital betrayal are linked together in the life of *Ulysses*' Dubliners. Double identity, sudden discovery, disguise, regret: these are themes that describe Bloom's situation as well – and perhaps Joyce's too.

When Joyce was asked, after many years of exile in Europe, whether he would ever go back to Ireland, his answer was a question: 'Have I ever left it?' (*JJ* 292). Ambivalent as it was, Joyce's tie to his native land, to its history and culture, is everywhere in his work. Dublin was perhaps the deepest point of contact, and throughout the writing of *Ulysses*, hundreds of miles away on the Continent, Joyce depended on his aunt Josephine Murray to supply him with vital local trivia. He asked her to check, for instance, 'whether there are trees (and of what kind) behind the Star of the Sea Church in Sandymount visible from the shore and also whether there are steps leading down at the side of it from Leahy's Terrace'.[7] To a certain extent a 1904 map of Dublin is as good a guide through *Ulysses* as Homer's *Odyssey*. It will at least decode, for the non-native reader, the insistent placing of characters at named streets, buildings, and monuments.[8] *Ulysses* describes a quintessentially urban world (though not an industrial one). Most of the action takes place in a public space, and most of the action is talk – the kind of talk that happens when men hang out together at street corners or in public bars. If a Dublin city map would be useful, so too would a Dublin voice, whose cadences are threaded into *Ulysses*' elastic English. The temptation is always there, in spite of one's mid-Atlantic (or other) blunders, at least to try to sound Irish.[9] Perhaps this is why the marathon 1982 Irish radio broadcast of the entire book, read by local actors, can be yet another major entryway into *Ulysses*. However, by voicing a reading it forces choices that print (Joycean print more than most) allows you to suspend.

I have spoken, so far, of the kinds of knowledge that you can bring to *Ulysses*: Homer's epic, the Western literary tradition, Joyce's earlier work, the Catholic and Irish cultural milieu, details of Dublin life, the sound of Dublin speech. The list goes on and on. But I have not yet considered the larger interpretive gestures by which that knowledge may be read into place, and by which *Ulysses* has been given shape. Or rather, shapes – for, Proteus-like, it has no single canonic identity. The current proliferation of critical languages allows us to see more clearly than was possible under a single dominant mode of criticism the extent to which a literary work's status and meaning are determined at least as much by communities of readers as by the intentions of writers. This is even more markedly so with *Ulysses*, which – among all the other things it does – undertakes an exploration and critique of reading. At many points it predicts the insights of current literary theory – though usually with far more wit and humour.

What I intend here is not to describe the various schools of criticism *vis à vis Ulysses*, but to provide something more general and schematic. I will propose that the initial moment in any reading is a decision about genre. What kind of a literary object is *Ulysses*? Three implicit answers have been offered: that it is primarily a poem; that it is really, still, a novel; and, most recently, that it is a 'text'. I shall use these general rubrics to introduce and to distinguish among lines of approach that continue to lead us into the work in interesting ways.

* * *

What would be entailed in a poetic reading of *Ulysses* and why would it be proposed in the first place? Of course, there are poems and there are poems. There is *The Odyssey*, and then there is Blake's 'London' – or Stephen's little lyric in 'Aeolus' (7.522–5). Each requires a different kind of reading. But some things may still be commonly assumed about the genre. To read a piece as a poem is to assume, first of all, that it uses language in special ways and is not to be taken literally (in contrast to the putative transparency of 'scientific', 'objective', or 'ordinary' language). These distinctions are by no means unproblematic. They have been disputed with considerable force on the grounds that all language is figurative, and that no utterance is free of intentions. For my purposes here, however, I will allow poetry its metaphorical privilege in order to highlight what many readers of *Ulysses* have found so striking: the liberties it takes with ordinary syntax and ordinary diction, its intense play with language, its metaphorical rather than narrative logic, its symbolism, its dense allusiveness.

Consider the opening paragraphs of *Ulysses*, with their unexpected images ('the light untonsured hair, grained and hued like pale oak'), their laconic yet symbolically portentous details ('a bowl of lather on which a mirror and a razor lay crossed'), and perhaps most notably, their quirky syntax: a way of arranging words within a sentence that keeps you pleasurably on edge, the way a poetic line does – though for different reasons since Joyce is not compelled by the poet's metrical clock (the one that often beats against the grain of prose-time). He is writing prose, undoubtedly, but a prose that takes unusual liberties: 'Halted, he peered down the dark winding stairs and called out coarsely . . . He faced about and blessed gravely thrice the tower, the surrounding land and the awaking mountains' (1.6–11). The initial 'halted', the strangely delayed 'gravely' and the ambivalent 'thrice' (does Mulligan bless each place three times?) are just a little 'off'. They make the sentences sound not wrong so much as foreign. One might argue that for Joyce, as for Stephen Dedalus in *A Portrait*, and indeed for any Irishman, English was both familiar and foreign, always an acquired speech. This complicated relationship allowed him a special insight into the fact that we are never at home in language, not even in our mother tongue. In spite of all our efforts to make the link between words and things seem irresistibly natural, language is profoundly artificial. The paradoxical force of poetry is that it is the most contrived and conventional of discourses, and yet it achieves an effect of perfect (i.e. perfectly appropriate, perfectly natural) utterance. Joyce's 'poetry' exposes that paradox to our gaze.

Consider the beginning of 'Calypso', the chapter in which Leopold Bloom makes his entrance. 'Mkgnao!' cries the cat, and then 'Mrkgnao!', and then again, loudly, 'Mrkrgnao!' (4.16, 25, 32).

'Miaow!' says Bloom later, answering back in standard English (4.462).
A certain position is being staked out here. The writer of *Ulysses* makes
it clear that, unlike Bloom, he has an obligation to the truth of that cat's
talk, and the ability to transcribe it. With the idiosyncratic 'Mkgnao'
and its variants Joyce claims the poet's prerogative to mint new words as
necessary. He also identifies the essential conventionality of language:
'Miaow' will never be quite the same again.

Since poetic language is taken to be densely and even cryptically
allusive, another reaction to 'Mrkrgnao' is worth noting here as well.
The Italian translator of *Ulysses* has seen in it a covert version of Mrkr,
the Greek spelling of Mercury, and thus a signal to the Homeric Hermes
which imbues it with epic significance.[10] Perhaps he too carries a
message to Bloom from the gods. Or maybe it is just a reminder of how
far Bloom's Dublin has fallen from the epic scale set by Homer. Or,
alternatively, 'Mrkrgnao' may be read as a reference back to the first
episode and to the explicitly mercurial Malachi, Buck Mulligan. Thus
Bloom's early-morning interlocutor is made analogous to Stephen's,
and inexorably a thread is drawn between the two protagonists. Note
that Stephen and Bloom do not really engage with each other until later
at night, in the 'Circe' chapter. And yet by the time they do so they will
already have been brought together, as here, by a long series of
rhetorical connections.

Here you begin to see the real force of the poetic model for *Ulysses*,
which is its vision of the work as a vast symbolic project whose logic is
metaphorical and allusive rather than narrative. Indeed, on the strictly
narrative evidence – i.e. how often Stephen and Bloom meet, and what
happens when they do – their relationship is marginal.

In its overwhelming desire for connections the poetic model
simultaneously simplifies and complicates the reading project. It allows
you to organize and construe the work, but only if, first, you recognize
it as a series of organizable terms. In this sense poetic readings are
radically suspicious for they assume that things are not as they seem
and that the truth lies under the surface. Everything must be raised up
to the same level of significance. (One repercussion is that the laughs in
Ulysses, and sometimes the gentle humour, tend to get translated out.
How seriously, after all, should you take the interchange between
Bloom/Ulysses and the feline Hermes?) This engenders a paradox. On
the one hand, poems are notoriously untranslatable – and *Ulysses*
certainly proves the rule. At every turn it places difficulties in its

translator's path, for every word, it seems, is linked to other words across pages and episodes in an intricate allusive network.[11] On the other hand, such language can never simply be taken literally. It does not so much resist translation as demand it. Thus to read *Ulysses* as a poem can be a long process of exegesis, or intralinguistic translation on the model A 'really is' B. A great many codes can make that equation possible; most notably the Homeric (as we have seen), the Jungian (by which *Ulysses'* particulars are given archetypal force and Stephen, Bloom, and Molly emerge as the essential psychic triad), and the theological. Take the fact that Molly's period starts some time at night after the events of 16 June. If you are persuaded that Joyce's Catholicism is deeply implicated in his work, then Molly does not simply begin to menstruate. The blood that threatens to stain the sheets ('O Jesus wait yes that thing has come on me . . . O patience above its pouring out of me like the sea' (18.1104–5, 1122–3)) will be 'intimately allied to the various consecrations throughout Dublin of Christ's blood and body'.[12] This coincidence (along with others) elevates Molly into the missing term in the trinity of Father (Bloom), Son (Stephen), and Holy Spirit, and it is most significant that, just when Father and Son come as close together as they will get ('Silent, each contemplating the other in both mirrors of the reciprocal flesh of theirhisnothis fellowfaces' (17.1183–4)), one of them is elucidating 'the mystery of an invisible attractive person, his wife Marion (Molly) Bloom, denoted by a visible splendid sign, a lamp' (17.1177–8).

The details fall into place, sometimes, with uncanny precision. It can be very satisfying to pattern *Ulysses* in this way. But to do so requires a continuous effort of translation and a willingness to bypass the more prosaic levels of signification. Or, to be more prosaic myself, to forget that Bloom and Stephen are standing in the back garden at Eccles street, about to take a companionable pee together. They look up at a second floor window and see 'the light of a paraffin oil lamp with oblique shade projected on a screen of roller blind supplied by Frank O'Hara, window blind, curtain pole and revolving shutter manufacturer, 16 Aungier street' (17.1173–6). Note that here the specificity of description is commercial, not religious. Note, too, that the moment of 'perfect unity' between Bloom and Stephen recalls an earlier mirroring in 'Circe' just after Boylan and Molly's voices are heard 'sweetly, hoarsely', and in lascivious union, and Bloom – 'eyes wildly dilated' – calls out: 'Show! Hide! Show! Plough her!' (15.3815). Bloom and Stephen then gaze into the mirror at Bella Cohen's. What they both see reflected back at them is *'The face of William Shakespeare, beardless . . . rigid in facial paralysis, crowned by the reflection of the reindeer antlered hatrack in the hall'* (15.3821–4). Not so much Holy Father and Holy Son, as fellow cuckolds – and perhaps fellow artists too – in a less than holy trinity. And yet, even in this counter-reading, elements from across the work are picked out and pulled together to construct a paradigm – in this case rather more earth-bound than spiritual, and certainly more attuned to scepticism than to faith – but a paradigm, nonetheless, feeding into a broadly poetic sense of the work.

In this version of *Ulysses*, sequence is less important than a synchronic and spatial mapping based on repetition: allusions, echoes, symbols, and archetypal patterns all being, essentially, modes of repetition which forestall the onward moving logic of narrative. But then, reading *Ulysses* is often a case of moving backward through the pages (to check a detail, note an echo, revise an interpretation) as much as forward. Like the verbal icons or the well-wrought urns of the New Criticism (which imaged poetry in this way for an entire generation) Joyce's 'poem' is to be taken whole, apprehended as a complex unity whose intricacy matches that of a vital organism and whose parts all co-exist in a single, ideal, moment of time.

To read *Ulysses* as a poem, finally, is to assume that it will reward scrupulous attention and that the intensity with which you focus on a short lyric may – no, must – equally be given to every page of this very long work. Nothing is contingent or insignificant. Bloom's comment on Molly's joke about Ben Dollard (that he has a 'bass barreltone' voice, punning on the fact that he has become fat as a barrel on Bass beer) holds for *Ulysses* as well: 'See, it all works out' (8.122). This offers both a daunting and a liberating prospect. How can you ever hope to master its densely interlocking verbal networks? But then, you can start anywhere, because everything matters equally, and meaning can exfoliate from any centre. On the whole, the first generation of Joyce's readers adopted the poetic model, and I suspect that most first readings of *Ulysses* will do so too, for it privileges the rage for order that motivates us when we first encounter a new work. It also gives us a strategy for beginning. While long sections of surrounding text may remain opaque, a single page, or paragraph, or even a few lines can generate enough of a sense that it does all work out – at least here – to keep us going.

*   *   *

Of all the genres, the novel is most resistant to definition – perhaps because it is always 'novel', or new, always a challenge to canonic forms. In this sense, *Ulysses* may be the most typical novel in world literature. However, it is also possible to speak of it as novelistic in a more conventional sense, as the kind of writing Virginia Woolf celebrates in 'Mr Bennett and Mrs Brown'. 'All novels', she says, 'deal with character, and . . . it is to express character . . . that the form of the novels, so clumsy, verbose, and undramatic, so rich, elastic, and alive, has been evolved.'[13] Indeed, it would be impossible to speak of *Ulysses* without referring to its characters, to what they do, and to the densely described society they inhabit.

The presence of a human figure in a landscape is irresistible. The viewer's eyes swerve toward it and make contact there, first. Similarly for readers of *Ulysses*, the force of character is compelling, though *Ulysses* does not 'give' them to us in quite the straightforward way we might expect. Helpful formulations like 'he said' or 'she thought' are usually absent. Oblique and even confusing attributions abound. At the same time, it tells us a great deal more than we are used to hearing. It does not avert its gaze when Bloom picks his toes and smells his fingers (17.1480–91). It follows him into the toilet and tracks the motions of his body and his mind with unembarrassed ease. 'Something new and easy. No great hurry. Keep it a bit' (4.501–2). The phrases apply three ways, it seems: to the story Bloom reads while sitting on the 'cuckstool', to Bloom's own sense of his bodily functions, and also to the narrative's languid pleasure in letting the words themselves come out. My point here is not merely that *Ulysses* breaches the borders of propriety. More than that: it can give the internal life of character with an extraordinary sense of intimacy. Indeed, if any literary catch-phrase still clings to *Ulysses* it is 'stream of consciousness'. However, you do not need to privilege that technique (which, in any case, is better termed 'interior monologue'), to see that reading character is a potent method for reading *Ulysses*. In the opening episodes, for instance, once you realize that much of what happens is happening inside Stephen's head (like the Oxford scene (1.165–75), or the visit to Aunt Sara's (3.70–104)), whole chunks of the novel become available. Instead of unnerving and frustrating shifts from one kind of language to another, even from one story to another, you recognize that you are tracking a mind in action and respond accordingly.

'Aeolus' is an interesting section to look at in this light. If you think
of the six preceding chapters as mechanisms that give you access to
character – to Stephen Dedalus and Leopold Bloom in particular –
'Aeolus' is immediately striking because it seems to turn its back on
both of them. To a great extent the progressive filling in of Bloom's and
Stephen's perspectives is what makes the early sections of *Ulysses*
intelligible. You hang on to them; you listen for their voices and they
lead you through the thicket of language. In 'Aeolus' that thicket is
specifically foregrounded. Set largely in a newspaper office, and filled
with talk about talk, the chapter is saturated with the languages of
rhetoric and of wind – an ironical gloss on Dublin's hot air. The sounds
of 'Aeolus' are insistent too, as the machinery of urban life drowns
out individual voices. The episode begins:

IN THE HEART OF THE HIBERNIAN
METROPOLIS

Before Nelson's pillar trams slowed, shunted, changed trolley, started for
Blackrock, Kingstown and Dalkey, Clonskea, Rathgar and Terenure, Palmerston
Park and upper Rathmines, Sandymount Green, Rathmines, Ringsend and
Sandymount Tower, Harold's Cross. The hoarse Dublin United Tramway
Company's timekeeper bawled them off:
—Rathgar and Terenure!
—Come on, Sandymount Green!
Right and left parallel clanging ringing a doubledecker and a singledeck
moved from their railheads, swerved to the down line, glided parallel.
—Start, Palmerston Park!   (7.1–13)

To come upon such an opening, especially after the intimacy of
'Hades', is as unnerving as suddenly discovering in the midst of a noisy
foreign city that you have lost your guide, that there is no one to speak
for you and no one whose language you understand. Bloom does turn
up again (by the third short section (7.26–7)), and Stephen somewhat
later (7.506), but as the talk in the newspaper office swirls around them,
and as the capitalized headlines repeatedly intrude, neither is allowed
his old status as *the* figure in the landscape. However, even though
Bloom and Stephen keep fading from view (and in subsequent chapters
they will do so even more), the novelistic lure of character remains. If
Bloom is absent for a good half of the episode (7.450–961), and Stephen
does not come in until half-way through (7.506), we begin to pay
attention to other voices in 'Aeolus'. To other entries and exits. To
other bursts of talk, and to other silences. Later chapters of *Ulysses* will

provide more sustained access to minor characters by speaking in their own language (for example, Gerty MacDowell in 'Nausicaa' and the sourly loquacious 'I' of 'Cyclops'). In 'Aeolus' the presentation is still dramatic and external, but the construction of character it makes possible is remarkably subtle. One of the effects of rereading *Ulysses* is that the noisy foreign city ceases to be quite so foreign and the talk that swirls about separates out into distinctly heard and comprehended sentences.

One of the voices heard in 'Aeolus' is J. J. O'Molloy's. He is by no means central to *Ulysses* – nor to this episode. Nevertheless, if you track him through this chapter you will have a good sense of the investment in character that moves *Ulysses* along. The minute he enters the scene Bloom provides a running commentary on his past and present situation. (And, of course, in a typically novelistic complication, the mere fact that Bloom does so, as if compelled to notice and to understand, adds to our construction of his character as well. He is not unlike a certain kind of novelist, for whom the smallest detail of dress or gesture can summon up a whole life story.) 'Cleverest fellow at the junior bar he used to be. Decline, poor chap. That hectic flush spells finis . . . What's in the wind, I wonder. Money worry' (7.292–4). When we use Bloom's mini-story as the magnet that picks up subsequent references to O'Molloy, the drama being played out emerges. J. J. O'Molloy has come to the newspaper offices with a single purpose in mind: to ask Myles Crawford for a loan. Characteristically for *Ulysses*, the actual request is never given in the text nor is the motive stated. It can only be inferred from Crawford's negative, but not particularly explicit, answer, and from O'Molloy's carefully orchestrated silences. '– *Nulla bona*, Jack', says Crawford, 'I'm up to here. I've been through the hoop myself . . . Sorry, Jack.' (7.996–8). Crawford's embarrassment at being asked and at intending to say no may well explain his histrionic reaction to Bloom, who interrupts the tête à tête by making his own request – or rather, Mr Keyes's: the tea merchant wants 'just a little puff' in exchange for renewing his advertisement. Crawford's rejection is loudly colourful, and in sharp contrast to his careful treatment of O'Molloy: '. . . he can kiss my arse . . . He can kiss my royal Irish arse . . . Any time he likes, tell him' (7.981, 991–2).

Once this scene of request and rejection is played out, O'Molloy's previous invisibility becomes perceptible. Consider his entry into the scene. He will not be drawn into conversation, even by the warm welcome of his fellow citizens (7.280–90). After minimal courtesies he responds with a silent shake of the head to Dedalus's greeting (7.290), fails to react to someone's 'You're looking extra', except perversely, by 'looking [instead] towards the inner door' and asking 'Is the editor [Myles Crawford] to be seen?' (7.296–8). Learning that Crawford is in his 'inner sanctum' he strolls to a desk and begins to look through a file. In effect he lapses into silence and invisibility until the editor reappears. Even then, he does not deign to respond to Ned Lambert's whispered remark (7.366), and only breaks into speech and motion after a direct greeting from Crawford:

—. . . Hello Jack . . .
—God day, Myles, J. J. O'Molloy said, letting the pages he held slip limply
back on the file.   (7.381–3)

He comes to life with Crawford's entrance, like an actor who steals the scene (otherwise full of noisy bombast) by the sheer quietness of his gestures – but like an actor for whom only part of the audience matters. He plays very deliberately to Stephen and Crawford, and to them only. He murmurs, he offers his cigarettes 'silently', he speaks 'gently', he murmurs again, he says 'quietly' and then again, 'in quiet mockery', 'smiling palely'. For a moment he speaks 'eagerly', but otherwise he keeps a cool control over himself, 'moulding his words' as he performs his role. He is poised, alert for the moment when he must call Crawford aside and pose the question. Even then, he throws it off, as if an afterthought. To Stephen:

—I hope you will live to see it published. Myles, one moment.
   He went into the inner office, closing the door behind him.   (7.907–8)

When he comes out the question will have been asked. We hear only the answer, which is fulsome but negative, and O'Molloy wastes no time upon it. 'J. J. O'Molloy pulled a long face and walked on silently' (7.1000). As before, others attempt to draw him in, but he will have none of it.

—I see [says Professor McHugh after Stephen's parable of the plums] . . .
Moses and the promised land. We gave him that idea, he added to J. J.
O'Molloy.

                                    . . .

   J. J. O'Molloy sent a weary sidelong glance towards the statue and held his
peace.   (7.1061–5)

The construction of a world in which characters 'really' live is so dense in *Ulysses* that even a marginal character like O'Molloy has his own complicated set of motives and gestures to move through – a kind of ballet that we can reconstruct and dance along with, even without the revealing inner speech that characterizes Bloom or Stephen. If, on first reading, 'Aeolus' seems to pull the rug out from under the novelistic table so carefully set in the preceding chapters, every rereading intensifies your sense of 'being there', and of that voyeuristic pleasure in overheard conversation that typifies the novel. No coincidence, perhaps, that the little drama being played out between J. J. O'Molloy and his fellow Dubliners repeats the larger drama of social mobility, of class and money, that animates the genre as a whole, and that certainly entangles Stephen in its logic. The interesting thing about 16 June 1904 is that for Stephen at least things might still go either way. He might yet become the artist – even the author of *Ulysses*, as some have argued. But O'Molloy's pointed recognition of him equally suggests that he has seen a fellow loser, and that his own artful, even elegant, performance prefigures what Stephen will become: a stylish cadger, and not particularly successful. Dramatically, too, O'Molloy's relative silence in 'Aeolus' echoes Stephen's in the opening pages of *Ulysses* and draws yet another thread between them. The paradigm thickens: a timely reminder that while poetic and novelistic readings are separable in theory, they are not necessarily so in practice.

* * *

Current literary study is anything but homogeneous. For the sake of argument, though, it might be described under the rubric 'textuality'. In a major interpretative shift, it 'thinks' the work in question as text, thus stressing its paradoxical identity as a web, a tissue, a signifying field, or even a process of signification, rather than a self-contained entity.[14] To speak of text is also to transgress generic and even literary distinctions. Advertising copy, novels, epic poems, and historical or philosophical writing are all, potentially, textual: *Ulysses*' plunder of a vast range of discourses – many of them flamboyantly extra-literary – comes immediately to mind. The text is Penelope's web: constantly made and unmade, an impossible weaving with ravelled selvedges. And Penelope too is made and unmade by such a text, for 'textuality' calls the reading subject into question.

The dictionary defines 'text' in a number of ways, not all of which are appropriate here. Indeed, the distinction between text (as authoritative, original writing) and commentary (secondary and presumably parasitical) is precisely what – for a textual reading – *Ulysses* undermines with such inventiveness. The various intertextual networks at play in 'Aeolus' gesture toward this blurring of borders. The 'Oxen of the Sun', to which I shall turn shortly, offers an even more elaborate example. You may also recall Bloom's cat in 'Calypso', whose 'Mrkrgnao' seemed to announce an essentially poetic project. But consider the complications. 'Mrkrgnao': a Greek version (Mrkr) of a Roman version (Mercurius) of a Greek god (Hermes). Translation upon translation, and curiously circular: the pure place of origins from which the poetic allusion draws its force is not quite as stable as one might think – nor as pure. Instead what we have is a web of reference points none of which is clearly privileged, and a putative text (Mrkr) which is itself a commentary. This perspective on 'Mrkrgnao' announces a rather different project.

A text is a 'theme or subject on which one speaks', a 'statement on which one dilates' (*OED*): never autonomous, never fully complete in itself, but always awaiting a reader/speaker who will call it out into life. It is most markedly at this point of symbiosis with a reader that *Ulysses* takes on its contemporary form as text. Without ever naming you directly *Ulysses* is constantly addressing you as its reader. There is no grand opening to an 'Idle reader . . .', as in *Don Quixote*. There is no 'Reader, I married him', as in *Jane Eyre*. But just as you tend to forget you have a body until some part of it malfunctions (what could possibly make a nose more obvious to its owner than a cold?), *Ulysses*, so full of moments of congestion and unease, foregrounds you as the reader in the text.

If the reading activity appropriate to poems and novels – indeed, to writing of all kinds – has been knowing or understanding, the one currently attached to texts is 'play'. The choice is telling. First of all, it invokes a particular kind of freedom within constraints, as when you might speak of the play of a hinge or of cogs in a wheel, the focus being on the inter-relationship between moving parts in a machine rather than on the stable and separate identity of any one part. It makes a great deal of sense to think of *Ulysses* in motion, its elements knowable only in relation to each other. One of the most relentless and yet exhilarating effects of the book is the way the verbal ground keeps shifting under you. Many readers have argued that *Ulysses* makes a major break with itself in the middle episode, 'Wandering Rocks'. It could also be argued that the experiments with style of the second half – powerfully anti-mimetic – are present from the beginning. And vice-versa: that even the most obviously subversive episodes (like 'Oxen of the Sun') sustain the commitment to point of view, character, and painstaking mimesis begun with 'Telemachus'. Either way, however, there is an acknowledgement that this play-full text is constantly differing from itself.

To speak of play in this sense, with all its attendant notions of machinery and construction, is clearly a provocation to any sense of the literary work as an organic entity, and in particular to the notion that like a natural organism a work like *Ulysses* will evince in each of its parts the same inevitable logic that motivates it as a whole. (These assumptions are central to the poetic model of *Ulysses*.) Instead the relationship of parts to whole, of microcosm to macrocosm, is understood as asymmetrical and contradictory. This is most strikingly the case in the extraordinary shifts that take place between (and sometimes within) episodes. There are certainly elements that hold the whole thing together: the reiteration of allusions, themes, motifs; the persistence of named characters; the chronological sequence of episodes that record events in Dublin, hour by hour, the morning of 16 June 1904, until early the following morning. But 'play' responds to the countervailing sense that the episodes do not so much share a common life as work together in contradiction. You might note here that textual readings tend to place the difficulties of *Ulysses* at the centre of their accounts, and to make them part of the solution rather than the problem to be explained (away).

Play is not merely *in* the text-system. The text must *be* played, like a musical score. Without the performance it is only black marks on a white page. But then, one might also ask: 'What are you playing at?' Play is never entirely faithful. Potentially at least, it is a kind of trifling with or fingering of the text – not paying it due respect. Certainly the notion of play is subversive, particularly to the authority of intentions and meaning. If the text is not a natural organism, or like one, then its author loses his old status as God-like creator. Play is anarchic, however. Its impulse is not imperialist. It does not simply seek to dethrone the writer in order to put the reader in his place.

To play is not only to perform but also to enjoy, to take ludic pleasure in the text, and with it. (I cannot stress enough how sheerly funny *Ulysses* can be.) At the same time, as anyone who knows children will confirm, play is intensely serious work. What is at stake is nothing less than the desire to honour, to pay homage to the gods by imitating them, whatever form they might take: Cowboys and Indians, Superman, or Mother. Indeed, there is more than that at stake, for the other side of imitation is subversive parody: the need to kill the gods. You play 'Mother' in order to steal her power and thus dethrone her. Or, at least, to see what it would be like if only that were possible.

The 'Oxen of the Sun' episode can be read in this light. Joyce, now a reader of the literary tradition, is playing at writing: doing and being Shakespeare, Milton, Pepys, Swift, Carlyle, Newman. At the same time, by overdoing them, he is in effect undoing them. The chapter's reader too is enmeshed in the play of making and unmaking, for a whole set of recognitions is required. You must, at the very least, recognize that the styles keep changing, and that they follow each other in chronological order. The joke falls flat if you do not play your part. The game becomes an absurd solitaire. A close look at the episode and at some of the readings it has elicited will give a more precise sense of how, and why, *Ulysses* and notions of textuality have gravitated towards each other.

Dublin's Maternity Hospital: ten p.m. Stephen has been drinking with his cronies for most of the afternoon and is now mired in a boozy debate with a group of medical students on the subjects of conception, contraception, and abortion. He is reminded at various points of his own struggle to engender a new literary life. Soon after the chapter begins, Bloom comes in. He has survived the hour of assignation between Molly and Boylan (four o'clock), but he has not returned home. Most recently ('Nausicaa'), in imitation of the fireworks display at Sandymount Strand, he has relieved some of his feelings. Gerty MacDowell – a young woman he does not know – has conveniently arranged herself so that he can look up her skirt, and with this encouragement he masturbates. By the time he reaches the hospital he is spent and makes few incursions into the rowdy talk around him. In another room in the hospital Mrs Purefoy labours hard and long to bring her child into the world. His birth is finally announced and soon afterwards Stephen and company go off to Burke's pub to prolong their drinking. Bloom hovers, paternal, close behind.

This sequence of events is simultaneously revealed and hidden by a series of narrative disguises that mimic English Literary History. The styles move forward in a chronological sequence leaving no identity stable in their wake. Bloom for instance is first gestured at as 'Some man that wayfaring was . . . Of Israel's folk' (14.71–2), 'that man mildhearted' (14.80), 'The man that was come in to the house' (14.111), then named as 'the traveller Leopold' (14.126), 'childe Leopold' (14.160), 'Sir Leopold' (14.169–70), each sighting caught up in a viscous 'linguicity' that makes it incompatible with the one that precedes it – or follows. 'And sir Leopold that was the goodliest guest that ever sat in scholars' hall and that was the meekest man and the kindest that ever laid husbandly hand under hen and that was the very truest knight of the world one that ever did minion service to lady gentle' (14.182–5) becomes, after various transformations, 'Calmer' explaining thunder to 'Young Boasthard' (Stephen) as 'a hubbub of Phenomenon' (14.436), and 'Leop. Bloom of Crawford's journal sitting snug with a covey of wags' (14.504–5). Later he stands accused as 'this traitor to his kind . . . [who] trembled for the security of his four per cents . . . [A] deluder of others . . . [A] censor of morals, a very pelican in his piety, who did not scruple, oblivious of the ties of nature, to attempt illicit intercourse with a female domestic drawn from the lowest strata of society!' (14.910–23). The indictment goes on. He 'is at his best an exotic tree which, when rooted in its native orient, throve and flourished . . . but, transplanted to a clime more temperate, its roots have lost their quondam vigour while the stuff that comes away from it is stagnant, acid and inoperative' (14.937–41). But then, 'No longer is Leopold . . . that staid agent of publicity and holder of a modest substance in the funds . . . He is young Leopold . . . That young figure of then is seen, precociously manly, walking . . . to the high school, his booksatchel on him bandolierwise' (14.1041–7). And so it goes, in constant flux, until the 'dear sir' invited to have a drink in Burke's ('Yous join uz?'), asks for 'ginger cordial', and is described by a medley of voices in terms that cast him as Hamlet's murdered and heartsick father. (The conversation recalls a bee-sting for which Dixon, one of the medical students, had treated him.) 'Got a pectoral trauma, eh, Dix? Pos fact. Got bet be a boomblebee whenever he wus settin sleepin in hes bit garten' (14.1472–3). Between the brackets of patriarch and baby, he is documented as Jew, self-employed, father of Milly, and bereaved friend: 'no fake, old man Leo . . . Vel . . . if that aint a sheeny nachez, vel, I vil get misha mishinnah . . . [T]he Bloom toff . . . Bloo? Cadges ads. Photo's papli, by all that's gorgeous . . . Pold veg! Did ums blubble bigsplash crytears cos fren Padney was took off in black bag?' (14.1524–56). The last sighting is posed as a question (possibly Stephen's): 'Whisper, who the sooty hell's the Johnny in the black duds?' (14.1575). The answer given is no more conclusive, not only because it casts Bloom inappropriately as the arch-sinner/Jew but also because it identifies him with a wrathful God in a single ambivalent pronoun: 'Hush! Sinned against the light and even now that day is at hand when he shall come to judge the world by fire' (14.1575–7). Who is the (lower-case) 'he' who shall 'judge the world'? Surely not 'that man mildhearted' 'that was the meekest man and the kindest that ever laid husbandly hand under hen'.

I have quoted at great length to recall the peculiarities of this episode. By the time you reach 'Oxen of the Sun' you are more than halfway through *Ulysses*. You might even be inured to the lack of a consistent style or even a 'base' style from which the writing digresses and to which it returns. Still, this episode ups the ante very considerably, for it shifts from one style to another at a disconcerting pace. Every paragraph or two a new voice makes itself heard. In doing so, and more particularly in linking its formal preoccupations (the growth of a literary tradition) with the sequence of events I have outlined, it performs 'textually' in interesting ways.

However, 'Oxen of the Sun' has often been explained in terms strikingly opposed to those of 'text'. Not insignificantly, it has also been the episode that readers have been most likely to resist and to resent.

The first temptation is to argue that the formal obsessions of 'Oxen of the Sun' are brilliantly adapted to its subject matter. Month by month in the womb a foetus develops to maturity. Century by century, beginning in a murky chaos (for what could be more opaque than the Saxon and Latinate constructions of the opening pages) the styles of English prose move ever forward into the present. The metaphor is profoundly organic, suggesting that the development of writing is like the gestation and birth of a human being and, implicitly, that the logic of *Ulysses* is similarly and inexorably 'natural'.

One of the most remarkable documents in Joyce criticism, partly because its author was himself a distinguished poet, partly because it was the last thing he wrote before lapsing into schizophrenia and silence, and partly because it pursues its hypothesis of perfect mimetic form with such inexorable and unrelieved passion, is A. M. Klein's 1949 essay, 'The Oxen of the Sun'.[15] For Klein, even the number of clauses in a section, or the numerical position of words in a sentence, add up (quite literally) to the hidden numbers of embryological and evolutionary life. Other readers have been more temperate, but Klein's passion speaks to something important in *Ulysses*: the sheer power of its will to order – or rather the seductive force with which it invites readers to pursue correspondences, coincidences, metaphors of all kinds. In the case of 'Oxen of the Sun' the analogy between language and biology can be so persuasive that what might otherwise seem erratic is taken to confirm and even to refine the paradigm. Thus, for instance, Stuart Gilbert takes care of certain deviations from strict literary chronology with the assurance that the growth of an embryo is not uniform either – that an eye, for example, 'may develop out of its term'.[16] The question remains of course whether the identification of particular styles with particular stages of foetal development does not push the concept of imitative form over the brink, into absurdity. As another of Joyce's early readers puts it: 'For what organic reason, if any, must Lyly represent the foetus in the third month, and Goldsmith in the sixth? And what's Bunyan to Mrs Purefoy, or Mrs Purefoy to Junius?'[17]

'Oxen of the Sun' is clearly a bravura performance of some kind. Perhaps what it represents though is not so much a history (whether biological or literary) as a moment of exhilaration and power on the part of its author. In this reading of the episode the argument shifts from a poetic fascination with metaphor to a novelistic focus on point of view, on the site of utterance, if you will, that organizes the pastiche of styles into a straight line with itself at the end: the point above and beyond all the others that is both a culmination and a point of origins. Anthony Burgess speaks with a fellow writer's admiration when he says that of all the episodes in *Ulysses* this is the one he would most like to have written: 'It is an author's chapter, a dazzling and authoritative display of what English can do. Moreover, it is a fulfilment of every author's egotistical desire not merely to *add* to English literature but to *enclose* what is actually there.' 'But', he adds – and it is a significant 'but' – 'it is a pity that Stephen and Bloom have to get lost in the process of glorifying an art that is supposed to be their servant.'[18] Writing as the site of mastery and servitude: is 'Oxen of the Sun' then a misconceived grab at power, as Burgess implies, or a much more deliberate challenge to what is 'supposed' to be? If Joyce is rewriting in the long line of literary history to show that he can more than do it all, that he can be Author of Authors, why are the imitations so uneven? Some scenes bear the master-mimic's touch: the Swiftean account of the Irish bull in an

English china shop (14.578–650), or Mulligan as 'le Fecondateur' and a Sterne-like Lynch (coyly tongue in cheek) discussing the French fashion for cloaks that keep 'a lady from wetting' (14.738–98). Other parodies are less convincing. The Dickensian moment, for instance, is so skewed that without the giveaway 'Doady' and the artful naming of all the babies after Dickens's own children you might well think yourself in a pulp-fiction interlude (14.1310–23). Clearly the advantage of privileging a perspective of 'Joyce the Prodigy' is that it organizes the multiple voices of this episode into the line of history that culminates in *Ulysses*. It also situates you, the reader, in a stable (and safe) place of admiration. But if you adopt this perspective you might have to admit, at some point, that Joyce was not quite the prodigy he claims or is claimed to be and that the chapter is an embarrassing lapse.

A textual reading, on the other hand, does not necessarily centre or stabilize the episode – either through an authorial (and loosely novelistic) point of view, or on a metaphor (loosely poetic) of organic life. Instead, it acknowledges that something disturbing is happening to the relationship between writing and the world it aims – perhaps – to represent. The cumulative effect is of seeing things at various removes, rather like the series of translations that renders the cat's 'Mrkrgnao' in 'Calypso' into a reminder of textual displacement and instability. Knowing something about the stages of composition for the chapter reinforces this impression, for Joyce's sources were less often the originals themselves than mediating texts like Peacock's selection of prose excerpts from Mandeville to Ruskin, and Saintsbury's *A History of English Prose Rhythms*, full of useful if unintended pointers to the would-be mimic.[19] Notably, drafts of the first long paragraph changed it from a fairly straight copy of Tacitus to something much closer to pastiche. A textual reading, attuned to the decentering play of languages, aligns itself with a reader in motion: not a fixed and discrete entity but a moving part of the textual machinery. More specifically in 'Oxen of the Sun' it rereads the central metaphor of birth to suggest that the reader is like Mrs Purefoy or like any woman in labour – her identity temporarily suspended and bound up in another's (the unborn child's, the text's), itself also amorphous and incomplete – thrust forward by an irrevocable logic toward 'the utterance of the word' (14.1390).

Paradoxically, but typically for *Ulysses*, the attempt to gain control, to put the various languages in their place, opens a Pandora's box of complicating and destabilizing pressures. Faced with the gaps between each style and the one that follows, you make a bridge by appealing to literary history. But every time you recall a pre-text a new gap opens up, this time between the imitation (which is often deliberately 'off' and keeps you at a distance), and the original it invokes (which draws you in, by memory, to an entire fictional world). But since the degree of parodic distortion changes at every turn, every new quotation makes you lose your footing in a new way. The episode is further complicated because not only the Joycean text shifts ground – so does each pre-text invoked by memory as it inscribes a different distance to the reader and to the fictional world. 'Pepys's' language, for example, might seem the spontaneous expression of reality, rendering words transparent and the reader invisible. 'Swift's' positions you in quite a different way, demanding your intervention as decoder. It makes it obvious that the relationship between words and meanings is not direct – that the story it tells of Lord Harry, farmer Nicholas, and the gelded bull requires interpretation. Reading 'Oxen of the Sun' you are in a kaleidoscopic space where every 'shake' of the writing creates a new cluster of relationships between language and its origins, language and its reference, language and its interpreter.

I have suggested that the episode plays an interesting game with its own authority. It plays, too, with the point of closure toward which every new parody seems to move as the line of literary history comes forward into the present. Play is distinguished from work because it is energy expended for its own sake. There is no ulterior motive. No pay-off is expected. In this sense at least reading 'Oxen of the Sun' can only be playful, for meaning (the hermeneutic pay-off) and closure (the plot's reward) are both promised and denied. Things certainly seem more intelligible as you progress toward the present but you do not simply move out of the murk of early time into a final clarity. At a certain point – ironically after 'the utterance of the Word' – the writing reverts to opacity. The last pages are among the most difficult in *Ulysses*. Obviously the verbal confusion matches the increasing drunkenness of Stephen and his friends. But the claim of mimesis does not answer the main question: why plot a history that returns to murky chaos?

The final pages play on the reader's sense of an ending as the call of closure for those in the pub is heard through the raucous blend of voices. 'Keep a watch on the clock. Chuckingout time . . . Ten to . . . Closingtime, gents . . . Time, gents . . . Time all . . . Night. Night'

(14.1452–3, 1471, 1534, 1544, 1561–3). The last paragraph, as we have seen, announces the apocalypse: '. . . even now that day is at hand when he shall come to judge the world by fire . . . *Ut implerentur scripturae*' – that the scriptures might be fulfilled (14.1576–7). The hot-gospelling diatribe that follows pulls out all the stops, invoking the prophetic entrance of Elijah (Matthew 17:9–11), the blood of the Lamb (Revelation 7:14 and 5:6–8), and the final gathering in of sinners that marks the Day of Judgement:

> Elijah is coming! Washed in the blood of the Lamb. Come on you winefizzling, ginsizzling, booseguzzling existences! Come on, you dog-gone, bullnecked, beetlebrowed, hogjowled, peanutbrained, weaseleyed fourflushers . . .! Come on . . .! Alexander J Christ Dowie, that's my name, that's yanked to glory most half this planet from Frisco beach to Vladivostock. The Deity aint no nickel dime bumshow . . . He's the grandest thing yet and don't you forget it. Shout salvation in King Jesus. (14.1580–8)

But this is a mock apocalypse. The second coming is utterly carni-valized; the revelation at the end is denied. And while the final verses of the Book of Revelation promise the quenching of thirst by the word of God, the Dubliners' indulgence in drink has quite another effect: writing is not so much fulfilled as thrust forward in its opaque materiality.

In its final gesture, the episode moves away from Stephen and Bloom. The closing paragraph says very little about them (except by suggesting that Bloom is the occasion for Elijah's second coming – but then, has he really sinned against the light?). They disappear until some pages later in the next chapter when Stephen, announced as 'the parson' and *'flourishing the ashplant in his left hand,'* crosses the stage followed by Bloom *'flushed, panting, cramming bread and chocolate into a sidepocket'* (15.67–73, 142–3). Something has happened at Westland Row Station, but neither 'Oxen of the Sun' nor 'Circe' chooses to reveal what it is – just as, in the other major plot of *Ulysses* (the one involving Bloom, Molly, and Boylan), the crucial moments between man and woman are not given. The closest you get to the assignation at four is Bloom's masochistic fantasy in 'Circe' and Molly's partial reprise in 'Penelope'. And as for its repercussions on the marriage, so little is said between husband and wife that readers continue to argue over what it all means. If Molly brings Bloom his breakfast in bed the next morning, does this mean (as some have argued) that she has learned her lesson and is restored to domestic happiness? Or does it rather mean that, like so many of her fellow Dubliners in *Ulysses*, she has misconstrued the words of another and heard only what she was ready to hear: 'breakfast in bed' (18.2) instead of Bloom's 'roc's auk's egg' (17.2328–9) murmured as he slips into sleep?

In 'Oxen of the Sun' the question of meaning is even more radically at issue because it is not simply a case of leaving certain events out of the narrative. Rather, the very possibility of making something present in language is subverted – comically so, for instance, in the account of the bull of Ireland and his seduction of every 'maid, wife, abbess and widow':

and the end [of the story] was that the men of the island . . . made a wherry raft, loaded themselves and their bundles of chattels on shipboard, set all masts erect, manned the yards, sprang their luff, heaved to, spread three sheets in the wind, put her head between wind and water, weighed anchor, ported her helm, ran up the jolly Roger, gave three times three, let the bullgine run, pushed off in their bumboat and put to sea to recover the main of America.
(14.639–46)

There is such sheer exuberance in the writing: but to what effect? Instead of each additional phrase enhancing the mimetic power of language (as each additional brush stroke on a canvas might increase your illusion of 'the real'), the accumulation of phrases is such that language itself is reified, and meaning (i.e. the thing 'out there' that language points to) recedes into the background. Before they even get out of the harbour, the men of Ireland capsize in a full sea of words. You may or may not agree with Burgess's rueful judgement that 'it is a pity that Stephen and Bloom have to get lost in the process of glorifying an art that is supposed to be their servant': he is nevertheless right to see that the expected hierarchy between words and a fictional world has been overturned. Closing time in 'Oxen of the Sun' discloses the loud and empty rhetoric of salvation – a twist on the biblical Elijah who learns that God's rule is established in a 'still, small voice' (I Kings 19:12). Perhaps, after *A Portrait of the Artist*, Joyce no longer sees himself as a kind of God, aloof, detached from his handiwork, paring his fingernails, and capable of revealing the world in all its meaning. The 'author' that seems to speak in 'Oxen of the Sun' is strangely unauthoritative – not so much a Joyce who parodies the past to proclaim his superiority, as a Joyce who involves the reader in the dilemma of language, and who is himself, like his characters and his readers, dispersed in language. Roland Barthes's account of textuality and its strategy of quotation is most appropriate to this episode. A multivalent text, he writes,

can carry out its basic duplicity only if it subverts the opposition between true and false, if it fails to attribute quotations . . . to explicit authorities, if it flouts all respect for origin, paternity, propriety, if it destroys the voice which could give the text its ('organic') unity . . . For multivalence . . . is a transgression of ownership.[20]

'Oxen of the Sun' speaks for the text/*Ulysses* in a number of ways. It plays on the themes of closure and disclosure but at the end of the line reveals very little, shifting its attention (and that of its readers) from the signified to the signifier. We are refused that moment of clear vision, 'as though face to face', promised by Revelation. The episode tries out style after style, discarding each in turn, never allowing one to take more than temporary precedence over another, and keeping its readers, always, off balance. And because there is no single language that provides and authorizes a meaning (neither one of the voices of the past nor the voice of Joyce standing above his creation), meaning can only be relational, produced in the spaces between languages – in their play. Most pointedly, however, by its impertinent manhandling of other writing (impertinent in the double sense: both cheeky and, variously, inappropriate or inaccurate), 'Oxen of the Sun' transgresses the principle of ownership on which both poetic and novelistic readings depend. The one assumes that all the elements in a literary work – however complex and paradoxical – ultimately cohere in a formal and thematic unity that the reader must discover. The other (in some ways only a more particular version of the first) assumes that the privileged unifying force is the human voice and individual psychology. To read *Ulysses* as a novel is to ask, at every turn, 'who speaks?' and, beyond that, 'what do these words say about the one who "owns" them?' To read *Ulysses* as a text is to be not a little perverse and focus instead on the places where connections come unstuck and the weaving frays, because it is precisely at such points that the playfulness of the text implicates the reader and allows itself to be seen.

'Oxen of the Sun', like *Ulysses*, is a contested terrain on which poetic, novelistic, and textual readings stake their claims. It offers ambitious answers to questions of formal and thematic unity. (Human, linguistic, and aesthetic life are all subsumed under an organic metaphor of growth and birth.) It sheds its kaleidoscopic light on Stephen and Bloom at a key moment in their (unwitting) search for each other, and with a crazy, strobe-light intensity that simultaneously illuminates and distorts, speeds up and slows down, it embeds them in a sharply observed social world. (Part of the fun of the episode is recognizing the players behind the rhetorical veils.) It also turns on itself, like Penelope's web, to unravel those illusions of originality, authority, and authorship, and to jostle those places of identity, upon which 'Literature' traditionally rests.

NOTES

1 'Ulysses, order and myth', *Dial* 75 (November 1923), 480–3; rpt. *CH I*, 268–71.
2 Hugh Kenner makes a similar point in his *Ulysses* (Baltimore: Johns Hopkins University Press, rev. edn., 1987), p. 28. Based on an extraordinary absorption and recall of Joyce's work, Kenner's study is full of insight.
3 *James Joyce's Ulysses* (London: Faber, 1930).
4 For a reading that works centrally with Linati's schema, see Richard Ellmann, *Ulysses on the Liffey* (London: Faber, 1972).
5 See, for example, William M. Schutte, *Joyce and Shakespeare: A Study in the Meaning of 'Ulysses'* (New Haven: Yale University Press, 1957) and Mary T. Reynolds, *Joyce and Dante: The Shaping Imagination* (Princeton: Princeton University Press, 1981).
6 A useful reference work is Weldon Thornton's *Allusions in 'Ulysses'* (Chapel Hill: University of North Carolina Press, 1961). See also Don Gifford, *'Ulysses' Annotated* (Berkeley: University of California Press, 1989). (Both works, of course, also refer to literary contexts.) Chs. 2–4 of this volume deal with some of the most important contexts of Joyce's work.
7 Postcard dated 5 January 1920, from Trieste (*Letters I* 135). Ellmann reports that Joyce 'had asked for the same information in another card a month or two earlier' (*JJ* 785).
8 See, for example, Clive Hart and Leo Knuth, *A Topographical Guide to James Joyce's 'Ulysses'* (Colchester: A Wake Newslitter Press, 1975), and Jack McCarthy, *Joyce's Dublin: A Walking Guide to 'Ulysses'* (Dublin: Wolfhound Press, 1986).
9 For a very useful account of Dublin English, see Anthony Burgess, *Joysprick: An Introduction to the Language of James Joyce* (London: André Deutsch, 1973), in particular ch. 2, 'The Dublin Sound'.

10 The translator is Giulio de Angelis, whose comment, cited by Sidney Alexander, is noted by Fritz Senn in 'Book of many turns', in Thomas F. Staley, ed., *'Ulysses': Fifty Years* (Bloomington: Indiana University Press, 1972), p. 46.

11 The difficulties *Ulysses* poses for translators, and the insights that their labours can provide, have been brilliantly explored by Fritz Senn; see chs. 1–3 of his *Joyce's Dislocutions: Essays on Reading as Translation*, ed. John Paul Riquelme (Baltimore: Johns Hopkins University Press, 1984).

12 Robert Boyle, S.J., 'Miracle in black ink: a glance at Joyce's use of his eucharistic image', in Staley, *'Ulysses': Fifty Years*, p. 47.

13 *Collected Essays*, I (London: Hogarth Press, 1966), p. 324.

14 For a concise presentation of the notion of 'text', see Roland Barthes, 'From work to text', in *Image-Music-Text*, ed. Stephen Heath (Glasgow: Collins/Fontana, 1977), pp. 155–64.

15 *Here and Now*, I, no. 3 (January 1949), 28–48.

16 *James Joyce's Ulysses*, p. 293.

17 Harry Levin, *James Joyce: A Critical Introduction* (London: Faber, 1944; rev. edn., 1960), p. 95.

18 *Re Joyce* (New York: Norton, 1968), p. 156. Published in Britain as *Here Comes Everybody: An Introduction to James Joyce for the Ordinary Reader* (London: Faber, 1965).

19 See J. S. Atherton, 'The Oxen of the Sun', in Clive Hart and David Hayman, eds., *'Ulysses': Critical Essays* (Berkeley: University of California Press, 1974), p. 315.

20 *S/Z*, tr. Richard Howard (New York: Hill and Wang, 1974), pp. 44–5.

7 *Finnegans Wake*

THE MATTER OF (WITH) *FINNEGANS WAKE*

riverrun, past Eve and Adam's, from swerve of shore to bend of bay, brings us by a commodius vicus of recirculation back to Howth Castle and Environs.

Thus begins James Joyce's last work, figuratively and thematically in mid-stream. The sinuous sentence, the swerving phrase, continues a journey: by water, by bodily fluid, by verbal fluency. If we, the readers, are encompassed in the ambiguous 'brings us', then we can begin to understand why the voice of that opening sounds so like the narration of a tour guide. For we have no way of knowing where we, as readers, are situated in this opening. Are we on a boat in the river Liffey in Dublin, or are we inside a human body; are we at the beginning of time, or in the eternal present of every human utterance? The opening of *Finnegans Wake* drops us, without map, clock, compass, glossary, or footnotes, into an unknown verbal country, and the voice of the tour guide, alas, speaks their language rather than ours, although we catch enough cognates to keep from drowning altogether in that verbal stream. The role of that tour guide is, in a sense, duplicated by the enterprise of this essay. Surely, no other existing literary work needs a 'guide' more sorely than James Joyce's *Finnegans Wake*, with its strange language, its neologisms, its generic ambiguity, the obscurity of its allusions, the mysterious status of its speech.[1]

The most helpful service a guide to *Finnegans Wake* might seem to offer would be to tell readers what the text is 'about'. But one of the many peculiarities of *Finnegans Wake* is that its content, what it is 'about', is indivisible from its form, from the language in which it is told. 'His writing is not *about* something; *it is that something itself*',

Samuel Beckett wrote in an early essay on the unfinished *Finnegans Wake*, then entitled 'Work in Progress' (Beckett, *Our Exagmination*, p. 14). By way of analogy, consider the disservice of the art critic who helps spectators understand a cubist painting by retrieving for them the residue of visible representation, the guitar and the bunch of grapes on the table, for example, and then encourages them to speculate on what the guitar, grapes, and table *mean*. Clearly something far more important is at stake in the cubist painting's distortion of representation, its spatial derangement, the play of textures, and the fragmentation of the spectator's point of view, than the significance of the objects that are represented. Cubist painting is not about goods and furniture, but about the relationship between media and the phenomenon of seeing.[2] Likewise, *Finnegans Wake* might be said to be 'about' not being certain what it is about: its subject is the nature of indeterminacy itself.

The indeterminacy of *Finnegans Wake* is created by the strange ontological conditions the work explores, particularly dreaming and dying, conditions that call the being of the self, and self-identity, into radical question. In dreaming, you no longer know who you are because you do not know if you are the self who thinks conscious thoughts, or the self who produces the strange, distorted, alien images of your dreams revealing that you know things you did not know you knew. In dying, you no longer know whether you are a being or a potential nothingness, and you are obliged to consider, while still in existence, what you will be when you cease to exist.

These cosmic indeterminacies of identity take the form in *Finnegans Wake* of an insistent questioning of everything throughout the text. Nearly every major chapter of the *Wake* is organized around an investigation, a trial, a quiz, a riddle, an inquisition, or some other state of uncertain knowing, that the reader must then duplicate in trying to make sense of the text. The questions seem to pursue problems of identity, as though the dreaming mind were trying to understand who or what it is by remembering and reliving what it desired, what it has done, and how it was judged. The quest for identity therefore tends to become a search for origins. The emotional impulses of dreams, while triggered by recent events and thoughts, must be sought, according to Freud, in forgotten or repressed childhood memories. The questing in *Finnegans Wake*, tracking identities to their sources, therefore takes on a historical character, both in an individual sense, as a return to childhood curiosity, desire, and games, and in a collective sense, as a 'memory' of historical and cultural events. The sons, for example, search for the secret of their identity in the hidden place in their mother's body that was their infantile home, 'the whome of your eternal geomater' (296.35), while their psychological struggles with their father take on historical form as famous military engagements, for example, the battle between Napoleon and Wellington rendered as a comical tour of the Wellington museum ('the Willingdone Musey-room') – 'This is the triplewon hat of Lipoleum. Tip. Lipoleumhat. This is the Willingdone on his same white harse, the Cokenhape' (8.15) [Wellington's white horse was named Copenhagen]. Because the dreaming mind can tap all the history, mythology, literature, and culture it has ever known, *Finnegans Wake* contains an enormous range of historical and cultural allusion that is disorganized, jumbled, and unimportant in itself, but very interesting for the way it assimilates to personal obsession and recapitulates personal experience.

Something like characters and something like narratives do emerge from the reading of *Finnegans Wake*, but it is difficult to be certain just how we learn about them. This partially reflects the way dream elements tend to be overdetermined. Because a dream is trying to tell the self things it does not want to know – its own guilty desires, for example – the dream's message must be indirect and takes disguised form as a kind of code. The difficulty and obscurity of the *Wake* text is therefore meant to baffle the dreamer rather than the reader. But to make itself understood at all, the text relies on endless repetition of its coded messages. Thus the names of the characters emerge slowly, tentatively, and *literally* in bits and pieces – that is, as initials or abbreviations. The figure of the father, for example, emerges as HCE (Humphrey Chimpden Earwicker, we eventually learn, or perhaps Harold Chimpden Earwicker), embedded in phrases that themselves contribute to our understanding of his place, work, familial functions, and the like: Howth Castle and Environs (3.03), hod, cement, and edifices (4.26), Haroun Childeric Eggeberth (4.32), happinest childher everwere (11.15), homerigh, castle, and earthenhouse (21.13), Humme the Cheapner, Esc (29.18).

Critics over time reduced the confusion of Wakean character identity by using little signs, called sigla, (see the footnote about 'The Doodles family, ⊓, △, ⊣, ×, □, ∧, ⊏ ' on 299 in II.2) that Joyce used in his working copies of the text in order to keep track of the different figures, to produce a sort of cast of characters. They include members of a family – father HCE, mother (ALP or Anna Livia Plurabelle), the twin sons Shem and Shaun, and the daughter Isabel or Issy – and their immediate society: two old domestic servants, a charwoman named Kate and an older manservant, four old men, and twelve pub customers. These figures are associated with certain recurring functions in the works: the father is fallen; the mother tries to save him; the twin sons fight each other, and, united, fight the father; the daughter, when not self-absorbed, comments wryly on the antics of the family; the four old men dispense wisdom; and the twelve customers in the pub criticize and gossip. But these identities are difficult to sustain during the actual reading of the text because the figures have many associative identities and functions, including mythical analogues from the Bible, Irish mythology, classical mythology, political history, opera, and literature. They are also identified with the geography of Ireland – HCE is the land of Dublin, ALP is the river Liffey that runs through it – and features of nature and landscape: Shem is tree, Shaun is stone, and Issy is a little cloud that has not yet become a river like her mother. Their relationships nonetheless appear to be dramatic: the father may desire the daughter, the sons may have caused the father's downfall, the mother may procure younger women for the father in an effort to restore his potency, the family and customers may have produced the father's fall purely with rumours and gossip.

But the story of this family does not unfold in an orderly, linear plot. Instead, there are family 'plots', as it were, dispersed among hundreds of little scenes, stories, fables, dialogues, anecdotes, songs, rumours, and plays, that are often versions of one another, and that are all versions of the same family conflicts. The wild incongruity of these vignettes and the sense of narrative excess they produce – as though we get too many stories with too many versions ('There extand by now one thousand and one stories, all told, of the same' (5.28)) – give the text much of its rollicking humour. They include, among many others, the tale of the prankquean who kidnaps Jarl van Hoother's children because he fails to guess her riddle; the writing of a funny but scurrilous ballad about improprieties HCE supposedly committed in Phoenix Park; an analysis of a smudged letter ALP, as a hen, apparently found in the dump; the triangle of Anthony, Caesar, and Cleopatra retold as the story of butter, cheese, and margarine; the image of Shem, the artist, as a stinking lowlife holed up in a house called 'The Haunted

Inkbottle'; children's sexual games at twilight told in the trope of flower pollination; the story of how Buckley shot the Russian General in the Crimean war; four old men watching the lovemaking first of Tristan and Isolde, and later of HCE and ALP in their marriage bed; a hilariously sacrilegious version of the *via crucis* (Christ's stations of the cross as he wends his way to his crucifixion), enacted by an obese, lecherous, and hypocritical Shaun; and the haunting swan song of ALP as, dying, she flows out to sea to rejoin her father, the wild ocean.

Each of these stories or tales or vignettes has its own narrative functions and stylistic charms. For example, one of the most delightful versions of the brothers' quarrel, the fable of the Ondt and the Gracehoper, is meant to function like a gospel parable excoriating the happy-go-lucky, feckless artist in favor of his thrifty, industrious twin. As the starving Gracehoper approaches the Ondt, presumably hoping for grace and money, he finds the fat, happy insect opulently esconced amid a ministering harem of female insects (Floh = flea, Luse = louse, Bieni = bee, Vespatilla = wasp):

Behailed His Gross the Ondt, prostrandvorous upon his dhrone, in his Papylonian babooshkees, smolking a spatial brunt of Hosana cigals, . . . as appi as a oneysucker or a baskerboy on the Libido, with Floh biting his leg thigh and Luse lugging his luff leg and Bieni bussing him under his bonnet and Vespatilla blowing cosy fond tutties up the allabroad length of the large of his smalls.   (417.10–20)

No wonder this insect intimacy ('As entomate as intimate could pinchably be') makes the Gracehoper 'aguepe with ptschjelasys', or agape with jealousy. The passage illustrates how Joyce effects overdetermination with 'portmanteau' words (introduced in Lewis Carroll's 'Jabberwocky') – for example, 'dhrone' as a throne for a drone. It also includes clever literary and musical allusions: for example, to the hookah-smoking caterpillar of *Alice in Wonderland* (although the Ondt smokes celebratory [Hosana] Havana cigars, or a French *cigale* or cicada); and to the amorous affairs (cosy fond tutties) of Mozart's *Cosi Fan Tutte*. The telling of the fable, then, does not just point a moral; it expresses, subjectively, what the painful lesson feels like by using the very funny sensuality of the scene to sharpen the Gracehoper's sense of deprivation and frustration. It also explores the enmity and grievances of brothers with very different temperaments, making it difficult for critics to resist seeing the fable as a parody of the exasperation of the thrifty and responsible Stanislaus Joyce with his profligate brother James.

THE DREAMING TEXT: 'ANNA LIVIA PLURABELLE'

Before going on to give the production history of *Finnegans Wake*, it might be useful to explore how a *Wake* chapter is created – not textually, how it is written, but imaginatively, how it was conceived. The last chapter of Book I, the 'Anna Livia Plurabelle' chapter, is considered the most beautiful and the most famous section of *Finnegans Wake*. This is a chapter narrated as a conversation between two gossipy washerwomen doing laundry on the banks of the river Liffey, which runs through Dublin. They gossip about Anna Livia Plurabelle and her husband, who has been indicted in some scandal, and as they delve into ALP's past, they also recount the course of the river Liffey, from its origin as a rivulet in the Wicklow Mountains, accumulating freight and debris as the woman accumulates lovers, responsibilities, and junk, until, laden with filth and life's griefs, she widens, at her delta, back out to the sea. Where did Joyce get the idea to write a chapter like this, and how is he able, technically, to give it its effects?

The anecdotal history of this chapter reveals how Joyce created a set of experiential fictions about its genesis that conceal his structural devices in order to promote its reading as poetry, as lyric. Joyce betrayed to an Italian journalist the controlling metaphor of the chapter, the woman as river:

> They say I have immortalized Svevo, but I've also immortalized the tresses of Signora Svevo. These were long and reddish-blond. My sister who used to see them let down told me about them. The river at Dublin passes dye-houses and so has reddish water. So I have playfully compared these two things in the book I'm writing. *(JJ 561)*

But it is worth noting that Joyce's experience is not *seeing* the tresses of Livia (ALP's middle name) Schmitz but rather *hearing* his sister describe them – so that his voyeurism is mediated by the female voice – 'was she marcellewaved or was it weirdly a wig she wore' (204.23). The sister was presumably Eileen Joyce, who lived with the Joyces in Trieste, and who might have described the beauty of Livia Schmitz's hair not to Joyce, but to her sister Eva, thus perhaps creating for him the interlocutory structure of the chapter: that of a male eavesdropping on the gossip of two women discussing another of their sex. 'O tell me all about Anna Livia! I want to hear all about Anna Livia. Well, you know Anna Livia? Yes, of course, we all know Anna Livia. Tell me all. Tell me now. You'll die when you hear' (196.01–06). The gossip of the washerwomen is never allowed to form a coherent story, however, because the red-haired woman they talk about keeps dissolving into the river: the waves of her hair become the waves of the water ('First she let her hair fal and down it flussed to her feet its teviots winding coils' (206.29–30)); her freckles the dappled light on the water surface ('why in the flenders was she frickled' (204.22–3); her dress the topological features of the water and its surrounding land ('a sugarloaf hat with a gaudyquiviry peak and a band of gorse for an arnoment and a hundred streamers dancing off it' (208.07–09); and her possessions and gifts the flotsam and jetsam riding the seafoam (German: Meerschaum) of her tides ('she raabed and reach out her maundy meerschaundize, poor souvenir . . . and wickerpotluck for each of them' (210.01–06)).

In another anecdotal confidence, Joyce once said that the structuring idea for the chapter was inspired by women washing clothes on both banks of the river Eure, whom he saw on a trip to Chartres (*JJ* 563). Joyce was no doubt delighted and moved by the washerwomen doing their laundry on the banks of the Eure. But the anecdote, with its fiction of a spontaneous and experiential source for the writing of 'Anna Livia Plurabelle', nonetheless serves to retard and divert our recollection that Joyce had written about washerwomen before in the *Dubliners* story 'Clay'. And, indeed, if we compare the two representations of washerwomen, in the ALP chapter and in 'Clay', we can see an intricately inverted structural relationship between them. 'Clay' introduces the washerwomen when they are finished with their washing: 'In a few minutes the women began to come in by twos and threes, wiping their steaming hands in their petticoats and pulling down the sleeves of their blouses over their red steaming arms' (*D* 100–1). All that is left of their laundering is the steam and the red of their arms and hands, before they pull their sleeves down and it is altogether effaced. *Finnegans Wake*, on the other hand, takes us behind the scene, as it were, and shows us what 'Clay' does not let us see and hear: what the washerwomen do and say when they work – literally and figuratively 'washing dirty linen in public'. The *Wake*'s washerwomen 'read' their laundry, drawing unflattering inferences from the stains, spots, and rips of the underwear of their clients, 'Look at the shirt of him! Look at the dirt of it! He has all my water black on me . . . I know by heart the places he likes to saale, duddurty devil!' (196.11–15). The washerwomen of 'Clay' probably talk about Maria behind her back, but because the story's narrator is so determined to put only the best face on Maria's environment, they are quickly dismissed as vulgar and unimportant, 'Mooney meant well though, of course, she had the notions of a common woman' (D 101). The washerwomen of 'Clay' are silenced except when quoted as singing Maria's praises.

Finnegans Wake takes what is background – or 'ground', in the way that term is used in visual representation – and transforms it into foreground or 'figure'. The washerwomen of Finnegans Wake are the figure that results from such a reversal, as Finnegans Wake, in a sense, turns 'Clay' inside out. The washerwomen's speech, repressed and silenced in 'Clay', is restored to the central narrative position as the dominant subjectivity of the ALP chapter. The thoughts, views, and expressiveness of the washerwomen is restored in the homely idiom and vulgar diction of their speech, 'Lordy, lordy, did she so? Well, of all the ones ever I heard! Throwing all the neiss little whores in the world at him!' (200.27–9). Their rhetorical function is reversed as well, as they now ferret out, and 'air', the little woman's secrets. However, ALP in the Wake benefits from the way dreams express wish-fulfilment: the virginal, loveless, childless little old maid in 'Clay' is transformed in 'Anna Livia Plurabelle' into the little wife with a generous sexual history and many children, the figurative 'proper mother' of 'Clay' (' – Mamma is mamma but Maria is my proper mother' (D 100)) turned into the literal mother of a nearly countless brood in Finnegans Wake. It is as though Finnegans Wake dramatizes the hidden wishes and fears of Maria in 'Clay', things the text of 'Clay' knew but could not tell us. 'Clay' describes Maria's homely little body dressed in chaste, drab garb; 'the diminutive body which she had so often adorned' (D 101) is ironically quite unadorned, the narrative verb notwithstanding. But Finnegans Wake reverses this description as if to gratify the woman's hidden desire for adornment in 'Clay', and the diminutive body of ALP is described in the Wake as elaborately bathed ('Then, mothernaked, she sampood herself with galawater and fraguant pistania mud' (206.30–1)), bejewelled ('Then she made her bracelets and her anklets and her armlets and a jetty amulet for necklace of clicking cobbles and pattering pebbles' (207.04–06)), and painted, 'a dawk of smut to her airy ey' and 'the lellipos cream to her lippeleens and the pick of the paintbox for her pommettes' (207.08–10). Maria's nondescript garb becomes on ALP the most outlandish costume in the world, as the little woman who, in her mousiness, is nearly invisible in 'Clay' is transformed into a gaudy, ridiculous, but decidedly eye-catching spectacle in *Finnegans Wake*.

The experiential fiction, that Joyce created 'Anna Livia Plurabelle' out of Chartrean washerwomen and Livia Schmitz's hair, lends the text a spontaneity that conceals the way he is manipulating, reversing, and inverting his own earlier textual material. Joyce thereby creates an oneiric verisimilitude, an illusion that the text is, as it were, dreamt, and that Joyce has himself absorbed and dissolved experience into the unconscious linguistic plenitude of his mind and, in a sense, 'dreamt' *Finnegans Wake*. The fiction of a text created spontaneously and in an *ad hoc* fashion, that is, written in the same way dreams are constructed, out of the transmutation of bits and pieces of experience and memory, was actively fostered by Joyce. He argued to Arthur Power that emotional, not intellectual, factors propelled his writing – 'Emotion has dictated the course and detail of my book, and in emotional writing one arrives at the unpredictable which can be of more value, since its sources are deeper, than the products of the intellectual method' (95) – and he described to Jacques Mercanton the serendipitous nature of his method, 'Chance furnishes me with what I need. I'm like a man who stumbles: my foot strikes something, I look down, and there is exactly what I'm in need of' (*JJ* 661). Archival research will no doubt continue to erode this fiction and suggest a far more deliberate procedure, but it will not alter the significance of Joyce's aim to disavow the rational writing, the puzzle-making construction, of his text. Joyce intended *Finnegans Wake*, I believe, to be 'the dream' of his earlier texts, as though his earlier texts contained hidden truths, secret feelings and desires, unconscious knowledge that the language 'contains' as possible interpretations, but that the narration itself, what the text 'says', does not articulate. *Finnegans Wake* in retrospect reveals the earlier text to have had an unconscious life (which we can equate with the potential of language), and which the *Wake* expresses or 'speaks', using the distorting, displacing, punning, poetic techniques of dream itself.

THE WRITING HISTORY OF *FINNEGANS WAKE*

The enormous strangeness of *Finnegans Wake*, and the difficulty this creates for the reader, have tended to produce two very different responses that have shaped the controversies of its public reception. During the course of its writing as 'Work in Progress', conflicting attitudes towards the *Wake*'s obscurity determined both the defections and the conversions among Joyce's friends. In some readers and critics, *Finnegans Wake*'s difficulty inspires the desire to master its meaning, an impulse that may disguise the wish that *Finnegans Wake* were really tamer and more conventional than it appears to be. But other readers and critics hail *Finnegans Wake*'s experimentalism and are delighted to treat it as an avant-garde work celebrating a revolution in modern language and literature. Such readers are content to accept the *Wake* as impossible to master or fully grasp, and the text's 'unreadability' becomes for them not an obstacle, but a cause for appreciation. In the last decade, this approach has regained some prominence, as *Finnegans Wake* was assimilated to post-modern literature and the theoretical interest it has generated. A brief account of the composition history, and, in the next section, the critical history of *Finnegans Wake*, will reveal the workings of these two tendencies in the way the aims and strategies of *Finnegans Wake* were reconstructed and assessed.

Joyce began writing *Finnegans Wake* early in 1923. His preparatory moves in December of 1922 included sorting out old notes for *Ulysses*, and Joyce claimed that the *unused* notes alone weighed twelve kilos! (*JJ* 545). This suggests, along with the evidence of the Buffalo Notebook VI. A (edited by Thomas E. Connolly as the 'Scribbledehobble' notebook) that *Finnegans Wake* is constructed, among other things, out of the earlier Joycean works, perhaps even with the earlier works serving as rubrics, although there is controversy about the degree of continuity between *Finnegans Wake* and Joyce's previous fictions. At the same time that old materials were being sorted out, Joyce had new ideas in gestation and got new research underway. He became enamoured with the *Book of Kells* at this time, and, as he had done in writing *Ulysses*, he once again used his aunt, Josephine Murray, as a source of domestic Dublin information, asking her to compile a notebook of 'curious types' (*JJ* 545). The first words Joyce wrote of *Finnegans Wake* were penned on March 10, 1923; by June 6 he was prepared to read aloud to friends the first sixty pages of the work. Before the year was over, the outlines for the first eight chapters that comprise Book I of *Finnegans Wake* were sketched out (*JJ* 555). This is the beginning of the *Finnegans Wake* story as Richard Ellmann narrates it in his biography of Joyce, in an account rich in anecdotal material. The labour occupied Joyce almost totally during sixteen years of his life in Paris, years marked by the growing acceptance and fame of *Ulysses*, but plagued also by frequent eye surgeries, increasing blindness, and mounting anxiety over his daughter's illness.

In reconstructing the compositional history of *Finnegans Wake*, one finds a tendency for the anecdotal and the archival evidence to bifurcate into two opposite versions, one stressing the random, *ad hoc*, free associative nature of his note-taking and textual assemblage, the other, Joyce's rational and architectural constructions. Joyce's friends the Nuttings were particular witnesses to his seemingly random methods. Myron Nutting reports greeting Joyce in the clinic during one of his convalescences, only to have Joyce pull out a composition block and write 'carriage sponge' upon it (*JJ* 566). The *non sequitur* is not explained. Joyce tended to learn an unusual word here, exchange an unusual anecdote there. He eavesdropped, like Shem, on conversations, and when he overheard Phyllis Moss tell Nora about her Irish donkey named Aulus Plautus, he put it into the *Wake* (*JJ* 565). He listened with ironic distance to his own conversations with people and reported them as farcical dialogues. To Harriet Shaw Weaver, for example, he reproduced his conversation with his ophthalmologist, Dr Borsch, in the absurd style of a Mutt and Jute dialogue (10 June 1923; *Letters III* 76).

But study of the notebooks and manuscripts themselves leads archival scholar Danis Rose to deduce a considerably more mechanical and logical system of composition from the evidence of the workshop materials (see *James Joyce's 'The Index Manuscript'*, General Introduction). He proposes that the *Finnegans Wake* text corresponds to units of words or phrases in the notebooks, and that these correspond to external sources, such as books and other literary material. But this model creates the image of a highly systematic procedure with a patently architectural result. In contrast to this master-builder model of Joyce's writing, David Hayman argues for considerable variation in Joyce's compostion practice, including the following procedures: '1. straight composition, 2. revise-and-complete, 3. episodic, 4. episodic fusion, 5. piecemeal or mosaic, 6. framing' (*First Draft Version*, p. 12). Questions about the compositional implications of the workshop materials will not be settled until the relationship of texts and notebooks is understood more clearly. But Rose's attempt to use composition practice to give the *Wake* an intertextual foundation, to have the text grow out of a web of literary and other textual sources, supports the venerable scholarly tradition begun by Hugh Kenner in

Dublin's Joyce, and brought to fruition in James Atherton's *The Books at the Wake: A Study of Literary Allusions in James Joyce's 'Finnegans Wake'*. Atherton's valuable study confirmed that for all of its fun and absurdity, *Finnegans Wake* is in some sense a very learned book, a book created out of and referring back to other books.

The creative act that shaped *Finnegans Wake* over such a long period of time was, no doubt, highly heterogeneous in nature. Its polyglossia resulted as much from Joyce's naturally hearing a variety of foreign speech in the several European countries he inhabited, as it did from deliberate research into arcane or exotic languages. His cosmopolitanism was balanced by a growing interest, in later life, for reappropriating Irish culture, tales, legends, and his own family lore, at a time when he was estranged from his native land, and this information (the *Book of Kells*, the legends of Finn MacCool and Dermot and Grania, the hagiography of St Patrick and St Kevin, the Danish occupation of Dublin and the battle of Clontarf, etc.) returned to him in inevitably estranged form. *Finnegans Wake* also reflects not only Joyce's solid, formal, Jesuit education, whose influence is still apparent in the Italian structural sources, orthodox and heretical, that contribute to the philosophical frames of the *Wake* – Dante, Bruno, and Vico, but also the more eclectic and eccentric erudition he accumulated along the way, that lets him dot the *Wake* with references to occult works and popular culture, Marie Corelli's *The Sorrows of Satan*, or the films of D. W. Griffith, for example.[3] He was influenced, I believe, by those of his friends excited by modernist experimentation and iconoclasm, and yet harked back to an older, more canonical tradition of subversive Irish literature, by referring to his countrymen Swift and Sterne, and his controversial contemporary, Oscar Wilde. Finally, Joyce clearly worked out the drafts of the *Wake* with some system and method for keeping track of the enormous body of external data he incorporated, as well as the internal, psychic logic he was developing; yet it seems he was still willing to respond to accidental stimuli and influences to keep the text's spirit fluid and surprising. The variety and range of his procedures and influences appear no less remarkable than the complexity of the text itself.

THE CRITICAL HISTORY OF *FINNEGANS WAKE*

As 'Work in Progress', *Finnegans Wake* first appeared in short extracts in a number of periodicals during the years before its ultimate publication in 1939.[4] As with *Ulysses*, Joyce experienced problems of censorship when English printers refused to set *Anna Livia Plurabelle*. But the incomprehensibility of the language created additional problems of the conflictual sort described earlier: as much as the linguistic and poetic strangeness made the text exciting for its experimentalism, its apparent lack of sense, and its failure to accommodate the reader's desire to understand, made Joyce enemies as well as friends for his new project. Many of those frustrated by the text reacted with hostility and destructive criticism. Pound wrote to Joyce of the Shaun episodes, 'Nothing so far as I make out, nothing short of divine vision or a new cure for the clapp can possibly be worth all the circumambient peripherization' (16 November 1926; *Letters III* 145); Joyce retaliated by making one of the titles of the 'mamafesta' in *Finnegans Wake* '*A New Cure for an Old Clap*' (104.34). Stanislaus Joyce called the effort 'the beginning of softening of the brain' (7 August 1924; *Letters III* 103), and even Harriet Shaw Weaver, his faithful benefactor and adviser, wavered. In print, Joyce's new work was attacked by Sean O'Faolain and Rebecca West. Other writer friends like H. G. Wells complained more privately: 'You have turned your back on common men, on their elementary needs and restricted time and intelligence and you have elaborated. What is the result? Vast riddles' (23 November 1928; *Letters I* 275).

But, paradoxically, the very strangeness of 'Work in Progress' that so infuriated some people, its uncompromising unconventionality, also made it converts who abetted its promotion. The publication of *Tales Told of Shem and Shaun* by the Black Sun Press resulted from a friendship with Harry and Caresse Crosby, connoisseurs of exoticism who considered themselves 'sun-worshippers'. They delighted in the text's exploration of 'otherness', and introduced Joyce to the Egyptian *Book of the Dead*, a text with great influence on the *Wake*. But Joyce's most important convert and new ally during the early days of writing *Finnegans Wake* was Eugene Jolas, who embraced the nascent text as a major document of his 'Revolution of the word', and published portions of it in *transition*. Jolas's manifesto for the 'Revolution of the word' included such directives as 'Time is a tyranny to be abolished', 'The writer expresses. He does not communicate', and 'The plain reader be damned' (*JJ* 588). Jolas armed Joyce with an aesthetic and intellectual rationale that made *Finnegans Wake* congruent with other avant-garde movements of his day.

This defence comes to fruition in the critical volume putatively commissioned and supervised by Joyce himself: *Our Exagmination Round his Factification for Incamination of 'Work in Progress'*, published by Shakespeare and Company in 1929, in which Jolas put Joyce in the company of Léon-Paul Fargue, Michel Leiris, André Breton, Gertrude Stein, and August Stramm (pp. 84–5). The contributors to this volume included, among others, the writer Samuel Beckett and the poet William Carlos Williams, and they were not insensitive to their inverted order as critics offering criticism of a literary work far in advance (a decade, as it happened) of its publication. Joyce playfully manipulated this perverse chronology along with other elements to give the volume a fictive feeling: he gave it a siglum (O) and a Wakean title that made the number of the twelve critics refer to the twelve customers, themselves versions of the twelve apostles, in the *Wake*'s pub, and included humorous, parodic letters ('Dear Mister Germ's Choice, in gutter dispear I am taking my pen toilet you know that . . . I have been reeding one half ter one other the numboars of "transition" in witch are printed the severeall instorments of your "Work in Progress"' (n.p.)). Joyce seemed to want to incorporate criticism of the work, insofar as he could control it in the work of his friends, as a kind of extra-textual chapter to his 'Work in Progress'.

But this humorous, fictive frame notwithstanding, the essays of *Our Exagmination* have a serious task in turning back the attacks on 'Work in Progress' by writers like Rebecca West, Wyndham Lewis, and Sean O'Faolain. The strategy of Joyce's friends was shrewd, for they refused the premises of the nascent *Wake*'s critics, and refused to supply the explications and explanations that appear to be demanded. Instead, they turn the argument around and attack the assumptions of Joyce's critics, O'Faolain's assertion of the immobility of English (p. 80), for example, or West's notion of Western art and literary history as preserved within a mould into which writers must fit themselves. 'She fails to fit Joyce to it', William Carlos Williams writes, 'She calls him, therefore, "strange", not realizing his compulsions which are outside of her sphere' (p. 185). The tendency of the essays as a whole might now legitimately be called 'deconstructive', for they dismantle notions of linguistic and literary structure. Samuel Beckett, for example, provides philosophical and philological antecedents for 'Work in Progress' in his essay on Dante, Bruno, and Vico, but in forms that announce them as inapplicable and inimicable. Beginning with the caveat, 'The danger is in the neatness of identifications' (p. 3), he proceeds to show how each of these figures modified or destroyed the nature of the 'pigeonholes', the traditional categories, conceptual frames, divisions and oppositions, that are conventionally required to make sense of history, theology, and language.

The bifurcated response Joyce's contemporaries gave 'Work in Progress', dismay at its incomprehensibility and delight at its unconventionality, continued after the formal publication of the finished work as *Finnegans Wake*, but with an important difference. The displeased response to the work's difficulty took on a positive and constructive form, and defection and outrage at the *Wake*'s crossword-puzzling were replaced by scholarly devotion and a commitment to find solutions. The next four decades saw the publication of a skeleton key, reader's guides, a short version, literary source studies, censuses, a gazetteer, a concordance, language lexicons, and foreign word lists and specialized studies of specific material in the text.[5] The underlying premise of this wealth of scholarship shaped a specifically positivistic vision of the textual nature of *Finnegans Wake* which assumed that the *Wake* was a semantic plenum whose excessive meaning would require an excess of philological scholarship to unpack. This approach entailed several problematic consequences for the reading and interpretation of the work. First, it implicitly promoted an indefinite deferral of attempts to read, interpret, and understand the work on the grounds that the scholarly tools were inadequate and incomplete. Second, it created a fiction of the reader's inevitable incompetence in the face of *Finnegans Wake*, an incompetence measured by implicitly postulating a hypothetical ideal reader who was a universal polyglot and polymath. The result has been *Finnegans Wake*'s status as an unreadable master-text whose function is the intimidation and humiliation of the common reader.

Eventually, the positivistic scholarship of *Finnegans Wake* articulated the narrative and 'plot' of the work sufficiently clearly to allow critics to begin tackling the more complex issues of its genre, its themes, its structure, and its purpose. In the work of the *Wake* critics of the 1960s, the critical conflict of wanting to master the work and make it understandable without negating its originality or denying its strangeness was dramatized in a series of interpretive studies. Bernard Benstock's *Joyce-Again's Wake*, for example, reads *Finnegans Wake* as a comic epic, making the genre elastic enough to accommodate the *Wake*'s excesses of meaning, and its many pluralities and shifting relativities. Clive Hart's *Structure and Motif in 'Finnegans Wake'* uses the structure of the baroque to argue for a clarity of outline beneath an excess of ornamental detail. The critics of the 1970s and early 1980s were able to relax their domesticating strategies toward the *Wake* even more, with the help of new metaphors for the work's experimental techniques. Patrick McCarthy's *The Riddles of 'Finnegans Wake'* explores the riddle not only as a thematic instance occurring through-out the chapters of the work, but as a philosophical device for exploring confusions of identity and resistances to self-knowledge. Jackson I. Cope, in *Joyce's Cities*, uses modern archaeological discovery both as a historical moment and as a metaphor for an incorruptible and perpetually present history to explain how erudition functions simultaneously in *Finnegans Wake*. David Hayman introduces a useful structural concept in the 'node', a point in the text where one finds 'coherent clusterings of motif-like materials' ('Nodality and the infra-structure of *Finnegans Wake'*, 136); while Fritz Senn uses chiefly verbal and discursive metaphors by speaking of the 'dislocutions' by which the later Joyce texts are destabilized. John Paul Riquelme, in *Teller and Tale*, uses the Möbius strip to represent the unorientability that characterizes our difficulty in reading *Finnegans Wake*. Finally, John Bishop's *Joyce's Book of the Dark* offers the most original metaphor of *Finnegans Wake*'s incomprehensibility by reducing the text, over and over, to all the different perceptions and experiences of the sleeping body.

By the 1970s the influence of French post-structuralism, which had been emerging in the journals *Tel Quel* and *Poétique* in the late sixties, was beginning to make itself felt in such Anglo-American assimilations as my own study, *The Decentered Universe of 'Finnegans Wake'*, and the work of Stephen Heath, Colin MacCabe, and Derek Attridge. However, as the appearances of Jacques Lacan and Jacques Derrida at the International Joyce Symposia of 1979 and 1984 made clear, the genetic relationship between *Finnegans Wake* and post-structuralist theory remains complex and ambiguous, with the *Wake* as both producer and product of French theory, and both stimulant and beneficiary of deconstructive thinking. Post-structuralist criticism of *Finnegans Wake* exhibited shadings from various critical orientations – political, psychoanalytical, feminist, and textual. Its most striking contribution was to rethink the position of *Finnegans Wake* in literary history, a resituation perhaps best characterized by Derek Attridge when he argues in *Peculiar Language* that its dramatization of the potentialities of all language should make *Finnegans Wake* central, not eccentric and peripheral, to literary history itself.

THE STRUCTURE OF *FINNEGANS WAKE*

The problem of how to construe the organization of *Finnegans Wake* as a whole remains vexing and difficult, although we increasingly realize that probably no Linati scheme, like the one that lent the organization of *Ulysses* such a satisfying ᵗnse of order and coherence, was possible for *Finnegans Wake* without falsifying its unconventional literary production. However, Samuel Beckett does produce a scheme for 'Work in Progress' that bears Joyce's imprimatur in the form of privileged information. The 'lovegame of the children', included in Beckett's 1929 essay, was not begun by Joyce until 1930 and not completed until 1932 (*JJ* 796): Beckett could only have had this proleptic information on Joyce's authority. The scheme presents a perfectly viable outline for *Finnegans Wake*:

Part 1 is a mass of past shadow, corresponding therefore to Vico's first human institution, Religion, or to his Theocratic age, or simply to an abstraction – Birth. Part 2 is the lovegame of the children, corresponding to the second institution, Marriage, or to the Heroic age, or to an abstraction – Maturity. Part 3 is passed in sleep, corresponding to the third institution, Burial, or to the Human age, or to an abstraction – Corruption. Part 4 is the day beginning again, and corresponds to Vico's Providence, or to the transition from the Human to the Theocratic, or to an abstraction – Generation.   (pp. 7–8)

But Beckett's qualifications virtually undo the scheme – 'The consciousness that there is a great deal of the unborn infant in the lifeless octogenarian, and a great deal of both in the man at the apogee of his life's curve, removes all the stiff interexclusiveness that is often the danger in neat construction' (p. 8).

The formulation of theme is less useful for *Finnegans Wake* than for other literary texts because the continual dissolution of narrative, image, and language in the *Wake* prevents the sort of positive representations that we construe as thematic material from taking shape. For example, Beckett's identification of Book 1 with Vico's Theocratic age does not take the form of a representation of God's governance – even though the text is dotted with the hundred-letter thunderwords taken to be the voice of God (or his cough, 'husstenhasstencaffincoffintussemtossemdamandamnacosaghcusaghhobixhatouxpeswchbechoscashlcarcarcaract' (414.19–20)) – but of a series of psychological and rhetorical effects in the chapter. God's law is indicated not in stories about God's law, but in the fear of transgression, the fear that a great sin has been committed, that shapes the narratives of investigation and persecution. In Joyce's earliest fictions we find the Theocratic age inscribed in the same way, in the authority-ridden ambience that produces the paranoid perceptions of 'The Sister's and the confessional pressures of *A Portrait of the Artist as a Young Man*. Indeed, the wake motif in the first chapter, the image of the fallen giant ('Fimfim fimfim. With a grand funferall. Fumfum fumfum' (13.15–16)), a Finnegan or Finn or HCE laid out for a wake, can be seen as 'The Sisters' turned inside out, with the occluded perspective – that of the corpse or the stiff – retrieved and represented. This first chapter of the *Wake* is an imaginative recreation of poor paralytic Father Flynn lying in his coffin, listening to his mourners keen ('Macool, Macool, orra whyi deed ye diie?' (6.13)) and speculate about his secret sins, perhaps the suspected syphilis imputed by critics, 'It has been blurtingly bruited by certain wisecrackers . . . that he suffered from a vile disease' (33.15–18). The sensibility that shapes the first book of the *Wake* is governed by dread of the discourse of the other, who may indeed be no more than the self, or the self's language, or the power of language to accuse, intimidate, and destroy. But the fear of what is heard – 'Hush! Caution! Echoland!' (13.05) – engulfs everyone and everything in Book 1, not only the fallen father, hounded by rumours of his sins, but also his family. In chapter 7, Shem, the dreamer's son, or the dreamer himself as young, is vilified by a malicious tongue ('Shem was a sham and a low sham' (170.25)). And the elusive ALP, the dreamer's wife, or the object of his desire, is herself captured, however fleetingly, by the gentler criticisms of the washer-women ('Ah, but she was the queer old skeowsha anyhow' (215.12)). Much of Book 1 of *Finnegans Wake* can be construed as the earlier Joyce fictions, 'The Sister's, 'Clay', 'Grace', and *A Portrait*, for example, turned inside out with the anxieties, fears, and tensions that underlie them foregrounded and magnified.

Beckett's suggestive remark, that Book 1 may explore the similarities between a paralytic ('lifeless'), sleeping, or dying old man and an unborn child (perhaps 'an overgrown babeling' (6.31)), makes even better sense if placed in the larger context of the ending of *Finnegans Wake*, Book IV. This last chapter of *Finnegans Wake* begins at dawn, at breakfast, as a new day beginning; but as the abstraction of 'Generation' announces, it is also about families and books beginning again, as the last page of *Finnegans Wake* might be thought to continue on the first page of *Finnegans Wake*. Book IV creates a curious, paradoxical image of dying not as a going forward into the future, or into nothingness, but rather as a regression into childhood and a return to the womb, a moving backwards in time, a rejuvenation that culminates in the absorption by the parent. This regression is suggested geographically and temporally by a metaphorical reversal of the idiomatic expression 'going west' as a term for dying (and thereby reverses Gabriel's westward journey at the end of 'The Dead'), by depicting dying as 'going east', toward sunrise rather than sunset, toward Egypt in a historical and cultural regression that returns us to the cradle of civilization (and, if we were to see Book IV *continued* in Book I, as a return to prehistory). Joyce's figure for this dying as a reverse of being born ('behold, he returns; renascenent; fincarnate' (596.03–04)) as a return to the womb and beyond, was prefigured in *Ulysses* by Stephen's image of linked navelcords, connecting each generation to the next by the fluid-carrying canal of the umbilicus, 'a commodius vicus of recirculation', all the way back, 'past Eve and Adam's' (3.01–02). Narratively and emotionally, then, we might picture Book IV as 'Telemachus' reversed: as Stephen's pain at separation and alienation from his mother is turned into its opposite, reconciliation figured as return to the womb by way of the metaphors of the navel and the maternal sea. The last chapter of *Finnegans Wake* depicts the son (in the guise of St Kevin floating on a raft through the waterways of Ireland) as reabsorbed into the fluid of the mother (who is both *mere* and *mer*, mother and sea, in Stephen and Mulligan's talk at the start of *Ulysses*), and ends with the mother's reabsorption into the oceanic semen of her father. This generational regression continues at the beginning of Book I, as that father's dying (perhaps many generations removed, now back at the beginning, at the time of Adam and Eve) is now pictured in reverse as an effort to become born. A more contemporary analogue for this concept of Generation as a process in reverse might be the one provided by Stanley Kubrick in the film *2001: A Space Odyssey*, in which the dying of the ancient astronaut is imagined as a regression into his form as a foetus.

Book II, in contrast to the predominantly ear, sound, and speech governed structure of Book I, continues the paranoiac fear of hearing

('Now promisus as at our requisted you will remain ignorant of all what you hear' (238.14)), but couples it with psychological fears grounded in the eye: in the fear of seeing either too little or too much, in the fear of ocular titillation and frustration on the one hand ('though if whilst disrobing to the edge of risk, . . . draw a veil till we next time' (238.16–18)), and, on the other, ocular shock ('I seen his brichashert offensive and his boortholomas vadnhammaggs vise a vise them scharlot runners and how they gave love to him' (352.04–06)). Because the controlling mode here is sight, the rhetorical structures of the chapters of Book II are very different, since discourse that takes the form of speech that is heard must be replaced with generic models that emphasize visual perception. Thus, the children's games of II.1 are structured around the modes of theatre, ballet, pantomime, and gesture language. The homework chapter, II.2, in which the quest for knowledge is represented as a voyeuristic exercise, the act of seeing forbidden sights, is expressed through modes of visually apprehended language: reading the book rather than hearing the lecture. Even in II.4, the reports of the four evangelists, or the four annalists of Irish history, emphasize a literal version of their role as 'witnesses', as they spy on the lovegames of Tristan and Isolde. But II.3, which presents a curious inversion of the eye-dominated chapter of the 'Cyclops' in *Ulysses*, augments its tales of forbidden and aggressive seeing (the shooting of the Russian General because the sight of him offends) with the aural modes of the radio broadcast, the tale, and the dialogue.

The first two children's chapters of Book II, especially, serve an interesting function in relation to some of Joyce's earlier texts, for they fill in gaps in *A Portrait* and *Ulysses* that exist because 'what the children saw', the children's perspective, is elided. There are a number of clues, for example, that would allow us to see the 'lovegame of the children' in II.1 as a filling in of what the little Caffrey twins, Tommy and Jacky, saw and felt on Sandymount strand, while Bloom and the older girls carry on their flirtations oblivious to the children's eyes. Likewise, there are clues that the little boy's quest in the 'Homework' chapter, II.2, to look at the female genitalia, perhaps the mother's in some displaced form, was the unnamed transgression for which little Stephen was threatened with such brutal ocular punishment in the opening pages of *A Portrait* – 'His mother said: – O, Stephen will apologise. Dante said: – O, if not, the eagles will come and pull out his eyes' (*P*8). In the 'Mime' chapter of the *Wake*, the eagles appear to have become the female eye, or its mirror, ready to retaliate for an unflattering voyeurism – 'If you nude her in her prime, make sure you find her complementary or, on your very first occasion . . . she'll prick you where you're proudest with her unsatt speagle eye. Look sharp' (248.03–06).

If Book I is the book of paranoid hearing and Book II the book of desirous looking, Book III might be called the book of deconstructive interpretation. The best analogue for the dissolution of divine authority and pretension in these chapters – the subversion of authoritative and didactic language in the form of sermons, epistles, commandments, benedictions and parables (the parable of the 'Ondt and the Gracehoper', discussed earlier, is here used as a sermon against profligacy) – can be found in Bloom's Messianic fantasies, his speeches announcing the New Bloomusalem and their disintegration amid the heckling of the rabble in 'Circe'. An even earlier analogue might be found in the *Dubliners* story 'Grace', with its quincunx configuration of evangelical figures around the bed of the fallen man, and their reappearance in the church retreat, evoking precisely questions of authoritative language, the Pope's *ex cathedra* pronouncements, powerful sermons and preachings, that the story itself subverts by drawing attention to its potential for error and hypocrisy. The *Wake* language of Book III, likewise, continually disintegrates into its opposite, as commandments reveal their libidinal motivations, and Shaun's discourse lapses into the speech of father and mother, as though his corruption were not only moral but also discursive and genetic. The function of Christology in the chapter appears to be the ironic dismantling of theocracy, as the human residue of Christ is exposed as the flawed, the prosaic, the trivial, in a regression to Vico's Human age. The last chapter of Book III, the witnessed lovemaking in the marriage bed of the Earwickers, represents the disintegration of the foundation of the symbolic order, the laws that govern sexuality and marriage in the form of psychological taboos as well as civil laws (see the absurd Roman domestic trial in the chapter), as the son disintegrates back into his genesis in the coitus of the parents. The second half of *Finnegans Wake* represents the undoing, by reversal, of the Oedipus complex: a reversal of the experience responsible not only for personal and social maturation, but also for the institution of law, patriarchy, and the symbolic order. This process of corruption as regression is then continued on an ontological level in the absorption into the mother's body, the return to the womb, that I previously described as the narrative movement of Book IV.

Now that so much of the scholarly apparatus for reading *Finnegans Wake* is in place, an exciting era in *Wake* scholarship and criticism is beginning. International co-operation among *Wake* scholars offers at least the potential for a wedding of philological information, archival research, and a sophisticated theoretical sense of the nature of textuality. The greater familiarity with *Finnegans Wake* of a generation of post-modern readers will yield, perhaps, a more comfortable relationship with a text whose modes of expression depart more drastically than usual from the conventions of realism and mimesis. And a more thorough assimilation of Freudian psychoanalytic premises may have prepared us better to confront an anarchic, unflattering, and alienating portrait of our dreaming selves, limned in the unfamiliar palette and the deranging perspectives of modern art. Whether readers choose to feel rebuffed and humiliated by this difficult text, or excited by its strangeness and stretched by its challenges, *Finnegans Wake* will measure their capacity for intellectual and imaginative adventure.

NOTES

1 Fortunately, there are several excellent guides available, if the reader wants to find out what *Finnegans Wake* is 'about' – how its narrative progresses (or regresses), how its themes exfoliate, how its characters proliferate, and how its language produces multiple meanings. I especially recommend Patrick McCarthy's essay on 'The structures and meanings of *Finnegans Wake*' in Bowen and Carens, *A Companion to Joyce Studies*.

2 Ellmann writes of Joyce's preparations for the writing of *Finnegans Wake*, 'He was interested also in variation and sameness in space, in the cubist method of establishing different relations among aspects of a single thing, and he would ask Beckett to do some research for him in the possible permutations of an object' (*JJ* 551).

3 The title of *Finnegans Wake* is taken from a popular song, the ballad of Tim Finnegan, the hod carrier with 'a tipplin' way', who falls from a ladder while drunk:

> One morning Tim was rather full,
>   His head felt heavy which made him shake,
> He fell from the ladder and broke his skull,
>   So they carried him home his corpse to wake.

A fight breaks out during the wake – ''Twas woman to woman and man to man' – and in the process a noggin of whiskey is thrown and strikes the bier, scattering over the corpse and waking him from the dead:

> Bedad he revives, see how he rises,
>   And Timothy rising from the bed,
> Says, 'Whirl your liquor round like blazes,
>   Thanam o'n dhoul, do ye think I'm dead?'   (*JJ* 543n)

4 See Jean-Michel Rabaté's summary of the *Wake*'s early publishing history in ch. 4 above (p. 89).

5 Clive Hart and Fritz Senn printed such notes and essays in *The Wake Newslitter* and *The Wake Digest*. For a list of other scholarly tools for explicating *Finnegans Wake* see 'Further reading' (pp. 291–2 below). Most of the material from earlier sources has been collected and collated in Roland McHugh's highly practical and user-friendly *Annotations to 'Finnegans Wake'*.

WORKS CITED

Atherton, James. *The Books at the Wake: A Study of Literary Allusions in James Joyce's 'Finnegans Wake'*. Rev. edn., New York: Paul P. Appel, 1974

Attridge, Derek. *Peculiar Language: Literature as Difference from the Renaissance to James Joyce*. Ithaca: Cornell University Press, 1988

Attridge, Derek, and Daniel Ferrer, eds. *Post-structuralist Joyce: Essays from the French*. Cambridge: Cambridge University Press, 1984

Beckett, Samuel, *et al. Our Exagmination Round His Factification for Incamination of Work in Progress* (1929). London, Faber, 1972

Benstock, Bernard. *Joyce-Again's Wake: An Analysis of 'Finnegans Wake'*. Seattle: University of Washington Press, 1965

Bishop, John. *Joyce's Book of the Dark: 'Finnegans Wake'*. Madison: University of Wisconsin Press, 1986

Bowen, Zack, and James F. Carens. *A Companion to Joyce Studies*. Westport, Connecticut: Greenwood Press, 1984

Connolly, Thomas E. *James Joyce's Scribbledehobble: The Ur-Workbook for 'Finnegans Wake'*. Evanston: Northwestern University Press, 1961

Cope, Jackson I. *Joyce's Cities: Archeologies of the Soul*. Baltimore: Johns Hopkins University Press, 1981

Hart, Clive. *Structure and Motif in 'Finnegans Wake'*. London: Faber, 1962

Hart, Clive, and Fritz Senn, eds. *A Wake Digest*. Sydney: Sydney University Press, 1968

Hayman, David. 'Nodality and the infra-structure of *Finnegans Wake*'. *JJQ* 16 (1979), 135–49

Hayman, David, ed. *A First-Draft Version of 'Finnegans Wake'*. Austin: University of Texas Press, 1963

Heath, Stephen. 'Ambiviolences: notes for reading Joyce'. In Attridge and Ferrer, *Post-structuralist Joyce*, 31–68

Kenner, Hugh. *Dublin's Joyce* (1955). Reprinted New York: Columbia University Press, 1987

MacCabe, Colin. *James Joyce and the Revolution of the Word*. London: Macmillan, 1978

McCarthy, Patrick A. *The Riddles of 'Finnegans Wake'*. Rutherford: Fairleigh Dickinson University Press, 1980

McHugh, Roland. *Annotations to 'Finnegans Wake'*. Baltimore: Johns Hopkins University Press, 1980

Norris, Margot. *The Decentered Universe of 'Finnegans Wake': A Structuralist Analysis*. Baltimore: Johns Hopkins University Press, 1976

Riquelme, John Paul. *Teller and Tale in Joyce's Fiction: Oscillating Perspectives*. Baltimore: Johns Hopkins University Press, 1983

Rose, Danis, ed. *James Joyce's 'The Index Manuscript': 'Finnegans Wake' Holograph Workbook VI.B.46*. Colchester: A Wake Newslitter Press, 1978

Rose, Danis, and John O'Hanlon. *Understanding 'Finnegans Wake': A Guide to the Narrative of James Joyce's Masterpiece*. New York: Garland Publishing, 1982

Senn, Fritz. *Joyce's Dislocutions: Essays on Reading as Translation*. Ed. John Paul Riquelme. Baltimore: Johns Hopkins University Press, 1984

A Wake Newslitter. Ed. Clive Hart and Fritz Senn. Essex: University of Essex, 1962–84

8 Joyce's shorter works

At first glance, Joyce's shorter works – his poems and epiphanies, *Giacomo Joyce*, and *Exiles* – seem to bear only the most tenuous relationship to the books for which Joyce has become famous. It is only by an exercise of the imagination that the epiphanies and *Giacomo Joyce* can even be called 'works'; Joyce published neither in its original form, choosing instead to loot them for the more ambitious undertakings that followed, and neither received the painstaking polish that Joyce lavished on his more ambitious productions. Only forty of at least seventy-one epiphanies are extant and their relationship to one another had to be reconstructed from manuscript evidence; the sketches that comprise *Giacomo Joyce* were similarly composed, arranged, and abandoned, but not destroyed. *Chamber Music*, although published in 1907, was orphaned when Joyce delegated the final arrangement of the poems to his brother Stanislaus. *Pomes Penyeach*, as the title suggests, is a modest offering of twelve and a tilly poetic 'fruits'. Only *Exiles* continued to hold Joyce's interest as an autonomous composition not destined for immediate verbal recycling.

The status of the shorter works as successful, original, or even finished compositions has always been in question; even in more subjective terms, however, they seem to offer few of the rewards of their longer and better known counterparts. First, and most damagingly, they are humourless; what humour may be discerned in them is bitter or ironic, inspired by pained defiance (as in 'Gas from a Burner') or jaded cynicism ('In my time the dunghill was so high' – *E* 43). Secondly, they are spare, denuded of the variable styles and elaborate contexts that make *Ulysses* and *Finnegans Wake* seem inexhaustible. Finally, they are easily dismissed as immediately derivative of both Joyce's experiences and his reading.

Although the brevity and earnestness of Joyce's minor pieces put them in opposition to the major ones, the relationship between the shorter and longer productions is much closer when viewed in structural and thematic terms. *Chamber Music*, the *Epiphanies*, and *Giacomo Joyce* are all composed of isolated, artistically rendered moments arranged to form a loose progression; the three acts of *Exiles* loosely divide thirteen unmarked scenes, each an intimate dialogue between two characters, stitched together by the conventions – both social and theatrical – of entrances and exits. The strategy of producing a longer and more complicated text by stringing together a series of formally self-contained units is essential not only to the design of *Dubliners*, where the structural building blocks are short stories, but also to the increasingly complex episodic structures of *A Portrait*, *Ulysses* and *Finnegans Wake*. In short, the minor works make it much more apparent that Joyce's technique – even in the longer texts – is in large part an imagist one, adapted from poetry to narrative and massively elaborated in the process.

If the shorter texts outline the basic structure of all Joyce's works, they also provide the simplest statement of Joyce's most characteristic themes, which are treated polyphonically in his longer compositions: themes of loss, betrayal, and the interplay of psychological and social experience. Strikingly, all of the shorter works record the experience of some loss: the *Epiphanies* seem to have been arranged to depict the loss of innocence; *Chamber Music* plays out the loss of youthful love, a theme picked up and translated into predominantly visual terms in *Giacomo Joyce*. Many of the poems in *Pomes Penyeach* echo the theme of lost youth, but the collection also includes more anguished treatments of different kinds of loss: in 'Tilly', a figurative loss of limb makes the dead speak; it is the illusion of beauty that is lost in 'A Memory of the Players in a Mirror at Midnight'. The list can be expanded to include loss of sight in 'Bahnhofstrasse', loss of life in 'She Weeps over Rahoon', loss of faith in 'Nightpiece', and loss of peace and security in the nightmarish 'I Hear an Army'; in the words of another 'pome', *'Tutto è sciolto'* (all is lost). *Exiles* is the most complicated of Joyce's briefer treatments of attrition, since it probes the loss of spontaneity in life and love, which the action of the play suggests is irreparable.

A less apparent symmetry between the shorter and longer works is in the careful balancing of subjective and objective experience. As Scholes and Kain point out, Joyce designed not one but two kinds of epiphanies – one narrative, one dramatic – and then interwove them into a single sequence.[1] The careful counterpointing of opposite perspectives – those of dream and observation – constitutes Joyce's earliest attempt to compensate for the distortion of 'parallax', the term for the inadequacy of a single vantage point that sparks Bloom's curiosity in *Ulysses*. The main problem with Joyce's characterization of both kinds of experience in the epiphanies is its *naïveté*: the imagination is always empowering, and outer experience invariably deflating. The narrative epiphanies celebrate the power of the author's mind; the dramatic epiphanies reduce the stature of those around him (*WD* 4). The epiphanies, like the manuscript novel that succeeded and partly incorporated them, present the nascent artist as an inevitable Hero.

As heroism is increasingly displaced by humour in Joyce's maturer works, his treatment of the relationship between fantasy and drama, desire and reality, also grows more complex.[2] *Giacomo Joyce* and *Exiles*, as narrative and dramatic treatments of problems that would later inform *Ulysses*, at first seem to constitute a two-phase attempt to represent the pain of betrayal from an internal and external point of view, respectively: that of the artist's mind and that of a more detached spectator. *Giacomo Joyce*, from such a perspective, resembles the narrative epiphanies in its depiction of the sensitive artist as dreamer, whereas *Exiles*, like the dramatic epiphanies, presents the artist exposing the imprecision and lack of integrity of those around him.[3]

The attempt to define *Giacomo Joyce* and *Exiles* in terms of the similarities and differences between the two kinds of epiphanies works only up to a point, however, since by the end of each text the oppositions between dream and drama, wish-fulfilment and satire, subject and object have begun to break down. *Giacomo Joyce* cannot sustain its status as pure fantasy; outer circumstances begin to impinge on its enclosed world when the object of Giacomo's gaze enigmatically announces her preference for a lesser man – '"Because otherwise I could not see you" . . . *Non hunc sed Barabbam!*' – and the speaker's imaginative superiority lapses into self-criticism: 'It will never be. You know that well. What then? Write it, damn you, write it! What else are you good for?' (*GJ* 16).

Just as the subjective cast of *Giacomo Joyce* dissipates in the strong light of fact, the objective, even clinical mood of *Exiles* yields to self-pity and hallucination. The upsurge of irrational forces begins when

Richard Rowan suddenly sees the hypocrisy of his high-toned opposition to any union between his friend and the mother of his child. He recognizes and confesses the hidden desire that prompted him to watch and passively abet their growing mutual attraction, as the play relentlessly pursues the treachery buried in the accusation of betrayal:

[I]n the very core of my ignoble heart I longed to be betrayed by you and by her – in the dark, in the night – secretly, meanly, craftily. By you, my best friend, and by her. I longed for that passionately and ignobly, to be dishonoured for ever in love and in lust, to be... . . . To be for ever a shameful creature and to build up my soul again out of the ruins of its shame.

(E 70)

Richard admits that his furtive desire to be betrayed was motivated, paradoxically, by pride, since Bertha has consistently used her faithfulness to shame him: 'She has spoken always of her innocence, as I have spoken always of my guilt, humbling me' (E 70). And as Richard is driven towards truth, he is also propelled into a nightmarish world of imagination, the world of Giacomo Joyce. Returning from his hour on the strand he tells Beatrice:

There are demons . . . out there. I heard them jabbering since dawn . . . The isle is full of voices. Yours also. Otherwise I could not see you, it said. And her voice. But, I assure you, they are all demons. I made the sign of the cross upside down and that silenced them.   (E 98)

Once we see that Giacomo Joyce and Exiles not only represent an opposition between inner and outer reality but also present complementary accounts of how that opposition breaks down, it is only a short step to an appreciation of how the two dovetail into the 'Circe' episode of Ulysses, which is both drama and fantasy, an extravagant celebration of the actor/viewer's superhuman dreams and subhuman instincts, his generous pride and shameful prejudices, and finally into Finnegans Wake.

The shorter works bear a marked resemblance to their longer counterparts in basic theme and structure, but they also reflect Joyce's characteristic readiness to appropriate the styles and voices of other writers. Whereas in his most famous works this appropriative tendency takes the form of parody or emerges through correspondences, in the slighter pieces it has been dismissed as simply derivative, as evidence of the influence exercised upon Joyce by Christian theology, Yeats, the Elizabethans, or Ibsen. All writing, of course, is derivative; the question that presses is whether a work represents a productive or reiterative reading of its sources: does it replicate the most familiar features of its parent texts, or does it reshape our awareness of those texts?

Not only are the shorter works derived (in part) from identifiable sources, but they, in turn, serve as sources themselves; Joyce reinterprets – and re-uses – them as readily as he uses any other material. And just as the dependence of Joyce's shorter works on the writings of his predecessors can easily obscure the extent to which our understanding of those other writings may change in reference to his, the dependence of Joyce's longer experiments on the shorter ones which frequently contribute to them raises a comparable problem of relation: how can we account for the disjunction between what the shorter works lack (humour, complexity, and a self-consciousness that is acutely philosophical rather than painfully self-dramatizing) and what they share with Joyce's other writings (seriatim structure, concern with betrayal, hunger for experience, and the appropriation of other writers' voices)? One solution is to sever any relationship between the slighter works and their famous siblings by asserting that the shorter works, unlike the longer ones, are unsuccessful on their own terms. Such a contention may be true, but its truth is to some extent irrelevant, since it is not purely on their own terms that any of these documents lay claim to our attention; their value stems largely from their incestuous relationship to other writing, their liminal status as threshold productions that mark the interstices between more apparently autonomous experiments. Whatever Joyce's shorter works have to offer they will not offer in isolation; on the other hand, if they are absorbed too completely into the rest of Joyce's writing we lose a vantage point for reinterpreting his other works. Like Joyce's longer texts, the shorter pieces simultaneously depend upon a larger written tradition and strain to break free of that tradition by exceeding it.

The shorter works are most fruitfully approached not only as half-realized versions of Joyce's more ambitious productions, but also as stilled frames in an ongoing process of reading and writing, a process that he parodied, practised and refined throughout a lifetime of experimentation with language. Like the manuscripts, the shorter works provide information indispensable for reconstructing the 'continuous manuscript' of Joyce's writing career,[4] an achievement that is both fluid and discontinuous, fragmented and whole. Unlike the manuscripts, though, which give insight into the arrangement of a published text by tracing the genesis of that arrangement and the false starts that help to define the finished shape, the shorter works preserve contextual as well as textual trials and errors: we see Joyce testing, not only phrases, but variant interpretations of problems like fidelity, combining the perspectives of different authors to create complex backdrops for his own treatments.

The most influential critical treatments of the shorter works show how easy it is to upset the fragile balance between a text's individuality and its applicability to larger contexts. In the case of the *Epiphanies*, the prose bits to which Joyce gave that name are too often digested into the general concept of 'epiphany'. In contrast, the critical focus on the poems, *Giacomo Joyce*, and *Exiles* has tended to be too narrowly biographical or literary. Whether the perspective is telescopic or microscopic, the attitude inclusive or dismissive, what is lost is the depth and flexibility that come from a less consistent, and more Joycean, sense of the continuity and discontinuity of relation.

EPIPHANIES

The main difficulty presented by the *Epiphanies* lies in the broad application of the word itself, which Joyce used not only to designate the slivers of life that he punctiliously preserved in prose and dialogue from 1900–1903, but also as a metaphor, drawn from classical and Christian myth, for the revelation of the spiritual in the actual. In Greek mythology, *epiphany* referred to the unexpected manifestation of the divine, and in Greek drama it was used to describe the sudden appearance of a god on stage. Christianity appropriated the term for liturgical purposes to commemorate the day that the Magi brought gifts to the Christ child (which represents the first manifestation of divinity to foreign travellers).

In the manuscript of *Stephen Hero*, where the term was first discovered, Joyce uses 'epiphany' both to describe his records of moments that blend triviality with significance and to designate the revelatory climax of aesthetic apprehension. He introduces the more local of the two meanings by describing his reaction to a fragment of overheard conversation:

A young lady was standing on the steps of one of those brown brick houses which seem the very incarnation of Irish paralysis. A young gentleman was leaning on the rusty railings of the area. Stephen as he passed on his quest heard the following fragment of colloquy out of which he received an impression keen enough to afflict his sensitiveness very severely.

The Young Lady – (drawling discreetly)...O, yes...I was...at the... cha...pel...

The Young Gentleman – (inaudibly)...I...(again inaudibly)...I...

The Young Lady – (softly)...O...but you're...ve...ry...wick...ed...

This triviality made him think of collecting many such moments together in a book of epiphanies. By an epiphany he meant a sudden spiritual manifestation, whether in the vulgarity of speech or of gesture or in a memorable phase of the mind itself. He believed that it was for the man of letters to record these epiphanies with extreme care, seeing that they themselves are the most delicate and evanescent of moments. (SH 210–11)

The collection of epiphanies receives further mention in *Ulysses*, where Stephen thinks to himself, 'Remember your epiphanies written on green oval leaves, deeply deep, copies to be sent if you died to all the great libraries of the world, including Alexandria? Someone was to read them there after a few thousand years, a mahamanvantara' (U 3.141–4). Several of Joyce's own epiphanies turned up among his papers and those of his brother Stanislaus, and it is Scholes and Kain's arrangement of these into a sequence based on manuscript evidence that constitutes what we now refer to as the *Epiphanies*.[5]

In *Stephen Hero*, after the narrator relates an epiphany and reveals Stephen's determination to collect them, Stephen goes on to explain the idea of epiphany in theoretical terms to Cranly. Epiphany, he argues, is the moment when the spiritual eye is able 'to adjust its vision to an exact focus' so as to apprehend 'the third, the supreme quality of beauty' in an object, its 'soul' or 'whatness', which the mind synthesizes from an appreciation of the first two qualities of beauty in the object, its integrity and symmetry:

After the analysis which discovers the second quality the mind makes the only logically possible synthesis and discovers the third quality. This is the moment which I call epiphany. First we recognise that the object is *one* integral thing, then we recognise that it is an organised composite structure, a *thing* in fact: finally, when the relation of the parts is exquisite, when the parts are adjusted to the special point, we recognise that it is *that* thing which it is. Its soul, its whatness, leaps to us from the vestment of its appearance. The soul of the commonest object, the structure of which is so adjusted, seems to us radiant. The object achieves its epiphany.   (SH 213)

When Joyce reworked this portion of Stephen's aesthetic theories for *Portrait* (*P* 212–13), he expunged any reference to epiphany, instead describing the moment of aesthetic apprehension as an experience of stasis.[6] The emphasis of Stephen's aesthetic theory is significantly different in *Portrait*; the goal of aesthetic apprehension is no longer presented as a semi-religious celebration of the spirit's ability to manifest itself through matter, but as a rare balance of spirit and matter, imagination and observation, an evenness of apprehension illustrated by the commingling of light and darkness in Shelley's image of a 'fading coal' (*P* 213).[7]

In philosophical and religious terms, epiphany represents an idealistic, even platonic belief in the superiority of the spirit, its ability to transcend materiality.[8] However, as Joyce's brother Stanislaus suggests, Joyce also used epiphany to signify a psychological revelation of repressed or subconscious truth through slips or errors. In his papers, arranged and edited by Richard Ellmann under the title *My Brother's Keeper*, Stanislaus writes:

> Another experimental form which [Joyce's] literary urge took . . . consisted in the noting of what he called 'epiphanies'; – manifestations or revelations. Jim always had a contempt for secrecy, and these notes were in the beginning ironical observations of slips, and little errors and gestures – mere straws in the wind – by which people betrayed the very things they were most careful to conceal . . . The revelation and importance of the subconscious had caught his interest.[9]

According to Stanislaus's account, the epiphanies began as satiric attempts to expose the pretensions of others, and they grew to include brief realizations of unconscious knowledge as it is unexpectedly unlocked by language or dream.

As Joyce matured, he lost the desire to exalt either spirituality or his own authorial privilege, and he increasingly valued more balanced representations of individual with shared realities. The *Epiphanies* fail to preserve such a balance; although they frequently invite us to entertain two opposed perspectives through puns or dialogue, one is always clearly preferred. In epiphany 32, for example, when Joyce juxtaposes the human race with a horse race, thereby foreshadowing the running puns of *Ulysses*, the human race clearly suffers by the comparison: '[H]uman creatures are swarming in the enclosure, moving backwards and forwards through the thick ooze'. In contrast to the vile human race is the distant, idealized horse race: 'A beautiful brown horse, with a yellow rider upon him, flashes far away in the sunlight'.

Criticism has tended to favour the concept of epiphany over the prose sketches that bear the same name. Lacking context themselves, the epiphanies have seemed less attractive in their denuded manuscript state than when decked out in the heavy robes of myth, religion, and aesthetics.[10] However, most critics have agreed that the importance of the manuscript epiphanies may be traced to a few of their most marked features: the absence of authorial commentary that also characterizes Joyce's later work; the division of the epiphanies into two types; their structure, a sequential ordering of fragments which has the effect of submerging 'plot'; the interplay of conscious and subconscious awareness; and their reappearance in the richer contexts of Joyce's subsequent works.[11]

The epiphanies evoke the desire and fear of discovery, but their exposures are all designed to prove the power and authority of the self over the external world. *Chamber Music*, as we shall see, transposes the theme of disclosure into a new key, taking it out of the psychological and mythic realm and into a private chamber, where attitudes of eroticism and morbidity are paramount.

THE POETRY

The nature of Joyce's poetic accomplishment may be momentarily pinned down only by a pointed definition of what exactly is meant by 'poetry' in the context of his career. If by poetry we mean a composition in verse that manages, paradoxically, to combine richness of applicability with verbal compactness, bridging public and private experience; if we are talking about poems on the order of Yeats's 'The Tower' or 'Among School Children', Joyce wrote no such poetry, although it could be argued that he realized comparably 'poetic' aims in prose. However, Joyce did not restrict himself to prose; his earliest efforts were primarily in verse, and by the end of his career he had written over one hundred poems, parodies, and poetic fragments. What distinguishes Joyce's poetry from that of someone like Yeats is that Joyce never used verse as a comprehensive form; he seldom strives to integrate different levels of meaning in a single metrical stroke. Instead, Joyce uses conventional poetic forms and meters as a way of *simplifying* emotional experience, whether in the form of a musical lyric, a satirical limerick, or an angry broadside. Versification allowed him to pare away complexity in favour of a simpler emotional and verbal expressiveness.

It is appropriate for a writer as contradictory as Joyce that his greatest poetry never assumes poetic form. Nevertheless, Joyce did write – and publish – two collections of verse, *Chamber Music* (1907) and *Pomes Penyeach* (1927), in addition to two earlier collections that he destroyed, and of which only fragments remain, *Moods* and *Shine and Dark*. In addition, he wrote numerous occasional poems, which tend to be comic or satirical – two broadsides, several limericks, regular quatrain poems, and quite a few poems designed to be sung to music.[12] His verses represent a wide variety of moods, from anguished nihilism or stung pride to lyrical wooing, but the range of emotion is not matched by a comparable flexibility in poetic technique. Joyce's verses are deliberately constructed, like everything he wrote, and they do manage to create some unusual local effects, many of which gather around Joyce's use of one particular word to magnetize the meaning of an entire poem, but his poems lack formal complexity or variation. For this reason, several critics have suggested that Joyce's poems are, more accurately, songs.

What differentiates Joyce's poetry most markedly from that of Yeats, and from his own most successful prose, is its paucity of voices and its propensity towards enclosure. *Chamber Music* might not be an inappropriate title for the majority of Joyce's metrical compositions; even the volume that bears that title is fairly representative of what Joyce achieved – and failed to achieve – in verse.[13] First of all, there is only one voice in *Chamber Music*, that of an alternately idealistic and sensual young lover. That voice serenades a conventionally golden-haired young woman who first appears playing the piano in her chamber (II). The burden of the lover's song is his desire to enter that chamber, which is a room, her heart, and metaphorically, of course, her womb. At first, the enclosed spaces that he longs to enter are depicted as warm and inviting, but after the poem that Joyce identified as the 'climax' of the sequence (XIV), those spaces cool and grow shadowy, increasingly representing the darker allure of sleep, and, ultimately, death.

At the outset of the sequence, the lover's desire for his beloved to 'unclose' herself to his love emerges by means of the analogies he sets up between his love songs and the music of the night wind, and between his beloved's hidden fire and the dawn. In the first poem, an anthropomorphized Love is wandering (like Yeats's 'Wandering Aengus') by the music along the river; in the next poem, it is the young woman's thoughts, eyes and hands 'That wander as they list', 'list' functioning both as an archaic word meaning 'inclination' and as a contraction of 'listen'. (The woman's frequent attitude of 'bending' or 'leaning' seems to figure a quite literal inclination, in this case her inclination to listen to the lover's songs and what they portend.) In poem III, the lover asks her if she has heard the natural and celestial music of 'the night wind and the sighs / Of harps playing unto Love to unclose / The pale gates of sunrise'. The next poem makes it clear that his music is designed to replicate the music of wind and harps, encouraging her to unclose *her* gate, at which he is singing. In V the gate is replaced by a window, which he urges her to lean through; in VI he openly expresses his desire to be 'in that sweet bosom', which, by the structural similarities that link the two stanzas, is also 'that heart' at which he softly 'knock[s]'. Images of enclosure grow brighter and less confining in successive poems: in VII, 'the sky's a pale blue cup'; in VIII, the 'chamber' is a sunny woodland; and in X it is a hollow. In poem XI, the dominant images of enclosure have been reduced in size and domesticated; the constraint of virginity is here represented by the snood that binds her hair and the stays that enclose her 'girlish bosom'. Picking up on the last word of XI, 'maidenhood', XII launches an argument against all 'hooded' or cautious counsel, particularly that of the hooded moon and the hooded Capuchin. Finally, in XIII, attention shifts back to the woman's chamber as the lover urges the 'Wind of spices whose song is ever / Epithalamium' to 'come into her little garden / And sing at her window' (compare Yeats, 'The Cap and Bells').

By poems XIV and XV, Love has indeed unclosed the gates of pale sunrise, thereby unlocking the potential for a son to rise; these dawn poems are also celebrations of consummated love. The speaker's love has shifted along the fault of rhyme to become a dove, image of the holy spirit, whom he bids, like the sun, to 'arise'. Although 'Eastward the gradual dawn prevails / Where softly-burning fires appear' (XV), the main impulse of the poems that follow XV is to escape the heat of the sun, whether into the 'cool and pleasant valley' of XVI (contrast the hollow of X), the 'deep cool shadow' of the dark pine-wood of XX (contrast the green and sunny wood of VIII), the prison of interwoven arms in XXII (contrast XI), the mossy nest of her heart (XXIII; contrast VI), the wasted sun and cloud-wrapped vales of XXV (compare VII), or the grave where 'all love shall sleep' (XXVIII). In XIII, the lover invited 'The wind of spices' into his beloved's garden to sing; in sharp contrast, XXIX describes 'Desolate winds that assail with cries / The shadowy garden where love is'. As the lover once knocked at the heart of his beloved, a 'rogue in red and yellow dress' is now knocking at a leaving tree (XXXIII) in mocking echo of springtime desire, and in XXXIV, the voice of the winter is at the door, crying to the Macbeth-like dreamer, 'Sleep no more'. This final poem in the sequence proper (Joyce wrote to G. Molyneux Palmer that XXXV and XXXVI are tailpieces, *Letters I* 67) is the only one in which voices begin to proliferate, as the voice within the lover's heart clashes with the voice of the winter outside his chamber, one crying 'Sleep now', the other forbidding further sleep. Appropriately, the music of the water has been displaced by 'noise' in XXXV, and choiring by a monotone. XXXVI is a literal image of nightmare that anticipates Joyce's punning treatment of nightmare in *Ulysses* and in *FW* 583.8–9: horses (mares?) come out of the sea – *mer* – at night, ridden by disdainful charioteers in black armour. The Love of the first poem has been supplanted by war, 'An army charging upon the land'; the idealized figure of garlanded peace ('Dark leaves on his hair') replaced with a multitude of embattled, shouting phantoms shaking in triumph their long, green hair.

The most influential treatments of *Chamber Music* have all arranged themselves around the linchpin of the title. William York Tindall reflects back on *Chamber Music* from the perspective of *Ulysses*, where Bloom thinks of chamber music as the music Molly makes when she urinates in a chamberpot (*U* 11.979–84). He connects this with the varying stories about how the title was chosen told by Herbert Gorman and Oliver St John Gogarty, both of which involve chamberpots as well, concluding with a strained interpretation of poems VII and XXVI as representations of micturition.[14] Tindall identified urination as one among many dimensions of the title's meaning, suggesting that it was also a sequence about wantonness – Elizabethan 'chambering'.

Chamber Music sparsely records a seduction and its chilly aftermath, but the main implication of its title is that it explores the musical possibilities of a small enclosed space. Joyce emphasized the musical nature of *Chamber Music* not only through the title but also by setting one of the poems to music himself (XI), and by encouraging Geoffrey Molyneux Palmer to set others: 'I hope you may set all of *Chamber*

Music in time. This was indeed partly my idea in writing it. The book is in fact a suite of songs and if I were a musician I suppose I should have set them to music myself' (*Letters I* 67). Stress on the music of the poems has recently been offset by Archie K. Loss's attention to its visual spaces – chamber and wood – in the context of Symbolist art, and by Chester Anderson's interest in its rhythmical gestures and rhetorical figures.[15] Such competing perspectives have made it easier to appreciate the economy with which the musical and spatial dimensions of the poems have been integrated. Technically, the stability and smallness of the poems' structure, together with the fact that they are all sung by the same voice, allow Joyce to explore, not the landscapes of Dublin, but a miniaturized interior chamber, which almost imperceptibly transforms itself into an image of the grave ('We were grave lovers', xxx). The external landscapes of the poem are all psychological and sexualized extensions of other inner chambers, a technique that Joyce learned from Yeats's *The Wind Among the Reeds*.

Poetry seems to have remained a slight vessel for Joyce, a vehicle for expressing emotions of isolation, or for preserving isolated moments. As the title suggests, *Pomes Penyeach* are not worth much individually; they are inexpensive offerings of private moments, one protective and delicate ('A Flower Given to my Daughter'), another arming the speaker against nostalgia for the simplicity and trust of childhood ('Simples'), but most agonized or despairing. As Herbert Howarth has suggested, Joyce's poems are the productions of a Henry Flower[16] (although 'A Memory of the Players in a Mirror at Midnight' could have been written by Virag); they are musical, nostalgic, and markedly senti-mental – Siren songs, such as the ones Bloom listens to and ultimately rejects in the 'Sirens' episode of *Ulysses*. Joyce betrays an awareness of the danger of such songs in 'Simples', where the speaker prays for an Odyssean sailor's 'waxen ear / To shield me from her childish croon'; the deficiency of his poems is their power to evoke a 'Flood' of nostalgia. Joyce never underestimated the power of simple song to seduce the sense and shipwreck the desire for life, which explains why, perhaps, a song from *Pomes Penyeach*, 'Nightpiece', was once the core of the 'Tristan and Isolde' episode of *Finnegans Wake*.[17] An early draft of the episode began as ironic marginalia that surrounds and eventually subsumes its sentimental center: the romantic, despairing poem of youth.

GIACOMO JOYCE

Like *Chamber Music, Giacomo Joyce* is a seduction piece. But if the 'Sirens' episode provides a context against which the power and danger of *Chamber Music* can be read, *Giacomo Joyce* is best read against 'Nausicaa', which takes painting rather than music as its technic. And if the danger of the music that seduces is a function of its univocality and its simplicity, *Giacomo Joyce* – against the background of 'Nausicaa' – shows that the danger of voyeurism is comparable to the seductive lure of the lyric. As *Chamber Music* lacks more than one voice, *Giacomo Joyce* lacks a view from more than one perspective: it is an example of what Joyce would later see as the distortion that results from failing to account for parallax.

Giacomo Joyce is a series of prose sketches formally akin to the narrative epiphanies. A fair-copy manuscript of sixteen pages transcribed onto eight oversized sheets of heavy paper, most probably in the summer of 1914, it is the only one of Joyce's writings to be set in Trieste, which is also where Joyce left it when he moved on to Zurich in 1915 (*GJ* xv, xi). The story – told through disjointed images rather than successive songs – loosely follows the lines of the story in *Chamber Music*, with emphasis falling once again on the waxing and waning of love, a waning that in this case seems to have something to do with the appearance of a rival. Unlike *Chamber Music*, however, *Giacomo Joyce* does not contain any suggestion that the love affair it chronicles – Joyce's relationship with one of the pupils to whom he taught English in Trieste, Amalia Popper – was ever anything more than an 'affair of the eye', and in this respect it anticipates 'Nausicaa'. However, its divergences from 'Nausicaa' are as important as its similarities: 'Nausicaa' provides two perspectives, that of the woman as well as the man, to Giacomo's one. Also in sharp contrast are the two accounts of the affair's climax. Unlike 'Nausicaa', in which Bloom's encounter with Gerty spends itself in a comically onanistic display of fireworks, *Giacomo Joyce* ends more bitterly when the object of the artist's gaze announces her preference for another man, for Barabbas (who is probably Popper's fiancé Michele Risolo) over Christ (Joyce) (*GJ* 16; see Mahaffey, '*Giacomo Joyce*', p. 406).

What is most notably missing in *Giacomo Joyce* is the perspective of the woman, a perspective that is so strategically provided in *Ulysses*.[18] Our first view of her is prefaced by a question – 'Who?' – and she emerges as a montage created by images of a pale face, furs, and quizzing glasses (GJ 1). Typical of the speaker's furtive mode of observing her is the sketch where he looks 'upward from night and mud', watching her 'dressing to go to the play' (GJ 6). His voyeurism grows more intimate as he pictures himself hooking her black gown, seeing through the opening 'her lithe body sheathed in an orange shift'. The shift shifts to a ship that 'slips its ribbons of moorings at her shoulders' and reveals her silver fishlike body 'shimmering with silvery scales' (GJ 7). She edges more closely towards Gerty MacDowell when, 'virgin most prudent', her 'sudden moving knee' catches her skirt back and the viewer sees 'a white lace edging of an underskirt lifted unduly' (GJ 9).

The animality or floral delicacy of her body is frequently available to the eyes of the beholder, but what is withheld are her thoughts, her anxieties, her dreams. This is even the case in the most bizarre sketch of the sequence, the interpolated dream scene that depicts her attacking him with a cold lust mingled with aggression:

– I am not convinced that such activities of the mind or body can be called unhealthy –

She speaks. A weak voice from beyond the cold stars. Voice of wisdom. Say on! O, say again, making me wise! This voice I never heard.

She coils towards me along the crumpled lounge. I cannot move or speak. Coiling approach of starborn flesh. Adultery of wisdom. No. I will go. I will.

– Jim, love! –

Soft sucking lips kiss my left armpit: a coiling kiss on myriad veins. I burn! I crumple like a burning leaf! From my right armpit a fang of flame leaps out. A starry snake has kissed me: a cold nightsnake. I am lost!

– Nora! –   (GJ 15)

Paradoxically, her coldness inflames and terrifies Joyce; she is portrayed as a snake whose very kiss injects him with venom, producing a fiery 'fang'. Here in active desire as elsewhere in passive reserve, she remains objectified.

Unlike Chamber Music, Giacomo Joyce seems to have been composed without any other listener (or viewer) in mind than 'Giacomo' himself. Partly because of its intense self-referentiality, the course of the imagined affair is difficult for a reader to trace without the aid of biographical information to flesh out the details, or without a guide to the use of unexpected literary allusions to string together disjointed patches of narrative. As a result, most accounts of Giacomo Joyce focus on biography or allusion, and the political implications of Joyce's project in *Giacomo Joyce* remain largely unexplored. It is not clear, for example, how Joyce's disturbingly ambivalent treatment of the young Jewish woman in *Giacomo Joyce* accords with his later presentations of women and Jews in *Ulysses*. The German graphic artist Paul Wunderlich has interpreted Joyce's interest in his student as erotic desire mingled with prophetic compassion for what would later be done to the Jews in Nazi-controlled Europe.[19] *Giacomo Joyce* plays on the incommensurability of artistic and social power, as well as that of sexual and racial privilege, but it does so in a way that protects Joyce's privilege as a man, a gentile and a writer. In *Exiles*, as well as in his maturer works, Joyce is quick to recognize such imbalances of power, devising a variety of strategies for drawing attention to them, but in *Giacomo Joyce*, as in the *Epiphanies* and *Chamber Music*, such privileges are protected by the fear of their reversal.

EXILES

Chamber Music and *Giacomo Joyce* record the passing of a carefully controlled passion, but reflect little or no compassion for the figure they idealize. In contrast, *Exiles*, like 'The Dead', aims at exposing the lack of compassion that precludes relationship. *Exiles* relentlessly exhumes the self-interest buried in conventions of love and friendship, pursuing its grim and hackneyed discoveries unrelieved by Joyce's characteristic humour. As Padraic Colum asserts in his introduction to the play (reproduced in the Penguin-Viking edition), the revelations of *Exiles* have a ritualistic decorum: 'In its structure, *Exiles* is a series of confessions; the dialogue has the dryness of recitals in the confessional; its end is an act of contrition' (*E* 11).

Interestingly, the only production of the play that has been generally acclaimed as successful, that of Harold Pinter at the Mermaid Theatre in London in 1970 (repeated by the Royal Shakespeare Company at the Aldwych Theatre in the following year), also stressed the quiet, threateningly conventional seriousness of the play. Bernard Benstock has described the effect: 'All the lines were read with precise politeness at a slow tempo, with little emotion ever allowed to violate the proprieties; an undertone of quiet menace pervaded throughout, giving a certain shape even to the most "innocent" lines; and no suggestion of Joycean irony was permitted in the interpretation. It was

magnificent, but it was not quite Joyce.'[20] Benstock questions the
authenticity of Pinter's interpretation because it conflicts with the
assumption that a Joycean text is necessarily ironic. It has never been
clear, however, whether *Exiles* is ironic, or whether, like the other
shorter works, its ironies are earnest ones.

Concerns about the seriousness of *Exiles* lie behind most critical
assessments of the promise or disappointment of the play. Which way
the needle of judgement points depends, in large part, on our
expectations. And that is fundamentally what the play itself is about:
the discovery that betrayal is only meaningful in response to a prior
expectation. Joyce's interest in the egotism of expectation and its
relation to treachery is even apparent in the political background of the
play. Although Richard disclaims any kinship with Archibald Hamilton Rowan (*E* 45), Richard's son Archie, who represents future
possibility, bears his name. Significantly, the historical Rowan's
notable distinction was to be labelled a traitor by both the English and
the Irish. Both expected him to support their side, but he did not take
sides unilaterally: he refused to help Wolfe Tone in his plans for the
revolution of 1798 after he saw the Reign of Terror in France, yet when
he returned to Ireland in 1803 he supported Catholic emancipation,
which brought the wrath of Peel down on him in 1825.[21]

In the play, Joyce's main characters are less aware than Hamilton
Rowan of the dependence of 'treachery' upon expectation: Robert
Hand expects Richard Rowan to be a patriot and a possessive lover;
when Richard violates these expectations, Robert subtly accuses him of
treachery, of having left his country (and his beloved) 'in her hour of
need'. Similarly, Richard expects Robert to be honest rather than
secretive about his desire for Richard's companion Bertha, an expectation which is as arbitrary, in a sense, as Robert's expectation that
Richard will fight for his 'property'. It is Richard, not Robert, who
values honesty, and it is Robert, not Richard, who is obsessed with
possession; the treachery of both is the assumption that the other
should share his own values. Does Bertha desire the freedom that
Richard wants for her? Does Richard want to be the proud and scornful
iconoclast that Beatrice Justice admires in him? Does Beatrice yearn to
be a cold, dead model for an exiled writer's work? Does Bertha want to
be the embodiment of Robert's 'dream of love'?

The possibility of love, or connection, remains shadowy in *Exiles*
because love is only possible when the expectations that strive to shape

it are confronted and dissolved. Joyce writes that Richard's jealousy 'must reveal itself as the very immolation of the pleasure of possession on the altar of love' (*E* 114), an attempt that Joyce seems to take very seriously (at times too seriously for optimum dramatic effect). Although the conclusion of the play is clumsily rhetorical (Richard is – for the first time in the play – seeing himself in a dramatic light, which reinforces his egotism), it takes the form it does partly because of its importance in the veiled contexts that inform Joyce's analysis of love in the play: his reading of Nietzsche, Wagner, and their disciple D'Annunzio, in particular.

Much of Joyce's reading centred on the destructiveness of seeking to possess another person in the name of love, of desiring to recreate the loved one in the creator's own image instead of accepting and appreciating the differences that necessarily divide lovers. In *The Case of Wagner* (which Joyce owned in Trieste), Nietzsche argues that even philosophers misunderstand the nature of love, refusing to see that what we call love is actually mortal hatred between the sexes. He claims that the only conception of love worthy of a philosopher is one that recognizes that people kill what they love by trying to possess it, citing José's destruction of Carmen as an example (see 'Scylla and Charybdis', where Stephen uses the same example to illustrate his theory of Shakespeare (*U* 9.1022–3)). He asserts that people demand a return for loving another person by wanting 'to *possess* the other creature'.[22] The lover insists on being loved in return, even though the demand results in the 'death' of the loved one. In *Exiles*, Robert yearns for such a 'death of the spirit', in sharp contrast to Richard's fear of it. Richard, wielding honesty as the weapon of his will to power, seems to be modelled partly on Nietzsche; Robert, with his equally strong will to illusion, owes many of his most distinctive characteristics to Wagner.[23]

The most obvious allusion to Wagner occurs at the beginning of the second act, when Robert moves to the piano to strum out Wolfram's aria in *Tannhäuser* (*E* 58). Like Wagner, whom Nietzsche characterized as an 'old robber', a 'seducer on a grand scale' (*Case* 42, 39), Robert stealthily tries to seduce Bertha, an attempt that Richard, attentive to the 'robber' in Robert's name, likens to the act of a thief in the night (*E* 61). Both Richard and Nietzsche describe the art of their former associates as the art of lying (*Case* 35, and *E* 39, where Richard calls Robert's leading articles lies). Most notably, Robert's 'dream of love' for Bertha echoes that of Wagner for Mathilde Wesendonck, wife of

Wagner's good friend Otto Wesendonck. Mathilde, like Bertha (and like Nora when Prezioso was wooing her), kept her husband informed of everything that happened between herself and her suitor.[24] Like Robert, who puts a pink glass shade on the lamp in his bedroom, telling Bertha, 'It was for you' (E 78–9), Wagner gave Mathilde a pink lamp shade in 1858 (Wagner to Wesendonck, p. 18). Robert says to Bertha in Exiles, 'And that is the truth – a dream? . . . Bertha! . . . In all my life only that dream is real. I forget the rest' (E 106). Similarly, Wagner writes to Liszt in December 1854:

> As I never in my life have quaffed the actual delight of love, I mean some day to raise a monument to this most beauteous of all dreams, wherein that love shall glut itself quite royally for once. In my head I've planned a Tristan and Isolde.
>   (Wagner to Wesendonck, p. li)

In the composition of Exiles, Joyce drew not only on Wagner's life – his dream of love for Mathilde Wesendonck – but also on the opera that expressed that dream. Joyce indicates in his notes that the idealized love of Robert and Bertha is indebted to that of Tristan and Isolde (E 123), a suggestion reinforced by the fact that in the 'Scribbledehobble' notebook for Finnegans Wake, Joyce entered notes on Tristan and Isolde under the heading for Exiles.[25] The most important (and least successful) import from Wagner's Tristan and Isolde is the wound that Mark claims Tristan has given him, which reappears to mar the conclusion of Exiles in the form of Richard's 'wound of doubt'. In Act II, when Mark asks Tristan why he has wounded him, Tristan tells him that he cannot truly tell, that what Mark would know can never have an answer (II: iii), an awareness that Richard already has in Exiles. When Bertha offers to tell Richard what has happened between her and Robert, he replies, 'I can never know, never in this world' (E 112; also 102).

The plot of Tristan and Isolde revolves around betrayal, as that of Exiles would later do in its shadow. Isolde accuses Tristan of having betrayed her by carrying her away from Ireland to the land of King Mark (I: iv, I: v); Brangäne betrays her mistress by giving her the love philtre instead of the death potion she requested; Isolde betrays her husband; Tristan betrays his friend and king; Melot betrays his 'truest' friend Tristan; Mark accuses Tristan of having betrayed him a second time by dying when Mark has come to 'prove his perfect trust' in him. In short, every character accuses every other of treachery, a situation duplicated in *Exiles*. Bertha accuses Richard of having left her when they were in Rome; Richard accuses Robert of trying to steal Bertha from him craftily and secretly; Robert accuses Richard of having abandoned those who depend on him in their hour of need.

Tristan and Isolde deliberately choose night-time, secrecy, illusion, and death over daylight, openness, truth, and life. As Brangäne warns them, love has put out the 'light' of their reason (II: i), and they persist in living in the darkness of a dream. Tristan's passionate desire for death, illusion, and night is shared by Robert; the gradual dimming of the lights during the scene in Robert's cottage between Robert and Bertha recalls the longing of both Tristan and Isolde for the torch to be extinguished, for the sudden darkness to envelop them, signalling Tristan to come to his beloved. Hatred of light and longing for death are the main themes of the famous love duet in the second act of Wagner's opera (II: ii). Night is the realm of dreams, and Tristan and Isolde embrace it, insisting that their dreams are the only reality.[26]

As in *Ulysses*, where the allusions to Homer criss-cross with references to Shakespeare's *Hamlet*, *Exiles* positions itself in relation to not one but two strikingly different authors. If the Wagnerian allusions shadow the relationship between Robert and Bertha, a second pattern of allusion serves to illuminate the relationship between Richard and Beatrice, a pattern which, as Beatrice's name suggests, derives from Dante. For Richard, as for Dante, Beatrice represents the story of his young life, his *Vita nuova*.[27] Aside from Beatrice's name, most of the allusions to the *Vita nuova* in *Exiles* are numerological. Dante meets Beatrice when he is nine, he sees her again nine years later, he has a vision of her at the ninth hour of the day, and she dies in June, which is the ninth month of the year by the Syrian calendar, in the year of her century in which the perfect number ten has been completed nine times. Dante's Beatrice dies in June of her twenty-seventh year; *Exiles* is set in June of Beatrice Justice's twenty-seventh year, and it has been nine years since the departure of Richard and Bertha that so changed all their lives (autobiographically, in June of 1912 it had only been eight years since Joyce left Dublin with Nora). The mysterious union between Bertha, now 'nine times more beautiful' (*E* 86), and Robert takes place at nine o'clock at night (*E* 83).[28]

Strikingly, the sensual relationship between Robert and Bertha, like the idealized one that links Richard and Beatrice, has no basis in reality: they are equally delusory. This is what gives the play its power, the gradual realization that there is no essential difference between Dante's Beatrice and Wagner's Isolde, that both are possessed in a way that threatens the life of each. Such a view represents a significant advance upon Joyce's way of thinking in April of 1912, when in answer to an examination question at the University of Padua he set up a weighted contrast between the medieval theologian and the modern journalist. In 'L'influenza letteraria universale del rinascimento', Joyce argued that 'The Renaissance . . . has put the journalist in the monk's chair: that is to say, has deposed an acute, limited and formal mentality to give the scepter to a mentality that is facile and wide-ranging.'[29] In this essay, Joyce illustrates the difference between the theologian and the journalist (whom he would later embody as Richard and Robert) with a comparison between Dante and Wagner, *Tristan and Isolde* and the *Inferno*. Joyce expresses a clear preference for Dante, who, he argues, builds the *Inferno* out of a gradually intensifying idea (the idea of hate), in contrast to Wagner, who expresses the opposite sentiment of love by linking it to sensations of the flesh:

A great modern artist wishing to put the sentiment of love to music reproduces, as far as his art permits, each pulsation, each trembling, the lightest shivering, the lightest sigh; the harmonies intertwine and oppose each other secretly: one loves even as one grows more cruel, suffers when and as much as one enjoys, hate and doubt flash in the lovers' eyes, their bodies become one single flesh. Place *Tristan and Isolde* next to the *Inferno* and you will notice how the poet's hate follows its path from abyss to abyss in the wake of an idea that intensifies; and the more intensely the poet consumes himself in the fire of hate, the more violent becomes the art with which the artist communicates his passion. One is the art of the circumstance, the other is ideational.   (Berrone, *James Joyce in Padua*, pp. 20–1)

Joyce's disdain for an art of the flesh (he goes on to claim that 'modern man has an epidermis rather than a soul' (Berrone, p. 21)) is still apparent in *Exiles*, but it has begun to break down. The ideal figure that once inspired him, as she inspired Dante, is portrayed as cold and dead; as Joyce suggests in the notes, 'Beatrice's mind is an abandoned cold temple in which hymns have risen heavenward in a distant past but where now a doddering priest offers alone and hopelessly prayers to the Most High' (*E* 119). Only Bertha suggests the possibility of life, combining uncommon receptivity with a practical-minded resistance to the desire of others to possess her.[30]

From a criticism of Wagner's sensuality as it contrasts with the ideality of a writer like Dante, Joyce arrived at a more balanced view of the relationship between ideal and real, partly through the writing of *Exiles*. *Exiles* unveils the power of the thinker as comparable to that of the seducer; if Robert has refreshed Bertha's awareness of her loneliness, Richard has confirmed Beatrice's suspicion that she too is isolated. The deadliness of idealization as a more subtle form of possessiveness is brought home in another work that Joyce draws on for *Exiles* that was itself influenced by the work of both Nietzsche and Wagner, Gabriele D'Annunzio's novel *The Triumph of Death*.[31]

The Triumph of Death details the mortal struggle between two lovers to possess one another, a struggle that culminates in murder-suicide of the kind Robert romantically longs for in *Exiles*: 'I want to end it and have done with it. . . To end it all – death. To fall from a great high cliff, down, right down into the sea. . . Listening to music and in the arms of the woman I love – the sea, music and death' (*E* 35). This is how the lovers die in *The Triumph of Death*, but the climax is anything but romantic: Giorgio and Ippolita have been listening to Wagner's *Tristan and Isolde* for two days, which transports them into 'a world of fiction'. He fears that she will enslave him through the power of desire, and he takes her to the edge of the sea: 'There was a brief but savage struggle, as between two mortal foes who had nourished a secret and implacable hatred in their souls up till that hour', and they crash 'down headlong into death, locked in that fierce embrace' (p. 315).

What Giorgio and Ippolita are struggling over is the power to possess – and to create – one another. From the outset, Giorgio is oppressed by the certainty that he can never possess Ippolita wholly (p. 5); like Gabriel in 'The Dead', he is jealous of the very memories that exclude him:

Suddenly a thought will strike me cold: what if I, unwittingly, should have evoked in her memory the ghost of some sensation felt once before, some pale phantom of the days long past? . . . You become remote, inaccessible; I am left alone in horrible solitude.   (pp. 6–7)

To forestall such infidelity, however inadvertent, he remakes her; as Ippolita meditates, 'In these two years he has transformed me – made another woman of me; he has given me new senses, a new soul, a new mind. I am his creature, the work of his hands' (p. 33). (In *Exiles*, Robert says to Richard of Bertha, 'She is yours, your work', *E* 62.) Later Ippolita repeats to him that she is wholly his creation (p. 119), and he succeeds in feeling 'the thrill of a creator': 'Giorgio had witnessed that transformation, so intoxicating to a lover of intellect – the metamorphosis of the woman he loves to his own image' (p. 141).

Giorgio's power to create and recreate Ippolita, his 'thrill' at creation, is a fantasy of possession. She has sacrificed herself to Giorgio's desire to possess her (p. 188), and he comes to see that he can transform her over and over again at will, into a goddess, an animal, a witch, or a snake: 'Her form is moulded by my desire, her shadow cast by my thoughts. Her aspects are protean as the dreams of fever' (p. 229). The narrator warns that 'his intelligence had reduced his mistress to a mere motive force to his imagination, and stripped her person of all value' (p. 235) (as Rubek did to Irene in Ibsen's *When We Dead Awaken*), but just at the point of his greatest triumph he discovers his greatest fear: she has an equal power over him. In his imagination, he hears her telling him that she knows the secret of her metamorphoses in his soul, that she knows all the words and the gestures that have the power to transfigure her in his eyes (p. 237). Both now long to destroy the person they cannot possess, and Wagner's opera serves as the prelude to the destructive consummation that both, in different ways, desire.

Although Ibsen also dramatizes the deadliness of power masked as love in *When We Dead Awaken*, the intensity of Joyce's exploration of the mortal combat between each of the four main characters in *Exiles* makes sense only in a larger intellectual context that includes Wagner, Nietzsche, and D'Annunzio as well as Ibsen. Moreover, *Exiles* celebrates what Ibsen could not, the refusal of lovers to be killed by the people who attempt to possess them; as Joyce writes in his notes, Bertha loves the part of Richard that 'she must try to kill, never be able to kill and rejoice at her impotence' (*E* 118), just as Richard loves and hates the living part of her that is open to experience. The most important aspect of *Exiles* is its implicit celebration of its characters' refusal to be buried in the snowy avalanche of Ibsen's despairing last play. The alternative to death, however, is acceptance, a hard-won acceptance of human difference that was to usher in *Ulysses*.

NOTES

1 Robert Scholes and Richard M. Kain, eds., *The Workshop of Daedalus: James Joyce and the Raw Materials for 'A Portrait of the Artist as a Young Man'* (Evanston: Northwestern University Press, 1965), pp. 3–4. Hereafter referred to as *WD*.

2 A duality also discussed by John Paul Riquelme in ch. 5 of this volume.

3 I have presented such an argument in *'Giacomo Joyce'*, in Zack Bowen and James C. Carens, eds., *A Companion to Joyce Studies* (Westport, Connect-icut: Greenwood Press, 1984), p. 393.

4 'Continuous manuscript' is Hans Walter Gabler's term for the successive autograph notations that he uses as the copytext for his edition of *Ulysses*. See Gabler's Afterword to *'Ulysses': A Critical and Synoptic Edition* (New York: Garland, 1984), pp. 1894–6.

5 Of the forty extant epiphanies, twenty-two (in Joyce's hand) are housed in the Poetry Collection at the State University of New York at Buffalo; transcriptions of these were published by Oscar Silverman as *Joyce's Epiphanies* (Buffalo: Lockwood Memorial Library, 1956). The twenty-five remaining epiphanies are at Cornell; all but one of these are from Stanislaus Joyce's commonplace book, and the remaining one (concerning Oliver Gogarty) is a rough draft in Joyce's own hand. Seven of the Cornell epiphanies are duplicates of those at Buffalo. When Peter Spielberg discovered that the Buffalo epiphanies have numbers on the versos that go as high as seventy-one, Robert Scholes and Richard Kain responded by ordering all the extant epiphanies into a sequence, which they transcribed and annotated (*WD*, pp. 3–51). Facsimiles of all of the epiphanies have since been published in *Archive 7*, *'A Portrait of the Artist as a Young Man': A Facsimile of Epiphanies, Notes, Manuscripts and Typescripts*, ed. Hans Walter Gabler. Shortly, the epiphanies will be available in a new edition together with the poems, the 1904 'Portrait' essay, and *Giacomo Joyce*; see James Joyce, *Poems and Epiphanies*, ed. Richard Ellmann and A. Walton Litz, with the assistance of John Ferguson (London: Faber, 1990).

6 Both Hugh Kenner and S. L. Goldberg argued that Joyce's omission represents a deliberate attempt on Joyce's part to weaken Stephen's aesthetic theories (see *Dublin's Joyce* (Bloomington: University of Indiana Press, 1966), ch. 9, and *The Classical Temper* (New York: Barnes and Noble, 1961), chs. 2 and 3), which prompted Robert Scholes to contest the meaningfulness of the term epiphany in a controversial article, 'Joyce and the epiphany: the key to the labyrinth?' *Sewanee Review* 72 (1964), 65–77.

7 Morris Beja attempts to get round the difficulty posed by the 'spiritual' nature of epiphany by redefining spirituality; see *Epiphany in the Modern Novel* (London: Peter Owen, 1971), p. 74.

8 Stephen admits as much in *Portrait*, when he tells Lynch that for a long time he thought Aquinas' third stage of apprehension signified 'symbolism or idealism, the supreme quality of beauty being a light from some other world, the idea of which the matter is but the shadow, the reality of which it is but the symbol', so that the goal of apprehension was 'the artistic discovery and representation of the divine purpose in anything' (*P* 213).

9 Stanislaus Joyce, *My Brother's Keeper*, ed. Richard Ellmann (London: Faber, 1958), pp. 134–5.

10 See, for just one example, Florence Walzl, 'The liturgy of the Epiphany season and the epiphanies of Joyce', *PMLA* 80 (1965), 436–50. Even Robert Scholes, who was through the greenness of the concept of epiphany when he transcribed and edited the manuscript epiphanies, asserts that 'the Epiphanies themselves for the most part bear out Stephen's condemnation of them. They are trivial and supercilious or florid and lugubrious, in the main. Their chief significance is in the use Joyce often made of them in his later works' ('Joyce and the epiphany', p. 73).

11 Morris Beja has found at least thirteen of the extant epiphanies in *Stephen Hero*, twelve in *A Portrait*, four in *Ulysses*, and one in *Finnegans Wake*. See Beja, 'Epiphany and the epiphanies', in Bowen and Carens, *A Companion to Joyce Studies*, pp. 710–13.

12 Several of Joyce's poems are literally songs, among the most interesting of which is 'Post ulixem scriptum' (to be sung to the tune of 'Molly Brannigan'). Most of the extant poems and poetic fragments are available in facsimile in *Archive* 1, ed. A. Walton Litz, and many are listed in Paul Doyle's bibliographical register of 'Joyce's miscellaneous verse' (*JJQ* 2 (1965), 90–6) and his addenda (*JJQ* 4 (1967), 71). One of the most influential arguments about the musical nature of *Chamber Music* is that of Herbert Howarth, 'Chamber Music and its place in the Joyce canon', in Thomas F. Staley, ed., *James Joyce Today* (Bloomington: Indiana University Press, 1966), pp. 11–27. On the similarity between *Chamber Music* and Elizabethan songs and airs, see Myra Russel, 'The Elizabethan connection: the missing score of James Joyce's *Chamber Music*', *JJQ* 18 (1981), 133–45.

13 *Chamber Music* does however pose uncharacteristic problems of attribution, since Stanislaus Joyce told W. Y. Tindall that both the title and the final arrangement of the poems were his. Joyce's arrangement of the twenty-seven poem sequence is that of the Gilvary manuscript: I, III, II, IV, V, VIII, VII, IX, XVII, XVIII, VI, X, XIII, XIV, XV, XIX, XXIII, XXII, XXIV, XVI, XXXI, XXVIII, XXIX, XXXII, XXX, XXXIII, XXXIV. The arrangement of the Yale manuscript is Stanislaus's: XXI, I, III, II, IV, V, VIII, VII, IX, XVII, XVIII, VI, X, XX, XIII, XI, XIV, XIX, XV, XXIII, XXIV, XVI, XXXI, XXII, XXVI, XII, XXVII, XXVIII, XXV, XXIX, XXXII, XXX, XXIII, XXXIV. See Litz, *Archive* 1.

14 William York Tindall, ed., *Chamber Music* by James Joyce (New York: Columbia, 1954), pp. 70–80. For Gorman's story about the title, see his *James Joyce* (New York: Farrar and Rinehart, 1939), p. 116; for Gogarty's, see his *Mourning Became Mrs. Spendlove* (New York: Creative Age Press, 1948), pp. 53–5, 57–60. According to Tindall, Stanislaus denied both

stories and recounted a third in a letter to Gorman, arguing that he (Stanislaus) had already chosen the title for the volume by the time the incident took place (Tindall, pp. 72–3).

15 Archie K. Loss, 'Interior and exterior imagery in the earlier work of Joyce and in Symbolist art', *Journal of Modern Literature* 8 (1980), 99–117, and Chester Anderson, 'Joyce's verses', in Bowen and Carens, *A Companion to Joyce Studies*, pp. 129–55.

16 See the reference to this article in note 12.

17 See *A First Draft Version of 'Finnegans Wake'*, ed. David Hayman (Austin: University of Texas Press, 1963), pp. 210–11.

18 In her excellent discussion of *Giacomo Joyce* in 'Shahrazade's Wake; The *Arabian Nights* and the Narrative Dynamics of Charles Dickens and James Joyce' (University of Pennsylvania doctoral dissertation, 1988), Henriette Power presents *Giacomo Joyce* as a power struggle between female physicality and male inscriptions. Power argues that Giacomo's attempt to capture a woman on paper takes the form of an artistic dismemberment, contrasting Giacomo's strategy with that of Bloom in 'Nausicaa' (pp. 162–80).

19 *Giacomo Joyce*, with introduction by Hermann Lenz (Dielsdorf: Mattheiu AG, 1976). The edition of ten lithographs was limited to 125 copies.

20 Bernard Benstock, *'Exiles'*, in Bowen and Carens, *A Companion to Joyce Studies*, pp. 361–2. See also J. W. Lambert's review of the Mermaid production in *Drama* 100 (Spring 1971), 21–3, and John Spurling's review of the Aldwych production in *Plays and Players* 19 (December 1971), 44–5, 88; a good overview may be found in John MacNicholas, 'The stage history of *Exiles*', *JJQ* 19 (1981), 9–26.

21 John MacNicholas, *James Joyce's 'Exiles': A Textual Companion* (New York: Garland, 1979), pp. 197–9.

22 Friedrich Nietzsche, *The Case of Wagner*, in *The Complete Works of Friedrich Nietzsche*, trans. A. M. Ludovici, ed. Oscar Levy, VIII (London: Allen and Unwin, 1911), p. 4. Hereafter referred to as *Case*.

23 In 'Joyce contra Wagner', John MacNicholas also suggests that Joyce 'superimposes Wagner upon Robert Hand' (*Comparative Drama* 9 (1975), 29).

24 *Richard Wagner to Mathilde Wesendonck*, trans. and pref. by William Ashton Ellis, 2nd ed. (1905; rpt. New York: Vienna House, 1972), pp. vi–vii.

25 Thomas E. Connolly, *James Joyce's Scribbledehobble: The Ur-Workbook for 'Finnegans Wake'* (Evanston: Northwestern University Press, 1961), pp. 75–85. See David Hayman's treatment of these notes together with some of the parallels between *Exiles* and Wagner's opera in 'Tristan and Isolde in *Finnegans Wake*: a study of the sources and evolution of a theme', *Comparative Literature Studies*, 1 (1964), 95–102.

26 In *Exiles*, Robert, like Tristan, is associated with darkness, unlike Richard who prefers the light; see Sheldon Brivic, 'Structure and meaning in Joyce's *Exiles*', *JJQ* 6 (1968), 38–9.

27 In Dante Gabriel Rossetti's illustrated edition of Dante's *La vita nuova* (Joyce owned the Italian version in Trieste), Rossetti argues that 'nuova', which means 'new', also connotes youth, which allows him to assert that Dante's *Vita nuova* is an 'autobiography or autopsychology of Dante's youth until about his twenty-seventh year' (*The New Life of Dante Alighieri*, trans. and illus. by Dante Gabriel Rossetti (New York: Russell, 1901), p. 25). See also Mahaffey, '*Giacomo Joyce*', pp. 408–9.

28 In 'Dante in Joyce's *Exiles*', *JJQ* 18 (1980), 35–44, Mary T. Reynolds asserts that the nine years Richard corresponded with Beatrice, in the light of her inspiration of him, constitute a significant reflection of the *Vita nuova*.

29 Louis Berrone, *James Joyce in Padua* (New York: Random House, 1977), p. 21.

30 Ruth Bauerle argues that Bertha is in fact the centre of the play; see 'Bertha's role in *Exiles*', in Suzette Henke and Elaine Unkeless, eds., *Women in Joyce* (Urbana: University of Illinois Press, 1982), pp. 108–31.

31 Gabriele D'Annunzio, *The Triumph of Death*, trans. Georgina Harding (London: Heinemann, 1898).

9 Joyce's text in progress

James Joyce claimed he lacked imagination. His artistry craved supports and scaffolds: structures from which and into which to be textured. Joyce's conception of art reached out and back to the medieval. Setting up the illuminators of the *Book of Kells* as his artistic ancestors (*JJ* 545), he strove for the intricacy and significant complexity of their design in the text of his writing.

In, as well as towards, his compositional crafting, Joyce was as much a reader as a writer of texts. Jesuit-trained, he was thoroughly schooled in the reading skills which he early exercised with catholicity on textbooks and dictionaries, curricular and extra-curricular literature, or the canonical Book of Books. Through reading, he penetrated to the philosophical foundations of the act of reading. 'Signatures of all things I am here to read, seaspawn and seawrack, the nearing tide, that rusty boot' (*U* 3.2–3). Anticipating long in advance the conceptualizations of present-day text theory, he discovered the structural and semiotic analogies of language-encoded texts and experience-encoded reality; and, in a desire like Stephen Dedalus's to grasp the wholeness and harmony of things (their *integritas* and *consonantia*) for the sake of illumination (their 'radiance', or *claritas* (*P* 212)), he taught himself to read streets and cities, landscapes, seashores or rivers, people, actions, events, dreams and memories, the randomness of everyday or the patterns (real or apparent) of history as texts in their own right.

Learning to read the world in this way was an act of intellectual self-liberation, and reading it in this way a new experience. Stephen Dedalus, exploiting Thomism for aesthetics and yet awaiting that new experience ('When we come to the phenomena of artistic conception, artistic gestation and artistic reproduction I require a new terminology and a new personal experience' (*P* 209)), mirrors James Joyce on the

213

very brink of turning reading into writing. To circumscribe, and thus make readable, the wholeness of things means to unlock them, in a kind of deconstruction, out of their apparently amorphous contingencies. Such unlocking turns into a morphologizing, or shaping, act. Through the constructive perception of things in their radiant wholeness, it makes them communicable, and thus writable. Hence springs a notion of writing as an act and process of transubstantiation ('In the virgin womb of the imagination the word was made flesh' (P 217)). The alternating pulse, and impulse, of deconstructive unlocking and constructive shaping as reading and writing is fundamental to Joyce's craft and art. As a governing principle, not only does it make available the external materials of literature and all manner of language-encoded pretexts, of history, autobiography, and everyday experience so as to render them integrable into the text-in-writing, the work in progress; but inside the boundary lines, too, that separate Joyce's text from all the pre-texts it absorbs, that text itself may be seen to be propelled – and thus, progressively self-generated – by constant and continuous acts of reading and rereading.

Notes, sketches, drafts, fair-copies, typescripts, and proofs have survived for Joyce's entire *œuvre*, albeit but fragmentarily for the early works, and with increasing comprehensiveness only from mid-*Ulysses* onwards. These workshop remains are sufficiently rich and varied to substantiate our general understanding of his mode of composition. One particularly illuminating instance of the complex interaction of the reading and the writing processes can be made out in the notes and drafts for *Exiles*. A surviving notebook contains trial fragments of dialogue and a number of passages of pragmatic, thematic, critical, and philosophic reflection on the play, its actions, its characters and their motivations, as well as on some of the audience responses envisaged; material which is all but unique from Joyce's pen.[1] Beyond this material, there are three sections – interspersed among the rest, but clearly of a common nature that sets them off and links them to one another – which enact the reading and writing itself. The first carries two initialized openings sequentially dated which also subdivide it into a reading and a writing phase: 'N.(B) – 12 Nov. 1913' and 'N.(B) – 13 Nov. 1913'. The initials provide the signal justification for our decoding approach: Joyce's companion Nora and the fictional character Bertha stand to be read in terms of each other.

Under 12 November are listed three strings of notes which, except that they are grouped under subheads ('Garter:', 'Rat:' and 'Dagger:'), thoroughly resemble the seemingly disjunct listings that sprawlingly cover the *Ulysses Notesheets*, and endlessly fill the *Finnegans Wake Notebooks*. Here, the organizing principle of the notes seems tolerably clear. They read Nora under aspects potentially to be written into the fictional character, role, and relationships of Bertha in the play. The first string of notes runs: 'Garter: precious, Prezioso, Bodkin, music, palegreen, bracelet, cream sweets, lily of the valley, convent garden (Galway), sea.'

Under 13 November follows a prose passage in four paragraphs. Progressively it incorporates these notes as jotted down the previous day, which shows it in part to be generated from them. In itself, it accomplishes the reading of Nora and Bertha in terms of each other in a mode of writing which from notes turns compositional and, as it unfolds, draws in an association of further pretextual significations. It is a sufficiently unfamiliar piece of Joycean prose to need citation in full:

Moon – Shelley's grave in Rome. He is rising from it: blond [.] She weeps for him. He has fought in vain for an ideal and died killed by the world. Yet he rises. Graveyard at Rahoon by moonlight where Bodkin's grave is. He lies in the grave. She sees his tomb (family vault) and weeps. The name is homely. Shelley's is strange and wild. He is dark, unrisen, killed by love and life, young. The earth holds him.

Bodkin died. Kearns died. In the convent they called her the man-killer. (Woman-killer was one of her names for me.) I live in soul and body.

She is the earth, dark, formless, mother, made beautiful by the moonlit night, darkly conscious of her instincts. Shelley whom she held in her womb or grave rises: the part of Richard which neither love nor life can do away with: the part for which she loves him: the part she must try to kill, never be able to kill, and rejoice at her impotence. Her tears are of worship, Magdalen seeing the rearisen Lord in the garden where He had been laid in the tomb. Rome is the strange world and strange life to which Richard brings her. Rahoon her people. She weeps over Rahoon, too, over him whom her love has killed, the dark boy whom, as the earth, she embraces in death and disintegration. He is her buried life, her past. His attendant images are the trinkets and toys of girlhood (bracelet, cream sweets, palegreen lily of the valley, the convent garden). His symbols are music and the sea, liquid formless earth in which are buried the drowned soul and body. There are tears of commiseration. She is Magdalen who weeps remembering the loves she could not return.

Palpably, the passage originates in autobiographical memory, which yet in the writing at once acquires literary overtones in the romantic conjunction of 'moon', 'Shelley's grave' and 'Rome' to which that memory has been atomized. It is the moonlight radiance of this initial romantic image which carries the writing forward. Strikingly, it exploits a fluidity, even indeterminacy of personal pronouns which may remind one of the calculated pronoun indeterminacies of 'Penelope'. 'He is rising from (the grave): blond [.] She weeps for him.' In one sentence, a reading of Nora's presumed emotional response at the poet's graveside is projected into character behaviour and motivation for the Bertha of *Exiles*: Bertha appears superimposed upon Nora. In the progress of the passage, their composite figure becomes further overwritten by pre-texts of myth and the Bible. In a counter-movement, Shelley is erased and successively overlaid by Bodkin, Kearns, I, and Richard. Was a character named Kearns envisaged as the counterpart in Bertha's memories of Michael Bodkin, the young man Nora had known as a girl, and whose early death and burial in Rahoon cemetery were the basis for the story of Michael Furey in 'The Dead'? In the published play, Bertha is not given an Irish past, and hence does not weep over Rahoon in a rewriting of previous readings of Nora from within the Joycean *œuvre*. The absence of this dimension from the finished text would seem to represent the deliberate curtailment of a potential inherent in the compositional writing. As the death-and-resurrection imagery pervasive in the notebook passage suggests, it is the Roman exhilaration in life which, even from the poet's grave, raises the buried Irish past. An extant set of draft fragments for *Exiles* shows that the autobiographical pre-text of the Roman experience passed through further rewritings that were not in the end incorporated in the play.[2] With them, the structuring of Bertha as a text of receding experiential memories was abandoned.

The two related passages in the notebook are each similarly prefixed by strings of notes, in a single and a double list respectively. The first one is 'Blister – amber – silver – oranges – apples – sugarstick – hair – spongecake – ivy – roses – ribbon' and the second one 'Snow: frost, moon, pictures, holly and ivy, currant-cake, lemonade, Emily Lyons, piano, windowsill', followed by 'tears: ship, sunshine, garden, sadness, pinafore, buttoned boots, bread and butter, a big fire'. The written-out prose sections that in each case follow do not acquire the multiplicity of pre-text reference, nor do they move the pre-text 'Nora' as far towards the text 'Bertha', as does the 'N.(B.)' passage of 13 November. Yet they reveal with greater stringency the functional interrelation of a record of reading (the notes) with the compositional writing which that record generates. The writing allows us to infer that the notes, again, 'deconstruct' a biographical pre-text. At the same time, the writing clearly does not write these notes back into the text from which it derives; it cannot, for example, be read as a straight, let alone simple, retelling of the pre-text story. Instead, the notes represent concatenations of 'germs' – as Henry James would have called them – from which autonomous texts originate. The autonomy, and incipient originality, of these texts – the fact that they may properly be said to be generated from the notes – is measurable by the distance they move beyond narration. What discernible telling there is in the expansion of individual key-word notes into narrative becomes subordinated to, as it is immediately overlaid by, writerly reflection on the 'flow of ideas', on modes of memory, mental processes, emotions, psychological motivation and repression, or the overt or hidden significance of behaviour.

The process of transforming reading into writing is laid open here as a labour of interpretation holding a potential for artistic creation which at any moment may become actualized in 'original' prose. Such creative transubstantiation of the notes, it is true, occurs only intermittently in these passages which, after all, remain notebook entries. Yet consider, for instance, what happens to the concatenated note segment 'ivy – roses – ribbon' in the subsequent writing:

Ivy and roses: she gathered ivy often when out in the evening with girls. Roses grew then. A sudden scarlet side in the memory which may be a dim suggestion of the roses of the body. The ivy and the roses carry on and up out of the idea of growth, through a creeping vegetable life into ardent perfumed flower life the symbol of mysteriously growing girlhood, her hair. Ribbon for her hair. Its fitting ornament for the eyes of others, and lastly for his eyes. Girlhood becomes virginity and puts on 'the snood that is the sign of maidenhood'. A proud and shy instinct turns her mind away from the loosening of her bound-up hair – however sweet or longed for or inevitable – and she embraces that which is hers alone and not hers and his also –

These eight sentences progress from a recall of a biographical given to the creation, via image and symbol, of the changing attitudes and moods of a young woman, who thereby – that is, by the constituent power of language – becomes imaginatively outlined as a fictional character. In the language itself, the transition is effected by a manner (or mannerism) of style that bears the hallmark of the James Joyce who wrote the fourth chapter of *A Portrait of the Artist as a Young Man*, *Giacomo Joyce* – or, indeed, the poems of *Chamber Music*. 'The snood that is the sign of maidenhood' comes from *Chamber Music*, XI. It parallels 'She weeps over Rahoon' in the preceding passage, the title of a poem which, though not published until 1927 in *Pomes Penyeach*, was written in 1913. The retextualization of pre-text from the *œuvre* is anything but an accident. On the contrary, it exemplifies one of the most significant, as well as one of the earliest and most persistent, among Joyce's authorial strategies.

Joyce tested his powers of structuring experience into language in the prose miniatures he wrote before 1904 and called 'epiphanies'.[3] While not the inventor of the genre, Joyce in adopting the epiphanic mode developed it and soon raised it to a significance within the evolving system of his aesthetics that has caused the idea of the epiphany to become largely associated with his name. Within the period of his main devotion to the form, a dialogue, or 'dramatic', type of epiphany appears to be followed by a set-piece-of-prose, or 'narrative', type; it is the latter type which resurfaces ten years later in the collection of prose miniatures entitled *Giacomo Joyce*. The dialogue epiphanies would seem to be strict records of observation and listening; the set-piece-of-prose epiphanies, by contrast, show increasing writerly concerns. If the dialogues are predominantly records of observational 'reading', the set-piece miniatures turn into writings of events, visions, or dreams.

When Joyce embarked upon his first novel, eventually to be published as *A Portrait*, he used the epiphany texts as pre-texts from within his own *œuvre*. The surviving epiphanies in holograph fair copy carry on their versos the vestiges of a sequential numbering. Uniform as it is, it gives no indication of representing the order of composition. Instead, evidently post-dating the fair-copying, it implies a rereading of the accumulated epiphany manuscripts, which resulted in a selection and serial linking of discrete items. Their serial contextualization acquires narrative potential. Ordered into a sequence, the selected epiphanies form the substratum of a story to be generated from them. The barest structure of epiphanies turned by concatenation into narrative may be exemplified from a brief section in part II of *A Portrait*. A string of three epiphanies, each beginning 'He was sitting' (*P* 67–8), tells of Stephen's visits to relatives and conveys the thematic motif of the squalor and insincerity he encounters. By way of the rereading implied in the ordering of pre-written units of text, experiences with an ultimate origin in the author's life become brush-strokes in the emerging portrait of the artist as a young man.

The author's life as a pre-text is, through intervening reading and writing processes, several times removed from the text of *A Portrait*. The pre-text from within the *œuvre* which *A Portrait* most pervasively exploits is *Stephen Hero*, the novel planned to extend to sixty-three chapters, yet abandoned after the completion of twenty-five chapters on nine hundred and fourteen manuscript pages.[4] The few planning notes that survive for *Stephen Hero* emphasize an organization of autobiographic pre-text to render it available for the fictional narrative. Towards *A Portrait*, *Stephen Hero* in its turn served as a notebook and quarry for words and phrases, characters, situations and incidents. Yet the ways in which, after the abandonment of *Stephen Hero*, *A Portrait* proves itself not so much a revision as a genuine rewriting of the Stephen Daedalus novel may be properly gauged only by the extent and complexity of its un-locking and consequent rewriting of pre-texts other than either *Stephen Hero* or, ultimately, the autobiographic experience.

In this respect, the writerly path from *Stephen Hero* to *A Portrait* is paved in *Dubliners*. The stories individually and as a co-ordinated collection show Joyce's developing concern with significant structures of form and matter in the writing, answering to a systematized reading of the pre-texts of Dublin, her streets and citizens, of Irish history, politics and society, of works of literature, theological doctrine or biblical tales. Joyce criticism has read from, or read into, the *Dubliners* stories a rich array of intertextual reference, as well as incipient examples of that mode of auto-referentiality – one might term it the *œuvre*'s intratextuality – which is to become so prominent in Joyce's later work. If there is critical justification to claiming as pre-texts the biblical tale of Mary and Martha for 'The Sisters', of the Irish political situation for 'Ivy Day', of the *Divine Comedy* for 'Grace', or of Dante or Homer for the macro-structure of the collection,[5] one may add that even the philosophy of Joyce's epiphany-centred aesthetics becomes rewritten as narrative when the many-layered epiphanies of 'The Dead' are made to occur on the night of the feast of the Epiphany – a fact of the story which, in its turn, is left to the reader epiphanically to discover.[6]

Moving beyond the trial experiment of *Dubliners*, it is *A Portrait* that first fully succeeds as a unified rewriting of intertwining pre-texts. In the semiotics of *A Portrait*, the author's life as well as the Daedalean, Christian, and Irish myths, the martyrdom of Stephen Dedalus, St Stephen, Icarus, Parnell, and Christ, the sinner's descent into hell and the artist's flight heavenward are held in mutual tension. What guarantees the balanced co-existence and cross-referential significance of the pre-texts is the tectonics of the writing, the novel's complex, intricate and firmly controlled structure. *A Portrait* marks an essential step in Joyce's art towards a dominance of structure and expressive form. Significantly, structure can be made out as a pre-writing as well as a post-writing concern. After interrupting *Stephen Hero* in the summer of 1905 with a view, presumably, to continuation, he utterly abandoned the early novel in 1907 from the artistic vantage-point gained in the completion of *Dubliners*, and specifically 'The Dead'. Thereupon, the earliest indications of Joyce's intentions in reworking the autobiographical novel concern its structure. He now proposes to write the book in five long chapters, which, even before the fact, is very different from a sixty-three-chapter *Stephen Hero*. In the course of writing, *A Portrait* appears to have gone through progressive phases of structuring. It is quite clear, even from the scant surviving manuscript materials, that, in their ultimate refinement, the complexities realized in the five-chapter novel as released for publication are the results of revisions-in-composition, that is to say, of rereadings of the text as it evolved in the workshop. While the five-chapter sequence was determined before the writing began, the overall correlation and multi-patterned chiastic centring of the novel's parts was, in an important sense, achieved in retrospect. Similarly, it was by a single revision in the first chapter of the fair-copy manuscript – in other words, by a late response of the author, as reader, to his own written text – that a potential of suggestive parallels inherent in the writing was turned into an actual correspondence in the text. A revision in the manuscript instituted the day on which Wells shouldered Stephen into the square ditch at Clongowes as the seventy-seventh day before Christmas. In 1891, the year of Parnell's death, this was Thursday, 8 October. Parnell died on 6 October, and his body was brought to Ireland to be buried, arriving at dawn on Sunday, 11 October. This, in the fiction, is the morning Stephen, at the infirmary, revives from a fever. Parnell dies so that Stephen may live. The synchronization of historical and fictional time was the precise result of one textual revision.[7]

It is prominently in a mode of rewriting within Joyce's own œuvre, as well as on the level of concerns about structure that predate the actual writing, that the beginnings of Ulysses first manifest themselves. We may discover its earliest formation by evaluating the relation of A Portrait to Stephen Hero, and by analyzing the process of rewriting and rethinking of written and unwritten Stephen Hero material in the light of Joyce's correspondence with his brother Stanislaus.[8] An early plan for Stephen Hero – one that seems to have been devised in conversation sometime in 1904, before Joyce's departure from Ireland – was to carry it forward to a tower episode.[9] Stephen Hero never reached that point. But the extant fair-copy of a Martello tower fragment from the Portrait workshop, dating presumably from 1912 or 1913, is evidence that, at an intermediary stage of the rewriting, a tower scene was still conceived for A Portrait. Its ultimate exclusion provided the material for the opening of Ulysses.

No doubt the Martello tower episode of Ulysses is different in execution and tone from whatever version of it would have entered A Portrait. Doherty's comment to Stephen in the fragment:

Dedalus, we must retire to the tower, you and I. Our lives are precious . . . We are the super-artists. Dedalus and Doherty have left Ireland for the Omphalos –[10]

would seem to imply an intention of figuring the concept of exile which concludes A Portrait into a retreat to the tower, where the young aesthetes, seeking unfettered freedom in an abandonment to Nietzschean élitism,[11] isolate themselves from society; or to preface Stephen's departure into an exile alone in the world by the attempt and failure of a retirement to the omphalos, the navel of friendship and art. The contextual ambience of A Portrait of course would hardly warrant the ironic view of an artistic revolt of the select in isolation which is implied from the outset in the Martello tower setting of the opening of Ulysses. It is only as it enters Stephen's consciousness of himself in Ulysses that the ironic detachment from his Daedalean flight – so hard to define, within the confines of A Portrait alone, as a dimension of meaning of the tale told – becomes manifest.

By being made to part company with Mulligan and Haines and

becoming a critical judge not only of others, but of himself, Stephen in *Ulysses* is rewritten as a character capable of action and reaction, one whom we accept as a self-searching Telemachus, within the fictional reality of his and Leopold Bloom's Dublin. Thus revised and refunctionalized in terms of the character realism as well as of the Odysseus myth of the new novel, he is made to look upon the Daedalean identification produced within the symbolic framework of the old one as a personal illusion. The authorial manner of the redefinition is significant for the new relation it provides between the narrative and the pre-text that is its governing myth. Whereas Stephen in *A Portrait* ardently aspires to Daedalean heights, neither Stephen nor Bloom in *Ulysses* possess any awareness of their mythical roles. These are communicated by means of narrative structures to the reader.

Stephen's recognition of himself as a foundered Icarus – 'Lapwing you are. Lapwing be' (*U* 9.954) – belongs to the library episode, or Hamlet chapter, 'Scylla and Charybdis', ninth of the eighteen episodes of *Ulysses*. This, it should be noticed, is a remarkably late point in *Ulysses* to refer back so outspokenly to *A Portrait*. We may assume that the chapter formed a section of the emerging novel's redefinition of Stephen before, by structural positioning, it entered into the functions of the Scylla and Charybdis adventure in the sequence of Odysseus'/Bloom's wanderings – where, even as it finally stands, it emphasizes the rock and the whirlpool more than the wanderer. This assumption also helps to explain in part the divergences in the early structural plans for *Ulysses*. In May 1918, Joyce told Harriet Weaver that, of the book's three main parts, the 'Telemachia', the 'Odyssey', and the 'Nostos', the first consisted of three episodes (*Letters I* 113). Yet three years earlier, upon completing a first full draft of the Martello tower episode, and with an initial outline of the whole probably quite freshly conceived, he had stated on a postcard written on Bloomsday 1915 to Stanislaus in awkward German that the 'Telemachia' was to comprise four episodes (*SL* 209). The fourth can hardly have been any other than Stephen's Hamlet chapter, prepared for by theme and hour of the day in the Martello tower opening. Thus the indication is strong that both these chapters, finally placed as the first and the ninth, belong to the vestiges of *A Portrait* carried over into *Ulysses*. The Hamlet chapter notably revolves on a restatement of Stephen's aesthetic theories, and it is not inconceivable that, at some stage and in some form of pre-textual planning, it might have been designed for a position in part v of *A Portrait* analogous to that which is in fact held there by the 'Villanelle' section. As an episode located inside the National Library, it might have fitted between the part v movements which by peripatetic conversations on themes divided between nationalism, literature, art, and aesthetics on the one hand, and religion on the other, lead up to the library steps, and away from them.

Together, the tower and library episodes show that the earliest writing for *Ulysses* from the autobiographical fountainhead originated in Joyce's endeavours – approximately between 1912 and 1914 – to define a line of division between *A Portrait* and *Ulysses*. As for the matter of Dublin, *Ulysses* reaches back to *Dubliners*, and to a time of conception in 1906. As we know from letters to Stanislaus (*Letters II* 190), a story to be named 'Ulysses' was planned for *Dubliners*, though it never got beyond a title. Yet there is a strong indication that its nucleus may be recognized in the sequence of the concluding night-time events in *Ulysses* (i.e. the brawl in Nighttown, and the rescue of Stephen by Bloom, who takes the injured and drunken young man back to his house in the early morning hours).[12] The emerging novel thereby possessed a point of departure, and a goal. A middle was provided by the simple act of foreshortening the 'Telemachia' as first planned, and moving the library chapter into a central place as the 'Scylla and Charybdis' episode of the Odyssean adventures. The redesigning took place before October 1916, when in a letter to Harriet Weaver (*Letters II* 387), Joyce declared that he had almost finished the first part – i.e. the 'Telemachia' – and had written out part of the middle and end. He had thus moored the pillars over which he proceeded to span the double-arch construction of *Ulysses*.

It is only from this point onwards in Joyce's writing career that reports and surviving evidence directly testify to his working methods. Passing over the cryptic post-1905 marking-up of the *Stephen Hero* manuscript, interpretable as related, though only obliquely, to the composition of *A Portrait*, and leaving out of further consideration the notes for *Exiles* as being less of a compositional than of a critically reflective nature, it is with *Ulysses* that for the first time we begin to catch glimpses of the author in the workshop. Frank Budgen gives lively accounts of how his writer friend, wherever he went, gathered scrap matter to go into the 'glorious Swiss orange envelopes' for later use in the book; of how Joyce worked with words in the manner of a

Byzantine mosaic artist; of how he encountered Joyce in search of the *mot juste*, as he (Budgen) presumed, but really seeking the 'perfect order of words in the sentence'.[13] What Budgen observed from the distance at which Joyce was careful to keep even him, and what he related with such evident sympathy, are labours and processes of writing essentially like those we have already analyzed. A deeper understanding of Joyce's creative artistry may be derived from the draft manuscripts themselves that survive from the *Ulysses* workshop.

The seminal manuscripts for *Ulysses* that Joyce speaks of in his letters are lost: for example, the first completed draft of 'Telemachus', of which Stanislaus was told on Bloomsday 1915 (*SL* 209), the draft materials of 'the beginning, middle and end' as achieved in 1915/16, or the 'nearly completed' 'Telemachia' of October 1916 (*Letters II* 387). The earliest extant *Ulysses* draft is a version of 'Proteus' (V.A.3 in the Buffalo Joyce collection). It is contained in a copybook which, by the evidence of its label, was purchased in Locarno. Dateable therefore to the autumn of 1917, which Joyce spent in Locarno finishing and fair-copying the 'Telemachia', the draft belongs to the final phase of work on the chapter.

Its derivation from lost draft antecedents is palaeographically indicated by the clean and fluent manner in which at least its opening is written out, before expansions, revisions, and second thoughts begin increasingly to overcrowd the pages and disturb the handwriting. Other extant draft manuscripts open similarly, notably 'Oxen of the Sun' (V.A.11) and 'Circe' (V.A.19). There is always in the appearance of the drafts some suggestion of a descent from pre-existing text. At times, the appearance is surely deceptive, for the probability is strong that, for example, the 'Cyclops' manuscript V.A.8, or the 'Nausicaa' copybooks Buffalo V.A.10/Cornell 56, are themselves first drafts. What this suggests is a manner of composition by which Joyce thought out at length, and in minute detail, the structures and phrasings of whole narrative sections before committing them to paper. The look which even first drafts have of being derived emphasizes the importance which the pre-writing processes had for Joyce's writing. To all appearances, his compositions were conceived and verbalized in the mind, as well as extensively, it seems, committed to memory, before being written out in drafts. These, consequently, immediately became the carrier documents of transmission. Holding the texts available for re-reading and revision, the author's manuscripts were his secondary *loci* of writing.

Extended periods of intense work on sometimes multiple drafts were the rule of his workshop. 'It is impossible to say how much of the book is really written', Joyce remarked to Harriet Weaver in May 1918. Beyond 'Hades', which was being typed at the time, 'several other episodes have been drafted for the second time but that means nothing because although the third episode of the *Telemachia* has been a long time in the second draft I spent about 200 hours over it before I wrote it out finally' (*Letters I* 113). 'The elements needed will fuse only after a prolonged existence together' (*Letters I* 128). In August 1919 he told John Quinn that a chapter took him about four to five months to write (*Letters II* 448). This was a fair statement at the time, and as an average it held true for all subsequent chapters except 'Circe', which required six months, and 'Eumaeus', which took only about six to eight weeks to complete from the earlier drafts. The work on 'Oxen of the Sun', for which three pre-faircopy draft stages are documented, Joyce estimated at one thousand hours (*Letters II* 465); his agonies over 'Circe' found expression in statements on the number of drafts written that vary between six and nine.

There is interesting circumstantial evidence that a physical release of energy promoted the release of Joyce's creative energy. For all the innumerable hours spent in libraries, at tables and desks or on top of beds with his notes and drafts spread out around him, Joyce was a peripatetic writer. The account he gives of his state in September 1921 is as extraordinary as it seems significant. Incessant writing and revising of *Ulysses* had precipitated a nervous breakdown which Joyce counteracted by cutting his sedentary hours from a daily sixteen to six or eight and taking twelve to fourteen kilometre walks along the Seine instead (*Letters I* 170). The result was not a slackening but, by all evidence, a concentration of the work on *Ulysses*: the final breakthrough towards the completion of 'Penelope' and 'Ithaca' (in that order) and the composition of the 'Messianic scene' for 'Circe' and the 'Metropolitan police' section for 'Cyclops' all date from September/October 1921.

In the light of Joyce's roamings along the Seine to give a final boost to the composition of *Ulysses*, the peripatetics of his artist *alter ego* Stephen Dedalus take on an added significance. In part V of *A Portrait*, Stephen Dedalus walks the streets of Dublin exercising traditional arts of memory, conscious as he is that the city's topography serves to recall his thoughts and emotions. In *Ulysses*, he walks along Sandymount strand writing a text of himself – for this, precisely, is the function to which the author puts the narrative technique he employs to verbalize the Stephen of 'Proteus'. If that text, though we may read it as Joyce's creation, never gets written down by Stephen himself, his roamings through much of the chapter also constitute the pre-draft peripatetics towards his own (plagiarized) poem which he eventually jots down on the strip torn from Deasy's letter.

Taking our cue from the creative situation thus mirrored in 'Proteus', we may attempt yet further to analyze the nature and procedures of Joyce's composition before he put pen to paper. From a survey of all extant manuscript materials for *Ulysses* – drafts and fair copies as well as revisions and additions to the chapters in typescript and proofs – the unwavering structural stability of most of the novel's episodes becomes strikingly noticeable. With the single exception of the 'Aeolus' chapter, recast in proof by the introduction of segmenting cross-heads, no episode changes shape, but retains the structural outline it possesses in the fair copy, regardless of how extensive the subsequent additions and revisions to its verbal texture. Moreover, except in the cases of 'Cyclops' and 'Circe' (to which we shall return), that structural outline is by and large already characteristic of an episode's earliest extant drafts. Again, structure appears to have been a concern even in advance of the physical writing, and it is tempting to infer that, in the mental creative process, the structural design preceded the verbal texturing. In so doing, the design could serve as a 'house of memory' for organizing the composition and situating all verbal detail as it accumulated. In the deployment of his creative artistry, Joyce thus cultivated a proleptic memory – as is indeed also manifestly indicated by the precision with which he is reported to have known where to place the materials collected in his orange envelopes, in notebooks, and on notesheets for insertion into the typescripts and proofs.

That the structure provided by the myth and epic narrative of the *Odyssey* preceded the text of *Ulysses* as a whole is patently true. Ezra Pound saw the *Odyssey* as a scaffolding for *Ulysses*, yet felt that, as such, it was of little consequence for the reader, since, as the author's private building device, it had been effectively dispensed with in the accomplishment of the novel itself. T. S. Eliot, in his rival early critique, showed a greater sensitivity to the intertextual dynamism actuated by the Homeric reference,[14] and his response to the mythic interaction has been thoroughly ramified by the progressive critical exploration of the many additional pre-texts which dynamize *Ulysses* in 'retrospective arrangements'.

'Proteus', again, proves instructive. To present-day criticism, it seems that the Homeric reference, far from being dispensable, best accounts for the chapter's fascinating elusiveness of style and character consciousness: on the levels of language and thought, the episode's effect is expressively Protean. At the same time, however, its structure, its design as a house of memory to hold a character consciousness verbalized in the language of an interior monologue, has also been felt to be largely elusive. Yet read on the level of its relationship to *Hamlet*, the episode appears to be retrospectively controlled by Stephen's parting gesture: 'He turned his face over a shoulder, rere regardant' (*U* 3.503). It re-enacts Hamlet's farewell to Ophelia 'with his head over his shoulder turned', which she so heart-rendingly recounts in Act II, scene i of the play. Shattered to the depths by his encounter with his father's ghost, Hamlet, cutting all ties of kinship and severing the fetters of love that bind him to Ophelia, walks out on his past. Stephen, who has been visited by the ghost of his mother, severs all ties of friendship and, unsure of the love of woman, walks on to evening lands. If thus, in the structure of bodily movement, the episode constitutes an imaginative rewriting of a reported scene from *Hamlet*, it was ultimately in a pre-text from within the *œuvre* that Joyce found a structure to contain both that movement and the Protean verbal texture. In *A Portrait*, Stephen's movement from childhood and adolescence to artistic self-sufficiency and exile is articulated in a structure of flying by the nets of 'nationality, language, religion'. In 'Proteus', an analogous triad of nets is conceived for Stephen to desire to fly by (as I have argued in detail elsewhere).[15] These, now, are family relations (Aunt Sara and Uncle Richie), religion (the lures of priesthood visualized in the seclusion of Marsh's Library), and exile (Patrice and Kevin Egan imprisoned in their Parisian exile). A pattern derived from *A Portrait*, therefore, may be recognized to control the conclusion of the 'Telemachia' in *Ulysses*. Yet in redeploying the pre-text of *A Portrait* to gain a design by which to organize the text of 'Proteus', it would seem that Joyce, too – rere regardant while moving onward – walked out on his own and Stephen's past as represented in *A Portrait of the Artist as a Young Man*.

If, for *Ulysses*, 'Calypso' and the introduction of Leopold Bloom constitutes a new departure carrying through to 'Lestrygonians' and leading to the novel's midpoint (in terms of chapter count) in 'Scylla and Charybdis', an auto-reflexivity of the novel itself – a redeployment of its own actualization of the Homeric design and of its earlier episodes in pre-text functions for its later ones – sets in with programmatic intent in 'Wandering Rocks'. Tenth of the book's episodes, it is the chapter by which, in a sense, *Ulysses* may be said to come fully into its own. 'Wandering Rocks' is a non-episode according to any Odyssean scheme, for it shapes an adventure Odysseus eschewed, choosing the path through Scylla and Charybdis instead. Not Bloom, therefore, nor of course Stephen, but *Ulysses* moves to the centre of the chapter's attention. Standing outside the plot structure of the myth, the episode functions like a pause in the action. Its relation to what precedes and what follows arises exclusively out of the text and design of the novel itself. What *Ulysses* realizes in 'Wandering Rocks' is a potential for alternative and variation held out in the *Odyssey*. At the same time, it frees itself, at a decisive juncture of its development, from structures of event and character prefigured for the episodes actualized in the epic. In artful ambivalence 'Wandering Rocks' does, and does not, step outside the Odyssean frame of reference for *Ulysses*. What it lacks is a textual substratum in Homer's epic to refer to. But exactly such a textual reference base had meanwhile become available in the new *Odyssey* of *Ulysses*.

In extending his *œuvre*'s text by the episodes of the novel in progress, Joyce was effectively, and significantly, broadening the basis for the combinatory play of reading and writing within that text, so characteristic of his art. Even in the process of being written, the text proved increasingly capable of oscillating between text and pre-text functions, and it is in 'Sirens', the episode succeeding 'Wandering Rocks', that such oscillation becomes codified. Structurally, an 'antiphon' of short fragments introduces the chapter, which then unfolds from these sixty segments, as if generated from them in sequence, theme, tonality, and mood. In terms of the author's writing techniques, it appears that here, finally, a typical Joycean set of notes (such as those for *Exiles* considered earlier) enters the published writing, so as to render explicit a dynamic dependence of text upon pre-text. A look into the manuscripts further reveals a thorough reciprocity of the text and pre-text relationship. By the manuscript evidence, the antiphon was prefixed to the entire chapter when the latter was already extant in fair copy. In other words: it was placed to give the appearance of generative writing notes, and arranged to be read as a set of reading instructions, but was in fact itself generated, and condensed into a set of reading notes, from a comprehensive reading of the fully realized chapter. The material evidence of the manuscript, therefore – a critical consideration of which, at this point, thus proves absolutely indispensable – renders wholly transparent, as well as functional to the accomplished composition, the interdependence of text and pre-text, and points to the ultimate circularity of their relationship.

A deepened sense of the peculiar strengths of his creativity thus becomes recognizable in and behind Joyce's work around the time of the launching into the second half of *Ulysses*. It appears that he perceived with increasing clarity the principle of self-perpetuation of his *œuvre*'s text which he now at length carried into his ongoing writing. In response to Harriet Weaver's unease at what she felt was 'a weakening or diffusion of some sort' in 'Sirens', Joyce – aptly for the chapter – chose a musical simile to express his sense of writing *Ulysses*: 'In the compass of one day to compress all these wanderings and clothe them in the form of this day is for me only possible by such variation which, I beg you to believe, is not capricious' (*Letters I* 129). The artistic principle of textual variation or self-perpetuation engendered Joyce's conception of his art as work in progress. This term, it is true, was a coinage of later years for the successive publication of the segments of text which were finally to coalesce into *Finnegans Wake*. But the attitude to the artistic production which it implies begins to govern the writing of *Ulysses* from 'Wandering Rocks' onwards, and would indeed appear to account most fully for the remarkable concomitant increase in surviving workshop materials.

It is hardly by accident – rather, it seems a manifest consequence of changed attitudes – that the majority by far of the documents which show *Ulysses* in progress have been preserved from about the spring of 1919 to January 1922, the time during which the book's second half was written and the whole was revised by such radical expansion of its text as to substantiate the later claim of all-encompassing encyclopedic dimensions for the novel. For the book's first half, we possess only the draft of the 'Proteus' episode – if, that is, we must assume the manuscript of ten large pages for 'Scylla and Charybdis' which was shown in 1949 at the La Hune exhibition in Paris is irretrievably lost.[16] But of the second half, draft manuscripts exist for every single one of the nine chapters.

As indicated above, these chapter drafts – some complete, some fragmentary – do not much differ in their nature from the 'Proteus' draft of 1917. Generally, they bear witness to a process of composition guided and controlled by a conception of design anticipating the writing. The fragmentary initial drafts for 'Cyclops' (V.A.8) and 'Circe' (V.A.19), however, are exceptions to this rule. In each case it appears that Joyce committed a text to paper earlier than usual in the compositional process, thereby providing us with some evidence for the evolving of chapter structures. What is particularly notable is that, even as fragments, the surviving 'Cyclops' and 'Circe' drafts divide into discrete narrative units. Such a framing of sub-episodes yet to be unified in an overall chapter design is an anticipation of the standard procedure of composition for *Finnegans Wake*. In terms of the writing of *Ulysses*, the initial drafts for 'Cyclops' reveal a struggle for a structure to contain and to sustain the opposition of the chapter styles of gigantism and realistic dialogue. Both the 'Cyclops' and the 'Circe' early fragments, moreover, are still indeterminate in their structural direction. The chapter designs later achieved at the fair-copy stage can in neither case be inferred from the initial drafts.

Complementary to the extant draft manuscripts for 'Proteus', and 'Wandering Rocks' to 'Penelope', are the compilations of note materials for the novel as a whole in copybooks widely separated by date: the Dublin/Trieste Alphabetical Notebook, begun around Christmas 1909, from which the material divides equally between *A Portrait* and *Ulysses*; the Zurich Notebook of 1918 (VIII.A.5), remarkable for its garnering of notes from Victor Bérard's *Les Phéniciens et l'Odyssée*, W. H. Roscher's *Ausführliches Lexikon der griechischen und römischen Mythologie*, Thomas Otway's plays, and Aristotle's *Rhetoric*, which Joyce consulted in the Zentralbibliothek in Zurich; a companion Zurich notebook recently rediscovered among the copies of notebooks prepared by Mme Raphael for Joyce's *Finnegans Wake* use; and the Late Notes for typescripts and galleys of 1921/1922 (V.A.2).[17]

Analogous in terms of format, yet preceding the 'Late Notes' in the order of compilation, there is, most particularly, the series of *Ulysses Notesheets*, which received the earliest attention and, among workshop materials, have elicited the most detailed discussion in Joyce scholarship.[18] Neither *Notesheets* nor 'Late Notes' can be taken to represent Joyce's original jottings, executed, as Frank Budgen records, on whatever surface material happened to be at hand. Instead, as has often been shown, they contain a systematic arrangement of what became the additions in Joyce's handwriting to the documents that survive from typescript to final proofs for the 1922 book publication – though they by no means account for all revision and rewriting in evidence on those documents. For the original jottings, no doubt, the orange envelopes served as sorting receptacles, and only after such pre-sorting – probably by episode, and within episodes apparently sometimes by theme or motif – did Joyce proceed to compile the extant *Notesheets* and 'Late Notes' arrangements.

The notesheet format appears to have been first found useful for 'Cyclops', the last episode written in the autumn of 1919 in Zurich, and 'Nausicaa', following in early 1920 in Trieste. If the reference to a 'recast of my notes (for "Circe" and "Eumaeus")' in the first letter to Harriet Weaver from Paris in July 1920 (*Letters I* 142) is again to notesheets, the format may have been induced by the need for light travelling. At any rate, it seems clear that the surviving notesheets represent extracts from the bundles of slips in the orange envelopes and did not supersede them. For when Joyce by far outstayed the short weeks or months he had originally expected to spend in Paris – specifically to write 'Circe' and 'Eumaeus' – one of his anxieties was to retrieve from Trieste 'an oil-cloth briefcase (total weight . . . estimated to be Kg 4.78), containing the written symbols of the languid lights which occasionally flashed across my soul'. 'Having urgent need of these notes in order to complete my literary work entitled *Ulysses*', he implored Italo Svevo to obtain them for him from the flat of Stanislaus (*Letters I* 154). He received them (*Letters I* 161) and used them in the composition of 'Ithaca' and 'Penelope' as well as for the great revisional expansions of the entire book in typescript and proofs.

Joyce's writing notes for 'Circe', we may be sure, were his garnerings from the fourteen episodes preceding the Nighttown chapter. It is common critical knowledge that 'Circe' essentially depends on Joyce's comprehensive and detailed rereading of the pre-text of *Ulysses* itself up to this point. Yet, curiously, little critical thought has been given to the significance of the rewriting of that text into the text of 'Circe'. Fundamentally, it conditions the chapter's mode of referentiality. Traditional notions of narrative referentiality are concerned with the empiric substratum of the fiction: fiction as written and read is assumed to refer to truth or probability in the real world of experience. Framed by such preconceptions, critics have struggled to define and distinguish strata of real action and of 'surreal' visions or hallucinations in

'Circe'. Yet the implications of the rewriting of *Ulysses* in 'Circe' are surely that the preceding narrative of Bloomsday is made to function as if it constituted not a fiction, but itself an order of empiric reality. This assumption allows us to perceive the episode's discrete narrative units as straightforward tales told, or dramatized. They lend new narrative surfaces to Leopold Bloom or Stephen Dedalus, whether as characters or as vehicles of consciousness, as well as to all other recurring personages, objects, events, and incidents that in 'Circe' realize new narrative potential from their fictionally real existence in the pre-narrative of Bloomsday. The combinatory virtuosity of the tales unfolded from the Bloomsday pre-text is often breathtaking, yet assumes a surreal quality only if we insist on their ultimate referability to empiric reality alone. If, instead, we accept a raising of the pre-narrative that so obviously engenders the episodes of 'Circe' to the level of absolute reality, or else – which is at least as intriguing – a 'lowering' of empiric reality to the state of relativity of fiction, we recognize the chapter's mode of referentiality as one that, rather than making the text conform to traditional notions of the rendering of reality in fiction, enlarges instead its field of reference so as properly to accommodate itself. Thus 'Circe' succeeds in challenging and modifying traditionally received and theoretically articulated notions of the referentiality of fiction. Its method of procedure would appear as the systematic extension of the generative, or regenerative, compositional process that from its very origins governed Joyce's work in progress.

In 'Circe', Joyce may thus be seen to embrace the full consequences of his creative artistry: by no other pre-text than that from within his own *œuvre* could he have rocked the foundations of traditional narrative. The challenge to narrative referentiality raised in 'Circe' is, in the conclusion to the novel, paralleled by a challenge to the historicity of fictional time. 'Penelope', I suggest, is a final rewriting from a rereading of the pre-text of *Ulysses* itself. The episode is organized from within a central consciousness, and the structural element of the preceding narrative which it rereads is that hierarchically superior, and thus external, consciousness of the text sometimes known as the 'Arranger'. Having in varying degrees made its presence felt through seventeen episodes, that superior and external consciousness is conspicuously absent from 'Penelope'. The Arranger's main function throughout these seventeen episodes has been to transform the *histoire* behind *Ulysses* into the *discours* of Bloomsday – but, aware of its function, we have as readers and critics throughout been as busily reversing its arrangement and transforming the 'discours' back into 'histoire', adjusting parallax, constructing biographies, mapping topographies, discovering untold episodes, and generally putting horses properly before carts. In 'Penelope', however, where the Arranger's functions are relinquished to a central consciousness internalized in the fictional character of Molly Bloom, we at last – amazingly and with amazement – give ourselves over to a flow of discourse characterized by that essential quality of discours, the dehistoricizing of history, or dechronologizing of time. As Molly thinks herself to sleep, we learn at last what it may mean to awake from the nightmare of history. In the rewriting of Ulysses in 'Penelope' – constituting a text designed to allow the consciousness of Arranger, of Molly Bloom, and of the reader to intersect in a narrative mode so clearly pointing the way to Finnegans Wake – we are taught, if we wish finally to learn, how to read the novel, which in its author's terms means how imaginatively to rewrite the pre-text of the Joycean œuvre.

The achievement of Ulysses set the stage for Joyce's last work. It was slow in starting, as each of his previous works had been. Yet within a few years, he began to publish it in segments.[19] During the sixteen years of its growth, he invariably referred to it as 'Work in Progress', withholding its final title – Finnegans Wake – until the moment of integral publication in 1939. Significantly, before entering into fresh reading and writing phases, he secured a basis from within his own œuvre by reassembling workshop materials from all his existing texts in the so-called 'Scribbledehobble' notebook (Buffalo VI.A.).[20] Beyond, the mass of Finnegans Wake notebooks holds overwhelming and as yet largely untapped evidence of his wide reading of the most heterogeneous array of source materials as pre-texts for the writings of the final extension to his œuvre's text.

Scholarship, at this level, is faced with a double impasse: on the one hand, the 'Books at the Wake'[21] yet to be traced through the notebooks are highly unpredictable; on the other hand, the notes assembled and cryptically condensed from them often seem, at present, next-to-illegible. Only when identification of a note source succeeds from the intermittent legible entries – if not by outright divination – does this in turn help to unlock the uncompromisingly private notebook graphics.

As Joyce's private material repositories, the notebooks are the mere preliminaries to all subsequent constitution of compositional text. The writing of *Finnegans Wake* itself from its pre-texts – whether or not encoded, successively, in related notebooks – passed through much the same stages as did that of *Ulysses*, albeit over an appreciably longer timespan; as it happens, Joyce's writing years from the beginnings on *Stephen Hero* to the conclusion of *Finnegans Wake* neatly divide in half with the publication of *Ulysses*. From the second half of his writing life, guided as it was by the notion of creative authorship as work in progress, such as it became now publicly declared in a title, we possess in abundance sketches and working drafts, fair copies, typescripts, segment publications and multi-revisional proofs that, even as they first emerge for sections and sub-sections that only eventually coalesce towards *Finnegans Wake*, relate in far more complex ways than anything to be observed in the organization of the writing for *Ulysses*. For sheer quantity, as well as for organizational intricacy, the sixteen years it took Joyce to wind off Work in Progress yielded a rich document legacy. Much more, however, the compositional and revisional testimony which the documents preserve appears unrivalled for its quality. But it is a qualitative testimony that has received very little critical exploration. Indeed, to do justice to Joyce's creative artistry in Work in Progress, Joyce scholarship may yet require a new critical outlook and a new corporate experience.

NOTES

1 Reproduced in *Archive* 11, ed. A. Walton Litz, 1–61, and inaccurately appended to *E* (148–60).
2 The fragments are reproduced in *Archive* 11, 64–85, and discussed in Robert M. Adams, 'Light on Joyce's *Exiles*? A new manuscript, a curious analogue, and some speculations', *Studies in Bibliography* 17 (1964), 83–105.
3 Those that survive, in manuscript, are reproduced in *Archive* 7, ed. Hans Walter Gabler. Special note should be taken of the recent bilingual edition: James Joyce, *Epifanie (1900–1904)*, ed. Giorgio Melchiori (Milan, 1982). See the discussion of the epiphanies by Vicki Mahaffey in this volume, ch. 8.
4 For a note on the available editions, see p. 129 above. Claus Melchior's Munich dissertation of 1987, '*Stephen Hero*: Textentstehung und Text. Eine Untersuchung der Kompositions- und Arbeitsweise des frühen James

Joyce' incorporates a freshly established text, due to be published in a critical edition.

5 See Hugh Kenner, 'Signs on a white field', in Morris Beja *et al.*, eds., *James Joyce: the Centennial Symposium* (Urbana: University of Illinois Press, 1986), pp. 209–19; Matthew C. Hodgart, '"Ivy Day in the Committee Room"', in Clive Hart, ed., *James Joyce's 'Dubliners': Critical Essays* (London: Faber, 1969), pp. 115–21 (as one essay among many that make the political point); Stanislaus Joyce, *My Brother's Keeper*, ed. Richard Ellmann (London: Faber, 1958), p. 225; Mary T. Reynolds, *Joyce and Dante* (Princeton: Princeton University Press, 1981), esp. p. 159; Brewster Ghiselin, 'The unity of Joyce's *Dubliners*', *Accent* 16 (1956), 75–88, 193–213.

6 See for example Bernard Benstock, '"The Dead"', in Clive Hart, ed., *James Joyce's 'Dubliners': Critical Essays* (London: Faber, 1969), pp. 153–69.

7 See Hans Walter Gabler, 'The Christmas dinner scene, Parnell's death, and the genesis of *A Portrait of the Artist as a Young Man*', *JJQ* 13 (1976), 27–38.

8 See Hans Walter Gabler, Preface to *Archive* 8, '*A Portrait of the Artist as a Young Man': A Facsimile of the Manuscript Fragments of 'Stephen Hero'*.

9 '[Cosgrave] says he would not like to be Gogarty when you come to the Tower episode' (*Letters II* 103).

10 *Archive* 10, 1219–22; cf. A. Walton Litz, *The Art of James Joyce* (Oxford: Oxford University Press, 1961), p. 133.

11 See Wilhelm Füger, 'Joyce's *Portrait* and Nietzsche', *Arcadia* 7 (1972), 231–59.

12 Richard Ellmann, in the Introduction to *Ulysses on the Liffey* (London: Faber, 1972), and in more detail in the Afterword to the old Penguin edition of *Ulysses* (Harmondsworth, 1968), has been the foremost spokesman for the hypothesis that the Nighttown episode essentially reflects the projected *Dubliners* story 'Ulysses'. Hugh Kenner, on the other hand, interprets the 'Calypso' to 'Wandering Rocks' sequence as the novel's expansion of a typical *Dubliners* story for which the title 'Ulysses' would have been appropriate (see Kenner, *Ulysses* (London: Allen & Unwin, 1980), p. 61).

13 Frank Budgen, *James Joyce and the Making of 'Ulysses', and Other Writings* (London: Oxford University Press, 1972); quotations on pp. 177 and 20. The comparison of Joyce to a Byzantine artist is Valery Larbaud's, from 'The *Ulysses* of James Joyce', *Criterion* 1 (1922), 102.

14 Ezra Pound, 'Paris Letter: *Ulysses*', *Dial* 72 (1922), 623–9; T. S. Eliot, '*Ulysses*, order and myth', *Dial* 75 (1923), 480–3 (reprinted in *CH I* 175–8).

15 Hans Walter Gabler, 'Narrative rereadings: some remarks on "Proteus", "Circe" and "Penelope"', in Claude Jacquet, ed., *'Scribble' 1: genèse des textes*, La Revue des Lettres Modernes, Série James Joyce 1 (Paris: Minard, 1988), 57–68.

16 Catalogued as no. 254 in *James Joyce, Sa vie, son oeuvre, son rayonnement* (Paris, 1949).

17 The entries from the Alphabetical Notebook are accessible in Robert Scholes and Richard M. Kain, eds., *The Workshop of Daedalus* (Evanston: Northwestern University Press, 1965); notebooks VIII.A.5 and V.A.2 have been transcribed, edited and discussed by Phillip F. Herring, *Joyce's Notes and Early Drafts for 'Ulysses': Selections from the Buffalo Collection* (Charlottesville: University Press of Virginia, 1977); as yet unpublished is Danis Rose and John O'Hanlon's edited and annotated transcription of the Madame Raphael notebook VI.D.7 (*VI.D.7: The Lost First Notebook*), which turns out to be derived from a companion notebook to VIII.A.5.

18 Phillip F. Herring, *Joyce's 'Ulysses' Notesheets in the British Museum* (Charlottesville: University Press of Virginia, 1972). The Notesheets were first discussed by Litz in *The Art of James Joyce* (see note 10).

19 See Jean-Michel Rabaté's summary in ch. 4 of this volume (p. 89).

20 Thomas E. Connolly, ed., *James Joyce's Scribbledehobble: The Ur-Workbook for 'Finnegans Wake'* (Evanston: Northwestern University Press, 1961).

21 The labourers on the notebooks for *Finnegans Wake* agree that the pioneering study by James S. Atherton, *The Books at the Wake* (London: Faber, 1959), may yet but scratch the surface of the litterheap of books that Joyce read and extracted from in the course of his Work in Progress. Knowing nothing about the *Finnegans Wake* notebooks (now available in *Archive*, vols. 29–43), Atherton did not develop refined standards of methodology to identify source books beyond the ones he discusses as 'major' ones. The pioneering study in this field is Danis Rose, ed., *James Joyce's 'The Index Manuscript': 'Finnegans Wake' Holograph Workbook VI.B.46* (Colchester: Wake Newslitter Press, 1977).

10 Joyce and feminism

I

Joyce and feminism – a difficult conjunction, a seemingly forced connection between a man who is quoted as saying, 'I hate women who know anything' and a movement that applauds women's intellects and rights. Perhaps the 'and' conjoins opposites, such as black and white? This would be the view of some feminists who see misogyny expressed in Joyce's representation of female characters, particularly Molly Bloom in *Ulysses*. Sandra Gilbert and Susan Gubar, for example, view Molly as 'a choice of matter over mind' ('Sexual linguistics', p. 518). They regard Woman in Joyce as confined to her body, excluded from the production of culture. Particularly in *Ulysses*, they see Joyce's language as the triumph of a patriarchal literary heritage. In short, and in pun, they 'refuse to be Mollified' (p. 519) by 'feminologist re-Joyceings'; they castigate those women critics who see in Joyce's subversion of social and literary conventions a natural alliance with feminism.

These harsh judgements are anticipated in Joyce's work itself, particularly *Ulysses* and *Finnegans Wake*, and even in his recorded dreams, all of which contain numerous examples of women accusing men of misleading and misrepresenting them. One of the best texts in which to examine these images of accusation is the 'Circe' or Nighttown episode of *Ulysses*, in which the characters act out many of their deepest desires and fears suppressed during the day. Women from Leopold Bloom's past and present accuse him of sexual innuendo, voyeurism, and defamation of character. For example, here is Martha Clifford, a typist with whom Bloom has conducted a titillating and secret correspondence after her response to an advertisement placed by him in the *Irish Times*:

MARTHA

(thickveiled, a crimson halter round her neck, a copy of the Irish Times *in her hand, in tone of reproach, pointing)* Henry! Leopold! Lionel, thou lost one! Clear my name.   (*U* 15.752–4)

'Clear my name', Martha cries reproachfully to her male betrayer/s, perhaps speaking for other female characters and readers who accuse the male writer of misunderstanding and misrepresenting women. In a chapter where transformations abound and identities slip and slide, Martha accuses a multiple male betrayer: Henry, the penname with which Bloom signs his secret letters to her ('Henry Flower' is the full signature); Leopold, Bloom's real first name which Martha never learns; Lionel, the male lead in Flotow's opera *Martha*. This composite list of male betrayers enjoined to 'clear' Martha's name suggests that perhaps 'James' (as in 'James Joyce') could be added to the list of men whose words to and about women endanger their reputations, and who might be challenged to redeem them.

Indeed, Joyce dreamt of Molly Bloom herself reproaching him for his prurient interest in women's 'business' and for his presumptuous attempts to lend voice to female desire. In a dream important enough for Joyce to relate in two different versions to two different friends (Herbert Gorman and John Sullivan), Molly Bloom herself rejects his attempts to represent her. In one version, Joyce said, 'Molly came calling on me and said, "What are you meddling with my old business for?" She had a coffin in her hand and said, "If you don't change this is for you"' (*JJ* 549). Here, Molly expresses her murderous anger toward her creator for his interest in woman's private, that is, sexual 'old' (smelly?) business. In another version of the dream, Molly flings a child's black coffin at Bloom (presumably Rudy's) and says, 'I've done with you.' Joyce, indignant, tries to intercede by delivering a 'very long, eloquent' and passionate speech 'explaining all the last episode of *Ulysses* to her.' Molly smiles at the end of Joyce's 'astronomical climax', then flings at him 'a tiny snuffbox, in the form of a little black coffin' and says, 'And I have done with you, too.' In recording this dream, Joyce explained that his godfather had given him a similar snuffbox when he attended Clongowes Wood College (*JJ* 549). Here Molly flings at him the symbol of intercourse, the coffin-shaped snuffbox that may remind us of the symbol of 'Plumtree's Potted Meat' in *Ulysses*. The snuffbox thrown in Joyce's face is also, as Joyce tells us, a patriarchal legacy. Molly cuts off her male critic as well as male creator, the one who tries to pen woman's desire and then has the audacity to explain it. It is as if the 'real' Molly accuses Joyce of offering a constructed woman as a naturalistic Everywoman.

Finally, as Bonnie Scott points out in *James Joyce* (p. 127), Anna Livia Plurabelle (ALP), the multi-formed female presence in *Finnegans Wake*, comments on Molly Bloom's ill treatment at the pen of their joint creator. ALP describes the 'Penelope' chapter of *Ulysses* as 'a colophon [last word] of no fewer than seven hundred and thirtytwo strokes tailed by a leaping lasso', in which 'the vaulting feminine libido' is 'sternly controlled and easily repersuaded by the uniform matteroffactness of a meandering male fist' (*FW* 123.05–10). Anna Livia ridicules the male writing which tries to 'lasso' the feminine libido (the 'lasso' is also the male pen) and the stern male fist that tries to grasp it (sexually and intellectually). This is the fist that makes Molly wait (like Penelope) the whole of *Ulysses* to be given 'the last word'.

II

How do these examples of female accusation, staged in Joyce's fiction and infiltrating his dreams, address the charges of feminist readers like Gilbert and Gubar, for example, who claim that women in Joyce are 'sentenced' to a purely material existence? These charges are compelling. For one thing, the history of male critical response to the women in Joyce, and to Molly in particular, seems to lend support to a charge of Joyce's confining women to their bodies: Molly has been read by influential critics as the womb (Tindall, *James Joyce*), Nature (Ellmann, *Ulysses on the Liffey*), and the goddess of the 'animal kingdom of the dead' (Kenner, *Dublin's Joyce*). And yet, this particular feminist reading ignores the way in which Joyce's texts partly deconstruct the symbolic, encoded forms of their own representations and expose the workings of male desire. Joyce's dream accounts and fictional passages implicitly acknowledge that the male writer's representation of woman is never 'objective', but rather involves a combination of *hubris*, assault, fascination, even envy. When men write to and about the 'Other', emotions are never expressed simply or directly. Feelings about the 'Other' are highly ambivalent, changeable, and disguised even from oneself. Desire circulates consciously and unconsciously through the writer's representation of the Other; art embeds this desire in the text.

In the 'Scylla and Charybdis' chapter of *Ulysses*, Stephen Dedalus describes his theory of artistic creation in a long disquisition on Shakespeare. According to Stephen, Shakespeare's plays are full of the torments in his life, especially sexual ones; he speaks of Shakespeare's plays as 'the creation he has piled up to hide him from himself' (*U* 9.475). Although Stephen's theory is grandiose and sometimes muddled, Joyce, too, believed that art is not simple self-expression or autobiography, but a complicated embedding, disguising, dispersing of the author and his desire in the text. Joyce's later work in particular reveals the ambivalent nature of writing, in relation to desire. In *Finnegans Wake*, Shem the Penman figures this dual nature of writing in the word 'squirtscreen' (*FW* 187.07), which captures the sense of writing as expression of the self (Shem's 'ink' is his own excrement) and self-defence (a squid squirts ink in self-defence); writing is a burst of expression ('squirt') but also a 'screen'. Perhaps writing is even a 'skirtscreen', by which the penman hides behind his mother's skirts or hides the female body; her body functioning as a defence against the anxiety of writing, or writing functioning as a defence against the power of her body. In 1904, Stanislaus Joyce wrote that it might be contended of James's style that he 'confesses in a foreign language' (*My Brother's Keeper*, p. 81). James came to realize that disclosure and disguise were inextricably linked, particularly in the arena of sexuality.

Thus a catalogue of misogynistic images or female stereotypes in Joyce's work fails to account for his undermining of the grounds of representation. And Gilbert and Gubar's emphasis on Joyce's linguistic 'puissance' and patriarchal mastery ignores his radical scepticism of the possibility of 'lassoing' essences, including that of the 'vaulting feminine libido'. Indeed, the deconstruction of presences poses a relationship between the metaphor of woman and a writing practice that disrupts patriarchal signature and conventions. Again, one can think of Joyce's dream of Molly, which seems to acknowledge that woman in writing is beyond his control and might stand for a play of language that always exceeds the writer's intention. Julia Kristeva links the disruption of patriarchal discourse in Joyce and some other avant-garde male writers with the feminine or maternal repressed by

Western culture: as Kristeva calls it, 'the inseparable obverse of [the writer's] very being, the other [sex] that torments and possesses him' (*Powers of Horror*, p. 208). This idea is anticipated in the description of *Finnegans Wake* as a 'letter selfpenned to one's other' (*FW* 489.33–4). If paternity is the 'legal fiction', as Stephen Dedalus says in 'Scylla and Charybdis', woman becomes the figure for illegitimacy, errancy, and forgery rather than patriarchal signature, a significance to which I will return.

III

Increasingly, Joyce's texts unmask male anxieties of women's power. In the earlier texts, these anxieties are represented as largely character based, the personal fears and desires of male characters like Stephen Dedalus or Gabriel Conroy; increasingly, however, the later texts reveal these fears to be inscriptions of cultural anxieties. Joyce shows that desire, like language, cannot be a purely personal phenomenon. At the beginning of *Ulysses*, Stephen says that history is a 'nightmare from which [he is] trying to awake', referring to his own past and Irish history. His latent reference to the profoundly troubling dream of Woman (the 'night-mare') is made more explicit when he jokes that the nightmare might give him a 'back kick' (*U* 2.377–9). *Finnegans Wake* reworks the image so as to expose the way in which culture validates male fear and subordination of the female. The nightmare reappears, this time explicitly as Woman being 'ridden' by male desire in the form of 'The galleonman jovial on his bucky brown nightmare' (*FW* 583.08–09). The 'galleonman's' joviality and casual assumption of the superior position does not mask the potential of the bucky 'night-mare' to bring unquiet dreams to her male rider. And, as Bernard Benstock has pointed out in regard to the struggle between the narrative voice and Margareen in Book I, chapter 6 of the *Wake*, the 'functioning narrator' undertakes 'ploys' in order to '''objectify'' – and therefore dispel – the strong feminine influence. By posing behind numerous journalistic styles and guises he seeks to prevent her female voice from usurping the directional tone' ('Twice-told tales', p. 105).

In exploring the institutionalization of cultural myths, Joyce exposed the power relationship suppressed within the binary oppositions that underwrite culture, i.e. the pairs of words like male/female and presence/absence in which one of the terms of the pair is privileged over the other. In unmasking the binary oppositions, Joyce is a precursor of deconstruction. Indeed, Jacques Derrida himself announces his debt to Joyce, especially *Finnegans Wake*, in 'Plato's pharmacy' (p. 88) and in 'Two words for Joyce'.

But in unmasking the power relations inscribed in culture and the workings of male fear and desire of the Other, Joyce implies that no one can stand outside this process. As Cheryl Herr puts it from a Marxist perspective (in *Joyce's Anatomy of Culture*), 'Joyce's fictions both operate within the philosophical structures that marked his early rearing and critique their ideological surface' (p. 9). Herr is speaking here of bourgeois ideology in particular, but her statement applies to patriarchal ideology in general. As Joyce's own dreams and letters attest, to expose the workings of male paranoia, desire, guilt, and ambivalence in one's fiction, is not necessarily to free one from the same feelings. Contending that Joyce exposes the workings of ideology and desire and subverts conventions is not the same as claiming that he completely transcends his own time. On the other hand, his scepticism of order, system, and style led to a radical critique of phallogocentrism, in which the disruptive metaphor of woman played an important part.

What I am describing is never an unambivalent progress toward a uniform idea or embodiment of Women. ALP's comment notwithstanding, Joyce's 'male fist' is neither 'matteroffact' nor 'uniform' when it comes to the feminine. Indeed, Joyce's representation of the feminine is often double-minded, containing the traces of past desires and fears. His 'critique' of the ideological surface of patriarchal culture in general, and his greater self-consciousness about the mechanisms of the cultural construction of the female, seem often to co-exist with the longing for a natural 'home' in the maternal body. To be more specific, although Joyce's work from *Dubliners* to *Finnegans Wake* moves toward a radical questioning of the notion of origin, it retains the signs of longing for just such an origin or home, a longing Stephen expresses when he calls mother love 'The only true thing in life', or when he imagines the 'strandentwining cable of all flesh' leading back to Edenville (*U* 3.37). Joyce, everywhere more self-conscious than his fledgling artist, still encodes in even the most post-modern of his works, *Finnegans Wake* and the latter parts of *Ulysses*, the desire for that place of birth, of origin, while simultaneously showing the impossibility of ever getting beyond culture, beyond language, to a natural, single 'home'.[1]

At times, this longing for an origin takes the form of a search for a 'natural' language. For example, according to Richard Ellmann, Joyce chose as analogue to the concept of perfect pitch in 'Sirens' 'Molly's natural comprehension of the hurdy-gurdy boy without understanding a word of his language' (*JJ* 439). Bloom sentimentally calls Molly's ability a 'Gift of Nature'. Joyce himself was fascinated by the idea of the 'secret' language of women. He kept a dream book in which he recorded some of Nora's dreams with his interpretations. In one such dream, Nora is lying on a hill amidst a herd of *silver* cows and is made love to by one cow. Joyce's sister Eileen appears. Joyce's interpretation of the dream is revealing:

That silver seems to her [Nora] a fine metal (and not a cheaper form of gold) shows a freedom from conventional ideas, a freedom more strongly shown by the fact that she feels no repulsion at being made love to by a female beast. Here there is no fear either of goring or of pregnancy. An experience more in life and therefore not to be avoided. Eileen appears as a messenger of *those secret tidings* which only women bear to women and the silver mountain torrent [an element in the dream], a precious and wild element, accompanies the secrecy of her messages with the music of romance.   (*JJ* 437; my italics)

Here Joyce fantasizes about a secret female language, an elsewhere outside patriarchal mastery, a kind of female annunciation ('no goring, no pregnancy'). Of necessity, it is an elsewhere whose very condition depends upon the exclusion of men. Paradoxically, woman represents an 'experience more in life' and therefore 'not to be avoided', yet an experience which the fallen Adam cannot have.

But the image of woman as the Truth of Nature is itself shown to be a fiction. As Stephen Heath reminds us in 'Ambiviolences' (p. 53), Anna Livia is the 'Bringer of Plurabilities' (*FW* 104.02). *Both* Woman as Nature and Woman as Fiction are conveyed in the name ALP – the source of every river *and* German for 'nightmare' (Alptraum), the dream and the nightmare from which the male writer cannot awake. Another phrase from *Finnegans Wake* condenses this longing for a source before language and the impossibility of arriving at that source. In his excellent work *Joyce's Book of the Dark*, John Bishop cites the following line from *Finnegans Wake*, applying it to the work as a whole: it 'make[s] you to see figuratleavely the whome of your eternal geomater' (296.30–297.01). He says 'the passage moves us behind the occulting and shame-invested "fig leave" (hence "figuratleavely") into a "momerry" of first "whome" ("womb", "home")' (p. 356). But it seems to me the 'figuratleavely' suggests not only the desire to remove the fig leaf to view the source, but also the inescapable *figuration* involved in the representation of Woman. If the desire to lift the veil of Woman is everywhere portrayed in the text, its impossibility is insistent. The 'misses in prints' (20.11) are never stripped of their 'feminine clothiering' (109.31) – one figuration leads to another, never passing beyond to a realm where the Truth of Woman is found.

In Joyce's works, then, woman is not revealed but constantly revised. Even epiphanies ('sudden spiritual manifestations') of women are rethought and rewritten. For example, the powerful image of the bird girl which sears Stephen's imagination in *A Portrait* is progressively deromanticized. That beautiful Irish muse with 'long slender bare legs' metamorphoses into the limping Gerty MacDowell, finally to become Biddy Doran the hen foraging in the midden heap in *Finnegans Wake*. The female is seen variously: she is ALP as the River Liffey, libidinously circulating through *Finnegans Wake*, ALP the letter writer, attempting to save her husband's reputation, and Issy, the daughter, whose letter threatens to expose her father's incestuous desires. She is both Nature and Culture, her body identified with both Mother Earth and the materiality of writing.

It is finally not as 'flesh-without-word' that Woman functions for Joyce most powerfully, but as an 'allaphbed' figuring the erotic and material potential of language. The phrase 'misses in prints' suggests the errancy and waywardness of language which for Joyce, particularly in his later works, is figured by women. Biddy Doran's midden heap in *Finnegans Wake* is an image of the contaminated, uncontrollable material of language, and the slipperiness of its sounds and associations. The female figures the comic, almost slapstick potential in language that eludes patriarchal control. Penelope as weaver, the hen as gatherer and scavenger, remind us of the texture of writing, its material body, its bricolage. Anna Livia is a thief, a retriever and interpreter of other people's language ('where in thunder did she plunder' (*FW* 209.12)). Her theft of language serves as a model of its citationality. She provides a figure for an illegality, something outside of the patriarchal rebellion that is a killing of the literary forefather by the male heir apparent. She offers, metaphorically, a way out of the discourse of Freudian rebellion, offers instead a term for the Derridean 'drift' in language.

Thus, although male rivalry and relationship dominate much of

Joyce's texts and filial rebellion is an enormously important figure as well as theme, the 'feminine' figured and as figure becomes increasingly important. One must recognize the danger of the 'genderization' of writing as feminine and of viewing the male avant-garde as writing the 'feminine', for the undecidability that characterizes 'feminine' writing might appear to reinscribe Woman in her old stereotypes. This seems to me always a danger in Joyce's work. But ultimately I believe that Joyce relied on stereotypical binary oppositions, as Stephen Heath says in 'Joyce and language' (p. 144), to 'deride and overturn them' by unmasking them and, further, by blurring the oppositions in the play of his language.

IV

In Joyce's early fiction, the staging of rebellion against the patriarchy exists still within some of its more dominant myths. For, although the early works explore cultural inscriptions of power, they seem less concerned with the role of the female in relation to patriarchal law. In *Dubliners* Joyce depicts the general entrapment of the 'submerged population' of Dublin, as Frank O'Connor once called it, the underclass victimized by its own pathetically limited expectations and by the masters – the British and the Church of Rome – that rule the country. Women do not figure prominently in the majority of these stories. When they do, as in 'Eveline' and 'Clay', they display the general Dublin 'paralysis' of their male counterparts, but, like the child in 'Counterparts', these women suffer by being the oppressed of the oppressed. Like the 'slavey' in 'Two Gallants', women in Dublin, 'good girls' included, wait for the favours of men. Even Gretta Conroy, whose vivid moment of romance is central to the story 'The Dead', is locked in her husband's story as well as his fantasy, and can reveal only glimpses of her own desire. The register of female roles is more limited than that of the males – overbearing mothers (Mrs Mooney, Mrs Kearney), repressed spinsters (the eponymous 'Sisters', Maria in 'Clay', Julia and Kate Morkan in 'The Dead'), frustrated wives (Gretta, Mrs Chandler), objects of fantasy (the girl in 'Araby'), the new political woman (Molly Ivors). The frustration of the female characters is signalled by this limited repertory of roles, but their marginality also arises from Joyce's basic scheme for the stories, to depict the stages of development from youth to maturity of a male protagonist.

The story of female development must be largely inferred: a character like Maria might be seen as the human consequence of Eveline's decision not to go with her sailor Frank; Mrs Kearney, the frustrated and manipulative mother in 'A Mother', might be what the pregnant and unwed Polly Mooney will become. Mrs Sinico in 'A Painful Case' is the fleeting image of what a woman could have meant in a man's life, a kind of Jamesian promise of the lived life. (Interestingly, it is the woman who dies as a result of the man missing his opportunity.) The significance of the female, however, is suggested in strange ways in *Dubliners* – in the seemingly misplaced title of the first story, 'The Sisters', which focuses on a young boy's fascination with a dead priest, or in 'The Dead', which itself might be called 'The Sisters', because the Morkan sisters, who play an auxiliary role in the plot, haunt the story almost like shades, with the thought of their impending deaths muted and displaced.[2]

In the early portraits of the artist, *Stephen Hero* and *A Portrait*, women seem to be once again cast in roles auxiliary to male development – as sexual tutors (the prostitute), muses (E.C., the bird girl), and symbols of the entangling snares the developing male must avoid (temptress of the villanelle, E.C., Dante with her hysterical Catholicism). The development of the Daedalean artist seems to entail a flight from women, particularly the mother, as a condition of growth. She is one of the 'nets' he must fly by. In order to enter the symbolic world of language and the Father, the boy must remove himself from 'the sufferings of women, the weakness of their bodies and souls' (*P* 245).

Joyce himself curtails the role of the female between *Stephen Hero*, the long unpublished novel in which both his mother and Emma Clery have explicit and extended roles, and the much shorter *Portrait*. May Dedalus, whose conversations are recorded in the earlier version of Stephen's story, is deprived of most of her lines and much of her role in *A Portrait*. And, as numerous critics have observed, Emma Clery is transformed from a character with a body and a name, to an object of mystery and intrigue – an ambivalent focus of desire, fear, and friendship whose presence – like the 'characters' of *Finnegans Wake* – is signified by her initials (E.C.).

It is as if the image of the female were abstracted by Joyce so that Stephen must incarnate it himself, for ultimately Stephen seeks to convert abstract beauty and desire into poetry. As he has his 'epiphany' of the bird girl at the end of part IV, Stephen feels 'her image pass into his soul for ever' (*P* 172). But he begins to realize that the image must pass out as well, if he is to be a 'priest of the eternal imagination' and transmute the spirit into a material image. The muse is crucial to this incarnation; somehow it is her spirit that must be embodied. One might say with Molly that all poets merely 'want to write about some woman', but the female is more than a topic here; she is projected as the muse of representation, of embodiment. Her image haunts his days and his nights, as he struggles to refine it into poetry.

In part V Stephen seeks to find an image for E.C., between temptress and muse, inspiration for a wet dream and for poetry. In the process of figuring her, the young artist hopes to capture her elusive power, yet, he questions his own images, disturbed that he cannot fully represent her. He tries first one, then another image, crossing out as he goes along, debating how to figure her in language. In the following passage, for example, he first clothes her in Elizabethan garb, then rejects the sluttish image he has summoned:

Eyes, opening from the darkness of desire, eyes that dimmed the breaking east . . . And what was their shimmer but the shimmer of the scum that mantled the cesspool of the court of a slobbering Stuart. And he tasted in the language of memory . . . dying fallings of sweet airs . . . and saw with the eyes of memory kind gentlewomen in Covent Garden wooing from their balconies with sucking mouths . . .

The images he had summoned gave him no pleasure. They were secret and enflaming but her image was not entangled by them. That was not the way to think of her. It was not even the way in which he thought of her. Could his mind then not trust itself? Old phrases, sweet only with a disinterred sweetness like the figseeds Cranly rooted out of his gleaming teeth. (*P* 233)

In the first passage Stephen searches for the 'right' image for Emma; in the second, he cancels out the image he has summoned from the literary stockpile. Like the 'figseed' plucked from Cranly's teeth, these phrases are leftover erotic (forbidden) fruit, conducive to erotic fantasy but not to poetry. Just like Molly Bloom in Joyce's dream, E.C. eludes Stephen's representation of her. 'Her image was not entangled' by his words, a strange phrase that suggests it is she now who flies by the nets.[3]

The maternal image, too, seems beyond Stephen's control, surfacing at a crucial moment like the return of the repressed. The moment occurs in *A Portrait* during Stephen's trip to Cork, his father's hometown, when he searches for his father's initials in a school desk. Instead, in the midst of his search for his paternal origins, he is startled to find the word 'foetus', carved in the desk like a scar. As Maud Ellmann says in a brilliant discussion of this episode, Stephen, searching for his father's (and thus his own) initials, discovers instead an image that draws him back to the body of the mother. In the midst of the scripting of the artist in the patriarchal tradition, the word leads back to 'a prior nameless unbegotten world'. The mother's anonymity flouts the name of the father. Her 'namelessness', Ellmann says, 'engraves itself upon the flesh [i.e. the navel] before the father ever carved his signature' ('Polytropic man', p. 96). 'The name of the father . . . necessarily entails a fresh unstained creation. The patronyms of all link back to that "creation from nothing" . . . which Stephen mocks and then repudiates. . . The scarletter on the belly tells another story, that has neither a beginning nor an end: that neither flesh nor words can ever say where they came from or claim a unitary origin' (p. 101). Ellmann rightly sees anonymity, rather than the authority of the proper name, in the maternal image. Maternity, then, is a different kind of 'fiction' than paternity, a fiction of a source before law and identity, the 'allaphbed' of Anna Livia. Stephen's discovery seems to have a significance in the narrative and his consciousness that is never fully explained or rationalized in the text. It is as if it were itself a kind of scar. Unlike the epiphany at the end of part II in which the prostitute initiates Stephen into sexual experience, the word 'foetus' cannot be assimilated to the pattern of the artist's quest. Indeed, the image of the artist as 'foetus' reverses the direction of development in an alarming way.

In *Ulysses*, too, Stephen is suddenly and gratuitously reminded of the maternal image in another scene which juxtaposes maternal mark with the name and seal of the father. In 'Nestor', scrawny Cyril Sargent, one of Stephen's students, copies out his sums; reminded of his own youth, Stephen gazes at an inkstain on the boy's face:

On his cheek, dull and bloodless, a soft stain of ink lay, dateshaped, recent and damp as a snail's bed.
    He held out his copybook . . . [A]t the foot a crooked signature with blind loops and a blot. Cyril Sargent: his name and seal.
    . . .

    Ugly and futile: lean neck and thick hair and a stain of ink, a snail's bed. Yet someone had loved him, borne him in her arms and in her heart. But for her the

race of the world would have trampled him underfoot, a squashed boneless snail . . . Was that then real? The only true thing in life? . . .
. . .

Amor matris: subjective and objective genitive. With her weak blood and wheysour milk she had fed him and hid from sight of others his swaddlingbands.   (*U*. 2.126–67)

The inkstain, the blemish on the face, is the mark of the mother's anonymity in the text. It reminds Stephen of maternal stain rather than the 'fresh unstained creation' of the father. Between birthmark and ink, the stain blurs the boundary between nature and culture. This scarletter reminds us that Moses, the child in swaddling bands, was shielded by a woman, his patriarchy dependent upon her protection. The wasted body of Stephen's mother appears throughout *Ulysses* to remind Stephen that one ignores the sign of the mother at one's peril. *Amor matris* is subjective and objective genitive – it works two ways.[4]

Throughout *Ulysses*, Stephen wrestles with the nightmare of his own history, especially its origin in the maternal body, his conception, the result of what he calls 'an instant of blind rut'. Indeed, Stephen's theory of literary creation in 'Scylla and Charybdis' and patriarchal literary culture itself in 'Oxen of the Sun' neutralize the power of the mother by effacing her role in culture.

In 'Scylla and Charybdis', Stephen speaks of the 'mystical estate' of fatherhood. Paternity, he says, may be a 'legal fiction', that is, only a fiction of origin, and yet it is the *founding* fiction of the Church of Rome and of Western civilization itself, including literary creation. In contrast, here, as in the 'Nestor' chapter, Stephen speculates that *amor matris* may be 'the only true thing in life', a product of nature instead of culture. The statement hides the complexity of the maternal image for Stephen. Moreover, although he acknowledges the mother's power, he renders it impotent; essentialized as Womb, she is excluded from participating in culture by means of her function as its unproblematic 'true' body. Stephen's theory of creation, then, pre-empts the role of the mother and leaves the male artist self-sufficient, free to create a world. If Joyce was intrigued with Nora's dream of a female language outside of patriarchal mastery, a kind of female annunciation without male interference, Stephen's myth of creation seeks to efface the role of the mother in the production of language.

As Dorothy Dinnerstein suggests in *The Mermaid and the Minotaur*, the invisibility of fatherhood paradoxically contributes to its power, as if man conceded to woman the visible and claimed for himself, compensatorily, the much greater world of the spiritual and invisible (p. 81).[5] She further suggests that patrilineage arises out of envy of woman's procreative power. In 'Oxen of the Sun' Stephen says (quoting the Gospel of John), 'In woman's womb the word is made flesh but in the spirit of the maker all flesh that passes becomes the word that shall not pass away. This is the postcreation' (U 14.292–4). He acknowledges the body of the mother only to appropriate its womb for paternal postcreation. Stephen acknowledges the reproductive power of the mother, but it is the paternal 'postcreation' of the word that produces true immortality.

In the 'Oxen of the Sun' chapter of Ulysses it is as if Stephen's defensiveness were played out across the span of literary history. The chapter represents the suppressed relationship between reproduction and textual production. The symbol of the chapter is the 'womb', and it applies to the chapter in two ways. In a sense, woman's womb funds the male discussion: it is the object of male debate and is praised, jeered at, legislated. In the changing styles of literary history, woman's economy changes as she is alternately valued and devalued, her body rhetorically flowered and deflowered. But the symbol of the chapter is also the womb in the sense that the womb is borrowed by male writers who are pregnant with the word. 'Oxen of the Sun' is the chapter most conducive to source-hunting for fathers whose signatures are hidden in the chapter's styles; it seems to suggest that Literature is the domain of the proper name, of paternity. Just like Mrs Purefoy, relegated to a place offstage during the male discussion, women seem to be excluded from cultural production.

But we sense as well that writing functions in part as 'skirtscreen', that is, as defence against the power of woman's body. Male anxiety surfaces despite the rhetorical styles that attempt to elide it, like the periodic sentences of Gibbon which almost obscure the birth of the Purefoy child. It surfaces in the explicit examples of male ambivalence toward the maternal image ('But thou hast sucked me with a bitter milk: my moon and my sun thou hast quenched for ever. And thou hast left me alone for ever in the dark ways of my bitterness: and with a kiss of ashes hast thou kissed my mouth' (U 14.377–80). It surfaces in the mention of Lilith, 'patron of abortion', a female fiction older than Eve, and one which was never tamed.

We are reminded of woman's body when Bloom stares at the red rubied triangle, the delta, on the bottle of Bass Ale, trademark or 'mademark' that figures so prominently in *Finnegans Wake*. The anonymous power of woman's body is felt within the chapter as a power to undo the male patronym. The power functions as a kind of illegitimacy that runs counter to the 'legal' fictions of patriarchal succession. And it is expressed in the spirit of errancy within the succession of styles that compromises the authority of the literary forefathers, in for example, anachronism and multiple allusion that deliberately subvert the integrity of the *pater* texts expropriated. (For specific examples, see Lawrence, 'Paternity, the legal fiction', p.47.) The pregnant word gives birth to too many meanings. It is this undermining of patriarchal authority and its connection with the mother that Gilbert and Gubar overlook in calling the chapter the triumph of patrolingualism (p. 534). If Joyce had wanted to write the epitome of the Egotistical Sublime, he could have done better.[6]

This spirit of the errancy and texture of language, the sense of language's body, bursts on stage in 'Circe' in no other than the body of Mrs Mina Purefoy upon which Father Malachi O'Flynn celebrates a Black Mass. *'On the altarstone Mrs Mina Purefoy, goddess of unreason, lies, naked, fettered, a chalice resting on her swollen belly. Father Malachi O'Flynn in a lace petticoat and reversed chasuble, his two left feet back to the front, celebrates camp mass'* (U 15.4691–95). Here we find a parody of the body of woman as unproblematic ground of culture, as pregnant Mrs Purefoy becomes the symbol of disruption (rather than 'pure faith', as her name suggests?). (And the injunction 'Be fruitful and multiply' is treated ironically, as unthinking obedience to the law is portrayed as irrational.) Stable forms merge into their opposites. With chalice on her body, a position recalling that of the dead priest, Father Flynn in 'The Sisters', Mrs Purefoy provides her body to Father O'Flynn for the Black Mass. Here is the 'abject' body of woman (to use Julia Kristeva's term), come back to haunt the priest of the eternal imagination who would expel it from the myth of postcreation and thus from language.

Ulysses, however, does contain two chapters in which woman's subjectivity is staged, chapters more in the spirit of Bloom's prurience and empathy than Stephen's fear. In 'Nausicaa' Joyce rewrote Stephen's epiphany on the beach, using, as Fritz Senn has shown in his essay 'Nausicaa', many details from the earlier episode. In fact, one can say that in 'Nausicaa', Joyce opened up the possibility of female desire only glimpsed in *A Portrait* in the young girl's frank gaze: 'She was alone and still, gazing out to sea; and when she felt his presence and the worship of his eyes her eyes turned to him in quiet sufferance of his gaze, without shame or wantonness' (*P* 171). From the perspective of *Ulysses*, this section from *A Portrait* now sounds like something Gerty could think as she watches Bloom. Only this time the dynamics are self-conscious, the topoi of desire scripted by the characters themselves. One effect of the transposition is deflationary, deromanticizing. If the eyes of Stephen's young girl 'call him' and 'his soul had leaped at the call' (*P* 172), Bloom responds to Gerty's gaze with a different kind of rise. The players have changed to Odysseus and Nausicaa, and the chapter carries an air reminiscent of Odysseus' embarrassment upon his naked intrusion on the young girls' play. It is an air that brings us close to the dynamics of desire in *Finnegans Wake*, a banality and hope-lessness that will return with Issy and Earwicker.

If in the 'Oxen' chapter we see the changing economy of woman's body encoded by the male pen in different ages, 'Nausicaa' presents that body clothed in the rhetoric of nineteenth-century popular romance. We are given the world in what Joyce described as a 'namby-pamby jammy marmalady drawersy' style of Victorian ladies' maga-zines (*Letters I* 135). The art of the chapter is painting, and indeed the scene on the beach is like a Victorian reproduction of woman's desire (a writing of 'what woman wants'). In the light of Derrida's work on postcards it is tempting to envision this scene as not even a painting but a postcard – a romantic, anonymous, mass-reproduced fantasy, the caption, perhaps, reading 'love loves to love love' (a line from 'Cyclops' perfect to 'Nausicaa'). Although it is Gerty's fantasy to the extent that she accepts the encoding of her desires in such language, even courts the titillation of euphemism and longs to have the 'suppressed meanings' in her look discovered, the fantasy is rooted in the patriarchal view. Gerty is 'troped' according to the dual roles of angel in the house and femme fatale. The free indirect discourse, blending the resources of first and third-person narration, suggests that the troping of her mind comes from outside as well as inside, providing the space of a separate view. Indeed, it is voyeurism that fuels Gerty's part of the chapter as well as Bloom's; Bloom watches Gerty watching him watch her. He projects his desires onto her, including his desire to be seen as exotic stranger rather than lonely Jew. Joyce once told Arthur Power, 'Nothing happened between [Gerty and Bloom]. . . It all took place in Bloom's imagination' (*Conversations with James Joyce*, p. 32).

I have previously written of this chapter as a puzzling instance of Joyce's condescending to a particular style, suggesting, as the preceding chapters have not, 'that there is some Olympian ground upon which the writer and reader can stand to be exempt from the charges of stupidity' (*The Odyssey of Style*, pp. 122–3). I now believe that the male gaze *is* contaminated by the 'namby-pamby . . . marmalady' style of romance, *is* implicated in just such a troping. Indeed, Joyce himself was 'implicated' in the encoded, banal desire circulating in this chapter, by a typically complicated set of revisions and mirrorings of life and art. Gerty MacDowell is based on Marthe Fleischmann, a young woman Joyce met in Zurich. In 1918 Joyce sent Marthe Fleischmann some love letters and a postcard addressed to 'Nausikaa', signed 'Odysseus' (see *Letters II* 426–36). As Heinrich Straumann records on the basis of an interview with Fleischmann, Joyce stared at her in wonder when he first saw her entering her apartment because she reminded him of the girl he had seen wading on the beach in his home country (*Letters II* 428). Thus, Gerty's desire is filtered through Joyce's desire for young 'Nausicaa', who in turn reminded him of his prior representation of the girl on the beach in Ireland and the 'bird-girl' in *A Portrait*.

It is in 'Penelope', however, that Joyce attempts to lend presence to woman's subjectivity in the flowing, unpunctuated sentences of Molly Bloom. As we have seen, Joyce's dream seems to acknowledge that woman and woman in writing is beyond his control, as the character he creates exceeds the boundaries he created. (One thinks of Issy in *Finnegans Wake* described as an 'uncontrollable nighttalker' (*FW* 32.07–08).) Therefore, Molly's chapter presents a dilemma: how can she represent what is beyond Joyce's control, language emanating from somewhere else, and still somehow provide an ending of the book and a release from the stark, patriarchal abstractions preceding it? How can she seem like a new beginning without seeming to offer a 'truth', the possibility of which the styles of the rest of the book have subverted?

Perhaps one can say that Molly represents the *problem of woman represented by the male pen*, a staging of alterity that reveals itself as masquerade. Patrick McGee says in *Paperspace:* 'Molly's word represents less what Joyce thought a woman was than what he could not think, possess, or come to be' (p. 188). The masquerade cannot represent something wholly outside the writer's knowledge, nor wholly outside the dominant discourse. Somewhere, between subject and object, Molly is figured as that which exists elsewhere, beyond the mastery of the male pen.[7]

This elsewhere, however, will be refigured, rewritten, repositioned, displaced in *Finnegans Wake*. For it was not until *Finnegans Wake* that Joyce wrote a whole book in which he tried to represent what could not be thought or possessed, a book, in other words, that does not limit the sign of the unthinkable or the other to the interstices and final chapters. For one thing, the concept of the interstitial loses its meaning in a book that so radically blurs the boundaries between inside and outside as well as the binary oppositions of male and female. The alphabet itself is gendered, its letters combining in transgressive ways. As Shari Benstock puts it in an article entitled 'Nightletters', woman's desire runs through the letters of the book signifying not a voice or presence, as has previously been suggested, but a writing always elusive, a desire that can never be possessed (p. 230).[8] And although Anna Livia, like Molly, has 'the last word', it returns us to the book's beginning. Indeed, the circulation of her 'untitled mamafesta' might be a figure for the wayward path of the writing of desire, a reminder that desire is always encoded and disguised, in letters 'selfpenned to the other'.

V

Joyce once wrote to Nora, 'I *know* and *feel* that if I am to write anything fine or noble in the future I shall do so only by listening at the doors of your heart' (*Letters II* 254). The combination of adoration and titillation in this image of Joyce as 'evesdropper' and 'earwitness' captures the complexity of his attitude toward women and suggests the kind of images with which he represented them. In a sense, Joyce's works are letters of desire to the female that circulate through the texts of culture, letters published for all the world to see. They are 'compromising letters' where women are concerned, just such a letter as Joyce referred to in a dream he recorded after the publication of *Ulysses*:

A young woman tells me with less and less indignation that I have written a compromising letter to her. The contents do not shock her much, but she asks me why I signed it 'Ulysses'. I affirm that I have done nothing of the kind; before I can swear to it she disappears. She was dressed in black. (*JJ* 548)

The dream suggests that *Ulysses* is the 'compromising letter'. The young girl denies that the contents of the book shock her, a denial that is suspect, given the shocked reaction of most early readers of the novel. Her shock is displaced onto the book's signature, 'Ulysses'. However, by a process of symbolic substitution, we can try to discover what the condensed symbol 'Ulysses' stands for. The title 'Ulysses' refers, of course, to the name of Ulysses, Latinized version of Odysseus, Greek counterpart to Leopold Bloom. Bloom's 'other' name, in his clandestine and 'compromising letters' to Martha Clifford, is Henry Flower. At the end of chapter 5 of *Ulysses*, Bloom imagines himself reclining in the tub, gazing at his penis, 'the limp father of thousands, a languid floating *flower*' (my italics). By a 'commodius vicus of recirculation' we can trace the disguised signature back to the phallus of its author. Despite displacement and other defences, the dream conveys Joyce's sense that he has exposed himself. Although he says that the girl becomes 'less and less' indignant, by a process of inversion typical of dreams, this probably suggests her increasing indignation and his increasing humiliation. 'I affirm that I have done nothing of the kind', Joyce defends himself in the dream. But strangely, he 'affirms' his denial, thus suggesting it is his guilt that he affirms. We might remember that in *Finnegans Wake* one of the names for James Joyce is 'Shame's Voice'.

Finally, in the dream the girl seems to question the substitution of the book's title for the author's signature, perhaps objecting that the private 'letter' of desire has itself been 'exposed' in the letters of the published book.

The dream draws on Joyce's correspondence with Marthe Fleischmann, the young woman with whom he was infatuated in Zurich. In the love letters he sent her, he 'disguised' his signature by signing his name with Greek 'e's' (just as Bloom signs the name Henry Flower in his clandestine letters to Martha Clifford). As we have noted, he also sent her a postcard (which was subsequently lost), written to 'Nausikaa' and signed 'Odysseus'. The 'compromising letter' in this case is in the form of a postcard, its message, as Derrida says in *The Postcard*, both exposed to the world and yet curiously encoded for deciphering by its recipient. The fact that it is now lost adds an ironic confirmation of the wayward path of desire. Heinrich Straumann, who first learned of the postcard by interviewing Marthe Fleischmann, bemoaned its loss, which he found 'particularly unfortunate in view of what the experience evidently meant to Joyce' (*Letters II* 429).

What it and similar experiences of the female 'meant' to Joyce is played out in Joyce's dreams, letters, unpublished drafts, and published works, and there is no simple way to decipher it. The desire is in no simple sense Joyce's; indeed, the substitution of the signature 'Ulysses' for that of 'James Joyce' in Joyce's dream functions to acknowledge that the desire encoded is neither singular nor merely personal. It is a desire variously woven through all the compromising, sent, suppressed, published, borrowed, and lost letters that he wrote to and about women.[9]

NOTES

1 I should add at this point that the genderization of his longing for home is double – for one can speak of it in patriarchal or matriarchal terms – a return, that is, to the Father or to the Mother. Later I will discuss in more detail the search for patriarchal origins.

2 In an interesting essay, Hélène Cixous looks beyond the quiet surface of 'The Sisters' to what she calls 'the nervous laughter of writing', a gratuitousness in the language that erupts in the text. This 'nervous laughter' might be a precursor of the kind of eruptions that occur in subsequent works by Joyce and suggests that the surface of *Dubliners* is less placid than former analyses of the stories have suggested. See Cixous, 'Joyce: the r(use) of writing'.

3 The imagery of lewd Elizabethans *without* its subsequent cancellation appears in *Giacomo Joyce*, an erotic, lyric work which recorded Joyce's obsession with a young female pupil in Trieste. Joyce wrote *Giacomo Joyce* simultaneously with the final chapters of *A Portrait*, but, as Richard Ellmann points out in his introduction to the publication of *Giacomo Joyce* in 1968, Joyce chose not to publish the intensely personal work. Instead he 'diffused' the 'spirit' of it into other works such as *Exiles, Stephen Hero, A Portrait*, and later *Ulysses* (*GJ* xxii; and see also ch. 8 of this volume). Perhaps Joyce felt the private diary-like jottings of *Giacomo Joyce* did not effectively veil the quality of his obsession, as if he had confessed not in a foreign language. It is as if he crossed out the false image twice, once when he decided not to publish it and once when he has Stephen disown it.

4 See my discussion of the subversion of patriarchal signature in 'Paternity, the legal fiction'.

5 This coding of the paternal as invisible and maternal as visible, while consistent with one equation in Western culture between the male and the spiritual and the female and the body, is contrary to the coding in psychoanalytic theory, where the possession of the phallus links the male to

the visible and normative and the absence of the phallus links the female to the invisible and the mysterious.

6 See also Jennifer Levine's discussion of this episode in ch. 6 of this volume.

7 Christine van Boheemen's discussion of related issues, *The Novel as Family Romance*, was published after the writing of this essay, but her chapters on Joyce provide an important contribution.

8 Benstock argues that the prevailing reading of women in the *Wake*, focusing as it has on women and voice, has ignored the link between women and writing.

9 I would like to thank my colleagues Robert Caserio, Kathryn Stockton, Barry Weller, and Meg Brady for their very insightful comments on my 'compromising letter' on Joyce and women.

WORKS CITED

Attridge, Derek, and Daniel Ferrer, eds. *Post-structuralist Joyce: Essays from the French*. Cambridge: Cambridge University Press, 1984

Benstock, Bernard. 'Beyond explication: the twice-told tales in *Finnegans Wake*'. In Morris Beja *et al.*, eds., *James Joyce: The Centennial Symposium*. Urbana: University of Illinois Press, 1986, pp. 95–108

Benstock, Shari. 'Nightletters: woman's writing in the *Wake*'. In Bernard Benstock, ed., *Critical Essays on James Joyce*. Boston: G. K. Hall, 1985, pp. 221–33

Bishop, John. *Joyce's Book of the Dark: 'Finnegans Wake'*. Madison: University of Wisconsin Press, 1986

Boheemen, Christine van. *The Novel as Family Romance: Language, Gender, and Authority from Fielding to Joyce*. Ithaca: Cornell University Press, 1987

Cixous, Hélène. 'Joyce: the r(use) of writing.' In Attridge and Ferrer, *Post-structuralist Joyce*, 15–30

Derrida, Jacques. *The Postcard: From Socrates to Freud and Beyond*. Trans. Alan Bass. Chicago: University of Chicago Press, 1987

  'Plato's pharmacy'. In *Dissemination*. Trans. Barbara Johnson. Chicago: University of Chicago Press, 1981, pp. 61–172

  'Two words for Joyce'. In Attridge and Ferrer, *Post-structuralist Joyce*, 145–59

Dinnerstein, Dorothy. *The Mermaid and the Minotaur*. New York: Harper and Row, 1963

Ellmann, Maud. 'Polytropic man: paternity, identity and naming in *The Odyssey* and *A Portrait of the Artist as a Young Man*'. In MacCabe, *James Joyce: New Perspectives*, 73–104

Ellmann, Richard. *Ulysses on the Liffey*. New York: Oxford University Press, 1972

Gilbert, Sandra M., and Susan Gubar. 'Sexual linguistics: gender, language, sexuality'. *New Literary History* 16 (1985), 515–43

Heath, Stephen. 'Ambiviolences: notes for reading Joyce'. In Attridge and Ferrer, *Post-structuralist Joyce*, 31–68

'Joyce and language'. In MacCabe, *James Joyce: New Perspectives*, 129–48

Herr, Cheryl. *Joyce's Anatomy of Culture*. Urbana: University of Illinois Press, 1986

Joyce, Stanislaus. *My Brother's Keeper: James Joyce's Early Years*, ed. Richard Ellmann. London: Faber, 1958

Kenner, Hugh. *Dublin's Joyce* (1956). Reprinted New York: Columbia University Press, 1987

Kristeva, Julia. *The Powers of Horror: An Essay on Abjection*. Trans. Leon S. Roudiez. New York: Columbia University Press, 1982

Lawrence, Karen. 'Paternity, the legal fiction'. In Robert Newman and Weldon Thornton, eds., *Joyce's 'Ulysses': The Larger Perspective*. Newark: University of Delaware Press, 1987, pp. 89–97

The Odyssey of Style in 'Ulysses'. Princeton: Princeton University Press, 1981

MacCabe, Colin, ed. *James Joyce: New Perspectives*. Brighton: Harvester, 1982

McGee, Patrick. *Paperspace: Style as Ideology in Joyce's 'Ulysses'*. Lincoln: University of Nebraska Press, 1988

Power, Arthur. *Conversations with James Joyce*, ed. Clive Hart. London: Millington, 1974

Scott, Bonnie Kime. *James Joyce*. Feminist Readings Series. Brighton: Harvester, 1987

Senn, Fritz. 'Nausicaa'. In Clive Hart and David Hayman, eds., *James Joyce's 'Ulysses': Critical Essays*. Berkeley: University of California Press, 1974, pp. 277–311

Tindall, William York. *James Joyce: His Way of Interpreting the Modern World*. New York: Charles Scribner's Sons, 1950

11   Joyce, modernism, and post-modernism

There are many kinds of modernism – one has only to think of the differences between Picasso and Kandinsky, Schoenberg and Stravinsky, or Joyce and Kafka to appreciate this. The number of books and articles devoted to attempts at defining the term is huge.[1] In what follows I wish to see Joyce's relationship to what is often loosely called the 'modernist movement' in a fairly simple way. First of all I look at his becoming 'modernist' in the most obvious sense – that is, by moving beyond his nineteenth-century predecessors. I then sketch his relationships to others who had diversely managed the same feat, and thus opened up an extraordinary avant-garde market-place of competing styles. Joyce made a contribution to this critical moment so great that he posed an acute problem to his successors: after *Ulysses* and *Finnegans Wake*, what types of expression in writing could possibly remain undiscovered? I end with some discussion of this problem, and its relation to post-modernism.

Modernist artists at the beginning of the century were to a large degree moved to this unprecedented freedom and confidence in stylistic experiment by what they saw as radically new ideas, current in that period, concerning consciousness, time, and the nature of knowledge, which were to be found in the work of Nietzsche, Bergson, Freud, Einstein, Croce, Weber, and others. And these ideas contested in a dramatic manner the beliefs of the older generation.[2]

This revolt focused on a 'transvaluation of all values'; and those who were most self-conscious about it tended to be followers of Nietzsche. Thus although he was generally sceptical about this sort of enthusiasm, Joyce thought of himself as a Nietzschean in 1904, when as 'James

Overman' he was all for neopaganism, licentiousness, and pitilessness (*JJ* 142, 162, 172; *Letters I* 23).[3] Thinkers like Nietzsche helped to sustain his opposition to those totalizing religious and philosophical frameworks characteristic of the nineteenth-century bourgeoisie. 'My mind rejects the whole present social order and Christianity' he tells Nora (*Letters II* 48), and his Stephen Daedalus is 'fond of saying that the Absolute is dead' (*SH* 211). Thus Joyce and many like him at this time (particularly Eliot) seem to have favoured that relativist opposition to the beliefs of the past which is one of the chief legacies of Pater and William James. Its symptoms were pragmatism, pluralism, and that most typical of modernist strategies, a sceptical irony. And so when the protagonist of *Stephen Hero* wishes to express feelings of love,

he found himself compelled to use what he called the feudal terminology and as he could not use it with the same faith and purpose as animated the feudal poets themselves he was compelled to express his love a little ironically. This suggestion of relativity, he said, mingling itself with so immune a passion is a modern note.

(*SH* 174: the 'feudal terminology' derives from Dante's *Vita nuova*.)

It is this scepticism concerning received ideas that Georg Brandes's *Men of the Modern Breakthrough* (1880), Ibsen, Björnson, Jacobsen, Drachmann, Flaubert, Renan, and J. S. Mill, all had in common. Joyce revered Brandes and was certainly influenced by Ibsen, Flaubert, and Renan. He documents his version of this intellectual revolt, amongst students 'who regarded art as a continental vice' (*SH* 38), most explicitly in *Stephen Hero* and *A Portrait*, which show how he extricated himself from the prevailing faiths of his contemporaries. But this rejection of religion and nationalism is not I think the most important part of the story concerning Joyce's turn-of-the-century scepticism. For it also resides, paradoxically enough, in his extraordinary attachment to fact. The 'scrupulous meanness' of *Dubliners* is his way of following Arnold in seeing things as they really are: and it is his realism which perpetually combats larger ideological commitments. A remark he made to Arthur Power is extremely significant from this point of view, and expresses an attitude which underlies his work through to the completion of *Ulysses*:

In realism you get down to facts on which the world is based; that sudden reality which smashes romanticism into a pulp. What makes most peoples' lives unhappy is some disappointed romanticism, some unrealisable misconceived ideal. In fact you may say that idealism is the ruin of man, and if we lived down to fact, as primitive man had to do, we would be better off. That is what we were made for. Nature is quite unromantic. It is we who put romance into her, which is a false attitude, an egotism, absurd like all egotism. In *Ulysses* I tried to keep close to fact.   (Power, p. 98.)

This Ibsenic destruction of illusions, and the charitable and humorous attitude Joyce brings to it, is of course implicit rather than overt in much of his work, and it has led to an obvious bafflement in his critics, both early and late, who have so far, with the two honourable exceptions of Richard Brown and Dominic Manganiello, not attempted to describe Joyce's attitudes to the doctrines or ideologies (other than Catholicism and nationalism) that were popular amongst his contemporaries.

Joyce's attitude to the modernist climate of ideas thus has largely to be inferred from his essentially solitary (and egotistical) experimentalism, and from our sense of the ideological risks it ran. For by the time he is writing *Ulysses* he has set himself the 'task' 'of writing a book from eighteen different points of view and in as many styles, all apparently unknown or undiscovered by my fellow tradesmen' (*Letters I* 167), and this stylistic diversity enshrines an essentially relativist attitude towards the 'truthful' depiction of reality. It makes an implicit stand against the ideological authority of the nineteenth-century novel, and of those other incorporative ideas which threatened him (as for example in the sermon of the *Portrait*). He thus uses modernist techniques, as Karen Lawrence argues, to adopt a 'series of rhetorical masks' which make us 'doubt the authority of any particular style'. The various methods of narrative in *Ulysses* are thus 'different but not definitive ways of filtering and ordering experience' (p. 9). For although Joyce obeys the underlying causal necessities of narrative, and is as obsessively concerned with accuracy as Proust, he also makes us see his history of a day within a number of stylistic frameworks, which are all relative to one another, and which often disrupt the conventions of word formation and syntax. This is the beginning of Joyce's 'revolution of the word', which is completed in *Finnegans Wake*.

II

Joyce's revolution towards this kind of sceptical relativism has its roots in the nineteenth century. Matthew Arnold makes a remark in his essay on Heine of 1863 which is distinctively echoed in Joyce:

Modern times find themselves with an immense system of institutions, established facts, accredited dogmas, customs, rules, which have come to them from times not modern. In this system their life has to be carried forward, yet they have a sense that this system is not of their own creation, that it by no means corresponds exactly with the wants of their actual life, that for them, it is customary not rational. The awakening of this sense is the awakening of the modern spirit.   (p. 109)

This confrontation with the customary is engaged with enthusiasm by modern writers like Nietzsche, Ibsen, Shaw, Marinetti, Kraus, Tzara, and others, in the name of a very different kind of rationality. But in allying himself with this movement of ideas, Joyce goes beyond Arnold in rejecting any desire for an overall metaphysical order, however tinkered with, in which 'culture' takes on the responsibilities of religion. He would probably have agreed with Wilde's comment: 'It is enough that our fathers believed. They have exhausted the faith-faculty of the species. Their legacy to us is the scepticism of which they were afraid' (pp. 1039–40). For Arnold's was always a confused and confusing demand, as T. S. Eliot pointed out: 'The total effect of Arnold's philosophy is to set up culture in the place of Religion, and to leave Religion to be laid waste by an anarchy of feeling' (p. 387). Through Stephen Daedalus in *Stephen Hero*, Joyce the Catholic confronts this loss of faith head on, while retaining, and secularizing, much of the vocabulary of religion, as, for example, his perplexing notion of 'epiphany' shows.

The tradition of thought descending from Arnold through Wilde and others was equally significant in legitimizing feelings of distance and alienation from a social and intellectual context. In displaying this tension in a young man Joyce was at one with many of his contemporaries, like Frank Wedekind in *Spring Awakening* (1891–2), Robert Musil in *Young Törless* (1906), André Gide in *L'Immoraliste* (1902), and Thomas Mann in *Tristan* and *Tonio Kröger* (1903), the latter of whom argues at one point as follows:

Literature is not a calling, it is a curse, believe me! When does one begin to feel the curse? Early, horribly early. At a time when one ought by rights still to be living in peace and harmony with God and the world. It begins by your feeling yourself set apart, in a curious sort of opposition to the nice, regular people; there is a gulf of ironic sensibility, of knowledge, scepticism, disagreement, between you and the others; it grows deeper and deeper, you realise that you are alone; and from then on any rapprochement is simply hopeless! What a fate!   (pp. 153–4)

The young Daedalus of *Stephen Hero* (1904–6) has very similar characteristics, and has also the highly Arnoldian awareness 'that though he was nominally in amity with the order of society into which he had been born, he would not be able to continue so' (*SH* 184). He defines his sense of the modern to his friend Cranly as an anti-traditional seeing of things as they really are, whose inspiration lies in science. But it is not perhaps the science one might expect:

The modern spirit is vivisective. Vivisection itself is the most modern process one can conceive. The ancient spirit accepted phenomena with a bad grace. The ancient method investigated law with the lantern of justice, morality with the lantern of revelation, art with the lantern of tradition. But all these lanterns have magical properties: they transform and disfigure. The modern method examines its territory by the light of day.   (*SH* 190)

Here is the Ibsenite Stephen, who has been told (admittedly by a priest) that his paper devoted to Ibsen on 'Art and Life' 'represents the sum of modern unrest and modern freethinking' (*SH* 96).[4]

Joyce and Stephen stand here at pretty well the same point of evolution, in 1906, just before the extraordinary stylistic transform-ation of *Stephen Hero* into *A Portrait of the Artist* (rather as Pound reduced a conventional thirty-line poem into the experimental and imagist two-line 'In a Station of the Metro'). But before this commit-ment to experiment of a recognizably modernist kind in the opening of *A Portrait*, Joyce manages what the other major modernists of the period also achieved: the complete recreative and parodic mastery of previous traditions.

It is this mastery which reveals the strongly conservative approach to art of the early modernists (as opposed for example to the futurists and dadaists who succeeded them). I am thinking here of Matisse's Impressionist and Picasso's Symbolist paintings; of Pound's recreation of the forms of the late nineteenth-century tradition, including the Browningesque monologue; of Stravinsky's neo-Debussyan im-pressionism in *The Firebird* (1909–10) and *King of the Stars* (1911–12), and of Schoenberg's writing of the symphonic poem *Pelléas and Mélisande* (1902–3) in a manner that deliberately exceeded in complex-ity the work of all his predecessors. All these early modernists thus work through Symbolism and its derivatives; and then go significantly beyond it, by inventing radically new languages for art. What they do not do is ally themselves to an avant-garde which expresses its revolutionary intentions in manifestos. In his work up to *Ulysses* Joyce makes this assimilation of tradition in a very similar manner, first producing a distinctly Chekhovian set of short stories, the last of which, 'The Dead', is profoundly Symbolist and Ibsenic at the same time; then manifesting in *A Portrait* the early modern metamorphosis of previous styles, by weaving the mental worlds and the verbal characteristics of Pater, Newman, and others into Stephen's consciousness. Here, as Lodge puts it,

Joyce varied his style to imitate various phases of his hero's narrative, . . . declared his secession from the fully readerly mode of narrative, and began his career as a fully-fledged modernist writer.   (p. 130)

An ironic gap is thus opened up between Stephen's self-emancipating thoughts as an arrogant young man and his poetic mimicry of his predecessors. This demands from the reader that awareness of allusion and split level of response that Eliot's 'Prufrock' before him and Pound's 'Hugh Selwyn Mauberley' after him also demand. It was indeed this stylistic self-consciousness and range of reference that Pound himself was so quick to notice in 1915:

His style has the hard clarity of a Stendahl or Flaubert . . . He has also the richness of erudition which differentiates him from certain able and vigorous but rather overloaded impressionist writers. He is able, in the course of a novel, to introduce a serious conversation, or even a stray conversation on style or philosophy without being ridiculous.   (*Letters II* 359)

This display reflects the reading of a well-informed and up-to-date young man; and it parallels Joyce's own. For he too had questioned conventional morality with the help of Ibsen and Shaw, and was in a position to judge D'Annunzio (temporarily) better than Flaubert by 1900. Between 1900 and 1902 he also read Zola, Hauptmann, Verlaine, Huysmans, and Tolstoy, and was guided through the Symbolist movement by Arthur Symons. He was thus familiar with the most challenging of realist writing, as well as with French Symbolism and its influence. Indeed he kept his devotion to early Yeats, especially *The Wind among the Reeds*, and the feebleness of his own (and Stephen's) poetic efforts shows that he did not get much beyond this late

Symbolist aesthetic in verse. Most significantly by the time he comes to write *A Portrait* he sees his work as going beyond that of writers in the realist tradition, like Hardy, Gissing, and Moore.

Nevertheless Joyce's *resistance* to certain contemporary ideas is of equal importance. His philosophical allegiances are to the pre-moderns, for example to Aquinas, for even when he is subverting Catholic dogma, one can feel that so far as Stephen's aesthetic theories go, he believes that the Scholastics have at least correctly formulated the categories with which we have to think (*SH* 81ff.). And although Joyce may have welcomed 'beauty' in Yeats and others (an old-fashioned Paterian aesthetic category to which he seems to have remained pretty loyal) and seen the advantages, in terms of extending the subject matter of literature, of the moral liberalism of Flaubert, Tolstoy, Hauptmann, and Ibsen, he was not going to fall entirely for those Schopenhauerian or Nietzschean or occultist ideas which intoxicated others of his generation in Europe. Thus as Stephen walks to the University (*P* 176ff.) he is attended by the ghosts of writers not very different from those available to Hardy's Jude in Christminster meadow: Hauptmann, Newman, Guido Cavalcanti, Ibsen, Ben Jonson, Aristotle, Aquinas.

Joyce's extraordinary fidelity to past time thus means that the *ideas* he presents in his books are not those of the modernist avant-garde. It is through his style that modernism is implied. And so it is the stylistic innovations of the opening and closing pages of *A Portrait* which launch Joyce into an original modernist experimentalism which is almost wholly unpredictable in terms of these earlier influences. A novelist deeply indebted to Joyce, Anthony Burgess, describes the montage of the book's opening pages as follows:

Prose and subject-matter have become one and inseparable; it is the first big technical breakthrough of twentieth-century prose-writing and, inevitably, it looks as if anybody could have thought of it. The roots of *Ulysses* are here – to every phase of the soul its own special language; *Finnegans Wake* must seem, not a wilful aberration from sense, but a logical conclusion from that premise.

(p. 50)

Faced with this sort of thing, the reviewer in the *Manchester Guardian* (March 1917) thought that 'there are ellipses . . . that go beyond the pardonable . . . [and] obscure allusions. One has to be of the family, so to speak, to "catch on"' (*CH I* 93). And the reviewer in *The New Age* had similar difficulties, commenting that '. . . his wilful cleverness, his determination to produce Kinematographic effects instead of a literary portrait, are due entirely to a lack of clarity'. For him, *A Portrait* seemed to be 'a mere catalogue of unrelated states' (*CH I* 110). It is precisely this initially baffling associativeness which is a central symptom of modernist writing. Joyce poses the same sorts of problems as we find in the poetry of Guillaume Apollinaire, Blaise Cendrars, Eliot, and Pound.

III

Joyce thus enters the experimental mainstream of modernism by an extraordinary display of technique, and not by any anterior commitment to some avant-gardist doctrine. Nevertheless, by the time he had published the earlier episodes of *Ulysses*, he could at the very least claim to have bequeathed to his successors new resources which were not simply matters of style. He had managed a distinctive reinvention of Symbolist experience through the 'epiphanic' moments of *A Portrait* and its aesthetic theory (*P* 208–13; epiphany is discussed explicitly in *SH* 216ff.), and he had revived and immeasurably extended the presentation of the 'stream of consciousness', which was previously to be found in Edouard Dujardin, whom he acknowledges, and in Arthur Schnitzler's *Lieutenant Gustl* (1901), of which he possessed a copy. By 1922 he had challenged all who wished to write after him by producing a designedly encyclopedic epic, whose sustained mythical parallelism raised in an acute form the post-Nietzschean and post-Jungian questions of the nature of history as repetition. He thus vastly extended the experimental repertoire available to the novelist; and also, paradoxically enough, influenced the general movement of the nineteen twenties back towards a conservative neo-classicism. We see Eliot attempting this assimilation of his work when he emphasizes Joyce's control and order and form, in his influential account of the Yeatsian 'mythical method' of the book (*CH I* 269–70).[5]

   These aspects of his work immediately influenced the Anglo-American modernist movement in general, including Eliot, as Ronald Bush and others have shown. Joyce's use of allusion to different cultural periods, which yet have an underlying coherence, leads to Eliot's 'Sweeney Among the Nightingales'; and similar considerations affect Pound's *Cantos* IV to VII (see Bush, pp. 207–43, and Sultan, *passim*). For by 1919 both Eliot and Pound had read the manuscript of 'Sirens', and their discussion of *Ulysses* must have had a considerable influence upon the former's 'Tradition and the individual talent', which is virtually a manifesto for a method which others might follow. Bush also discerns the influence of the 'Nestor' episode of *Ulysses* on Pound's *Cantos* v and vi, and on Eliot's 'Gerontion', which seems to respond to Stephen's remark, 'History . . . is a nightmare from which I am trying to awake' (*U* 2.377). Pound had wanted 'Gerontion' to resemble his own work more closely in its fragmentation, but Eliot happily seems to have defended its underlying Joycean coherence.

Pound had had doubts concerning 'Sirens' and so did not see anything more of Joyce's work till the 'Circe' episode came to him in April 1921. He and Eliot thought it magnificent. It is thus Joyce's *Ulysses* which may well have been the crucial impetus to the major work of Pound and Eliot in this period, and have provided some of the central aesthetic principles governing their work and their interaction at this time.

The influence of *Ulysses* as an experimental achievement seems to have been undoubted from the beginning; and its influence on writers like Virginia Woolf, William Faulkner, John Dos Passos, Alfred Döblin, Hermann Broch, Vladimir Nabokov, and others has been ably demonstrated by R. M. Adams. But its relationship to the modernist movements which surrounded its making is much more doubtful. Of course it is an obvious fact of literary history that Joyce's critical reputation partly stood or fell with that of his early modernist supporters, like Pound and Eliot, and his later surrealist ones, like Eugene Jolas and Philippe Soupault. And even his detractors, like Wyndham Lewis, managed to focus upon central issues in his writing (to judge by the strong response to *Time and Western Man* in *Finnegans Wake*). Joyce seems nevertheless to have been extremely reticent in his critical judgements on his modernist contemporaries. Ellmann records positive judgements on André Gide's *Caves du Vatican*, Wyndham Lewis's *Tarr*, and little else. Joyce seems to have been interested enough in Eliot to parody him (see *JJ* 572, 495), but he does not seem to have much liked Pound's work beyond the relatively conservative *Cathay* (*JJ* 661).

I suspect that although Joyce knew about other types of modernist experimental activity, he was not going to be drawn on them, as his silence at the end of the following exchange with Budgen shows:

'Does this episode ['Cyclops'] strike you as futuristic?' said Joyce.
   'Rather cubist than futurist', I said, 'every event is a many-sided object. You first state one view of it and then you draw it from another angle to another scale, and both aspects lie side by side in the same picture.'

(Budgen, pp. 156–7)

The contents of his library in 1920, as reported by Ellmann (*Consciousness*, pp. 97ff.), are consistent with the restriction of his interest to those ideas which could have influenced his characters at that point in the moral history of his country at which he chose to place them. Thus, for example, his chief sources for the interpretation of Homer are Butler, Bacon, and Bérard, rather than Frazer and the Cambridge School, whose use of comparative anthropology and construction of a 'primitive mentality' was becoming so influential. Eliot was far more self-consciously up to date in his view of myth as a cultural phenomenon. We only find Gide, Jens Peter Jacobsen, Lawrence, Lewis, Heinrich Mann, Woolf, Bergson, and Nietzsche (and, as we shall see, Freud) amongst those of his books which could be thought to have been of much interest to the avant-garde of his time. The one truly avant-gardist text he possessed, Marinetti's *Enquête internationale sur le vers libre et Manifeste du Futurisme* (1909), does not seem to have inspired him. This sort of evidence is hardly conclusive, however, for Joyce was very likely far more aware of what was 'going on' than the extant evidence would suggest, and it will be up to future critics to advance parallels to contemporary art more convincing than those in the current literature (see, for instance, Loss, *Joyce's Visible Art*). Indeed, I suspect that he was very well-informed when he needed to be for his own purposes; his remark to Stanislaus in a letter of 15 July 1920 is significant, for he is well able to support his assertion that the 'Odyssey is very much in the air here' [Paris] by references to Anatole France, to Fauré's *Pénélope*, to Giraudoux, and to Apollinaire's *Les Mamelles de Tirésias* (*Letters III* 10). It seems, then, that so far as his experimental techniques were concerned Joyce was very good at disguising the sources of his inspiration. As Budgen remarks,

There are hints of all practices in *Ulysses* – cubism, futurism, simultaneism, dadaism and the rest – and this is the clearest proof that he was attached to none of the various schools that followed them. At one time in Zürich . . . I quoted to him one full-sounding phrase I had learned: 'Noi futuristi italiani

siamo senza passato.' 'E senza avvenire', said Joyce. Any other doctrine would
have called forth the same comment. ['We futurists are without a past.' 'And
without a future.']   (p. 198)

It is the *ideology* of avant-garde movements which Joyce finds
irrelevant to his purposes; and my judgement is that he quickly
appropriated all available modernist techniques, while keeping himself
well clear of the often inflated claims for 'simultaneity', the 'destruction
of the past', and so on, of the manifestos. Although his earlier readers
thought they could discern such influences upon him (so that in 1923
Ernest Boyd, for example, compares his work to that of Romains and
the Unanimists, while maintaining that 'its form is more akin to the
German Expressionists' (*CH I* 304)), there are no obvious modernist
sources for the leading candidates, such as the Nighttown episode,
which indeed makes use of what seem to be the techniques of stage
presentation, and on occasion the abbreviated 'telegraphic' language,
of much German expressionist drama.

Joyce's work thus has to be placed within the modernist tradition by
critical comparison rather than through the study of its direct
influence. The presentation of the city as subject in *Ulysses*, for
example, fits into just such a sequence, descending in the twentieth
century through Jules Romains' *La Vie unanime* (1907), Biely's
Petersburg (1913), and many other works. Joyce celebrates the city as
they do, rather than seeing it as alienating, in the manner of sociologists
like Ferdinand Tönnies and Georg Simmel at the turn of the century,
and more pessimistic writers than he, from Gissing and Conrad through
to Döblin's *Alexanderplatz*. The poets' treatment of the city similarly
divides between optimistic celebrants like Apollinaire and Cendrars,
and pessimists like Rilke, Heym, and Benn. In their light however
Stephen Dedalus strikes us as a Baudelairean flâneur from a less
troubled age. This designedly retrospective tone is sustained by Joyce
to prevent too facile an accommodation of his work to artistic activity
contemporary with its writing. Thus the 'Aeolus' episode is clearly
'modernist' in its interest in the newspaper and its use of headlines, an
interest affirmed by Apollinaire, Cendrars and, most noisily, by
Marinetti, who sees the city as a site for new modern materials which
are juxtaposed to one another like 'the great newspaper (synthesis of a
day in the world's life)' (Apollonio, *Futurist Manifestos*, p. 96). But
Joyce's use of this topos is also deeply traditional, as the episode

explores the art of rhetoric back to the Greeks (see Vickers, *In Defence of Rhetoric*, pp. 387–404). It is this synthesis of past and present, rather than a merely ironic or satirical juxtaposition of the 'classical' and the modern (as in Eliot), that seems to me to be one of Joyce's most distinctive achievements.

His presentation of many events taking place simultaneously within a single time-span, or presented in different parts of the text and then unified in the mind of the reader (through an apprehension of 'spatial form') as he or she grasps the interactive life of a great city, also seems to have obvious affinities with the unanimism of Romains, the 'dramatism' of Barzun, and the much vaunted 'simultaneism' of Cendrars's *Prose du Transsibérien*, all of which emphasized the rhythmical and cinematic techniques of montage to express city life. Cendrars summarizes these tendencies in his 'A.B.C. du Cinema' (1919), when he asks for a

Remue-menage d'images. L'unité tragique se déplace. Nous apprenons. Nous buvons. Ivresse. Le réel n'a plus aucun sens. Aucune signification. Tout est rhythme, parole, vie. Il n'y a plus de démonstration. On communie.[6]

The simultaneism of 'Wandering Rocks' seems to be as virtuosic a treatment of this sort of theme as could be imagined, and Joyce's ambition with respect to it immense: 'If I can get to the heart of Dublin I can get to the heart of all the cities in the world' (*JJ* 505). But his inspiration may also have been directly cinematic, and influenced by concepts of montage as we find them in Eisenstein (with whom he discussed the possibility of turning *Ulysses* into a film, *JJ* 654) and others. Indeed the *Evening News* pointed out in 1922 that 'his style is in the new fashionable kinematographic vein, very jerky and elliptical' (*CH I* 192), and Carola Giedion-Welcker compares *Ulysses* to 'the cinematic-technical transmission' of futurism (*CH II* 442). This judgement is hardly surprising, for the language of *Ulysses* can be at least as 'poetic', and fragmented in its presentation of the isolated or juxtaposed image, as that of avant-garde poets like Marinetti, who used a 'simultaneist' and juxtapository technique. Joyce's work thus parallels that of Apollinaire (in 'Zones' and 'Vendémiaire') and Cendrars (in his *Pâques à New York* (1912) and *Prose du Transsibérien* (1913)), or German city poets like Van Hoddis, Lichtenstein, and Stadler.

After Joyce, in the work of writers like Dos Passos, Döblin, and Musil, these techniques are variously adapted to the theme of city life, often enough in the light of Eliot's judgement that Joyce had given order to what he called, with inappropriate pessimism, 'the immense panorama of futility and anarchy which is contemporary history' (*CH I* 270). Eliot wholly fails to appreciate the progressive and optimistic elements in Joyce's thinking, and his view is surely more applicable to his own *Waste Land* or (minus the myth) to a work like Dos Passos's *Manhattan Transfer* (1925).

IV

As my frequent references to contemporary critics have already shown, it is to the history of Joyce's reception that we have to turn in order to appreciate how he was located with respect to the modernism of his contemporaries. For Joyce never made avant-gardist propaganda for his own work; though he was willing (as in *Our Exagmination*) to leave that to others. So far as the critical understanding of *Ulysses* is concerned, the prime documents to emerge after these initial critical reactions are Budgen's memoir, *James Joyce and the Making of 'Ulysses'*, and Gilbert's *James Joyce's Ulysses*, but the latter at least is more a work of exegesis than an apology for *Ulysses'* position within the modern movement. They are nevertheless the main sources for the establishment of *Ulysses* as a central text within the high modernist period after the First World War.

The criticism of the reviews is by and large disappointing in its lack of sophistication; moral shock rationalized by reference to Freud seems to have formed the staple of many early attempts to relate Joyce to contemporary goings-on. He is thus 'completely anarchic' and 'in rebellion against the social morality of civilisation' according to Middleton Murry (*CH I* 196); and he 'deliberately ignores moral codes and conventions' according to Holbrook Jackson (*CH I* 198). Gosse thought that Joyce was 'a sort of Marquis de Sade, but he does not write so well' (*CH I* 313).

Objections like this last to the 'poetic' juxtapositions and alogicalities of Joyce's prose miss the point. For the reader is expected to rationalize Joyce's use of language by reference to the great change in assumptions concerning our mental life which was proclaimed (though not invented) by the modernists. This is the essentially post-Freudian assumption that there is an intelligible, and revelatory, *rationale* for the association of apparently disjunct ideas. This was much attacked at the time, for example by Max Eastman, as a mere 'cult of unintelligibility', of which he also accuses Hart Crane, e. e. cummings, and Gertrude Stein (*CH II* 489).

There seems nevertheless to have been considerable agreement with Edmund Wilson's claim (in the *New Republic*, 1922) that *Ulysses* was the 'most faithful X-ray ever taken of the ordinary human consciousness' (*CH I* 228). Wilson develops this claim in his account of the modern movement (as essentially post-Symbolist) in *Axel's Castle*:

> Joyce is indeed really the great poet of a new phase of human consciousness. Like Proust's or Whitman's or Einstein's world, Joyce's world is always changing as it is perceived by different observers and by them at different times.   (p. 221)

This rather obvious reaction gets on to much more controversial ground with the assumption that Joyce's work was somehow designedly Freudian. Thus an early approving review by Joseph Collins claimed that *Ulysses* 'would seem to substantiate some of Freud's contentions' (*CH I* 223), and the *Daily Express* in 1922 perhaps articulated the ordinary reader's sense of what Freud stood for by pointing out that it displayed 'all our most secret and unsavoury private thoughts' (*CH I* 191). Mary Colum even more confidently proclaimed that it was a 'book written on the subconscious method' (*CH I* 234), and the *Sporting Times* review reported that 'Nausicaa' had been defended in New York as 'the unveiling of the subconscious in the Freudian manner' and thus as un-aphrodisiac (*CH I* 194).[7] In this context perhaps the judgement of Holbrook Jackson, that 'every action and reaction of his [Bloom's] psychology is laid bare with Freudian nastiness', and that 'much of the action of *Ulysses* is subconscious' (*CH I* 199), and of Ford Madox Ford that it was 'a volume of dream interpretations by Freud' (*CH I* 277), might have struck the contemporary literate reader as authoritative.

There are of course two aspects of this type of judgement: clearly Joyce would have known that he had provided excellent examples for psychoanalytic interpretation, which claims to interpret all sorts of neurotic behaviour. But it is a separate question to decide on the nature of any Freudian influence on him.[8] It was not until he was living in Trieste that Joyce read Vico (*JJ* 340), Freud on Leonardo, Ernest Jones's Freudian study, *Hamlet and his Problems*, and Jung's 'The significance of the father in the destiny of the individual', and he probably learnt more about psychoanalysis from Ettore Schmitz, the author of *La coscienza di Zeno*, whom he came to know there. But he concluded that Freud was in any case anticipated by Vico, and claimed, in a peculiar return to the Catholicism he had rejected, to prefer the confessional as a mode of self-revelation.[9]

Thus although Stephen refers to the 'new Viennese school' in the library scene, and the 'Circe' episode could certainly be said to incorporate, as Freud said dreams would, the events of the previous day, and to reveal various complexes and fears in the main characters (see Hoffmann, pp. 137ff.), Joyce's *moral* attitude to psychoanalysis (like that of D. H. Lawrence) seems to have been very hostile, at least in the period of *Ulysses*. For although he admitted, in attacking the notion that there was a moral to be found in *Ulysses*, that he had 'recorded . . . what you Freudians call the subconscious', he went on to say 'but as for psychoanalysis it's neither more nor less than blackmail' (*JJ* 524; and compare Ellmann, *Consciousness*, pp. 54ff.). *Finnegans Wake* on the other hand is clearly indebted to psychoanalysis, to which it frequently alludes. A Freudian interpretation of its language, and a Jungian one of its myths and symbols, seems inevitable.[10]

V

As our brief discussion of the psychology of Joyce's characters shows, it is one of the most obvious features of his work from *A Portrait* on that he withdraws the presence of the omniscient author who stage-manages the reader's judgement, in favour of a focus upon a particular consciousness. Joyce of course found this move from the external to the psychologically inward in the novel as mediated by James, Meredith, and Butler, and it was already part of the continental tradition in Chekhov, Maupassant, Huysmans, Jacobsen, D'Annunzio, Bourget, and Turgenev. And in developing it in modernist terms he extends a tradition which runs through Conrad, Mann, Proust, and Gide. As Quinones points out, Bloom like Marcel in *A la recherche du temps perdu*, Hans Castorp in *The Magic Mountain*, Tiresias in *The Waste Land*, Birkin in *Women in Love*, Jacob in *Jacob's Room*, and Clarissa Dalloway in *Mrs Dalloway*, is a 'reflective, passive, selfless and tolerant witness'. And 'the creation of these complex central consciousness constitutes one of the major achievements of modernism' (pp. 95ff.).

These developments entailed a fundamental change in the traditional conjunction between author and (realist) literary text.[11] For Joyce the authority of the text, as an 'omniscient' documentary work in a 'transparent' relationship to its subject matter, is displaced to various rhetorics or styles which are nominally independent of the author as a reliable source of knowledge. This relationship is at its most extreme in *Finnegans Wake*. Like James, Mann, Conrad, and Gide, Joyce displaces that critical relation to society, which had previously been expressed by the author as narrator, to the evocation of a particular consciousness within the text.

It is this concentration on the subjective which, paradoxically enough, freed modernists like Joyce to achieve another aim, not obviously compatible with it: that of the aesthetic autonomy of the experimental work. For it is not simply the nature of passing states of consciousness of the world that become interesting to modernists under the influence of thinkers like William James, Bergson, Freud, and Ernst Mach, but also the way in which the hidden consciousness of the artist *behind* the text may *implicitly or indirectly* display his or her own formal procedures. It is this hidden thematic patterning that is so completely missed by Wyndham Lewis in his polemic concerning the Bergsonian treatment of time in relation to consciousness in modernism, and makes ridiculous his accusation that Bloom and Stephen are 'overwhelmed in the torrent of matter, of *nature morte*. This torrent of matter is the Einsteinian flux. Or (equally well) it is the duration flux of Bergson' (*CH I* 362).

The first and essential step towards this state of affairs for the modernists involved a confrontation with the techniques of the realist text, a confrontation which is at its most extreme in *Finnegans Wake*. It entailed a radical withdrawal from established modes of representation; for nearly all the major experimental works of the early modernist canon deviate from a previous consensual language, and often enough also from common sense. Music abandons the natural 'Pythagorean' language of tonality, cubism abandons the naturalist methods of Renaissance perspective and the facts of vision of the Impressionists. The alogical poetry of Apollinaire, Gottfried Benn, and others, and the stream of consciousness writing of Joyce, Dorothy Richardson, Woolf, and the surrealists, abandons that language of rational control which had been so heroically exercised in the introspections of the protagonists of the nineteenth-century novel. Hence the deep contrast (which is not simply a matter of the earlier censoring of sexual material) which we find if we compare Isobel Archer in James's *Portrait of a Lady* and Dorothea Brooke in George Eliot's *Middlemarch* with Molly Bloom, let alone Anna Livia Plurabelle.

The exploration of consciousness from this point of view forced literary modernists further and further, through Dada and surrealism, into that 'crisis of language' which derives from the work of Hölderlin and Mallarmé, and Rimbaud's *Lettres du voyant* (1871): 'Trouver une langue; du reste, toute parole étant idée, le temps d'un langage universel reviendra!'[12] As George Steiner remarks, this does no less than proclaim a new programme for language and literature (p. 177). And in *Finnegans Wake* Joyce simply bypasses Dada and surrealism in rising to Rimbaud's challenge. He presents us with a universal accretion of *all* languages, and of the underlying myths inherent in their metaphorical structures.

This revolution was prepared by the simple rejection in *Ulysses* of those consensual metadescriptions, emerging from a narrator, which are typical of the realist mode. It is thus hardly surprising that Colin MacCabe and others who write within a post-structuralist framework have made 'the experience of language' central to their interpretation of Joyce, early and late. Thus in 'Sirens' 'the nature of language becomes the concern of the text'; 'Cyclops' is a 'montage of discourses'; and *Finnegans Wake* 'turns around the connexion between writing and sexuality' (MacCabe, pp. 54, 64, 79ff., 90, 133). Joyce's night book, founded in the philosophy of Vico, nevertheless met with resolute opposition from its early readers, and most hurtfully from his brother Stanislaus, who called it 'drivelling rigmarole', 'unspeakably wearisome', and 'the witless wandering of literature before its final extinction' (*Letters III* 102–3). In his attempt to promote it through *transition* and through the apostolic twelve critics of the *Exagmination*, Joyce was forced into a rare alliance with the avant-garde and its doctrines.[13]

The *Wake* was conceived at the climax of the high modernist revival of formally extremely complicated works. These often aim at a kind of formal self-containment which facilitates the expression of an autonomous world, and thus revert to the Symbolist notion of the Mallarméan 'Grand Livre', the culminating encyclopedic masterpiece. Thus Beckett tells us that 'His writing is not *about* something; *it is that something itself*' (Beckett *et al.*, p. 14), and Jolas proclaims:

The new artist of the word has recognised the autonomy of language and, aware of the twentieth century current towards universality, attempts to hammer out a verbal vision that destroys time and space.

(Beckett *et al.*, p. 79)

This claim that the experimental work can emancipate itself from the substructure of experience itself, and hence from the causal structures that underwrite all realism, is echoed by Marcel Brion, who argues that *Ulysses* is 'one of the Einsteinian miracles of the relativity of time', leading inexorably to the *Wake*, which he says is 'essentially a time work' (Beckett *et al.*, pp. 30–1).

Joyce's project thus resembles that of works like Berg's *Wozzeck* (1922), Schoenberg's *Moses and Aaron* (1930–2), Duchamp's *The Bride Stripped Bare by her Bachelors, Even* (1915–23), and ultimately of even so conservative a work as Eliot's *Four Quartets* (1943), all of which thrive on occult hidden orders, which are independent of the usual mimetic aims associated with a particular content. What his book also has in common with music, rather than with the language of his predecessors and successors, is the aim of reinventing the basic elements of the language of his art, in what McAlmon called 'an esperanto of the subconscious' (Beckett *et al.*, p. 110). He thus superimposes the languages and stories of many races, under which are supposed to lie the simplest of (Viconian) mythical narratives. For rather as pitches freed from traditional tonal relationships manage to enter into hitherto prohibited relationships with one another, and so to require the invention of wholly new principles for their ordering (which may also involve the revival of neo-classical forms as underlying structure, as in Berg), so Joyce invents a vocabulary which allows the words of different languages to interact.

This analogy with music is one that Joyce himself was inclined to exploit (*JJ* 703), and McAlmon tells us that 'he wishes to believe that anybody reading his work gets a sensation of understanding, which is the understanding which music is allowed without too much explanation' (Beckett *et al.*, pp. 110–11). Indeed this parallel is turned to with relief by nearly all the early commentators on the *Wake*, who are not so much concerned to situate it in the context of the (declining) modernist culture of its time, as to attempt baffled exegesis and to defend its language. Even Beckett says that it is 'not only to be read. It is to be looked at and listened to' (Beckett *et al.*, p. 14). This procedure realizes for Joyce an 'aesthetic of the dream' wholly independent of everyday experience, in which 'the forms prolong and multiply themselves, where the visions pass from the trivial to the apocalyptic, where the brain uses the roots of vocables to make others from them which will be capable of naming its phantasms, its allegories, its allusions', as he put it to Edmond Jaloux (*JJ* 559).

VI

The circumstances of its early publication (and the later fortunes of surrealism in post-modern literature) have led to the *Wake*'s being seen as an attempt at a revolution in society through the word; as an act of liberation. It has thus had a long run as a fosterer of these sorts of hopes – in our time through the doctrines of the *nouveau romanciers* and the critics associated with them (see, for example, Sollers, pp. 7ff.), and through the doctrines of Julia Kristeva concerning the 'revolution in poetic language'. She thus sees the *Wake* as an example of the unconsciously motivated 'chora', which manages to evade that phallogocentric discourse of the Lacanian 'Symbolic Order' which dominates our waking lives – a view to which MacCabe also seems sympathetic (see pp. 147–51).

This kind of apologia for Joyce's book marks a very important point of transition from modern to post-modern writing, which is centrally concerned with the artificiality of modes of discourse, with intertextuality, and with that attack on mimesis which transforms 'real Matter-of-Fact' into a 'matter of fict' or 'the matter of ficfect' (*FW* 532.29). As Brian McHale, who has provided us with an outstanding account of the rhetoric of post-modern fiction, puts it,

Molly Bloom's soliloquy notoriously represents the 'stream of consciousness', but Anna Livia is the thing itself: the personification of the River Liffey, she literalizes the metaphor 'stream of consciousness'. Just as her discourse seems to sweep up all language in its stream, so it also sweeps up the projected world of this text: there is no stable world *behind* this consciousness, but only a flux of discourse in which fragments of different, incompatible realities flicker into existence and out of existence again, overwhelmed by the competing reality of language.

Postmodernist fiction, in short.   (p. 234)

Like the work of Robbe-Grillet and others, this project is less concerned by its own self-contradictions than by the game-like process of writing itself, and this is a metaphor Joyce uses in writing to Harriet Weaver: 'I know that it is no more than a game, but it is a game that I have learned to play in my own way. Children may just as well play as not. The ogre will come in any case' (*Letters III* 143–4).

As Joyce's rather sad remark suggests, *Finnegans Wake* was, by comparison with *Ulysses*, neglected in its time; but in a period in which post-Saussurean dissemination, and play theories of experimental fiction, have come in to their own, it stands as the initiator of a new tradition, leading to writers like Ray Federman, Ronald Sukenick, Gilbert Sorrentino, and Donald Barthelme. For them as for Joyce 'the text produces a derisive hesitation of sense, the final revelation of meaning being always for "later"', as Stephen Heath puts it (p. 31). In this process as enacted by Joyce and his recent successors, the confident articulating subject (the author) is broken down as he runs through a multiplicity of styles and produces a text shot through with intertextual relationships. The 'declamatory personality' (Flaubert's term) founders in the vacillation of the play of forms, sliding through them and retraceable only in the terms of sham, forgery, and citation. Thus Heath concludes that

in a sense, *Finnegans Wake* is to linguistics as Saussure's *Anagrammes* are to the *Cours de linguistique générale*, a radical contestation of the knowledge of his language constructed by the subject.   (pp. 33, 57)

It is thus hardly surprising that one of the best interpretations of this work to date, by Margot Norris, sees the book in relation to the post-Saussurean structuralism that in fact succeeded it, to Lévi-Strauss, to Lacan, and to Derrida. Jean-Michel Rabaté similarly interprets the *Wake* in the light of thinkers who come after it, like Lévi-Strauss, Eco, and Barthes, using notions like the 'scriptible' and 'serial thought' (pp. 79ff.). And Derrida himself praises the *Wake* as a 'great paradigm', in which Joyce

repeats and mobilizes and babelizes the (asymptotic) totality of the equivocal, he makes this his theme and his operation, he tries to make outcrop, with the greatest possible synchrony, at great speed, the greatest power of the meanings buried in each syllabic fragment, subjecting each atom of writing to fission in order to overload the unconscious with the whole memory of man: mythologies, religion, philosophies, sciences, psychoanalysis, literatures.

(p. 149)

It is the extraordinary achievement of John Bishop's work that he manages to realize some of this complexity, at the same time as saving the *Wake* as an intelligible reading experience.

The relationship of *Finnegans Wake* to pre-war modernism is thus tenuous; but it has served as a major source of inspiration to post-modernists, not alone to writers and theorists but also to musicians (such as Pierre Boulez, Luciano Berio, and John Cage) who have like Joyce been concerned to invent alternative languages for their art, and who have wished to turn even further away from the consensual forms of discourse in the society which surrounds it. And it has been equally influential upon the growth of post-structuralist literary theory and philosophy since the 1960s, providing a text that exemplifies many of its concerns.

Joyce's work perpetually challenges us to appreciate and bring to light the formal manoeuvres of the hidden hand, of the parodist of past styles in *A Portrait*, of the inventor and Arranger of eighteen new ones in *Ulysses*, and of the celebrant of the occult orders hidden within that most subjective of experiences, the dream, in the *Wake*. He is adamant that all of his methods can be explained and justified: 'If you take a characteristic obscure passage of one of these people [modern writers] and asked him what it meant, he couldn't tell you; whereas I can justify every line of my book' (*JJ* 702). This challenge is always a joy to meet. For some, he always plays fair and preserves consistency, as those proponents of the realistic novel, or of the reconstruction of a lost Dublin underlying *Ulysses*, or of the coherent plot underlying *Finnegans Wake*, would be the first to affirm. For others, and more recently, his inconsistencies are of equal interpretative importance.

Joyce indeed wanted to be interpreted; in this he follows one of the central aims of early modernism, which was to attract an audience which was willing to attempt to decode the relationships between stylistic medium and message. His works, from *Stephen Hero* to *Finnegans Wake*, mark in this respect the essential steps in the evolution of literature from the Symbolist epoch to the post-modern; and it should be added, that whatever our mode of interpretation may be, in reading Joyce we are perpetually entertained by the most humorous and charitable of all twentieth-century writers.

NOTES

1 Some relevant distinctions are attempted in Chefdor, Quinones, and Wachtel, pp. 1–15.
2 See, for example, Hughes, pp. 63ff. The classic account of modernist tendencies as Oedipal revolt is to be found in Schorske's *Fin de Siècle Vienna*; this generational model has appealed to many historians of the period, for example Wohl in Chefdor, Quinones, and Wachtel, pp. 66–79.
3 There is also a mixture of Zarathustra and Marx in Joyce's 'A Portrait of the Artist', a short autobiographical piece written in 1904 and submitted to *Dana*. See Scholes and Kain, *The Workshop of Daedalus*, pp. 56–74. It is discussed in Manganiello, *Joyce's Politics*, pp. 67–72. See also ch. 3 of this volume.
4 The paper corresponds to Joyce's own on 'Drama and Life' of October 1899, delivered in January 1900 (see *JJ* 71–2). It is according to Manganiello the work of a 'socialist artist' (pp. 44–5).
5 Of course Joyce favoured classicism on his own definition from the start. See *SH* 83, and Goldberg, *The Classical Temper*.
6 'Swirling jumble of images. Tragic unity is displaced. We learn. We drink. Drunkenness. The real no longer has any sense. No meaning. Everything is rhythm, speech, life. There are no more proofs. We're all in communion' (Cendrars, *Aujourd'hui*, p. 254). See also Kern, pp. 67–88.
7 This was broadly correct; see *JJ* 502ff., esp. 503. The 'pink 'un' concluded nevertheless that *Ulysses* was 'sordidly pornographic' and 'immensely dull' (*CH I* 194).
8 Hoffman's account in *Freudianism and the Literary Mind* is still the best discussion of this topic, and its conclusions are largely negative concerning positive influence in *Ulysses*. But see also Schechner's *Joyce in Nighttown*, and Klaus Reichert's discussion of Freud in ch. 3 of this volume.
9 He discusses the *Five Lectures on Psychoanalysis* and Freud's doctrines concerning slips of the tongue with a friend – which emerge, for example, in Bloom's saying 'the wife's admirers' rather than 'the wife's advisers' in *Ulysses* (12.767) – as early as 1913 (*JJ* 340), and he recorded Nora's dreams and his own interpretations of them (*JJ* 436ff.). But he refused analysis by Jung (though later accepted it for his own daughter) (*JJ* 466, 676).
10 See Hoffman, pp. 122ff. and 139ff., Norris on dream in *The Decentered Universe*, pp. 98–119, and, most impressively, Bishop, *Joyce's Book of the Dark*, pp. 15–18 and 179ff. Bishop emphasizes the comparison with, and prior indebtedness to, Vico.
11 See Butler, 'Joyce and the Displaced Author', and Mahaffey, *Reauthorizing Joyce*.
12 'Find a language; for the rest, since all speech is idea, the time of a universal language will return!'

13 Thus many of the points made in Jolas's *Manifesto of the Word*, heavily reliant as it is on Blake and Rimbaud, could be applied to the *Wake*, especially the declarations numbered 3 to 6. See *JJ* 588.

WORKS CITED

Adams, Robert M. *AfterJoyce*. New York: Oxford University Press, 1977

Apollonio, Umbro, ed. *Futurist Manifestos*. London: Thames and Hudson, 1973

Attridge, Derek, and Daniel Ferrer, eds. *Post-structuralist Joyce: Essays from the French*. Cambridge: Cambridge University Press, 1984

Arnold, Matthew. 'Heinrich Heine'. In *Lectures and Essays in Criticism*, ed. R. H. Super. Ann Arbor: University of Michigan Press, 1962

Beckett, Samuel, *et al. Our Exagmination Round His Factification for Incamination of Work in Progress* (1929). London: Faber, 1972

Bishop, John. *Joyce's Book of the Dark: 'Finnegans Wake'*. Madison: University of Wisconsin Press, 1986

Brown, Richard. *James Joyce and Sexuality*. Cambridge: Cambridge University Press, 1985

Budgen, Frank. *James Joyce and the Making of 'Ulysses'* (1934). London: Oxford University Press, 1972

Burgess, Anthony. *Here Comes Everybody: An Introduction to James Joyce for the Ordinary Reader*. London: Faber, 1965

Bush, Ronald. *The Genesis of Pound's Early Cantos*. Princeton: Princeton University Press, 1976

Butler, Christopher. 'Joyce and the Displaced Author'. In W. J. McCormack and Alistair Stead, eds., *James Joyce and Modern Literature*. London: Routledge, 1982, pp. 54–74

Cendrars, Blaise. *Aujourd'hui*. Paris, 1931

Chefdor, Monique, Ricardo Quinones, and Albert Wachtel, eds. *Modernism*. Urbana: University of Illinois Press, 1986

Derrida, Jacques. 'Two Words for Joyce.' In Attridge and Ferrer, *Post-structuralist Joyce*, 145–59

Eliot, T. S. *Selected Essays*. London: Faber, 1951

Ellmann, Richard. *The Consciousness of Joyce*. London: Faber, 1977

Gilbert, Stuart. *James Joyce's Ulysses* (1930). New York: Random House, 1955

Goldberg, S. L. *The Classical Temper: A Study of James Joyce's 'Ulysses'*. London: Chatto and Windus, 1961

Heath, Stephen. 'Ambiviolences: notes for reading Joyce'. In Attridge and Ferrer, *Post-structuralist Joyce*, 31–68

Hoffman, Frederick J. *Freudianism and the Literary Mind*. 2nd edn., Baton Rouge: Louisiana State University Press, 1957

Hughes, H. S. *Consciousness and Society: The Reorientation of European Social*

282   CHRISTOPHER BUTLER

Thought, 1890–1930. London: McGibbon and Kee, 1967

Kern, Stephen. *The Culture of Time and Space, 1880–1918*. London: Weidenfeld and Nicolson, 1983

Kristeva, Julia. *Revolution in Poetic Language*. Trans. Margaret Waller. New York: Columbia University Press, 1984

Lawrence, Karen. *The Odyssey of Style in 'Ulysses'*. Princeton: Princeton University Press, 1981

Loss, Archie K. *Joyce's Visible Art: The Work of Joyce and the Visual Arts*. Ann Arbor: UMI Research Press, 1984

Lodge, David. *Modes of Modern Writing*. London: Arnold, 1977

MacCabe, Colin. *James Joyce and the Revolution of the Word*. London: Macmillan, 1979

Mahaffey, Vicki. *Reauthorizing Joyce*. Cambridge: Cambridge University Press, 1988

Manganiello, Dominic. *Joyce's Politics*. London, Routledge, 1980

Mann, Thomas. *Tonio Kröger*. In *Death in Venice, Tristan, Tonio Kröger*. Trans. H. T. Lowe-Porter. Harmondsworth: Penguin, 1955

McHale, Brian. *Postmodernist Fiction*. London: Routledge, 1987

Norris, Margot. *The Decentered Universe of 'Finnegans Wake': A Structuralist Analysis*. Baltimore: Johns Hopkins University Press, 1976

Power, Arthur. *Conversations with James Joyce*, ed. Clive Hart. London: Millington, 1974

Quinones, Ricardo. *Mapping Literary Modernism: Time and Development*. Princeton: Princeton University Press, 1985

Rabaté, Jean-Michel. 'Lapsus ex machina'. In Attridge and Ferrer, *Poststructuralist Joyce*, 79–102

Schechner, Mark. *Joyce in Nighttown: A Psychoanalytic Inquiry into 'Ulysses'*. Berkeley: University of California Press, 1974

Scholes, Robert, and Richard M. Kain. *The Workshop of Daedalus: James Joyce and the Raw Materials for 'A Portrait of the Artist as a Young Man'*. Evanston: Northwestern University Press, 1965

Schorske, Carl Emil. *Fin de Siècle Vienna: Politics and Culture*. London: Weidenfeld and Nicolson, 1980

Sollers, Philippe. 'Pourquoi je suis si peu religieux'. *Tel Quel* 81 (Fall, 1979), 7–25

Steiner, George. *After Babel: Aspects of Language and Translation*. London: Oxford University Press, 1975

Sultan, Stanley. *Eliot, Joyce and Company*. New York: Oxford University Press, 1988

Vickers, Brian. *In Defence of Rhetoric*. Oxford: Oxford University Press, 1988

Wilde, Oscar. *Complete Works*. London: Collins, 1966

Wilson, Edmund. *Axel's Castle*. New York: Charles Scribner's Sons, 1931

Further reading

The number of books and articles about Joyce is enormous and ever-increasing; the quantity of secondary material not directly concerned with Joyce but relevant to his work is even larger. None of these publications is without value, but none of them need be regarded as essential. The bibliographies mentioned below give comprehensive lists, and the chapters of this volume refer to specialized works of particular relevance to their topics. What follows is a highly selective set of suggestions for the interested reader, with an emphasis on works that will provide useful information or critical stimulation. Apart from the sections on Joyce's own texts and on bibliographies, the order studies. In 1992, the copyright on several of Joyce's works expired, and a number of new editions have been announced.

TEXTS

Chamber Music (1907). New York: Columbia University Press, 1954; London: Cape, 1971. The US edition is edited by William York Tindall. See also *Poems and Shorter Writings* below.

Dubliners (1914). Text corrected by Robert Scholes. New York: Viking, 1968; London: Cape, 1967. Text further corrected for the Viking Critical Library edition, ed. Robert Scholes and A. Walton Litz (New York: Viking, 1969), which also includes explanatory notes and critical essays. Several reprints of this text in the USA and UK.

A Portrait of the Artist as a Young Man (1916). Ed. Chester G. Anderson. New York: Viking; London: Cape, 1964; and several reprints. This text was reprinted in the Viking Critical Library edition, ed. Chester G. Anderson (New York: Viking, 1968), which also includes the 1904 'Portrait of the Artist' and other supplementary material.

283

Exiles (1918). New York: Viking, 1951; London: Cape, 1952. Several reprints in USA and UK.

Pomes Penyeach (1927). London: Faber, 1933, reprinted 1966. See also *Poems and Shorter Writings* below.

Ulysses (1922). Ed. Hans Walter Gabler with Wolfhard Steppe and Claus Melchior. New York: Random House; London: Bodley Head; Harmondsworth: Penguin, 1986. This edition is based on the three-volume Critical and Synoptic Edition published in New York and London by Garland in 1984, keeping its chapter-by-chapter line-numbering, which makes precise references possible. Most readers will buy the paperback edition, published by Random House in the USA and Penguin in the UK – but note that of the two Penguin editions only the 'Students' Edition' includes line-numbering. (New readers may skip the somewhat reductive Preface by Richard Ellmann.) The new text has provoked much discussion, and we can expect more corrections to be made in future editions; readers should remember, however, that there can be no such thing as a 'definitive' text of a work with a compositional and publishing history as complex as that of *Ulysses*.

Finnegans Wake (1939). New York: Viking; London: Faber, 1939; many subsequent reprintings. Some parts of *Finnegans Wake* appeared as separate publications in earlier versions before 1939; the work as a whole was known as 'Work in Progress' prior to publication. Unlike *Ulysses*. *Finnegans Wake* has never been re-edited or reset; this means that all printings follow the same pagination and line-division as the original one, with only very minor discrepancies arising from corrections. It also means that the current text has many errors (but the notion of 'error' is even more problematic in the case of the *Wake* than in the case of *Ulysses*).

Stephen Hero (posthumous, 1944). Ed. Theodore Spencer, rev. John J. Slocum and Herbert Cahoon. Norfolk, CN: New Directions, 1963; London: Cape, 1969. Published in the UK as a Triad/Panther paperback in 1977. See the comment on this text in ch. 5, note 5, above.

Giacomo Joyce (posthumous, 1968). Ed. Richard Ellmann. New York: Viking; London: Faber, 1968. See also *Poems and Shorter Writings* below.

Letters. Ed. Stuart Gilbert (vol. I) and Richard Ellmann (vols. II and III). New York: Viking; London: Faber, 1957, 1966. These volumes also contain some useful supplementary material, including (in vol. II) a list of Joyce's addresses and a detailed chronology of his writings, and are well indexed.

Selected Letters. Ed. Richard Ellmann. New York: Viking; London: Faber, 1975. The *Selected Letters* includes some correspondence not printed in the three volumes of the *Letters*.

Critical Writings. Ed. Ellsworth Mason and Richard Ellmann. New York: Viking; London: Faber, 1959; reprinted Ithaca: Cornell University Press, 1989. This volume brings together Joyce's lectures and essays on a variety of topics, chiefly literary and political.

Poems and Shorter Writings. Ed. Richard Ellmann, A. Walton Litz, and John Whittier-Ferguson. London: Faber, 1991. (This volume includes all the poems, the unpublished epiphanies, the 1904 essay 'A Portrait of the Artist', and *Giacomo Joyce*.)

The James Joyce Archive. Ed. Michael Groden, Hans Walter Gabler, David Hayman, A. Walton Litz, and Danis Rose with John O'Hanlon. 63 vols. New York: Garland, 1977–9. This massive set of facsimiles collects virtually all the surviving pre-publication material relating to Joyce's works.

The Portable James Joyce. Ed. Harry Levin. Rev. edn., New York: Viking/Penguin, 1966. A useful collection of Joyce's shorter works: *Dubliners*, *A Portrait*, *Exiles*, and the poems, together with brief selections from *Ulysses* and *Finnegans Wake*. Published in the UK by Cape and Panther/Triad as *The Essential James Joyce*.

Œuvres. Readers of French should note that the first volume of the Pléiade Complete Works has appeared, superbly edited by Jacques Aubert with full textual and explanatory notes (Paris: Gallimard, 1982). It contains – in translation – all the poems and epiphanies, *Dubliners, Stephen Hero. A Portrait, Giacomo Joyce, Exiles*, the critical writings, a selection of letters, and other manuscript materials.

BIBLIOGRAPHIES

Slocum, John J., and Herbert Cahoon. *A Bibliography of James Joyce, 1882–1941*. New Haven: Yale University Press, 1953; reprinted Westport, CN: Greenwood, 1971. A comprehensive bibliography of Joyce's own writings.

Deming, Robert H. *A Bibliography of James Joyce Studies*. 2nd edn., Boston: G. K. Hall, 1977. A full listing of works on Joyce.

Staley, Thomas F. *An Annotated Critical Bibliography of James Joyce*. Brighton: Harvester, 1989. A brief guide through Joyce criticism.

Rice, Thomas Jackson. *James Joyce: A Guide to Research*. New York: Garland, 1982. A detailed annotated bibliography up to 1981.

Brockman, William S., 'Current JJ Checklist'; Will Godwin, 'Annual James Joyce Checklist.' Lists of recent primary and secondary material (including reviews), published in *JJQ* and *Joyce Studies Annual* respectively.

GENERAL WORKS

Introductions to Joyce

Levin, Harry. *James Joyce: A Critical Introduction* (1941). Rev. edn, New York:
New Directions Press, 1960. An early but still valuable approach to Joyce.
Benstock, Bernard. *James Joyce*. New York: Frederick Ungar; London:
Lorrimer, 1985.
Parrinder, Patrick. *James Joyce*. Cambridge: Cambridge University Press,
1984.
Burgess, Anthony. *Joysprick: An Introduction to the Language of James Joyce.*
London: André Deutsch, 1973.
Bowen, Zack, and James F. Carens, eds. *A Companion to Joyce Studies.*
Westport, CN: Greenwood, 1984. A full, if unwieldy, survey of Joyce's
life and works, and of the industry he set going, by eighteen Joyceans.

For reference

Deming, Robert H., ed. *James Joyce: The Critical Heritage*. 2 vols. London:
Routledge, 1970. A selection of critical writings on Joyce from 1902 to
1941.
Benstock, Shari, and Bernard Benstock. *Who's He When He's at Home: A James
Joyce Directory*. Urbana: University of Illinois Press, 1980. A directory of
the named individuals in Joyce's works other than *Finnegans Wake* (for
which see Glasheen, below).
Hodgart, Matthew J. C., and Mabel P. Worthington. *Song in the Works of
James Joyce*. New York: Columbia University Press, 1959. Includes
Finnegans Wake, which the following more laboriously detailed study
does not.
Bowen, Zack. *Musical Allusions in the Works of James Joyce: Early Poetry
Through 'Ulysses'*. Albany: State University of New York Press; Dublin:
Gill and Macmillan, 1975.

Critical studies

Chace, William M., ed. *Joyce: A Collection of Critical Essays*. Twentieth-
Century Views. Englewood Cliffs, NJ: Prentice-Hall, 1974. Includes some
of the most famous essays on Joyce.
Bloom, Harold, ed. *James Joyce: Modern Critical Views*. New York: Chelsea
House, 1986. A number of important essays, from Beckett to Ferrer, many
of them quite advanced. Includes pieces by Jennifer Levine, Raymond
Williams, Fredric Jameson, and Karen Lawrence.

Kenner, Hugh. *The Stoic Comedians: Flaubert, Joyce, Beckett*. Berkeley: University of California Press, 1962. Joyce in a tradition of writers who wrest comedy from the limitations of discourse.

Joyce's Voices. London: Faber, 1978. A readable study of the indeterminacies of narrative voice.

Litz, A. Walton. *The Art of James Joyce: Method and Design in 'Ulysses' and 'Finnegans Wake'*. London: Oxford University Press, 1961, rev. 1964. A useful guide to Joyce's working methods.

Kenner, Hugh. *Dublin's Joyce* (1955). Reprinted New York: Columbia University Press, 1987. A kaleidoscopically rich book, both tendentious and illuminating; the chapter on *A Portrait* – 'The *Portrait* in perspective' – has been particularly influential.

Senn, Fritz. *Joyce's Dislocutions*. Ed. John Paul Riquelme. Baltimore: Johns Hopkins University Press, 1984. Subtle readings that raise, freshly and undogmatically, the large questions about Joyce.

Henke, Suzette, and Elaine Unkeless, eds. *Women in Joyce*. Urbana: University of Illinois Press; Brighton: Harvester, 1982.

Attridge, Derek. *Peculiar Language: Literature as Difference from the Renaissance to James Joyce*. Ithaca: Cornell University Press; London: Methuen, 1988. Chs. 5 and 6 on *Ulysses*; chs. 7 and 8 on *Finnegans Wake*.

MacCabe, Colin, ed. *James Joyce: New Perspectives*. Brighton: Harvester; Bloomington: Indiana University Press, 1982. Reflects some of the new directions taken in Joyce studies during the 1970s; includes essays by Seamus Deane, Jean-Michel Rabaté, Fritz Senn, and Stephen Heath.

Mahaffey, Vicki. *Reauthorizing Joyce*. Cambridge: Cambridge University Press, 1988.

Riquelme, John Paul. *Teller and Tale in Joyce's Fiction: Oscillating Perspectives*. Baltimore: Johns Hopkins University Press, 1983.

MacCabe, Colin. *James Joyce and the Revolution of the Word*. London: Macmillan; New York: Barnes and Noble, 1979.

Beja, Morris, *et al.*, eds. *James Joyce: The Centennial Symposium*. Urbana: University of Illinois Press, 1986. Includes papers by Seamus Deane, Maud Ellmann, Margot Norris, and Jean-Michel Rabaté.

Benstock, Bernard, ed. *The Augmented Ninth: Papers from the Ninth James Joyce Symposium*. Syracuse: Syracuse University Press, 1988. Includes papers by Jacques Derrida and Julia Kristeva.

Jacquet, Claude, ed. *'Scribble' 1: genèse des textes*. La Revue des Lettres Modernes, Série James Joyce 1. Paris: Minard, 1988. A collection of essays in English and French, including work by Jacques Derrida, Jean-Michel Rabaté, Hans Walter Gabler, and Klaus Reichert.

Attridge, Derek and Daniel Ferrer, eds. *Post-structuralist Joyce: Essays from the French*. Cambridge: Cambridge University Press, 1984. Includes essays by Hélène Cixous, Jean-Michel Rabaté, Stephen Heath, and Jacques Derrida.

Rabaté, Jean-Michel. *James Joyce, Authorized Reader*. Baltimore: Johns Hopkins University Press, 1991. A translation of *James Joyce: Portrait de l'auteur en autre lecteur* (Petit-Roeulx: Cistre, 1984).

On Joyce's contexts

Deane, Seamus. *A Short History of Irish Literature*. London: Hutchinson, 1986. *Celtic Revivals: Essays in Modern Irish Literature*. London: Faber, 1985.
Scott, Bonnie Kime. *Joyce and Feminism*. Bloomington: Indiana University Press; Brighton: Harvester, 1984. Especially valuable for its discussions of Joyce's relation to early feminism, and of the women who played an important role in Joyce's creative life.
Garvin, John. *James Joyce's Disunited Kingdom and the Irish Dimension*. Dublin and London: Gill and Macmillan, 1976.
Hutchins, Patricia. *James Joyce's Dublin*. London: Grey Wall Press, 1950.
Kain, Richard M. *Dublin in the Age of William Butler Yeats and James Joyce*. Norman: University of Oklahoma Press, 1962.
Manganiello, Dominic. *Joyce's Politics*. Routledge: London, 1980. A study of Joyce's attitudes towards and involvement in the political movements of his time.
Read, Forrest, ed. *Pound/Joyce*. New York: New Directions, 1967. Over sixty letters from Pound to Joyce, with linking commentary, together with Pound's critical essays on Joyce; an entertaining insight into one of modernism's most significant relationships.
Brown, Richard. *James Joyce and Sexuality*. Cambridge: Cambridge University Press, 1985. A thorough discussion of the discourse of sexuality that informed Joyce's treatments of the subject.
Herr, Cheryl. *Joyce's Anatomy of Culture*. Urbana: University of Illinois Press, 1986. Joyce's relation to Dublin working-class culture, with special attention given to newspapers, pantomime, and sermons.
Kristeva, Julia. *Desire in Language: A Semiotic Approach to Literature and Art*. Trans. Thomas Gora, Alice Jardine, and Leon S. Roudiez. New York: Columbia University Press; Oxford: Blackwell, 1980. Joyce figures among other writers in Kristeva's theory of a pre-rational language tapped by the literary text.

DUBLINERS AND A PORTRAIT

For reference

Gifford, Don. *Joyce Annotated: Notes for 'Dubliners' and 'A Portrait of the Artist as a Young Man'*. 2nd edn., Berkeley: University of California Press, 1982.

Bidwell, Bruce, and Linda Heffer. *The Joycean Way: A Topographic Guide to
'Dubliners' and 'A Portrait of the Artist as a Young Man'*. Dublin:
Wolfhound Press; Baltimore: Johns Hopkins University Press, 1982.
Contains maps and photographs as well as descriptions.
Füger, Wilhelm, ed. *Concordance to James Joyce's 'Dubliners'*. Hildesheim and
New York: Georg Olms, 1980.
Hancock, Leslie. *Word Index to James Joyce's 'Portrait of the Artist'*.
Carbondale: Southern Illinois Press; London: Feffer and Simons, 1967.

The making of *A Portrait*

Scholes, Robert, and Richard M. Kain. *The Workshop of Daedalus: James Joyce
and the Raw Materials for 'A Portrait of the Artist as a Young Man'*.
Evanston: Northwestern University Press, 1965. Manuscript material and
discussion.

Critical studies

Beja, Morris, ed. *'Dubliners' and 'A Portrait of the Artist as a Young Man': A
Casebook*. London: Macmillan, 1973.
Hart, Clive, ed. *James Joyce's 'Dubliners': Critical Essays*. London: Faber; New
York: Viking, 1969. Includes essays on each of the stories.
Staley, Thomas F., and Bernard Benstock, eds. *Approaches to Joyce's 'Portrait':
Ten Essays*. Pittsburgh: University of Pittsburgh Press, 1976. Includes
valuable essays by Hugh Kenner and Hans Walter Gabler, among others.
Brown, Homer Obed. *James Joyce's Early Fiction: The Biography of a Form*.
Cleveland: Press of Case Western Reserve University, 1972.

ULYSSES

For reference

Gifford, Don. *'Ulysses' Annotated*. Berkeley: University of California Press,
1989. A revised edition of the 1974 work, which met with some criticism
for its inaccuracies.
Thornton, Weldon. *Allusions in 'Ulysses': An Annotated List*. Chapel Hill:
University of North Carolina Press, 1968.
Hart, Clive, and Leo Knuth. *A Topographical Guide to James Joyce's 'Ulysses'*.
Colchester: A Wake Newslitter Press, 1975, rev. 1986. Entertaining and
informative maps, with commentary and list of addresses.
Schutte, William M. *Index of Recurrent Elements in James Joyce's 'Ulysses'*.
Carbondale: Southern Illinois University Press, 1982. A useful tool for
tracing the web of cross-references and repetitions in *Ulysses*.

Steppe, Wolfhard, with Hans Walter Gabler. *A Handlist to James Joyce's 'Ulysses'*. New York: Garland, 1986. A computer-generated concordance, produced in conjunction with the 1984 edition of *Ulysses* and keyed to its line-references.

The making of *Ulysses*

Budgen, Frank. *James Joyce and the Making of 'Ulysses'* (1934). Bloomington: Indiana University Press, 1960; London: Oxford University Press, 1972 (with additional articles). An anecdotal account of the years of *Ulysses'* construction by a friend of Joyce's, incorporating many of Joyce's own suggestions.
Groden, Michael. *'Ulysses' in Progress*. Princeton: Princeton University Press, 1977. A study of Joyce's work on *Ulysses*, and his shifting conception of the book.
Herring, Phillip F., ed. *Joyce's 'Ulysses' Notesheets in the British Museum*. Charlottesville: University Press of Virginia, 1972.
Joyce's Notes and Early Drafts for 'Ulysses': Selections from the Buffalo Collection. Charlottesville: University Press of Virginia, 1977.

Critical studies

Gilbert, Stuart. *James Joyce's Ulysses* (1930). Rev. edn., London: Faber, 1952; New York: Random House, 1955. An influential study whose interest lies partly in the fact that Joyce assisted in its composition; since it was designed to gain acceptance for *Ulysses* among a sceptical audience it exaggerates the book's learned allusiveness.
Hart, Clive, and David Hayman, eds. *James Joyce's 'Ulysses': Critical Essays*. Berkeley: University of California Press, 1974. Eighteen critics discuss one chapter of *Ulysses* apiece; a mixed bag.
Kenner, Hugh. *Ulysses*. Rev. edn., Baltimore: Johns Hopkins University Press, 1987. Sharp observations and strong opinions make this a lively and illuminating short study.
Lawrence, Karen. *The Odyssey of Style in 'Ulysses'*. Princeton: Princeton University Press, 1981. Focuses on the feature of *Ulysses* that many earlier commentaries glossed over: its striking shifts in style.
Thomas, Brook. *James Joyce's 'Ulysses': A Book of Many Happy Returns*. Baton Rouge: Louisiana State University Press, 1982.
Boheemen, Christine van. *The Novel as Family Romance: Language, Gender, and Authority from Fielding to Joyce*. Ithaca: Cornell University Press, 1987. *Ulysses* discussed in relation to the English novel's perennial exclusion of 'woman'.

FINNEGANS WAKE

For reference

McHugh, Roland. *Annotations to 'Finnegans Wake'*. Baltimore: Johns Hopkins University Press, revised edition, 1991. McHugh's highly convenient handbook gathers together the work of many scholars, including those (not listed here) who have produced lexicons of a number of the languages used in the *Wake*. But it does not claim to be either 'exhaustive' or 'definitive'.

Glasheen, Adeline. *Third Census of 'Finnegans Wake': An Index of Characters and Their Roles*. Berkeley: University of California Press, 1977. A remarkably full and lively directory of people's names in the *Wake*.

Atherton, James S. *The Books at the Wake: A Study of Literary Allusions in James Joyce's 'Finnegans Wake'* (1959). Rev. edn, Mamaroneck, NY: Paul P. Appel, 1973. A pioneering and still useful guide to the major books and authors exploited in the *Wake*.

Hart, Clive. *A Concordance to 'Finnegans Wake'* (1963). Reprinted Mamaroneck, N.Y.: Paul P. Appel, 1973. An invaluable tool, which lists not only all the 'words' of *Finnegans Wake* in the forms in which they appear, but meaningful parts of those 'words', and other words suggested by these 'words'.

Mink, Louis O. *A 'Finnegans Wake' Gazetteer*. Bloomington: Indiana University Press, 1978. A detailed guide to the place-names in the *Wake*.

The making of the *Wake*

Higginson, Fred H. *Anna Livia Plurabelle: The Making of a Chapter*. Minneapolis: University of Minnesota Press, 1960. Six draft versions of the 'ALP' chapter of the *Wake*.

Connolly, Thomas E., ed. *James Joyce's Scribbledehobble: The Ur-Workbook for 'Finnegans Wake'*. Evanston: Northwestern University Press, 1961. Not free from transcription errors, but a fascinating glimpse of Joyce's compositional methods.

Rose, Danis, ed. *James Joyce's 'The Index Manuscript': 'Finnegans Wake' Holograph Workbook VI.B. 46*. Colchester: A Wake Newslitter Press, 1978. A meticulous edition of one of the most important of the workbooks out of which the *Wake* was constructed.

Critical studies

McHugh, Roland. *The 'Finnegans Wake' Experience*. Dublin: Irish Academic Press, 1981. A down-to-earth account of one person's encounter with the *Wake*, together with glimpses of the Joyce industry in operation.

Beckett, Samuel, et al. *Our Exagmination Round His Factification for Incamination of Work in Progress* (1929). Reprinted London: Faber; New York: New Directions, 1972. A collection of pieces on the earlier parts of the *Wake*; orchestrated by Joyce, it is of considerable historical interest, and continuing critical value – especially the essay by Samuel Beckett.

Norris, Margot. *The Decentered Universe of 'Finnegans Wake': A Structuralist Analysis*. Baltimore: Johns Hopkins University Press, 1976. Developments in literary theory in the 1960s and 70s – for which Joyce's work was an important catalyst – bear fruit in this valuable account of the *Wake*'s matter and method.

Rose, Danis, and John O'Hanlon. *Understanding 'Finnegans Wake': A Guide to the Narrative of James Joyce's Masterpiece*. New York: Garland, 1982. An attempt to reduce the simultaneous meanings of the *Wake* to a linear narrative; like all such attempts, it seeks to undo what Joyce laboured to achieve, but it can be useful if treated critically. Based on a somewhat rigid theory of the relationship between the workbooks and the final text, which is not necessarily important for the reader.

Hart, Clive. *Structure and Motif in 'Finnegans Wake'*. London: Faber, 1962. Especially useful on repeated motifs.

McHugh, Roland. *The Sigla of 'Finnegans Wake'*. London: Arnold; Austin: University of Texas Press, 1976. Raises interesting questions about the 'characters' of the *Wake*.

Bishop, John. *Joyce's Book of the Dark: 'Finnegans Wake'*. Madison: University of Wisconsin Press, 1986. Particularly good on Joyce's use of Vico and the Egyptian *Book of the Dead*; less convincing as an attempt to make the whole of the *Wake* fit one interpretative framework.

BIOGRAPHY

Joyce, Stanislaus. *My Brother's Keeper: James Joyce's Early Years*, ed. Richard Ellmann. New York: Viking; London: Faber, 1958. A vivid biographical account of Joyce by a brother three years younger.

The Complete Dublin Diary, ed. George Healey. Ithaca: Cornell University Press, 1971. James figures largely in this diary kept by Stanislaus.

Power, Arthur. *Conversations with James Joyce*, ed. Clive Hart. London: Millington; New York: Columbia University Press, 1974.

Potts, Willard, ed. *Portraits of the Artist in Exile: Recollections of James Joyce by Europeans*. Seattle: University of Washington Press, 1979.

Ellmann, Richard. *James Joyce*. Rev. edn., New York: Oxford University Press, 1982. A mass of raw material transmuted into a magisterial biography; inevitably, the portrait of the artist that emerges is a reflection of Ellmann's as well as Joyce's views, and it has been challenged in matters both of detail and of general bias.

Maddox, Brenda. *Nora: A Biography of Nora Joyce*. London: Hamish Hamilton; Boston: Houghton Mifflin, 1988. (The American edition bears the misleading subtitle *The Real Life of Molly Bloom*.) An important complement and corrective to Ellmann's biography of Joyce.

Bradley, Bruce. *James Joyce's Schooldays*. Dublin: Gill and Macmillan, 1982.

CURRENT JOURNALS

James Joyce Broadsheet. Reviews, illustrations, and comment; published three times a year. The School of English, University of Leeds, Leeds LS2 9JT, England.

James Joyce Literary Supplement. Twice a year. Reviews and features. Department of English, P.O. Box 248145, University of Miami, Coral Gables, FL 33124, USA.

James Joyce Quarterly. Scholarly articles on Joyce, together with book reviews, notes, and lists of recent publications. University of Tulsa, Tulsa, OK 74104, USA.

Joyce Studies Annual. A yearly collection of essays on Joyce, initiated in 1990. P.O. Box 7219, University Station, The University of Texas at Austin, TX 78713, USA.

James Joyce "Newestlatter". A newsletter sent to members of the James Joyce Foundation, which also organizes an International James Joyce Symposium every two years. Membership enquiries to The International James Joyce Foundation, English Department, Ohio State University, 164 W. 17th Ave., Columbus, OH 43210, USA. Subscriptions to the above journals are also available through the Foundation.

Index